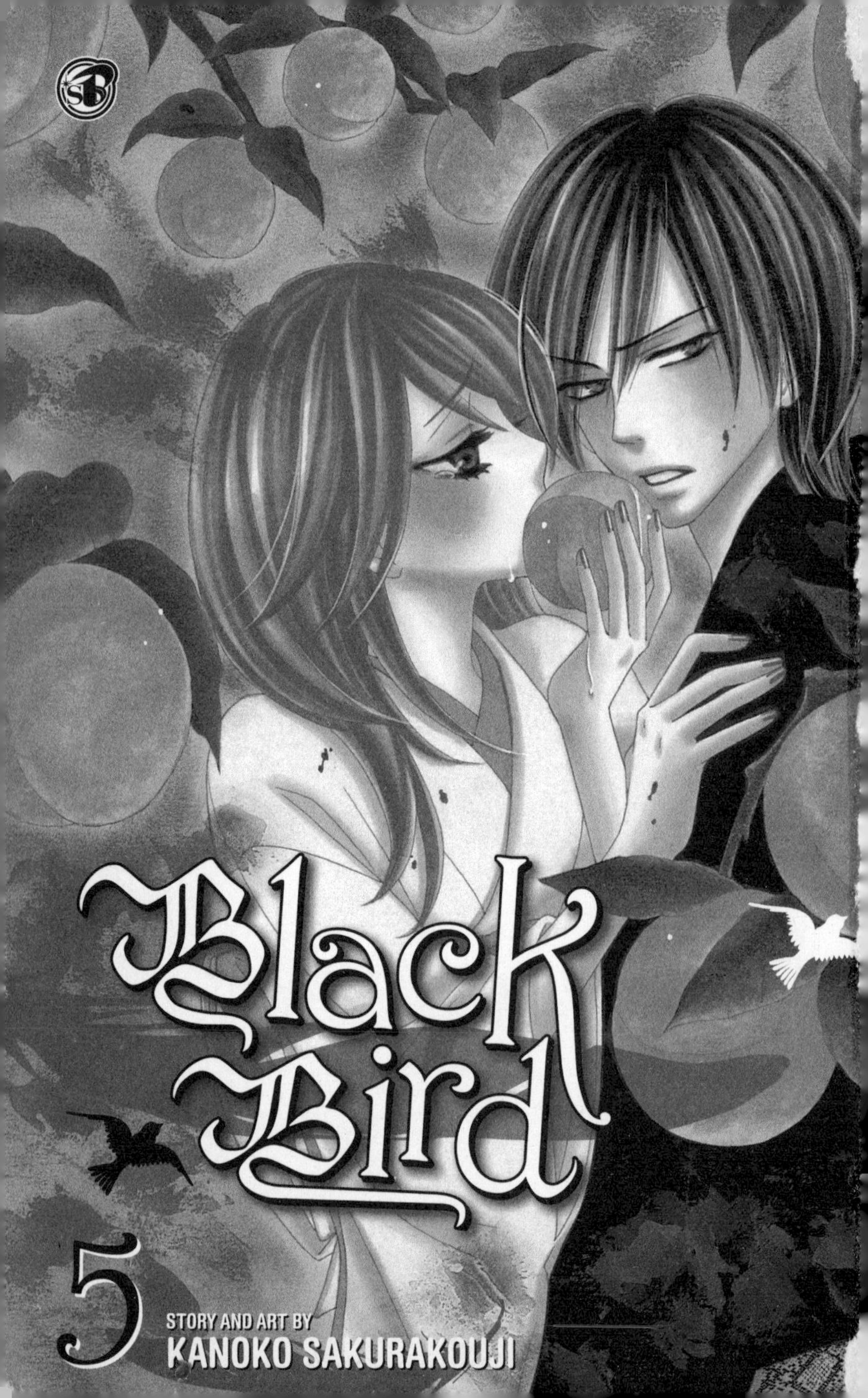
Black Bird
5
STORY AND ART BY
KANOKO SAKURAKOUJI

Black Bird

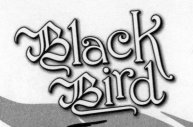

CONTENTS

CHARACTERS

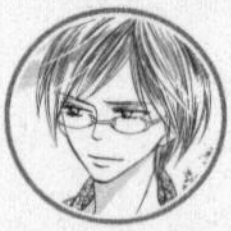

TADANOBU KUZUNOHA
Kyo's close friend since childhood. Current leader of the Kitsune clan.

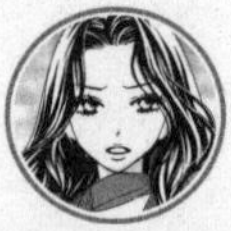

RENKO JONOUCHI
Tadanobu's girlfriend. Like Misao, she can see demons.

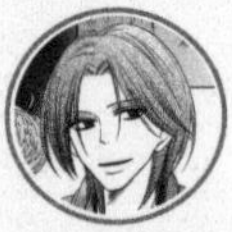

SHO USUI
Kyo's older brother and a member of the Eight Daitengu. He is also known as Sojo. He is currently incarcerated after injuring Misao in an attempt to gain leadership of the clan.

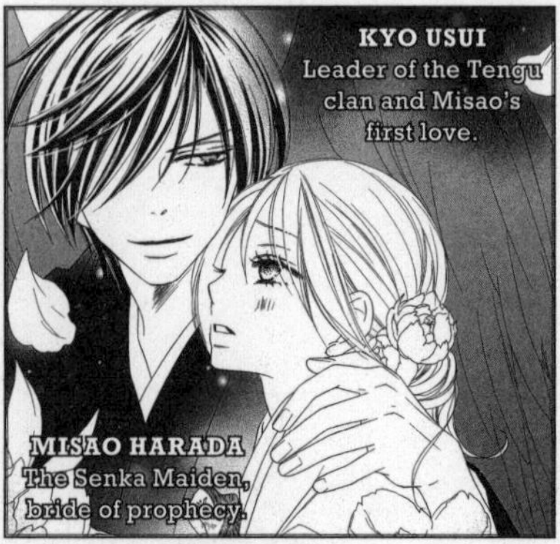
KYO USUI
Leader of the Tengu clan and Misao's first love.
MISAO HARADA
The Senka Maiden, bride of prophecy.

THE EIGHT DAITENGU
Kyo's bodyguards. Their names designate their official posts.

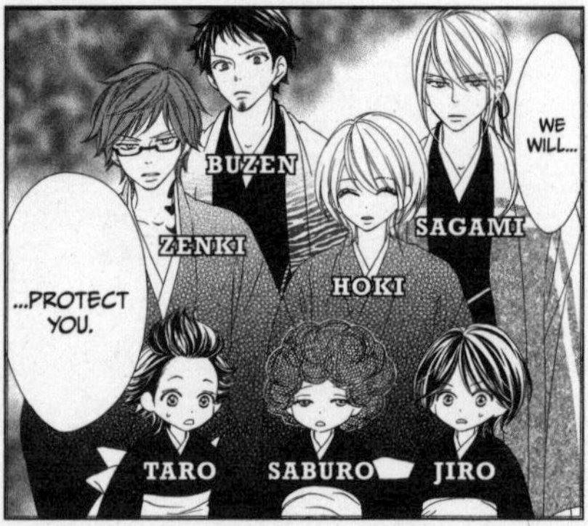
WE WILL...
...PROTECT YOU.
BUZEN
SAGAMI
ZENKI
HOKI
TARO
SABURO
JIRO

STORY THUS FAR

Misao can see spirits and demons, and her childhood sweetheart Kyo has been protecting her since she was little.

"Someday, I'll come for you, I promise." Kyo reappears the day before Misao's 16th birthday to tell her, "Your 16th birthday marks 'open season' on you." She is the Senka Maiden, and if a demon drinks her blood, he is granted a long life. If he eats her flesh, he gains eternal youth. And if he makes her his bride, his clan will prosper...

Misao discovers that Kyo is a *tengu*, a crow demon, with his sights firmly set on her. But Kyo's older brother Sho, who was denied the leadership of the Usui clan because of his cruelty, schemes to take Misao for himself. Kyo protects Misao from his brother's machinations and imprisons Sho. Now that his leadership is secure, Kyo's advisors encourage him to bed Misao quickly. But no one knows what the consequences will be if Misao, a human, has sex with a demon... and the answer can only be found in the *Senka Roku*, a secret record held by the Kuzunoha kitsune clan.

Unfortunately, the *Senka Roku* is stolen by unknown demons during a battle between Tadanobu, the new leader of the Kuzunoha, and Kyo. Tadanobu warns, "If you want to spend the rest of your life with that girl... you must never have sex with her."

What will Kyo do?!

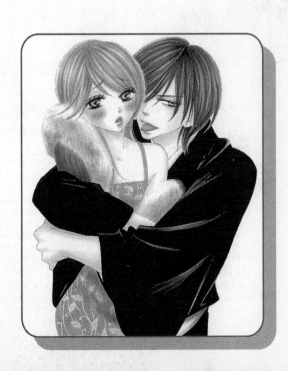

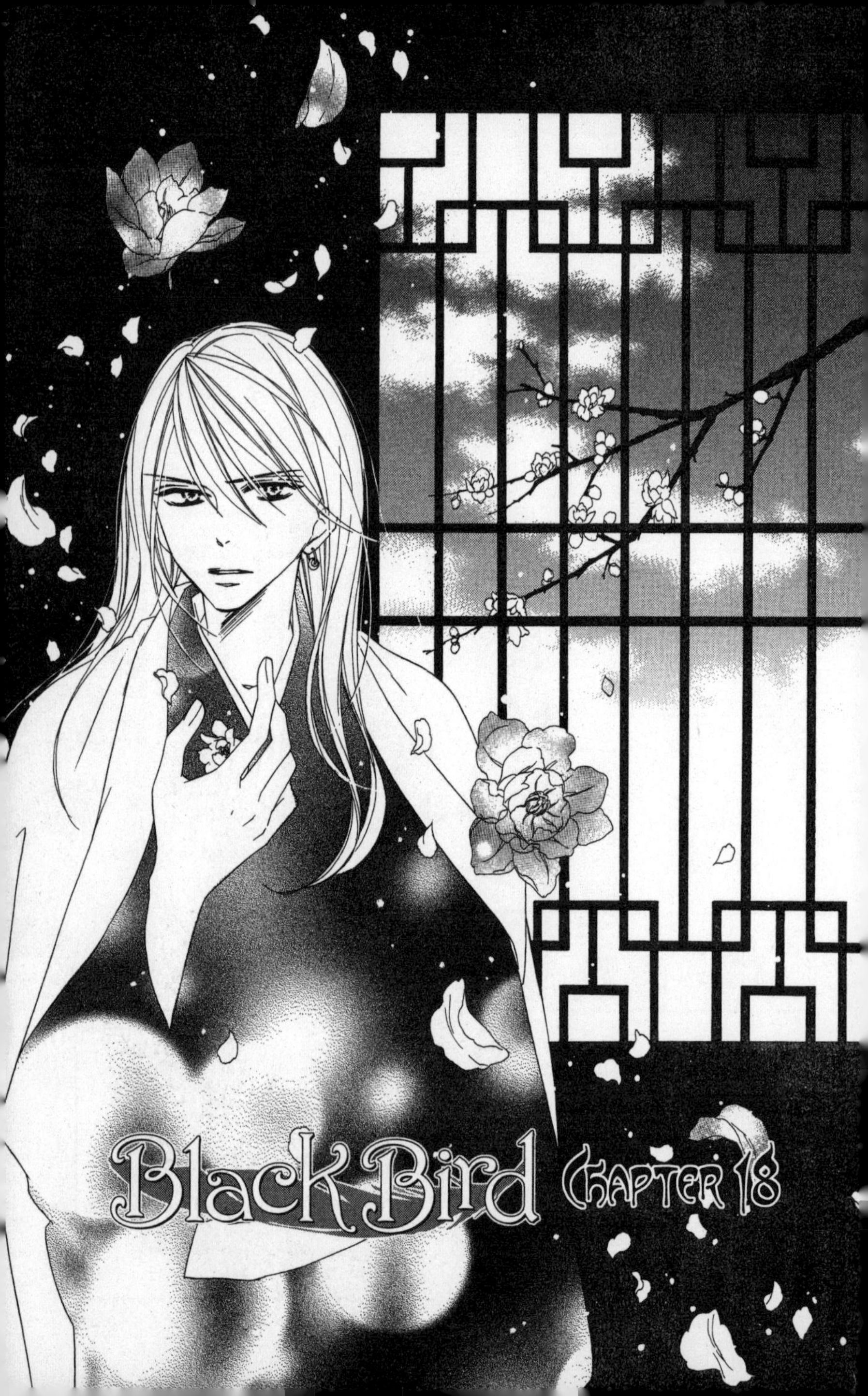
Black Bird
Chapter 18

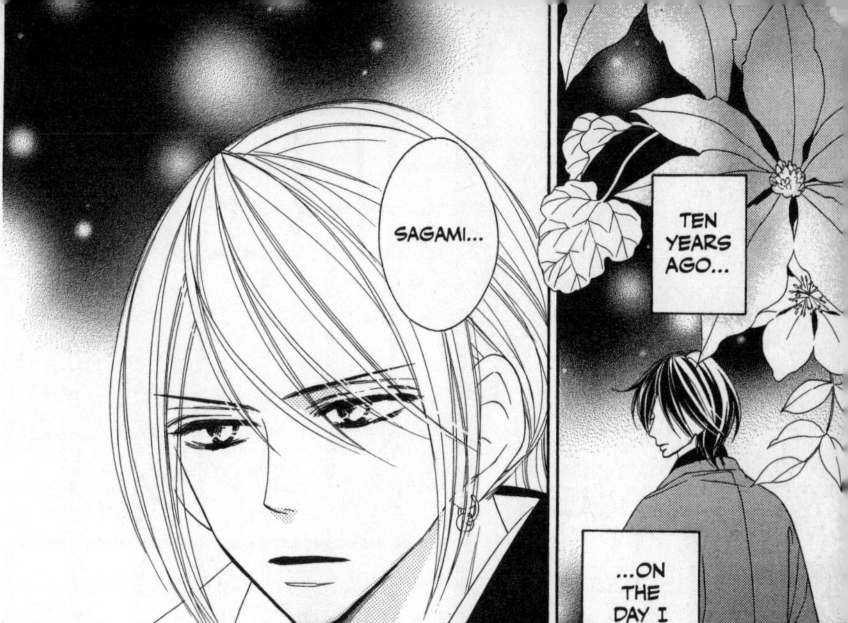
TEN YEARS AGO...
...ON THE DAY I BECAME LORD KYO'S ATTENDANT...
HOW ARE THINGS WITH KYO AND THE SENKA MAIDEN?
SAGAMI...
...I MADE UP MY MIND.

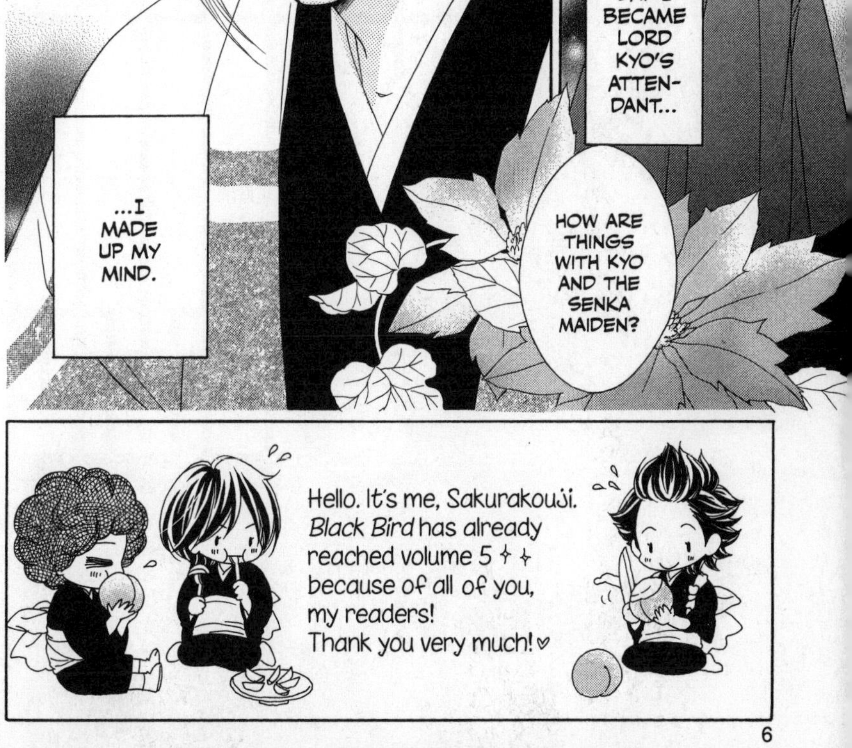
Hello. It's me, Sakurakouji. *Black Bird* has already reached volume 5 ✧✧ because of all of you, my readers! Thank you very much! ♡

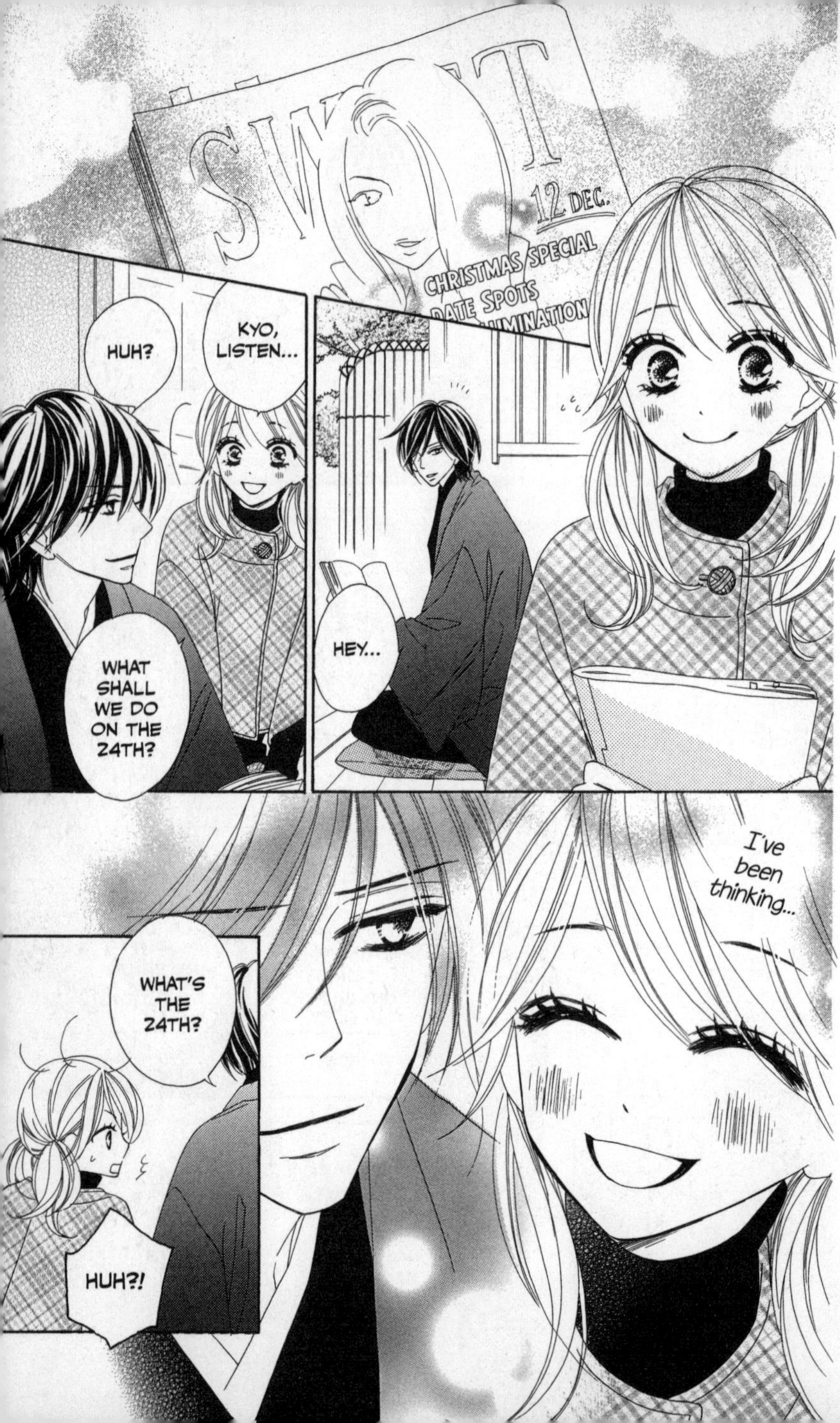
12 DEC.
CHRISTMAS SPECIAL
DATE SPOTS
HEY...
KYO, LISTEN...
HUH?
WHAT SHALL WE DO ON THE 24TH?
I've been thinking...
WHAT'S THE 24TH?
HUH?!

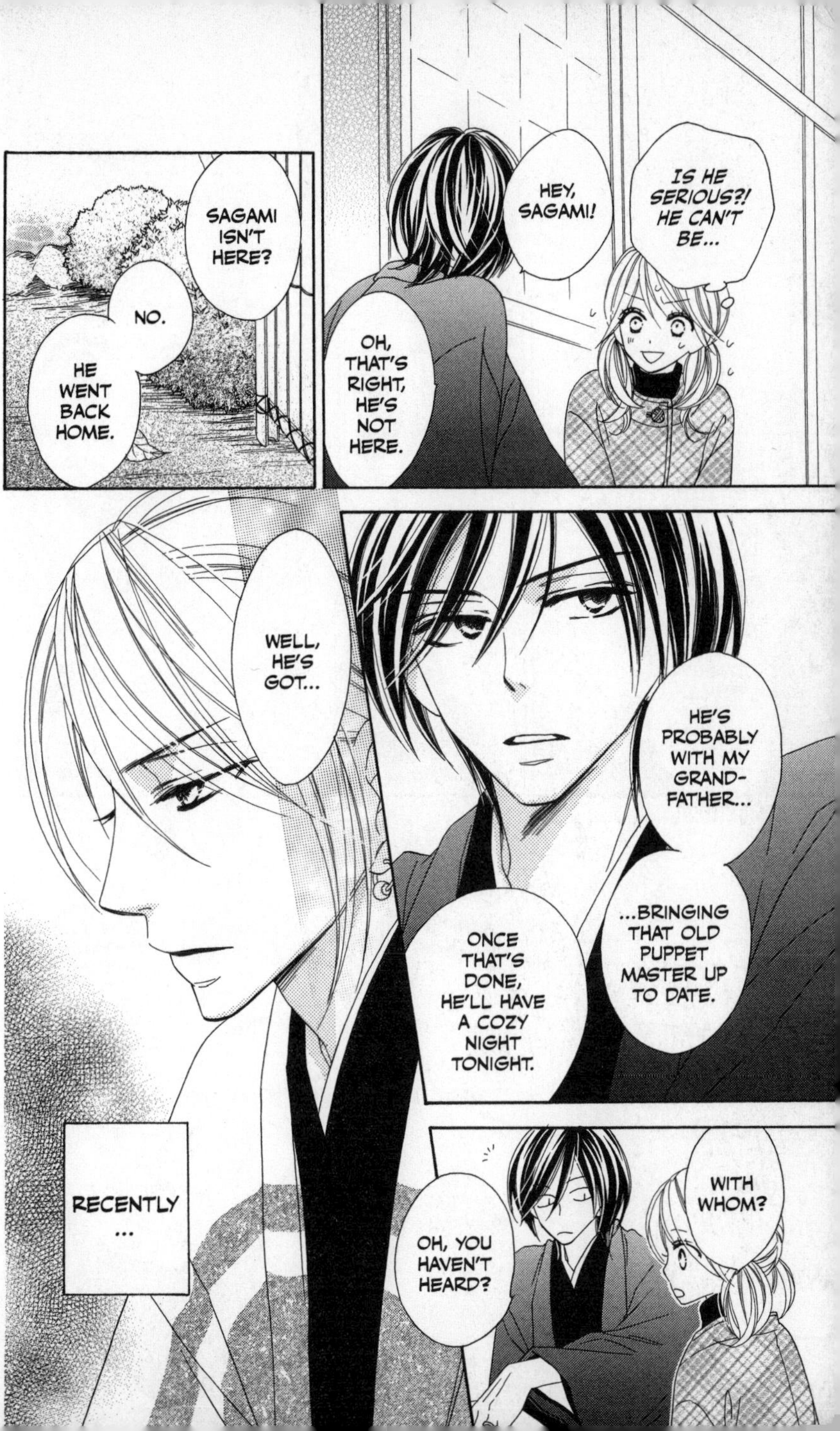
IS HE SERIOUS?! HE CAN'T BE...
HEY, SAGAMI!
OH, THAT'S RIGHT, HE'S NOT HERE.
SAGAMI ISN'T HERE?
NO.
HE WENT BACK HOME.
HE'S PROBABLY WITH MY GRAND-FATHER...
...BRINGING THAT OLD PUPPET MASTER UP TO DATE.
ONCE THAT'S DONE, HE'LL HAVE A COZY NIGHT TONIGHT.
WITH WHOM?
OH, YOU HAVEN'T HEARD?
WELL, HE'S GOT...
RECENTLY ...

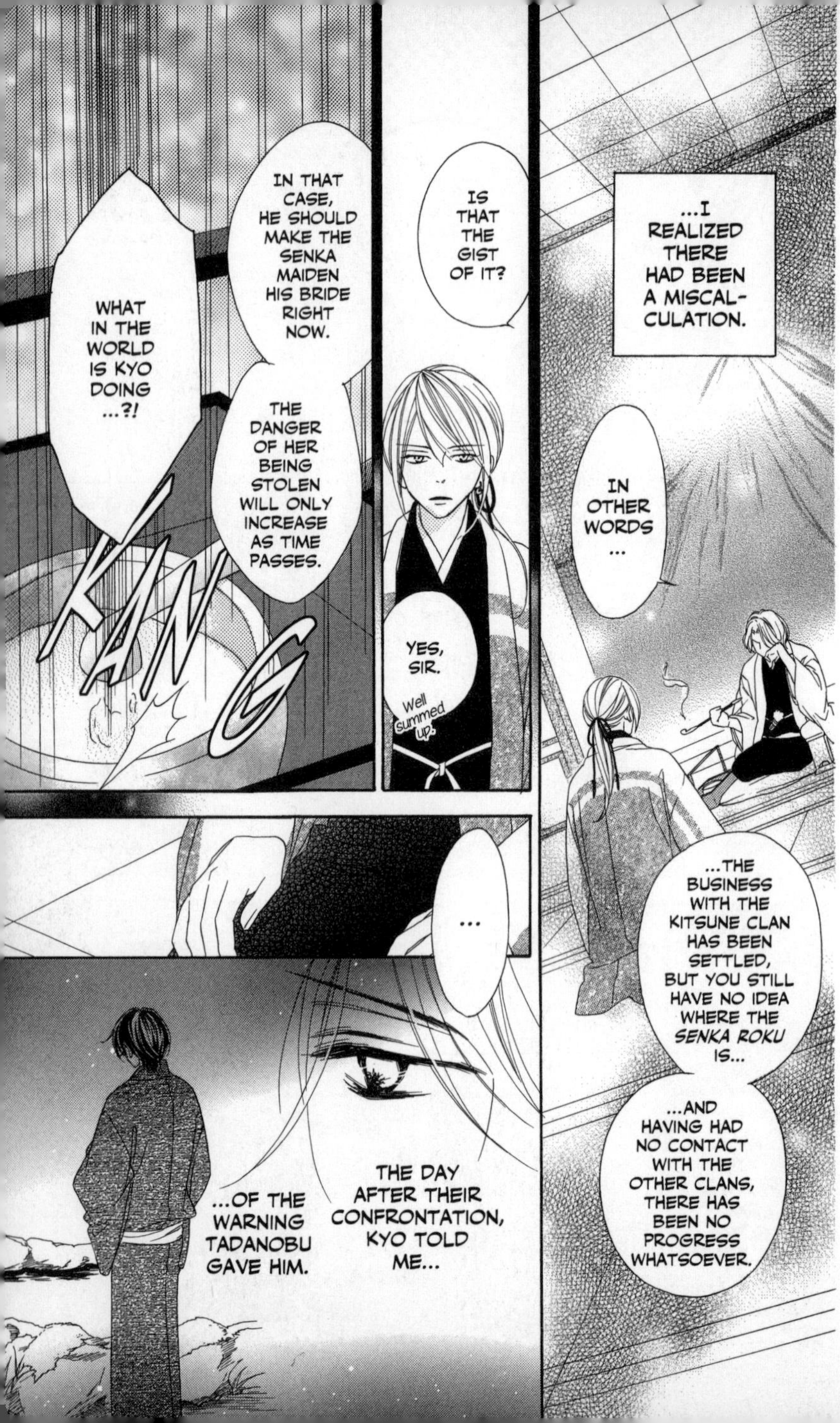
...I REALIZED THERE HAD BEEN A MISCALCULATION.
IN OTHER WORDS...
...THE BUSINESS WITH THE KITSUNE CLAN HAS BEEN SETTLED, BUT YOU STILL HAVE NO IDEA WHERE THE *SENKA ROKU* IS...
...AND HAVING HAD NO CONTACT WITH THE OTHER CLANS, THERE HAS BEEN NO PROGRESS WHATSOEVER.
IS THAT THE GIST OF IT?
YES, SIR.
Well summed up.
IN THAT CASE, HE SHOULD MAKE THE SENKA MAIDEN HIS BRIDE RIGHT NOW.
THE DANGER OF HER BEING STOLEN WILL ONLY INCREASE AS TIME PASSES.
WHAT IN THE WORLD IS KYO DOING...?!
KANG
...
THE DAY AFTER THEIR CONFRONTATION, KYO TOLD ME...
...OF THE WARNING TADANOBU GAVE HIM.

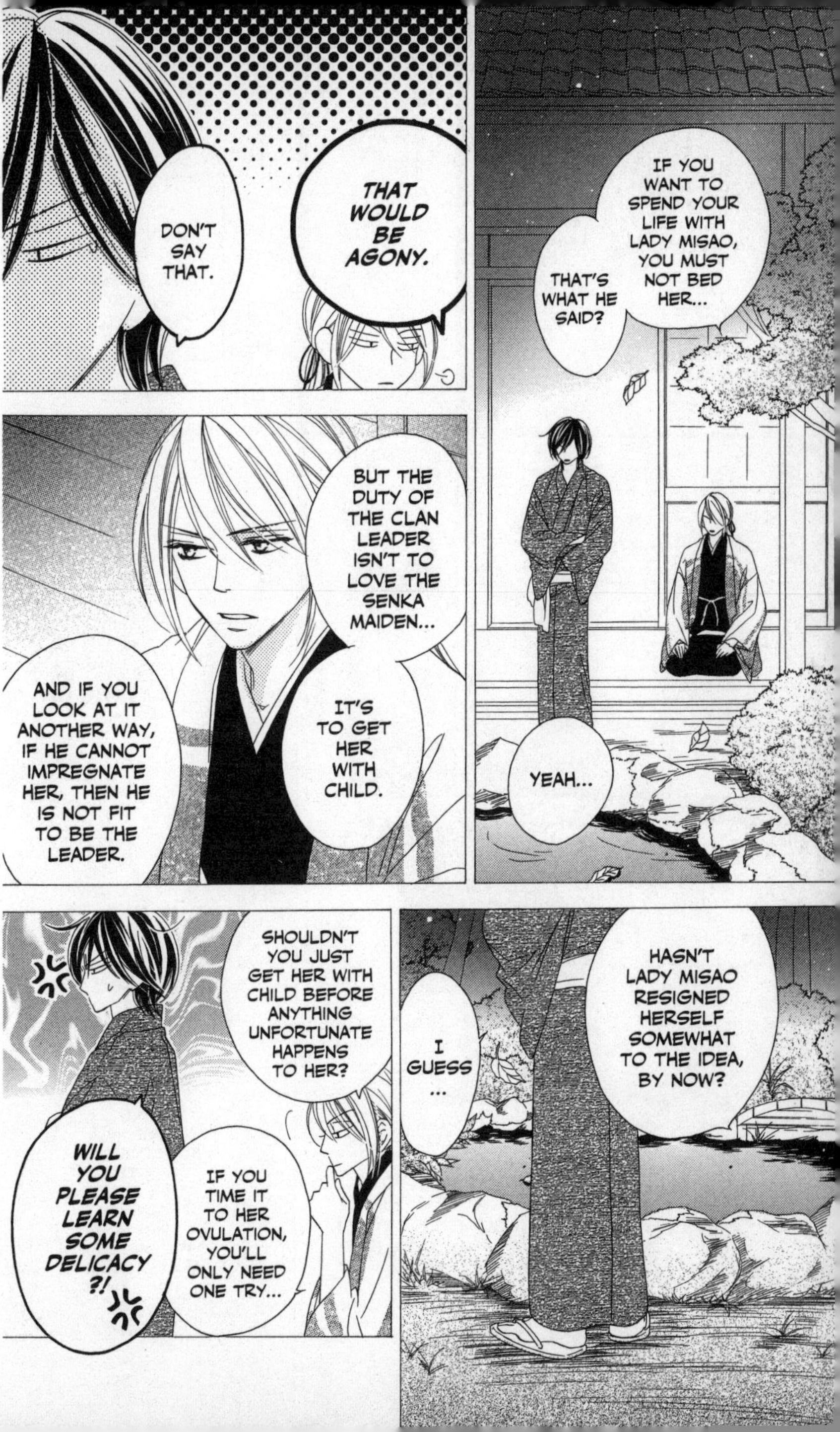
IF YOU WANT TO SPEND YOUR LIFE WITH LADY MISAO, YOU MUST NOT BED HER...
THAT'S WHAT HE SAID?
YEAH...
THAT WOULD BE AGONY.
DON'T SAY THAT.
BUT THE DUTY OF THE CLAN LEADER ISN'T TO LOVE THE SENKA MAIDEN...
IT'S TO GET HER WITH CHILD.
AND IF YOU LOOK AT IT ANOTHER WAY, IF HE CANNOT IMPREGNATE HER, THEN HE IS NOT FIT TO BE THE LEADER.
HASN'T LADY MISAO RESIGNED HERSELF SOMEWHAT TO THE IDEA, BY NOW?
I GUESS...
SHOULDN'T YOU JUST GET HER WITH CHILD BEFORE ANYTHING UNFORTUNATE HAPPENS TO HER?
IF YOU TIME IT TO HER OVULATION, YOU'LL ONLY NEED ONE TRY...
WILL YOU PLEASE LEARN SOME DELICACY?!

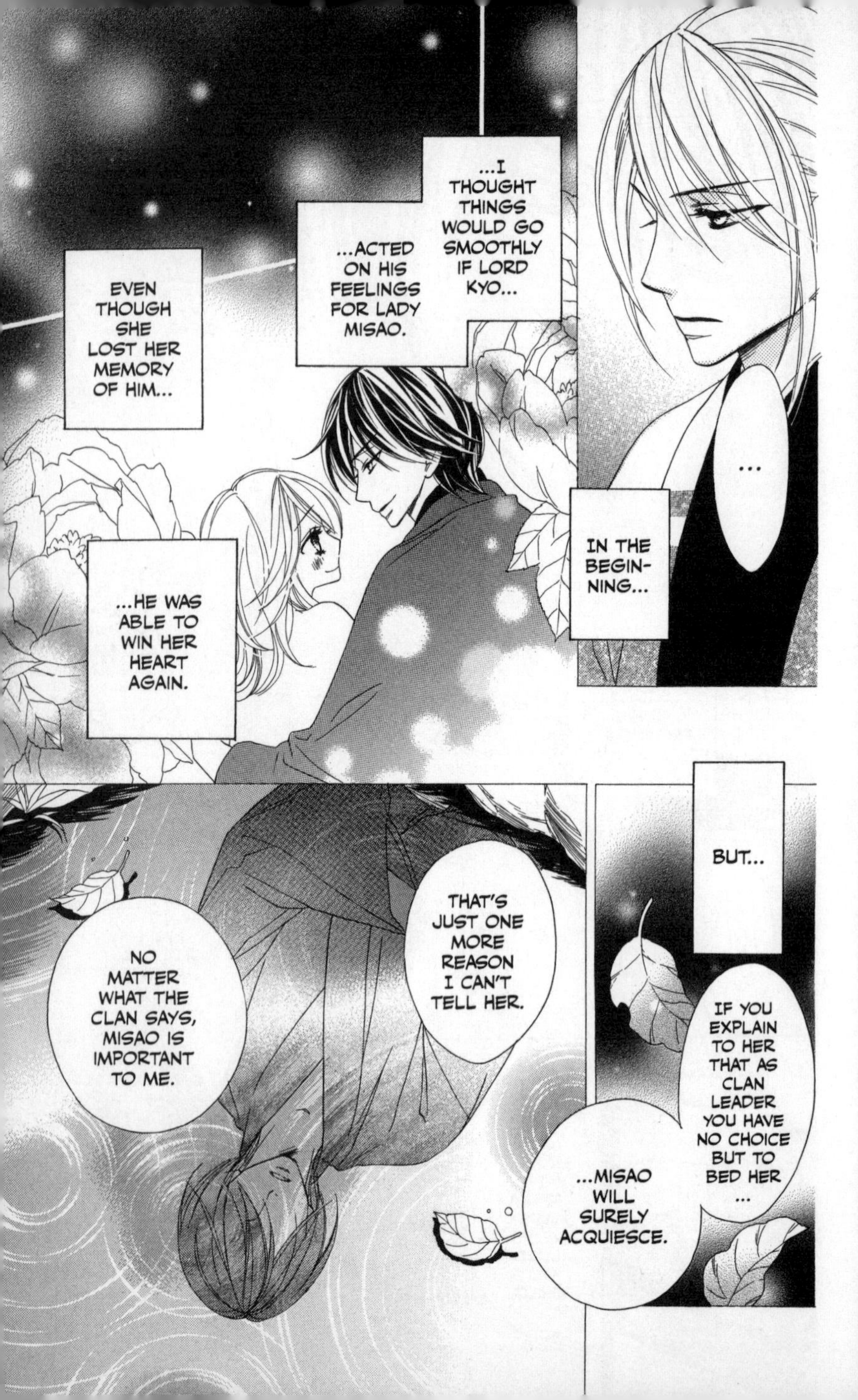
...
IN THE BEGINNING...
...I THOUGHT THINGS WOULD GO SMOOTHLY IF LORD KYO...
...ACTED ON HIS FEELINGS FOR LADY MISAO.
EVEN THOUGH SHE LOST HER MEMORY OF HIM...
...HE WAS ABLE TO WIN HER HEART AGAIN.
BUT...
IF YOU EXPLAIN TO HER THAT AS CLAN LEADER YOU HAVE NO CHOICE BUT TO BED HER ...
...MISAO WILL SURELY ACQUIESCE.
THAT'S JUST ONE MORE REASON I CAN'T TELL HER.
NO MATTER WHAT THE CLAN SAYS, MISAO IS IMPORTANT TO ME.

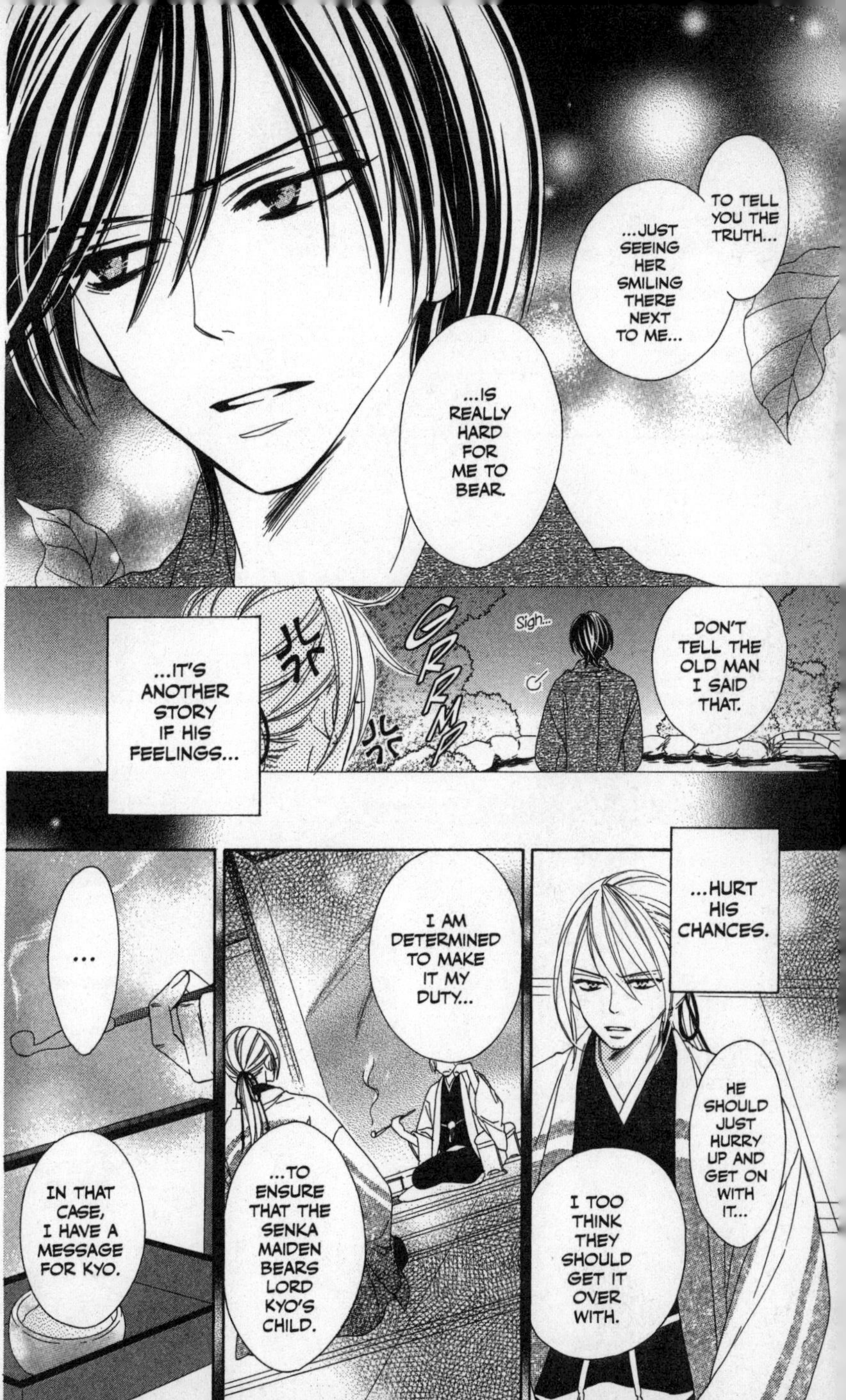
TO TELL YOU THE TRUTH...
...JUST SEEING HER SMILING THERE NEXT TO ME...
...IS REALLY HARD FOR ME TO BEAR.
DON'T TELL THE OLD MAN I SAID THAT.
Sigh...
...IT'S ANOTHER STORY IF HIS FEELINGS...
...HURT HIS CHANCES.
HE SHOULD JUST HURRY UP AND GET ON WITH IT...
I TOO THINK THEY SHOULD GET IT OVER WITH.
I AM DETERMINED TO MAKE IT MY DUTY...
...TO ENSURE THAT THE SENKA MAIDEN BEARS LORD KYO'S CHILD.
...
IN THAT CASE, I HAVE A MESSAGE FOR KYO.

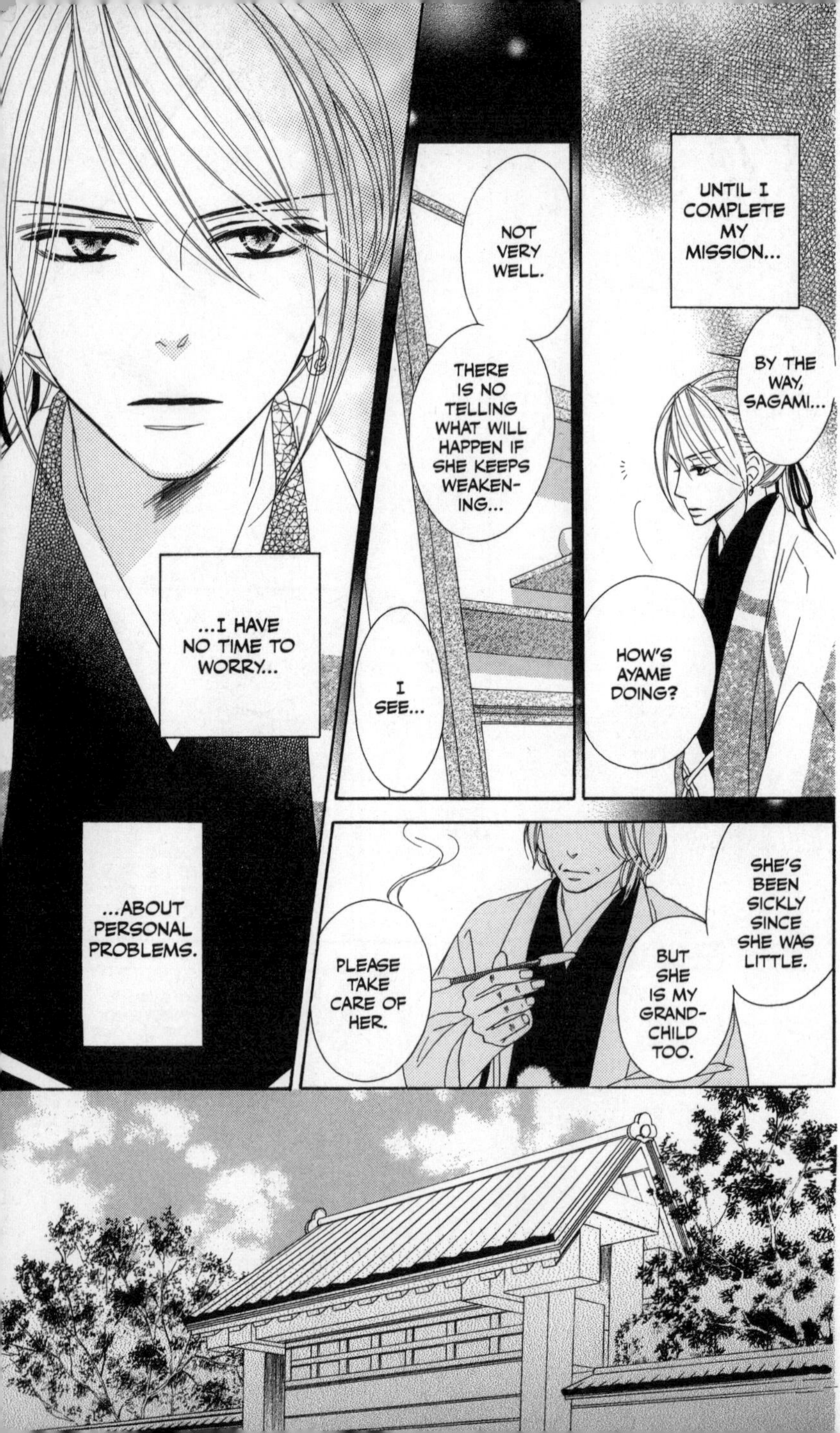
UNTIL I COMPLETE MY MISSION...
BY THE WAY, SAGAMI...
HOW'S AYAME DOING?
NOT VERY WELL.
THERE IS NO TELLING WHAT WILL HAPPEN IF SHE KEEPS WEAKEN-ING...
I SEE...
SHE'S BEEN SICKLY SINCE SHE WAS LITTLE.
BUT SHE IS MY GRAND-CHILD TOO.
PLEASE TAKE CARE OF HER.
...I HAVE NO TIME TO WORRY...
...ABOUT PERSONAL PROBLEMS.

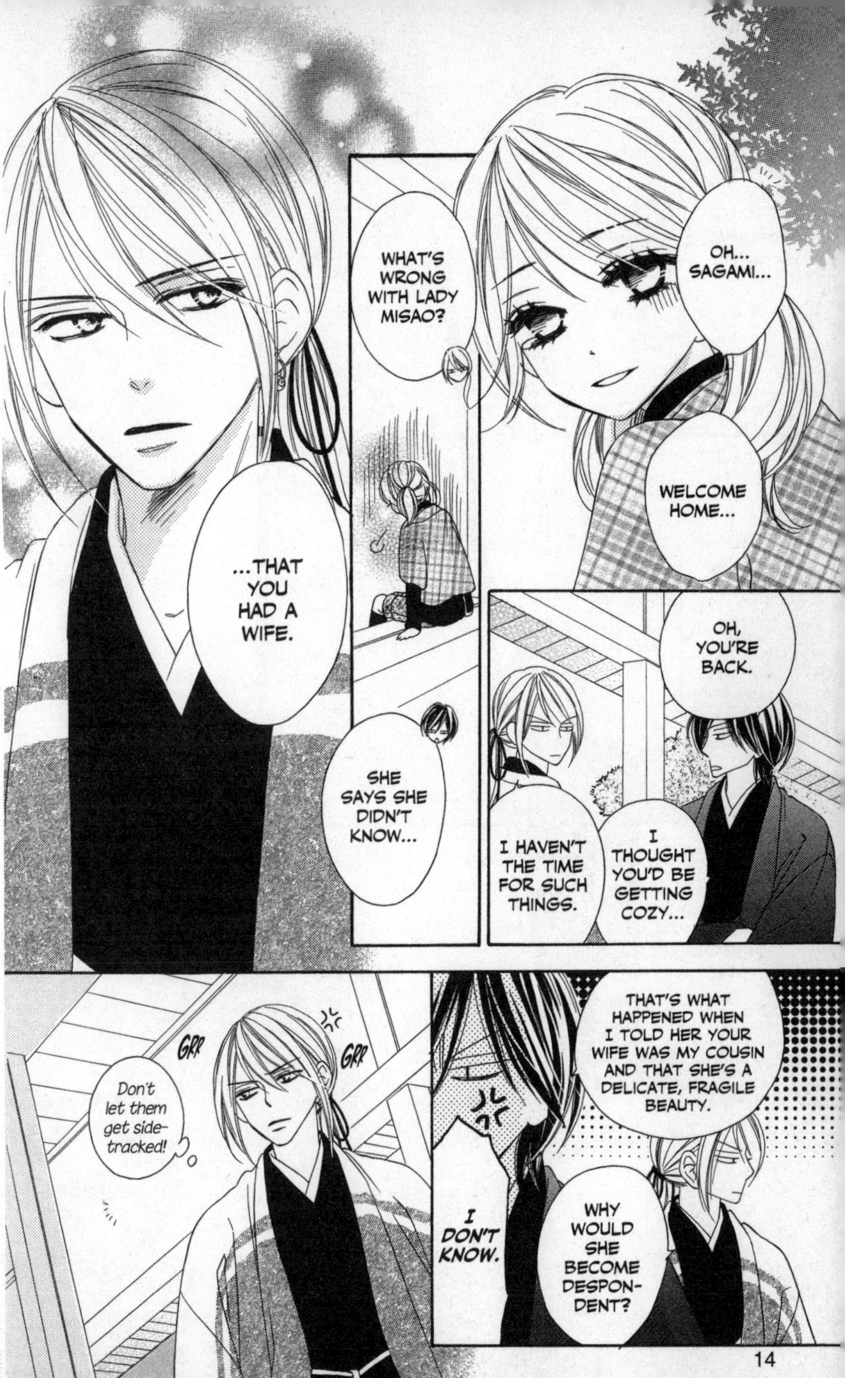
OH... SAGAMI...
WELCOME HOME...
OH, YOU'RE BACK.
I THOUGHT YOU'D BE GETTING COZY...
I HAVEN'T THE TIME FOR SUCH THINGS.
WHAT'S WRONG WITH LADY MISAO?
SHE SAYS SHE DIDN'T KNOW...
...THAT YOU HAD A WIFE.
THAT'S WHAT HAPPENED WHEN I TOLD HER YOUR WIFE WAS MY COUSIN AND THAT SHE'S A DELICATE, FRAGILE BEAUTY.
WHY WOULD SHE BECOME DESPONDENT?
I DON'T KNOW.
GRR
GRR
Don't let them get side-tracked!

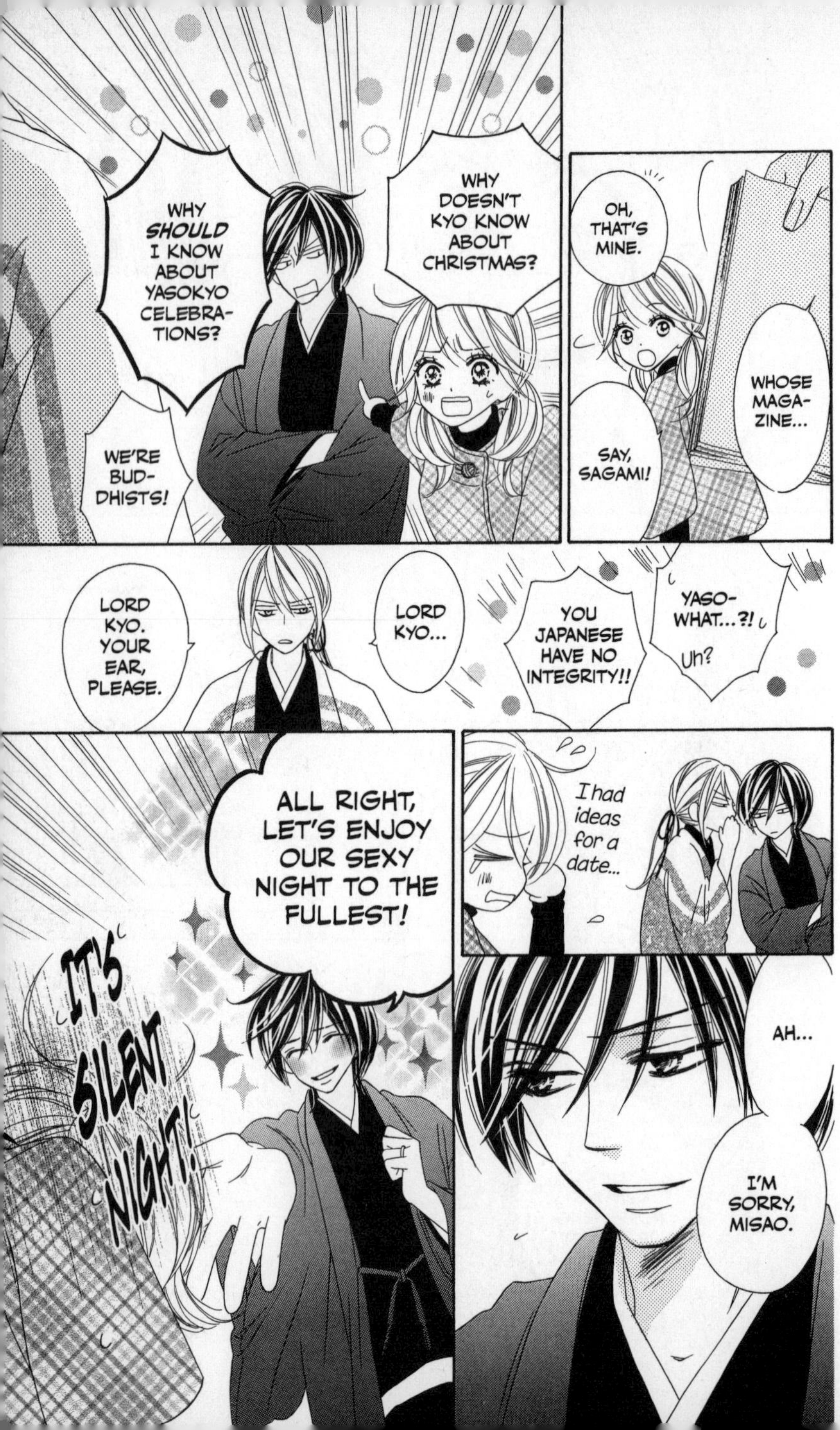
SAY, SAGAMI!
WHOSE MAGA-ZINE...
OH, THAT'S MINE.
WHY DOESN'T KYO KNOW ABOUT CHRISTMAS?
WHY *SHOULD* I KNOW ABOUT YASOKYO CELEBRA-TIONS?
WE'RE BUD-DHISTS!
YASO-WHAT...?!
Uh?
YOU JAPANESE HAVE NO INTEGRITY!!
LORD KYO...
LORD KYO. YOUR EAR, PLEASE.
I had ideas for a date...
AH...
I'M SORRY, MISAO.
ALL RIGHT, LET'S ENJOY OUR SEXY NIGHT TO THE FULLEST!
IT'S SILENT NIGHT!

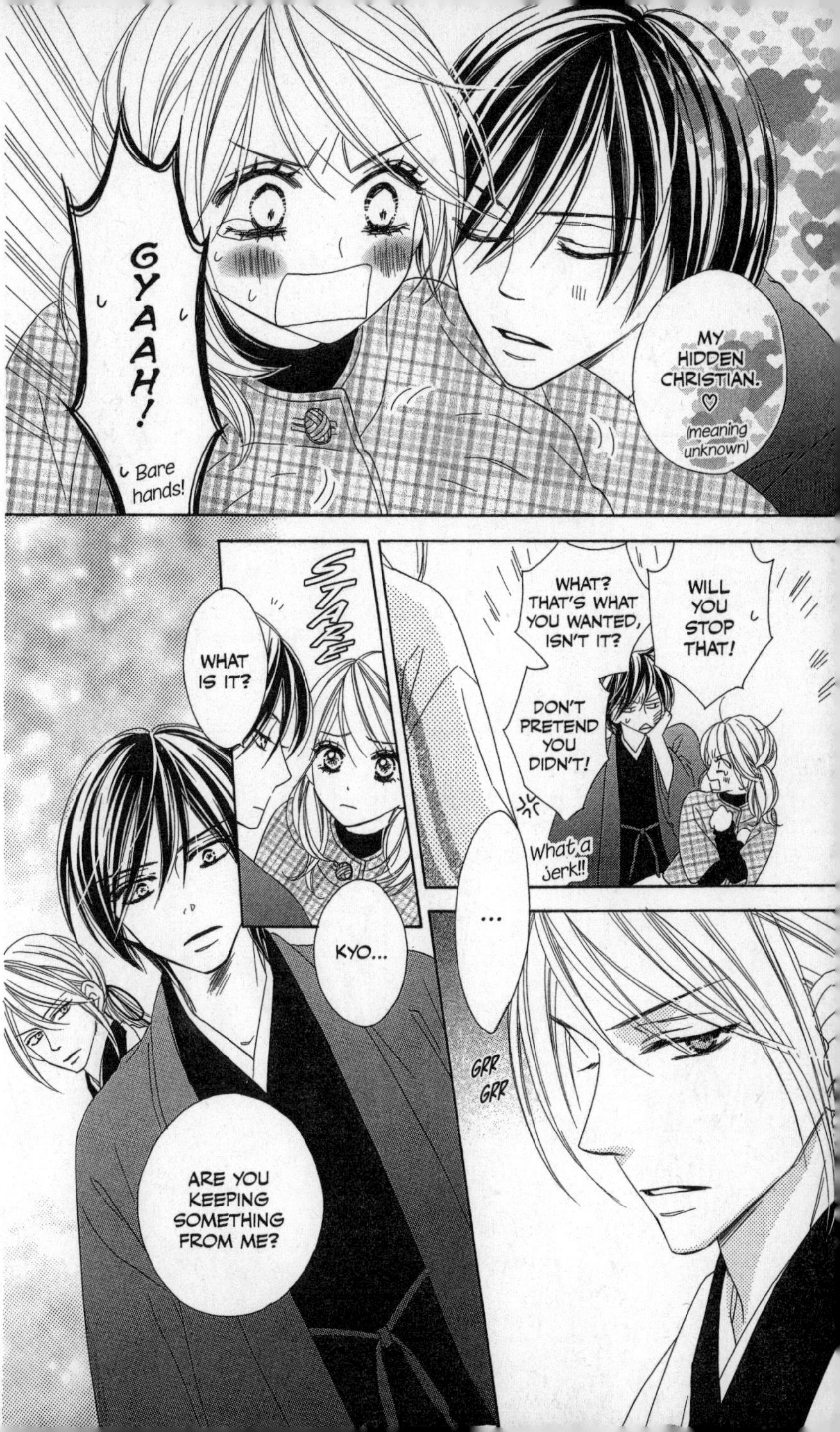
MY HIDDEN CHRISTIAN. ♡
(meaning unknown)
GYAAH!
Bare hands!
WILL YOU STOP THAT!
WHAT? THAT'S WHAT YOU WANTED, ISN'T IT?
DON'T PRETEND YOU DIDN'T!
What a jerk!!
STARE
WHAT IS IT?
...
GRR GRR
KYO...
ARE YOU KEEPING SOMETHING FROM ME?

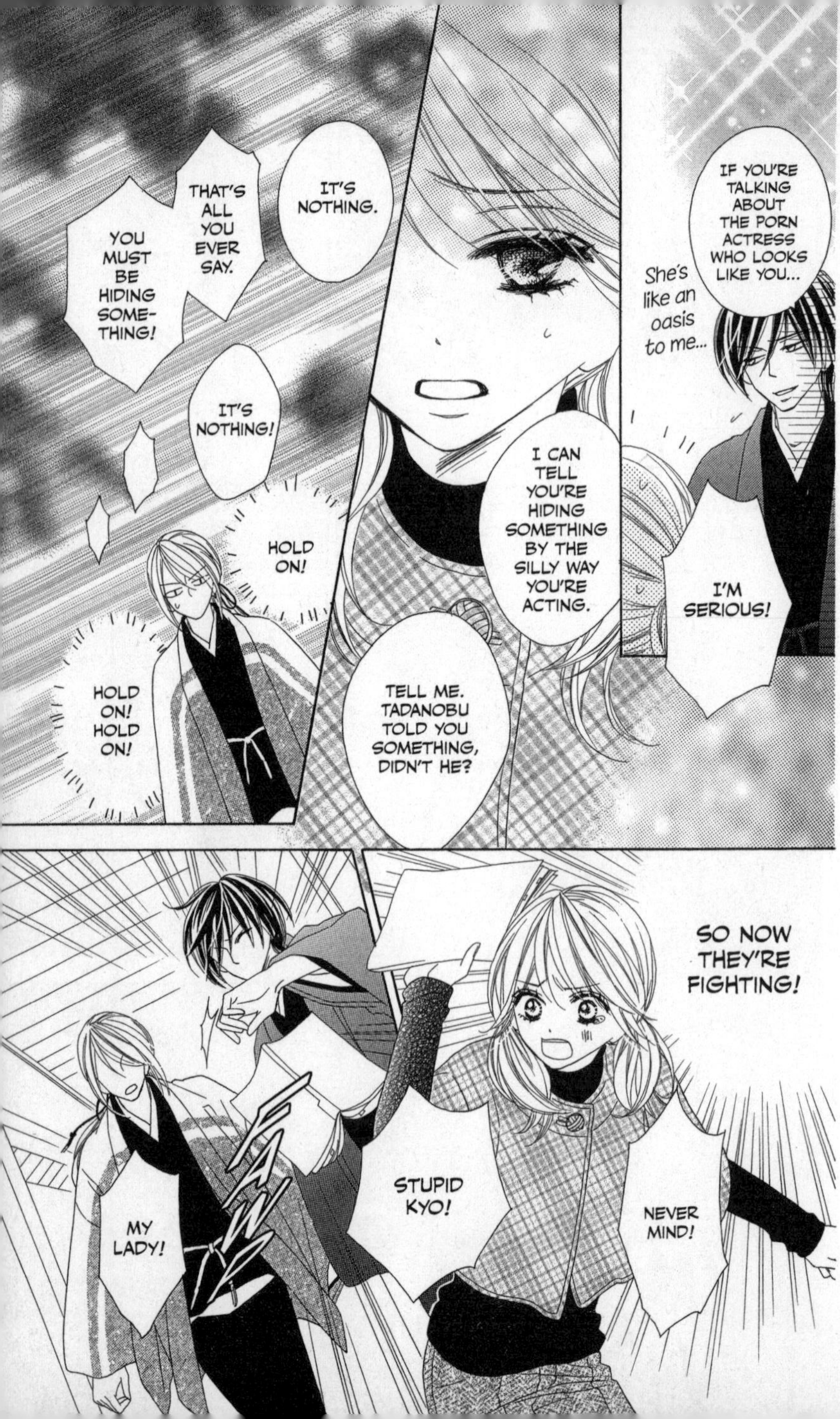

IF YOU'RE TALKING ABOUT THE PORN ACTRESS WHO LOOKS LIKE YOU...
She's like an oasis to me...
I'M SERIOUS!
I CAN TELL YOU'RE HIDING SOMETHING BY THE SILLY WAY YOU'RE ACTING.
TELL ME. TADANOBU TOLD YOU SOMETHING, DIDN'T HE?
IT'S NOTHING.
THAT'S ALL YOU EVER SAY.
YOU MUST BE HIDING SOME-THING!
IT'S NOTHING!
HOLD ON!
HOLD ON! HOLD ON!
SO NOW THEY'RE FIGHTING!
NEVER MIND!
STUPID KYO!
MY LADY!

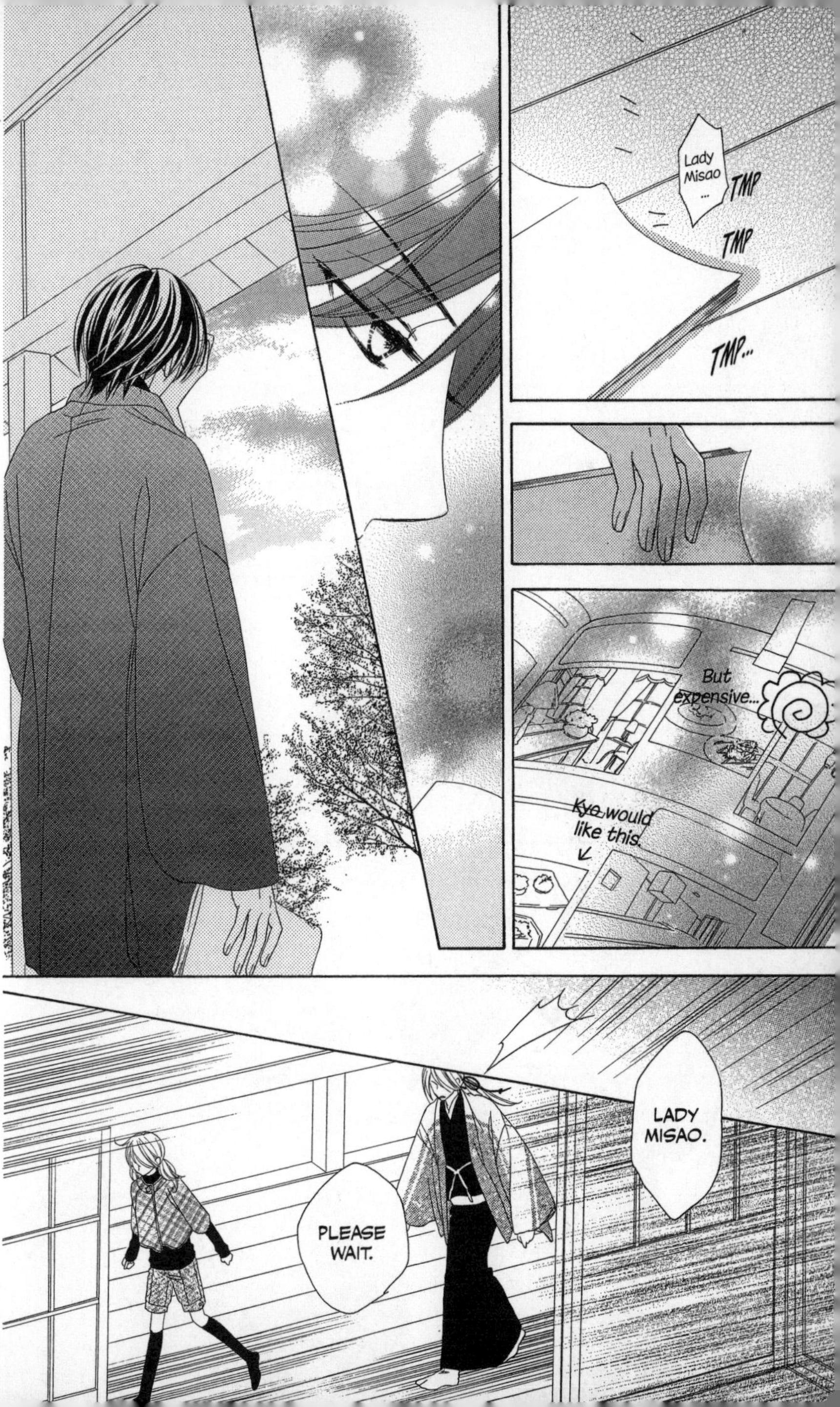
Lady Misao...
TMP
TMP
TMP...
But expensive...
Kyo would like this.
LADY MISAO.
PLEASE WAIT.

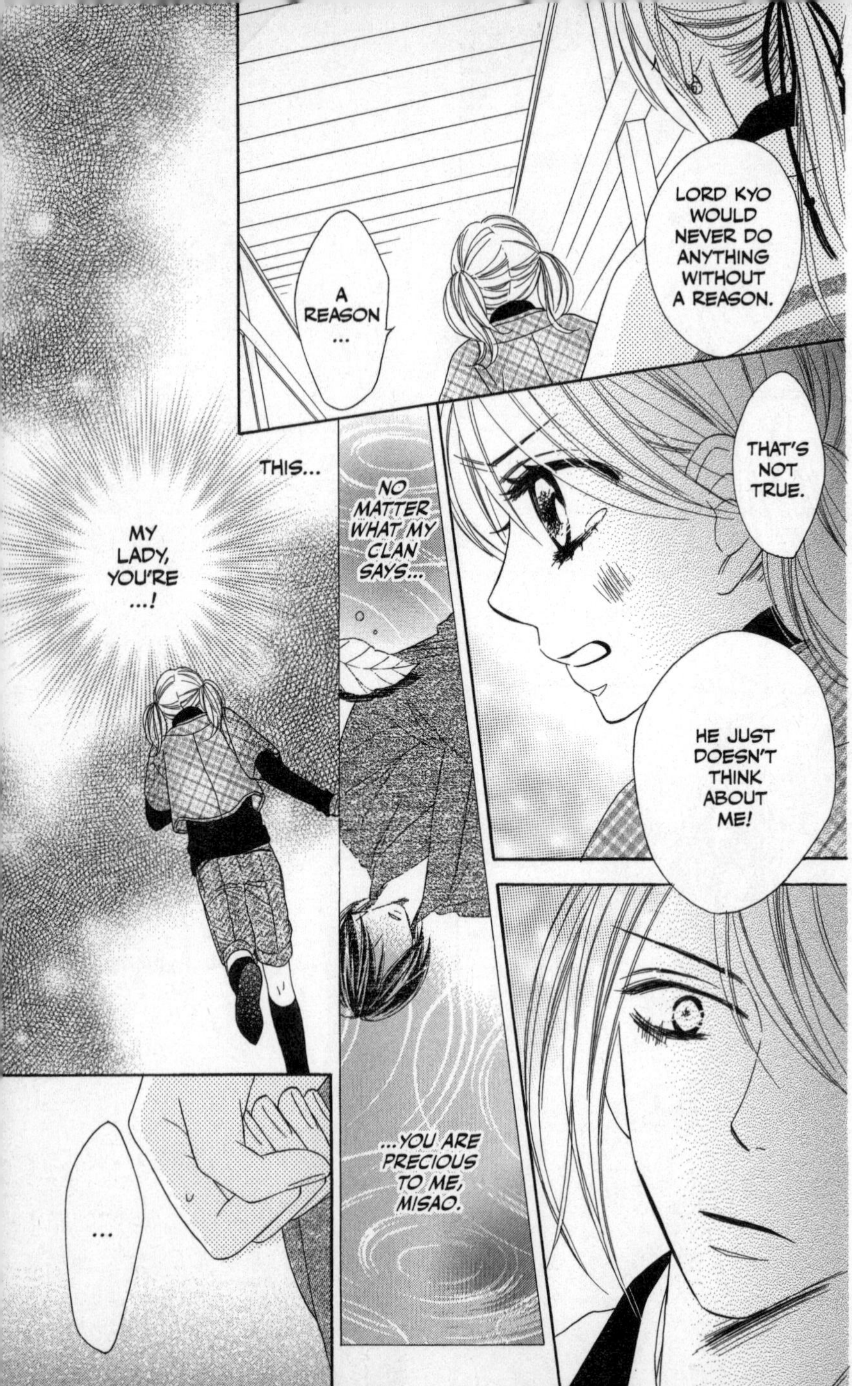
LORD KYO WOULD NEVER DO ANYTHING WITHOUT A REASON.
A REASON ...
THAT'S NOT TRUE.
HE JUST DOESN'T THINK ABOUT ME!
NO MATTER WHAT MY CLAN SAYS...
...YOU ARE PRECIOUS TO ME, MISAO.
THIS...
MY LADY, YOU'RE ...!
...

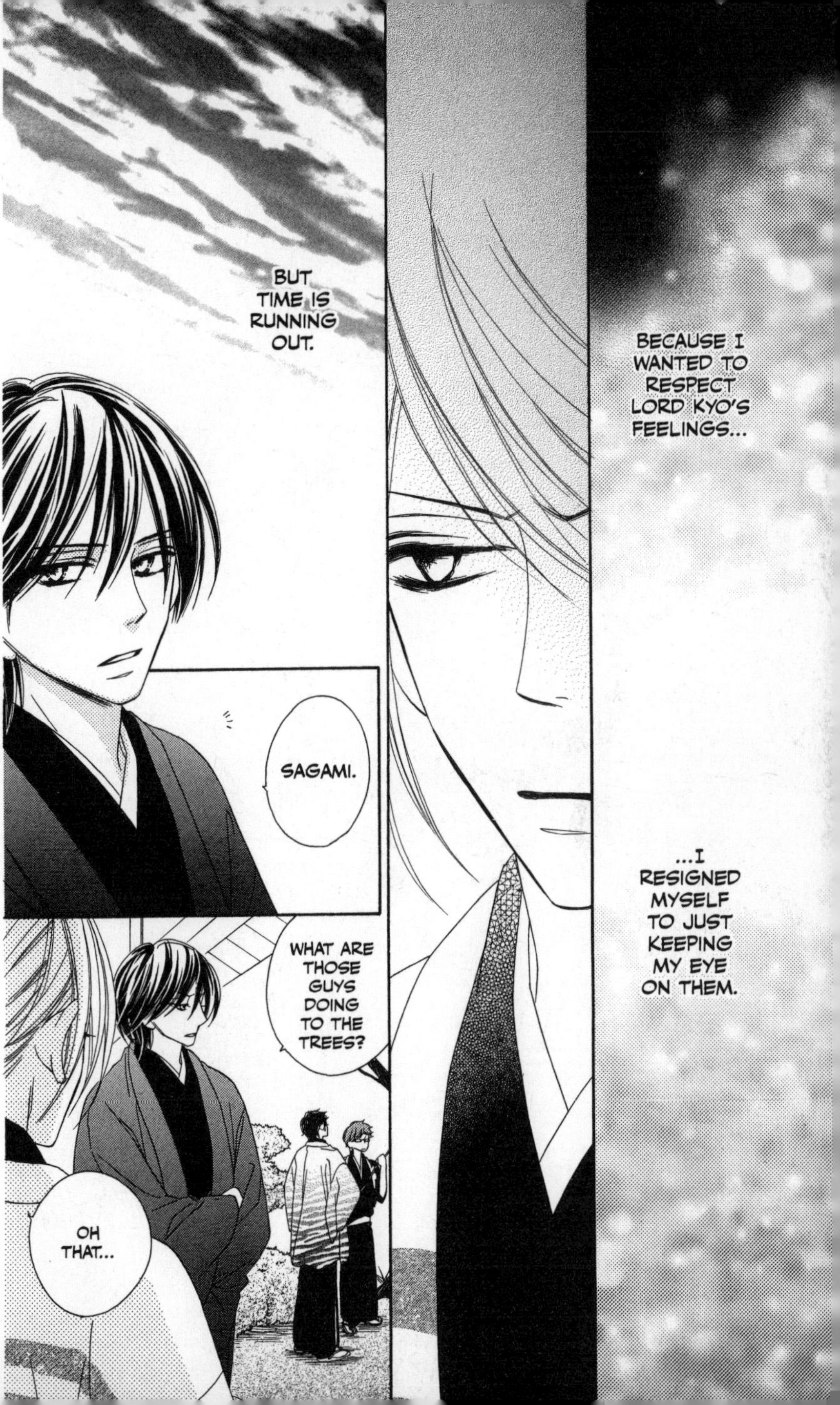
BECAUSE I WANTED TO RESPECT LORD KYO'S FEELINGS...
...I RESIGNED MYSELF TO JUST KEEPING MY EYE ON THEM.
BUT TIME IS RUNNING OUT.
SAGAMI.
WHAT ARE THOSE GUYS DOING TO THE TREES?
OH THAT...

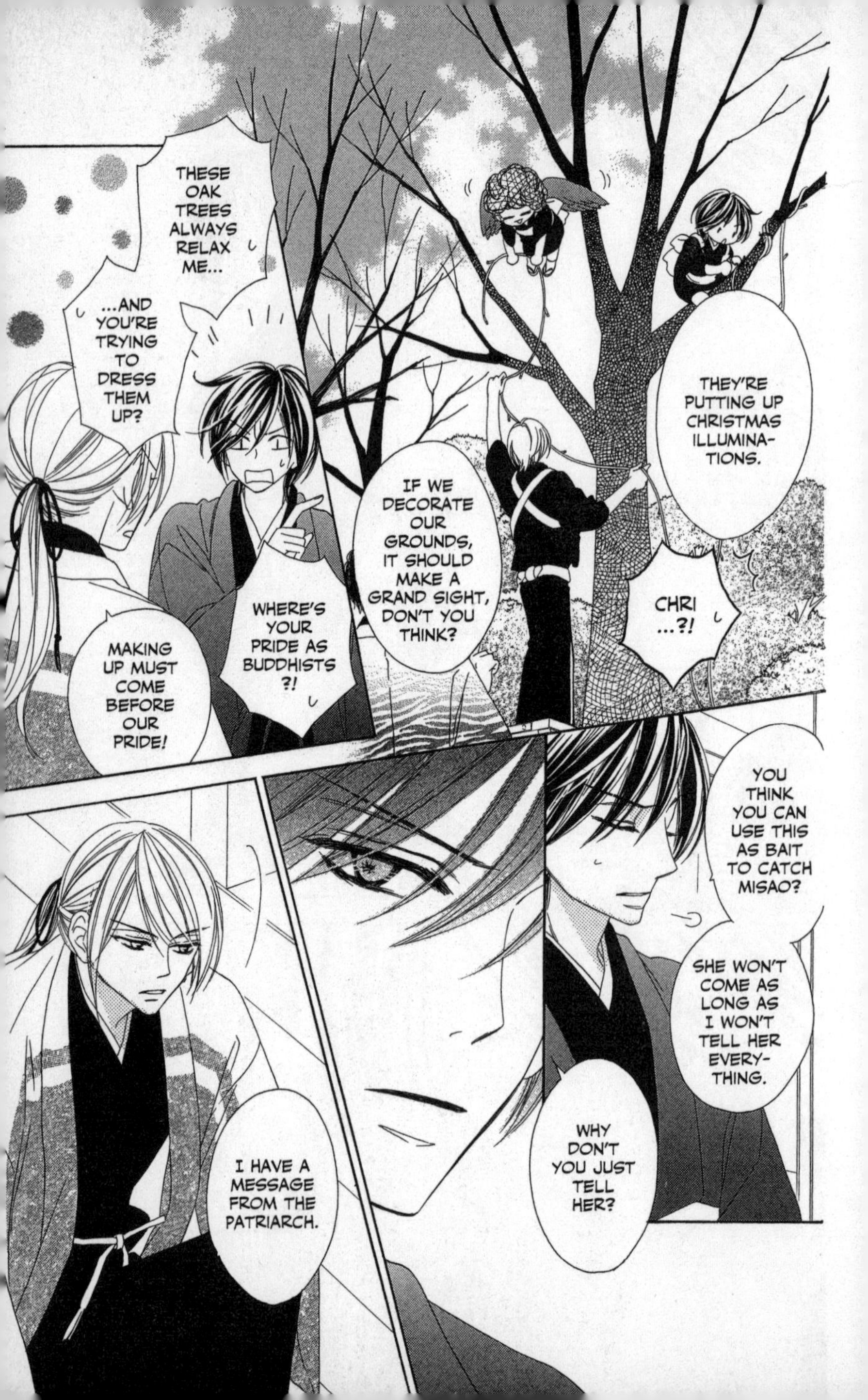
THEY'RE PUTTING UP CHRISTMAS ILLUMINATIONS.
CHRI ...?!
IF WE DECORATE OUR GROUNDS, IT SHOULD MAKE A GRAND SIGHT, DON'T YOU THINK?
THESE OAK TREES ALWAYS RELAX ME...
...AND YOU'RE TRYING TO DRESS THEM UP?
WHERE'S YOUR PRIDE AS BUDDHISTS ?!
MAKING UP MUST COME BEFORE OUR PRIDE!
YOU THINK YOU CAN USE THIS AS BAIT TO CATCH MISAO?
SHE WON'T COME AS LONG AS I WON'T TELL HER EVERY-THING.
WHY DON'T YOU JUST TELL HER?
I HAVE A MESSAGE FROM THE PATRIARCH.

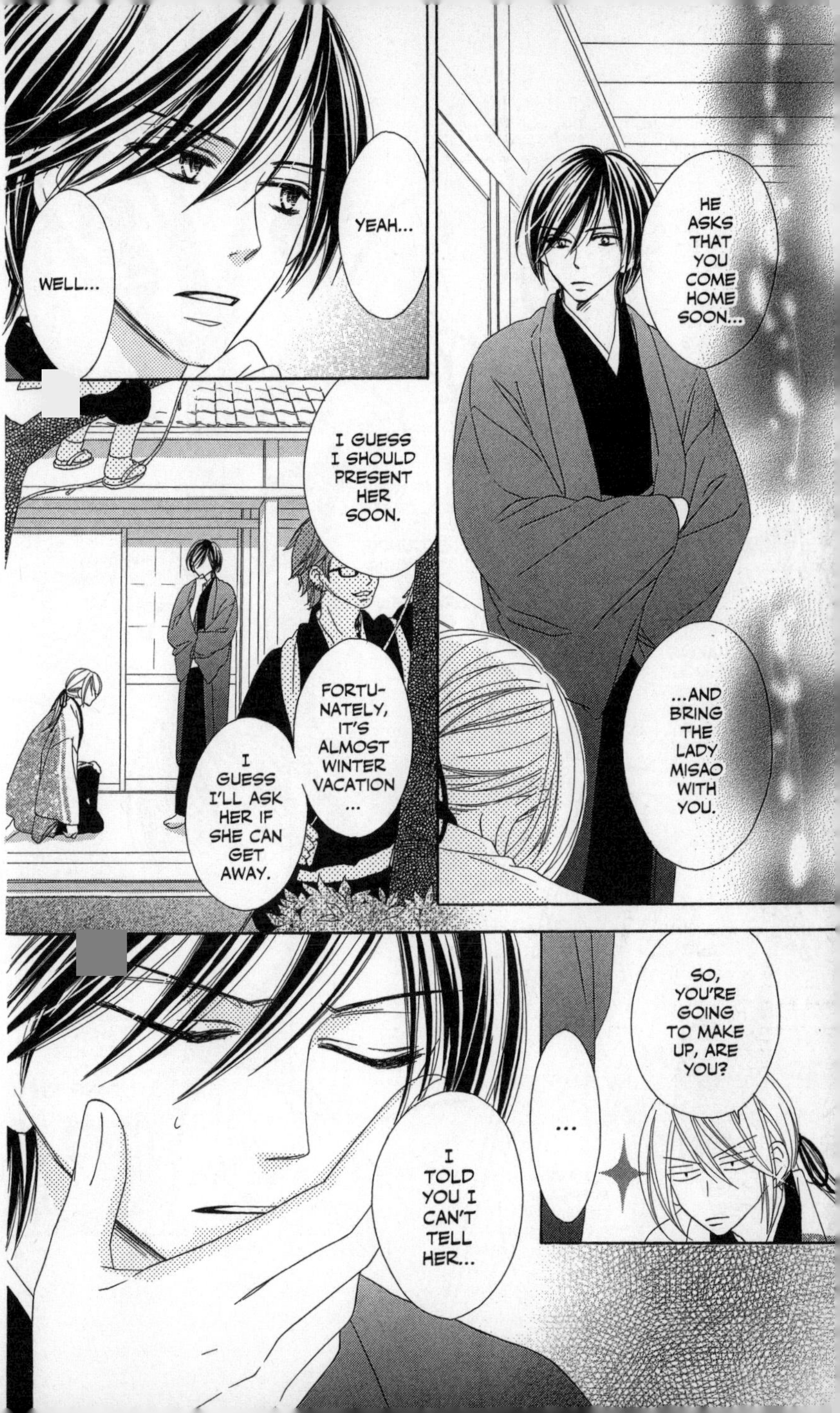
HE ASKS THAT YOU COME HOME SOON...
...AND BRING THE LADY MISAO WITH YOU.
YEAH...
WELL...
I GUESS I SHOULD PRESENT HER SOON.
FORTUNATELY, IT'S ALMOST WINTER VACATION...
I GUESS I'LL ASK HER IF SHE CAN GET AWAY.
SO, YOU'RE GOING TO MAKE UP, ARE YOU?
...
I TOLD YOU I CAN'T TELL HER...

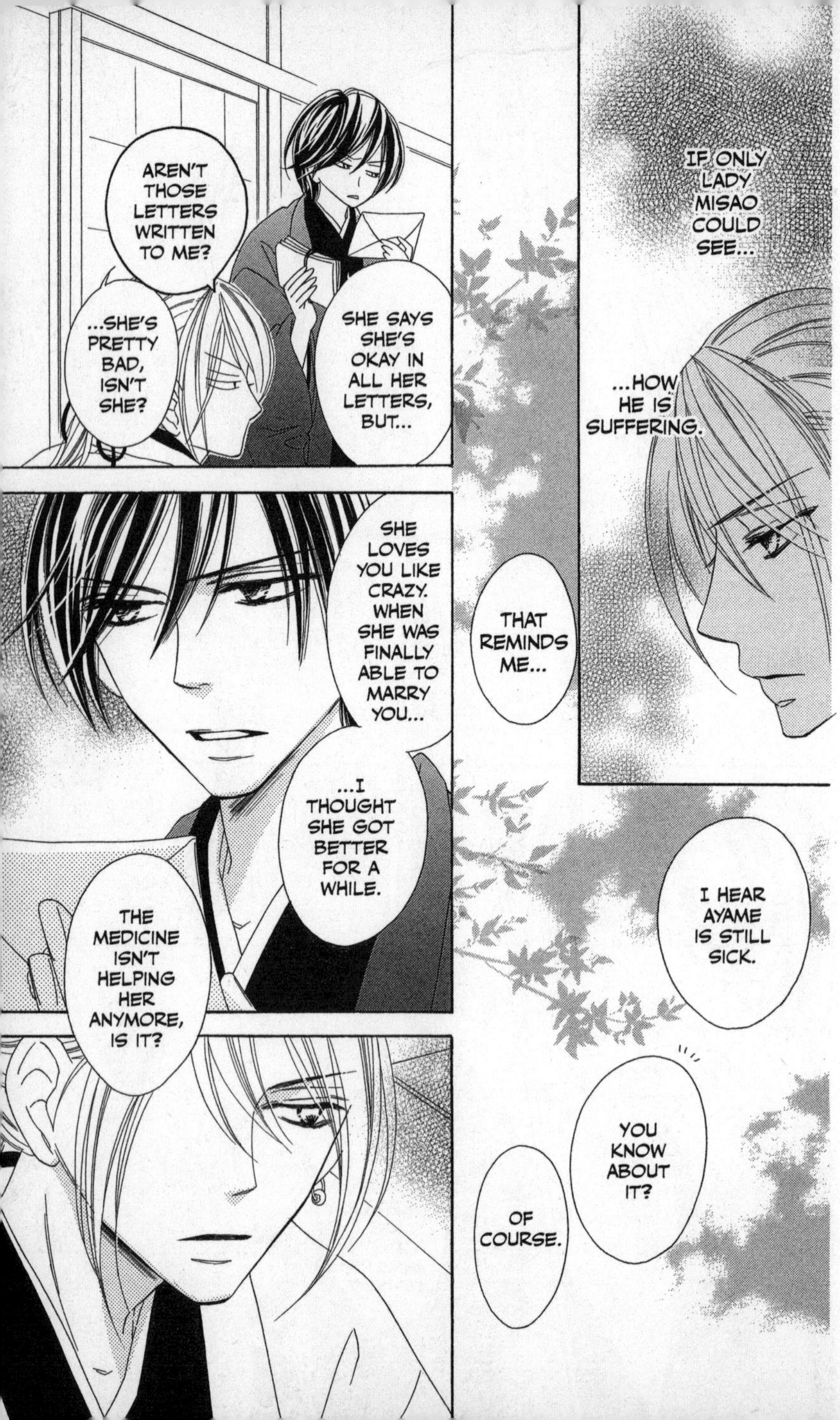

IF ONLY LADY MISAO COULD SEE...
...HOW HE IS SUFFERING.
THAT REMINDS ME...
I HEAR AYAME IS STILL SICK.
YOU KNOW ABOUT IT?
OF COURSE.
AREN'T THOSE LETTERS WRITTEN TO ME?
SHE SAYS SHE'S OKAY IN ALL HER LETTERS, BUT...
...SHE'S PRETTY BAD, ISN'T SHE?
SHE LOVES YOU LIKE CRAZY. WHEN SHE WAS FINALLY ABLE TO MARRY YOU...
...I THOUGHT SHE GOT BETTER FOR A WHILE.
THE MEDICINE ISN'T HELPING HER ANYMORE, IS IT?

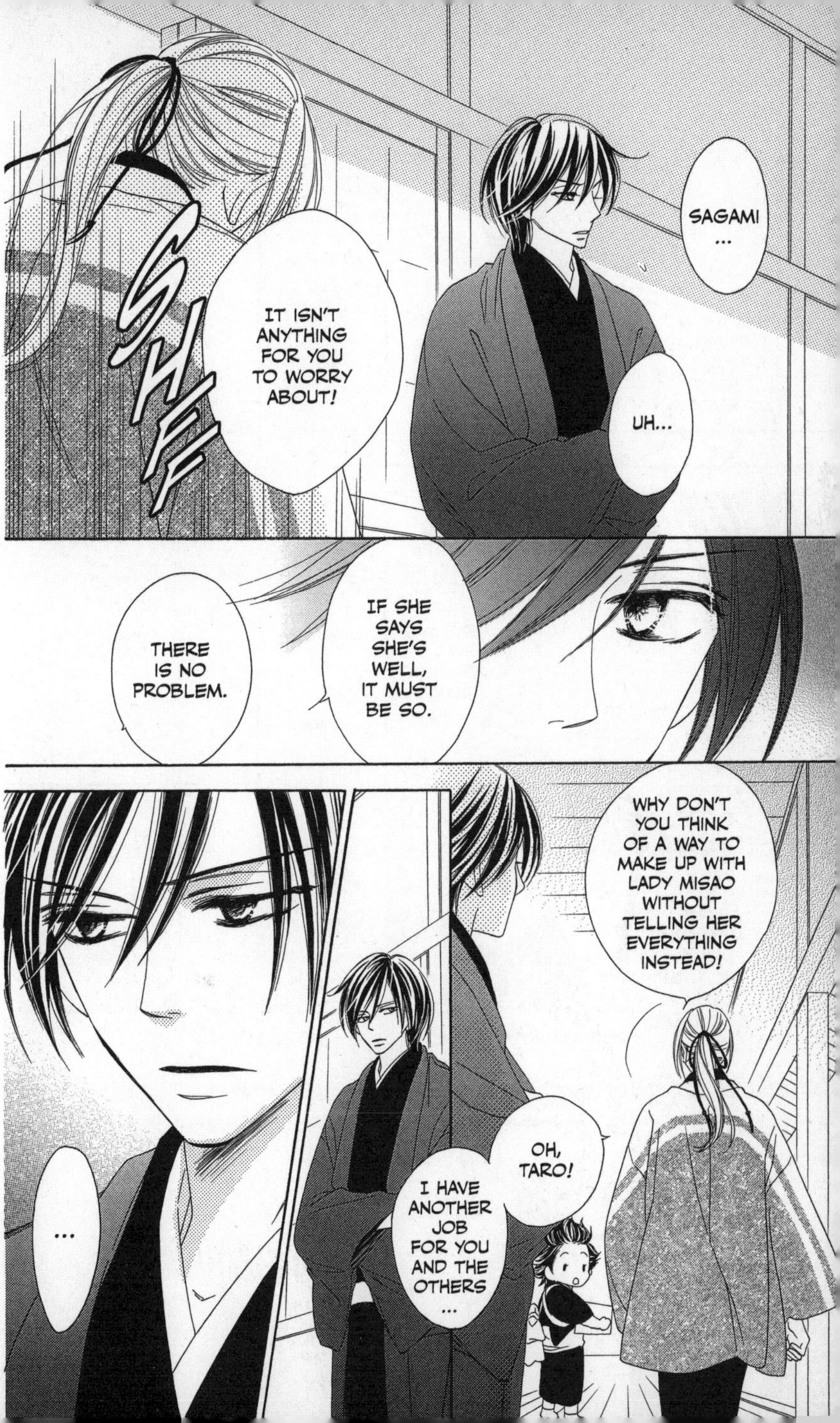
SAGAMI ...
UH...
IT ISN'T ANYTHING FOR YOU TO WORRY ABOUT!
SHFF
IF SHE SAYS SHE'S WELL, IT MUST BE SO.
THERE IS NO PROBLEM.
WHY DON'T YOU THINK OF A WAY TO MAKE UP WITH LADY MISAO WITHOUT TELLING HER EVERYTHING INSTEAD!
OH, TARO!
I HAVE ANOTHER JOB FOR YOU AND THE OTHERS ...
...

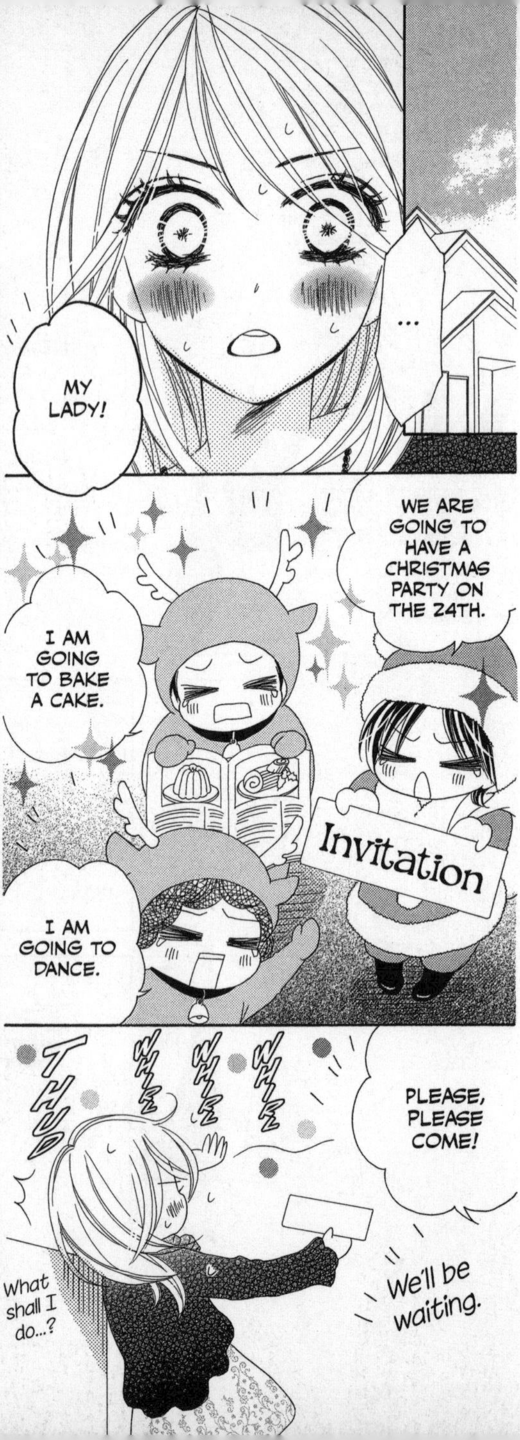
...
MY LADY!
WE ARE GOING TO HAVE A CHRISTMAS PARTY ON THE 24TH.
Invitation
I AM GOING TO BAKE A CAKE.
I AM GOING TO DANCE.
PLEASE, PLEASE COME!
WHEE
WHEE
WHEE
THUD
We'll be waiting.
What shall I do...?

It's fun drawing the kids in costume. Or rather, just drawing the kids is fun.

That reminds me—except for Taro, I haven't done character introductions for the kiddies, or the others in the Eight Daitengu either.

I've completely missed my opportunity. I gave you their ages and heights, but is that enough...?

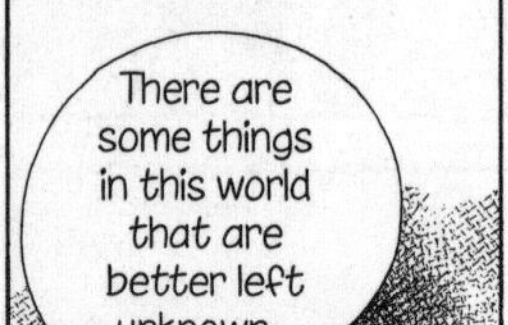
There are some things in this world that are better left unknown...
HEE HEE HEE...

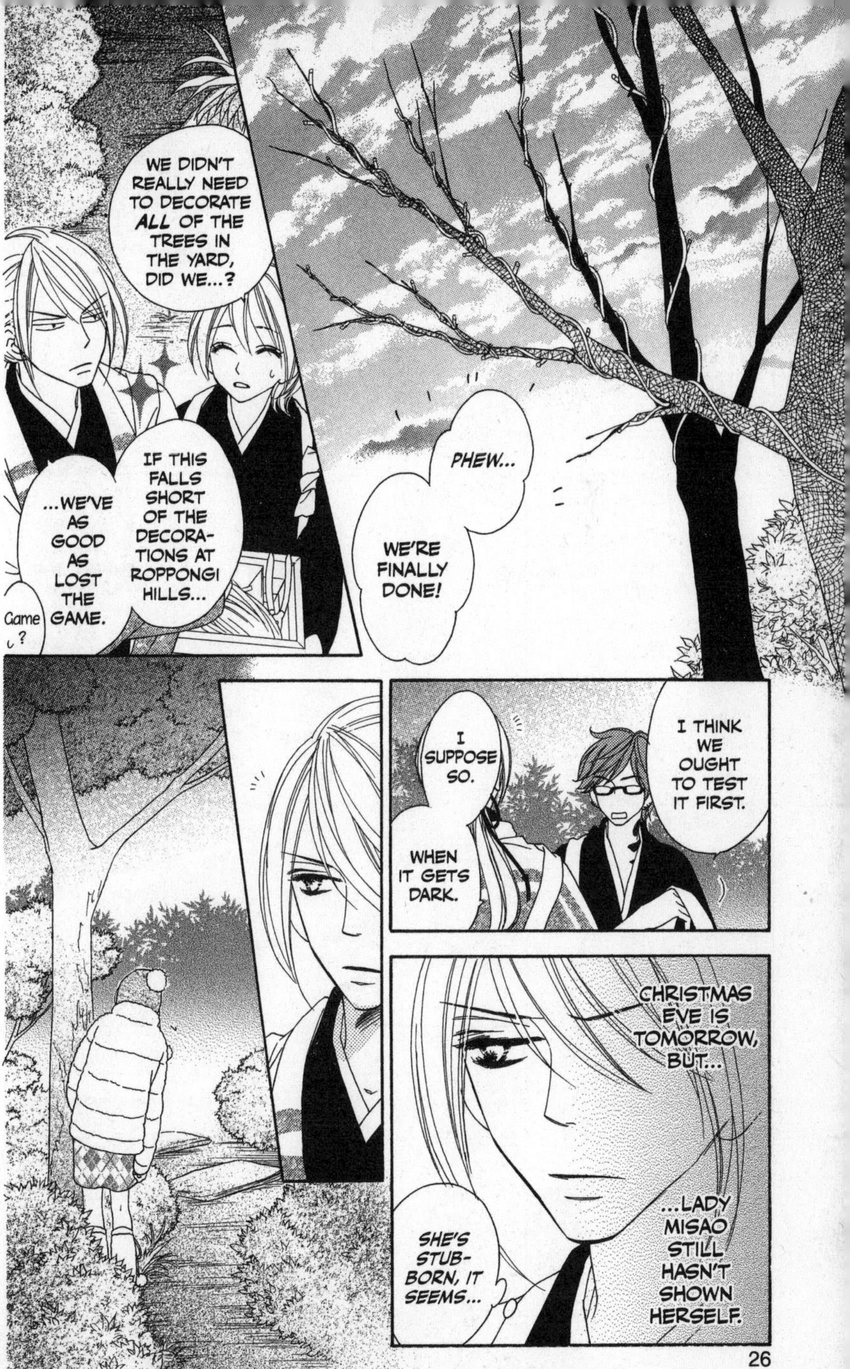
PHEW...
WE'RE FINALLY DONE!
WE DIDN'T REALLY NEED TO DECORATE ALL OF THE TREES IN THE YARD, DID WE...?
IF THIS FALLS SHORT OF THE DECORATIONS AT ROPPONGI HILLS...
...WE'VE AS GOOD AS LOST THE GAME.
Game ?
I THINK WE OUGHT TO TEST IT FIRST.
I SUPPOSE SO.
WHEN IT GETS DARK.
CHRISTMAS EVE IS TOMORROW, BUT...
...LADY MISAO STILL HASN'T SHOWN HERSELF.
SHE'S STUBBORN, IT SEEMS...

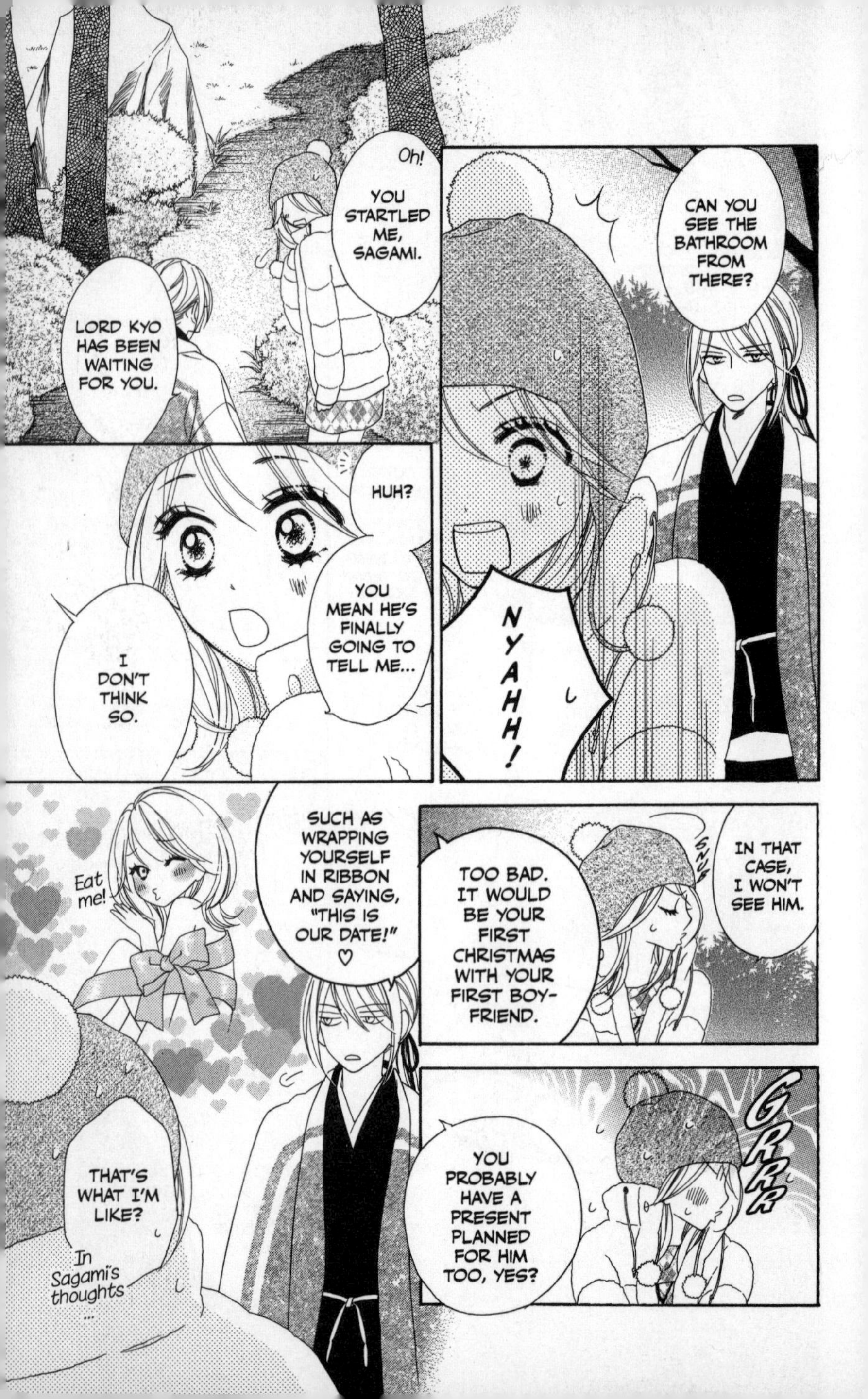
CAN YOU SEE THE BATHROOM FROM THERE?
NYAHH!
Oh!
YOU STARTLED ME, SAGAMI.
LORD KYO HAS BEEN WAITING FOR YOU.
HUH?
YOU MEAN HE'S FINALLY GOING TO TELL ME...
I DON'T THINK SO.
IN THAT CASE, I WON'T SEE HIM.
SNUB
TOO BAD. IT WOULD BE YOUR FIRST CHRISTMAS WITH YOUR FIRST BOY-FRIEND.
YOU PROBABLY HAVE A PRESENT PLANNED FOR HIM TOO, YES?
GRRRR
SUCH AS WRAPPING YOURSELF IN RIBBON AND SAYING, "THIS IS OUR DATE!" ♡
Eat me!
THAT'S WHAT I'M LIKE?
In Sagami's thoughts...

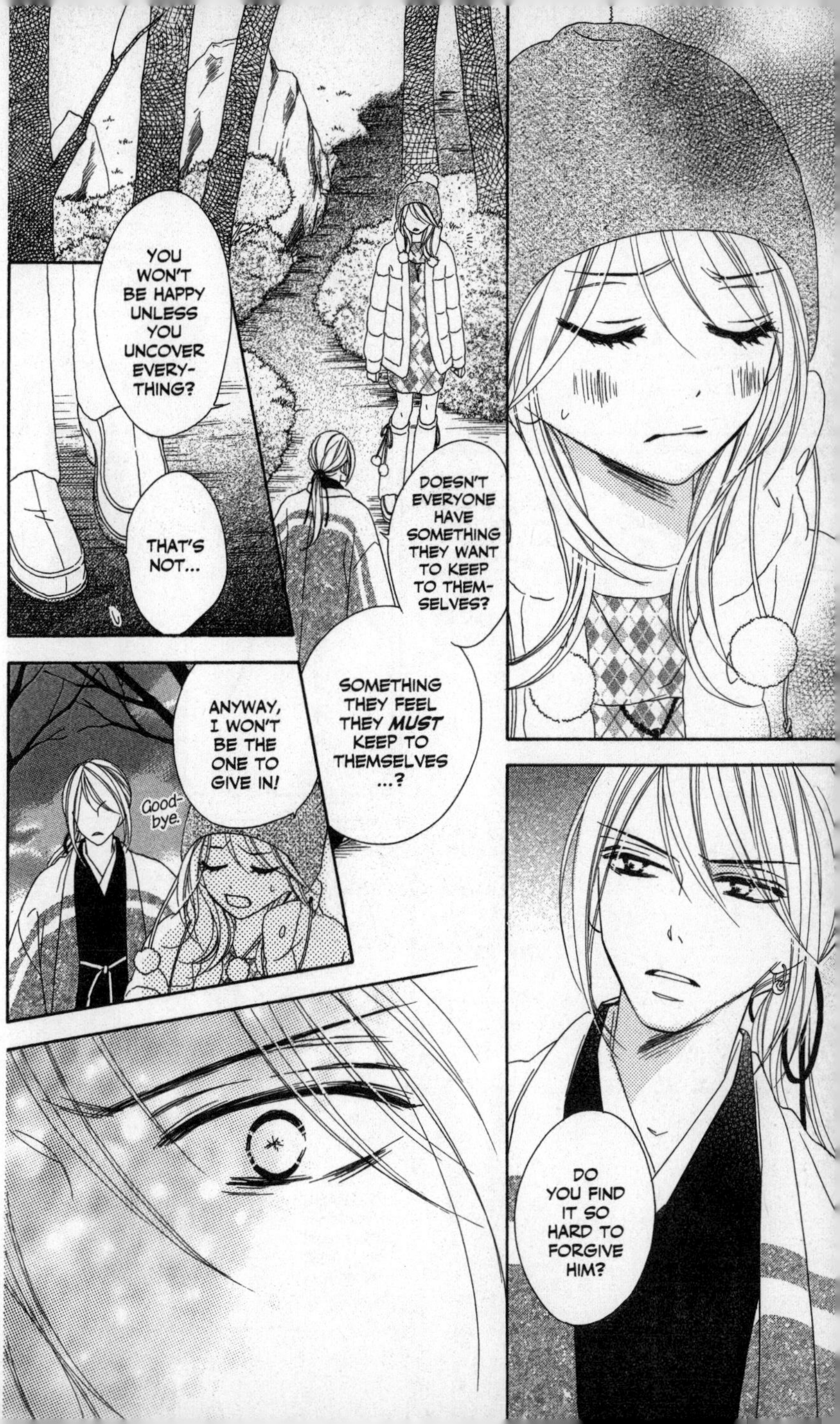
YOU WON'T BE HAPPY UNLESS YOU UNCOVER EVERY-THING?
THAT'S NOT...
DOESN'T EVERYONE HAVE SOMETHING THEY WANT TO KEEP TO THEM-SELVES?
SOMETHING THEY FEEL THEY *MUST* KEEP TO THEMSELVES ...?
ANYWAY, I WON'T BE THE ONE TO GIVE IN!
Good-bye.
DO YOU FIND IT SO HARD TO FORGIVE HIM?

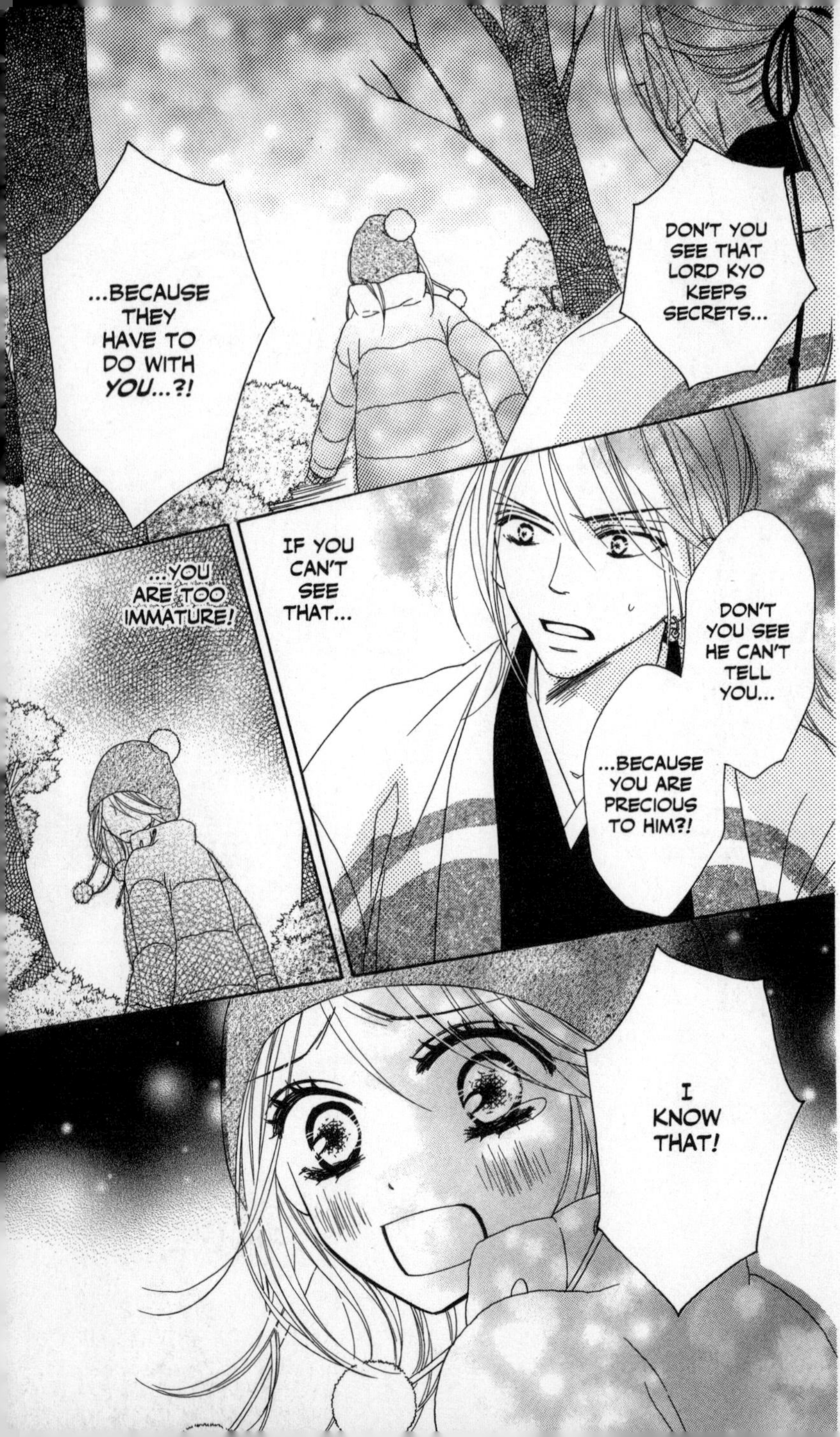
DON'T YOU SEE THAT LORD KYO KEEPS SECRETS...
...BECAUSE THEY HAVE TO DO WITH *YOU*...?!
DON'T YOU SEE HE CAN'T TELL YOU...
...BECAUSE YOU ARE PRECIOUS TO HIM?!
IF YOU CAN'T SEE THAT...
...YOU ARE TOO IMMATURE!
I KNOW THAT!

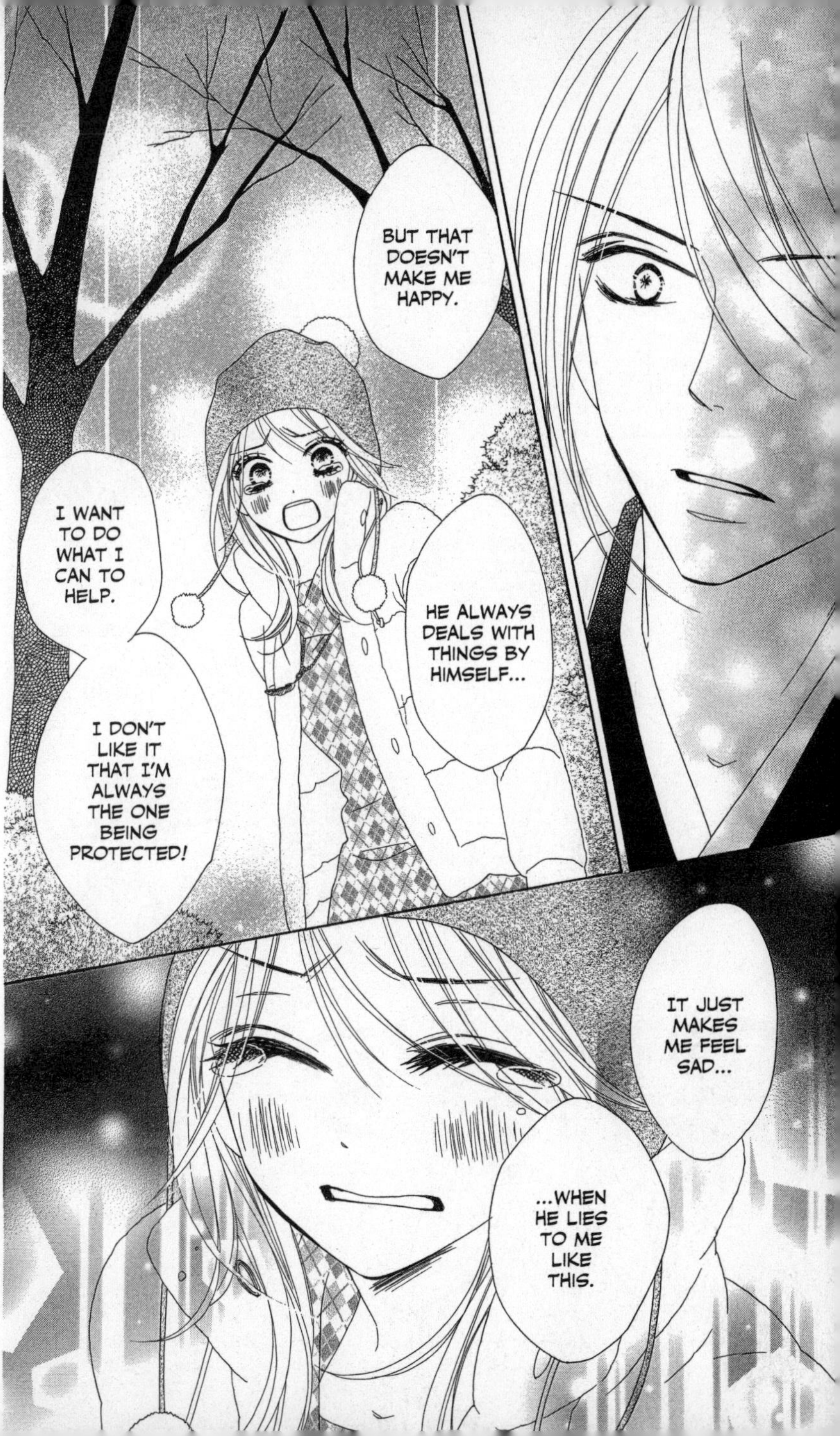
BUT THAT DOESN'T MAKE ME HAPPY.
HE ALWAYS DEALS WITH THINGS BY HIMSELF...
I WANT TO DO WHAT I CAN TO HELP.
I DON'T LIKE IT THAT I'M ALWAYS THE ONE BEING PROTECTED!
IT JUST MAKES ME FEEL SAD...
...WHEN HE LIES TO ME LIKE THIS.

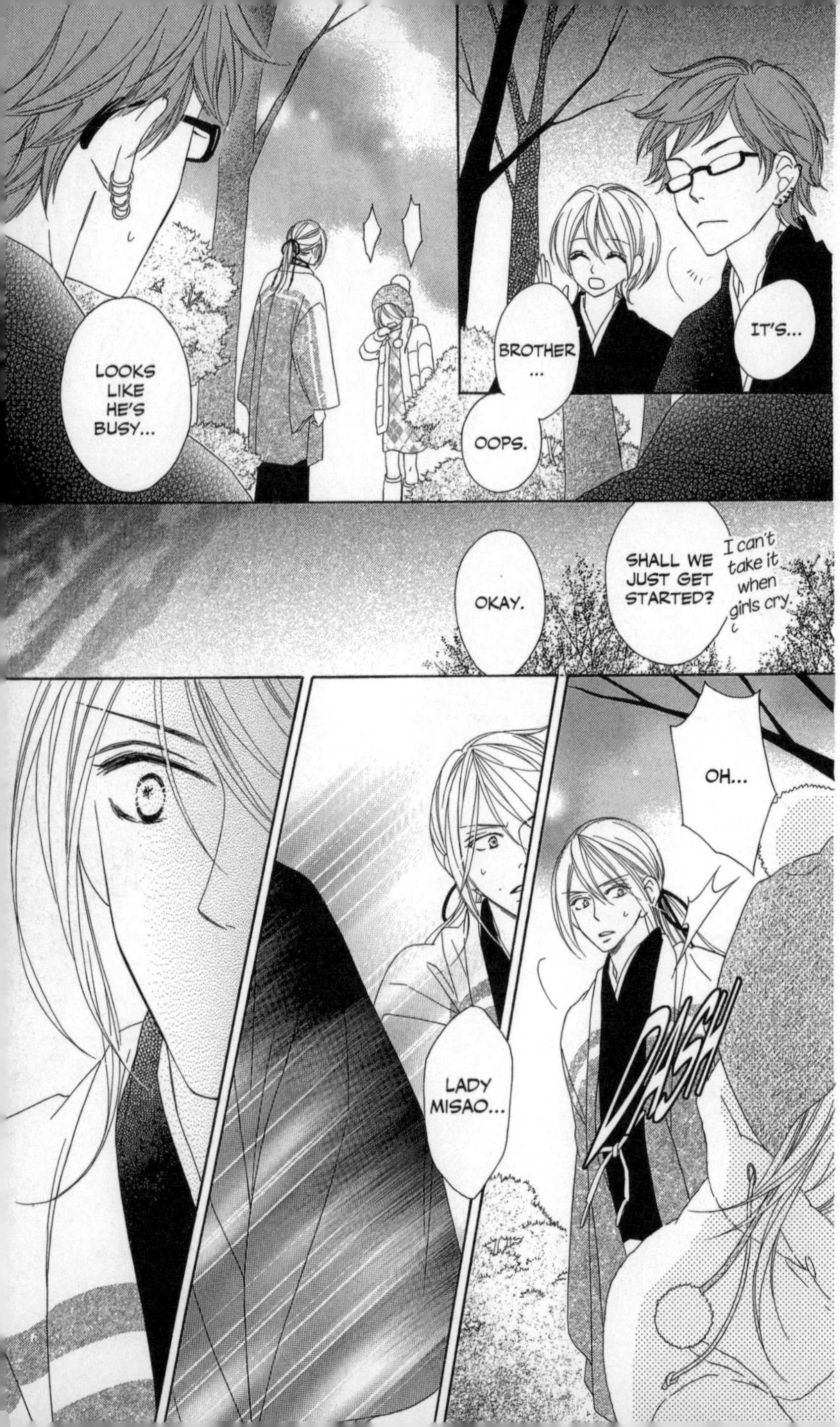
IT'S...
BROTHER ...
OOPS.
LOOKS LIKE HE'S BUSY...
I can't take it when girls cry.
SHALL WE JUST GET STARTED?
OKAY.
OH...
DASH
LADY MISAO...

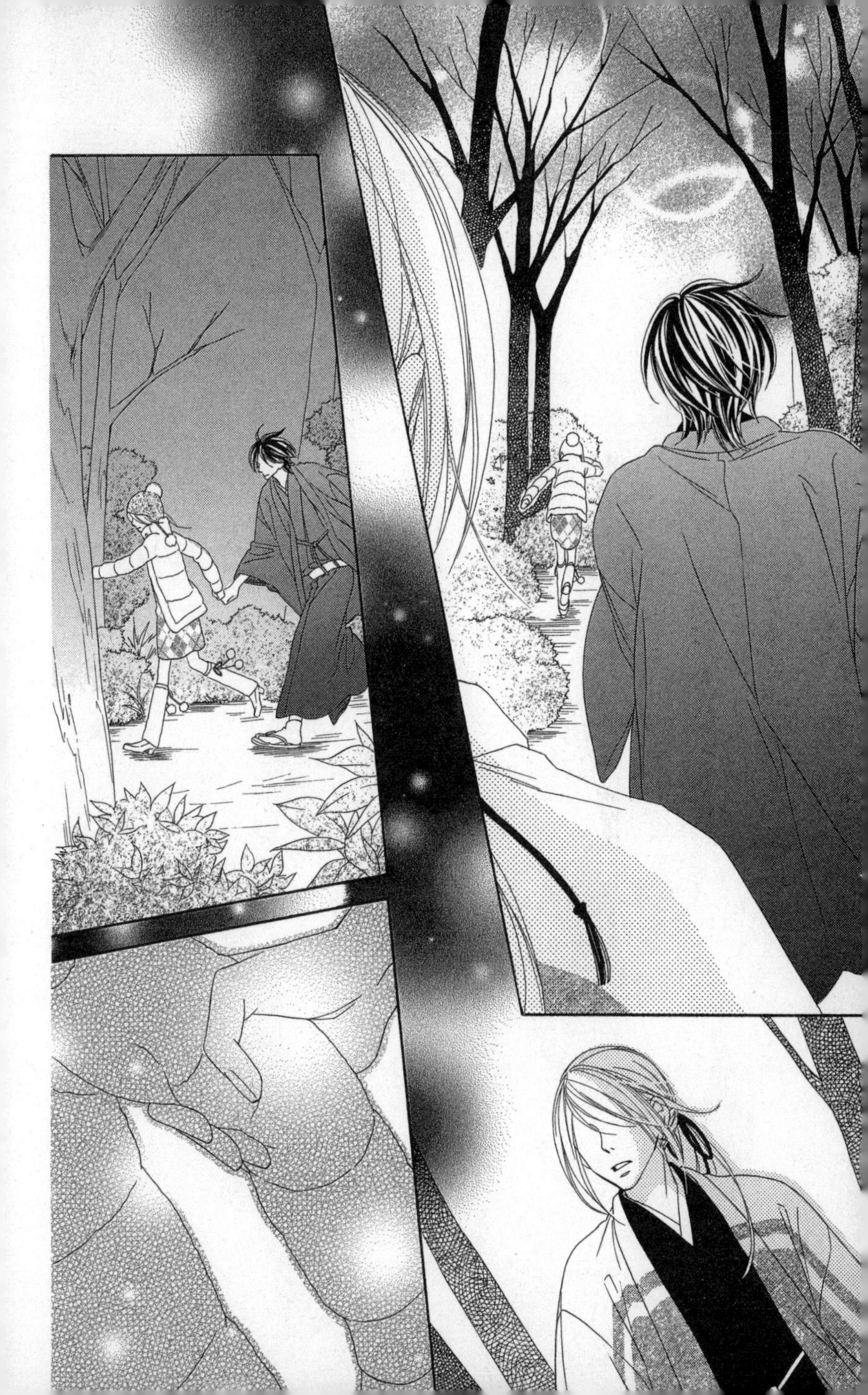

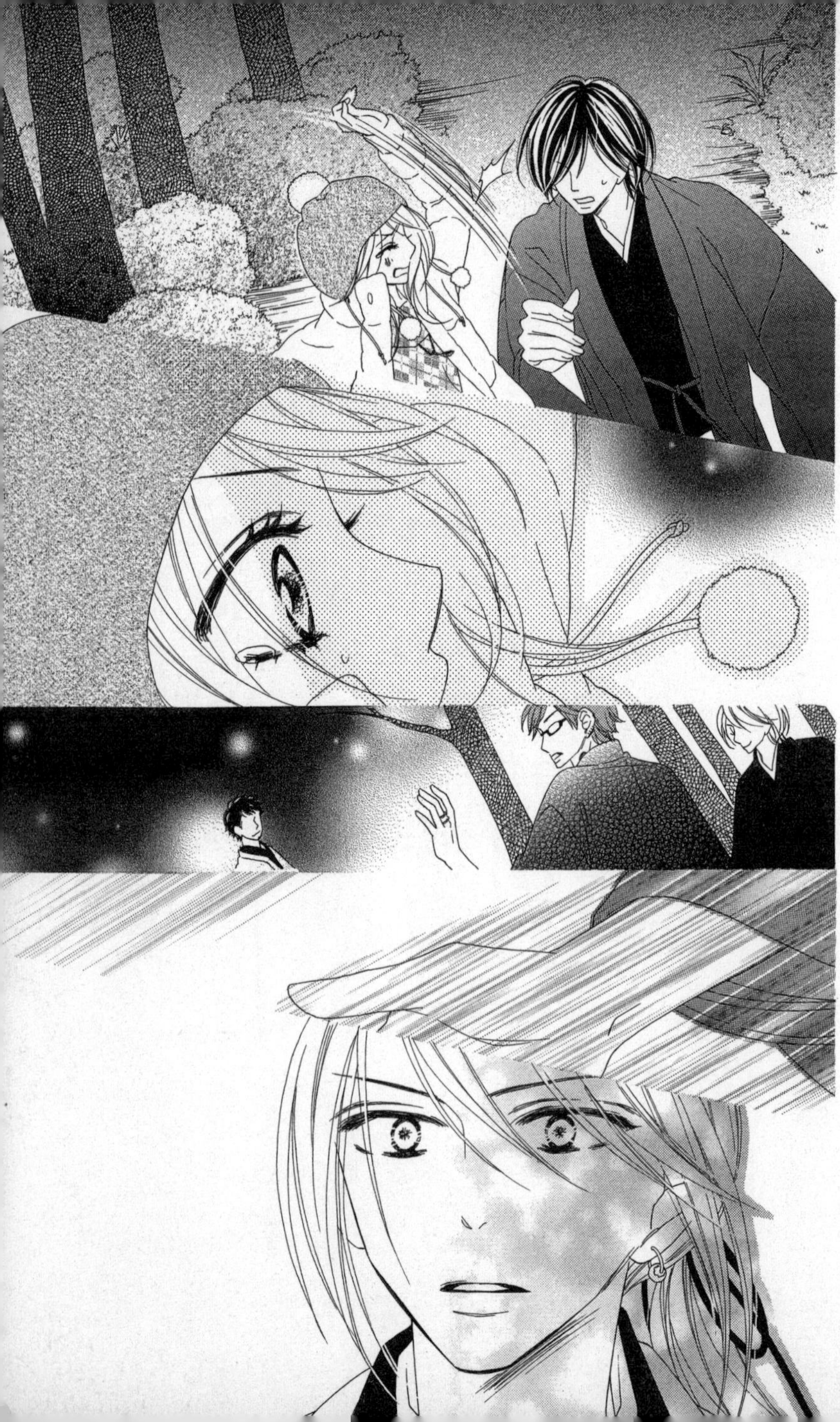

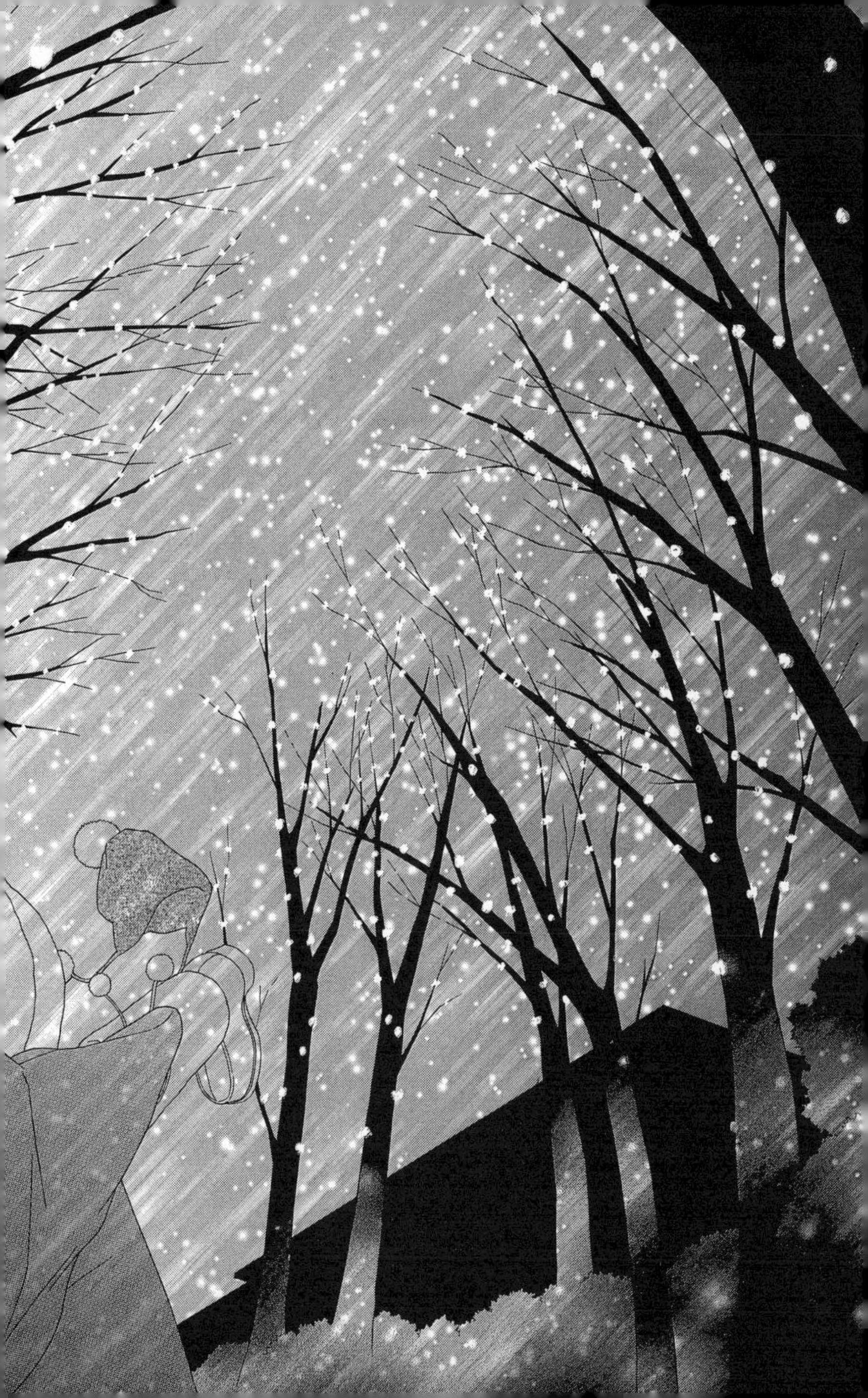

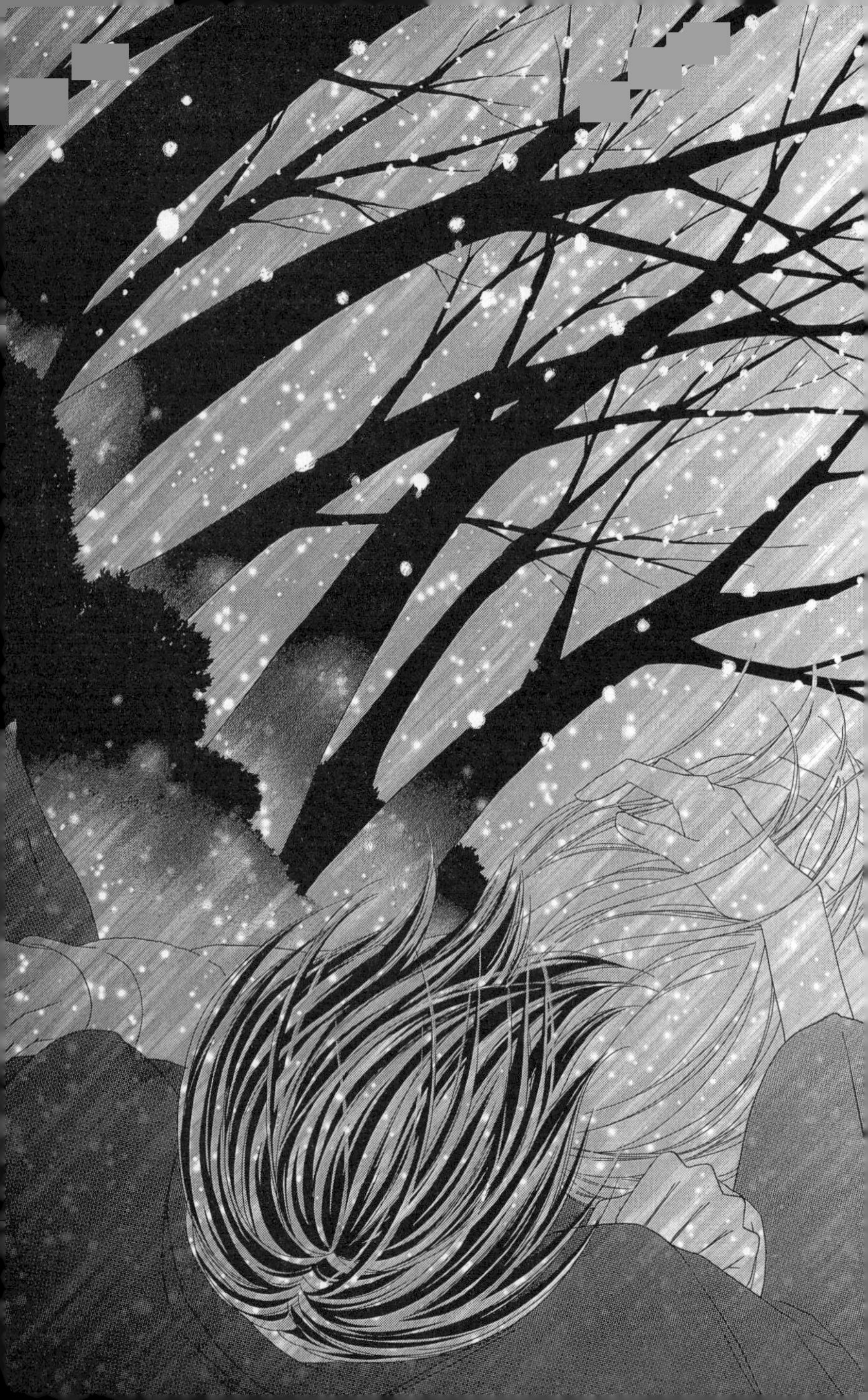

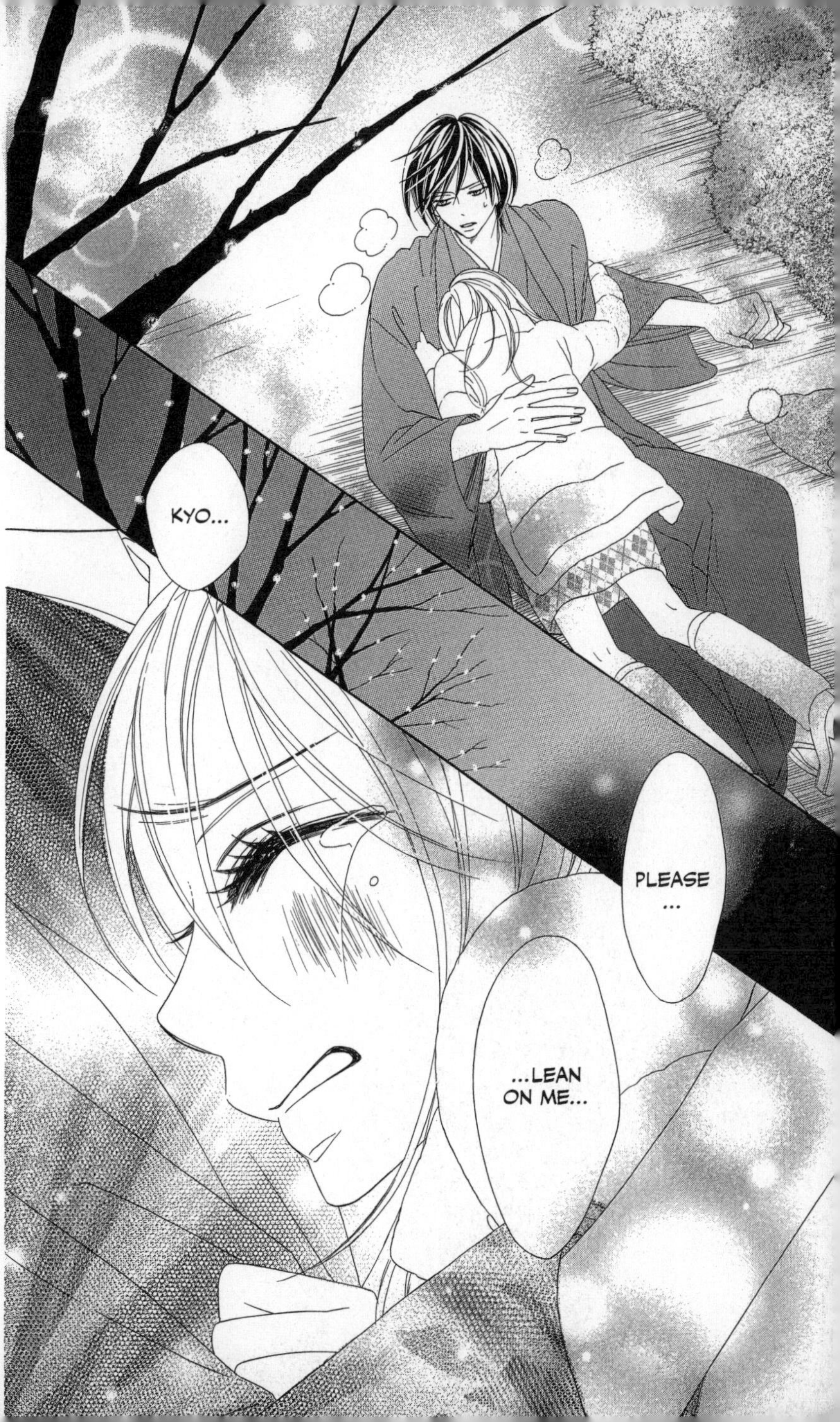
PLEASE ...
...LEAN ON ME...
KYO...

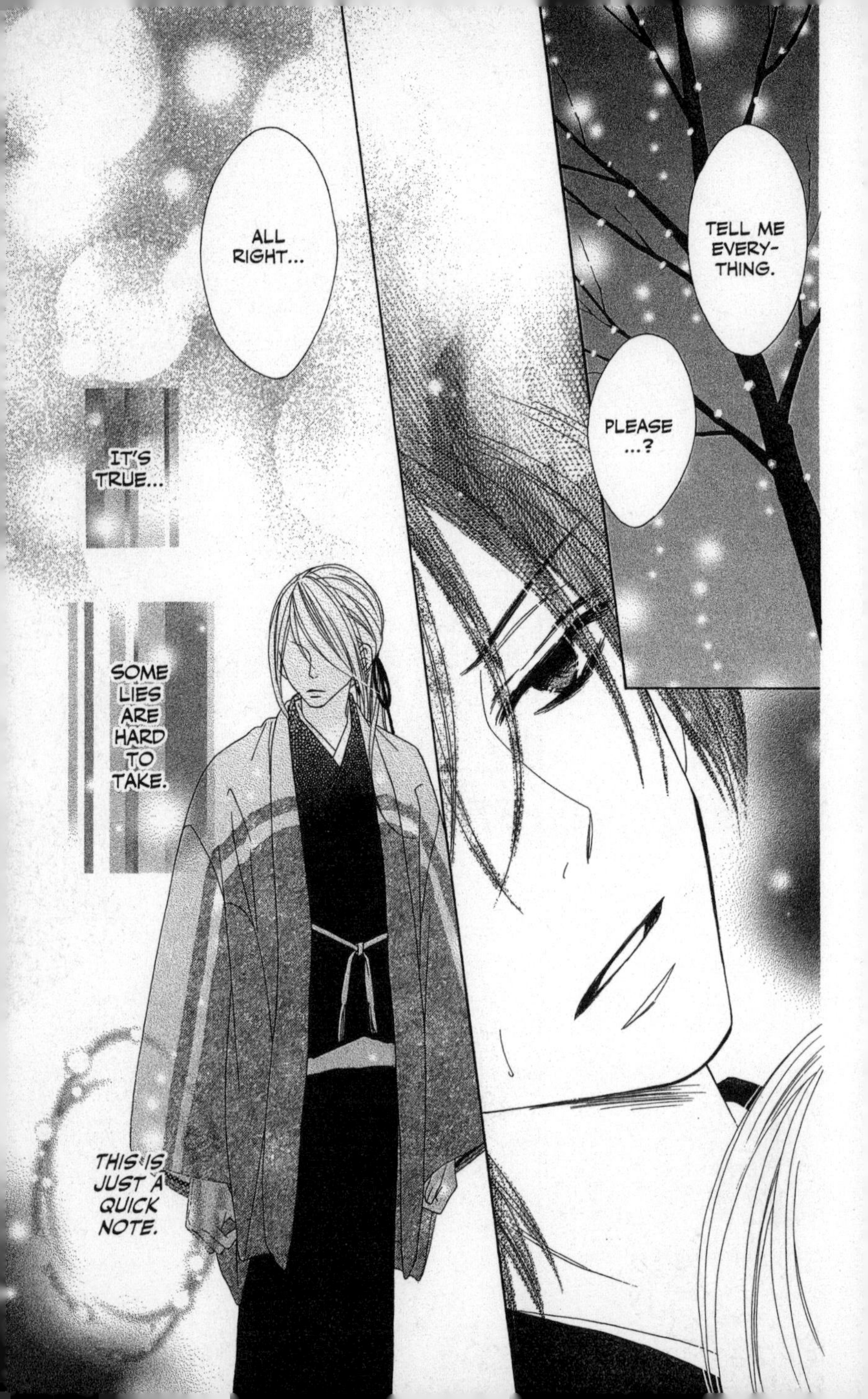
TELL ME EVERY-THING.
PLEASE ...?
ALL RIGHT...
IT'S TRUE...
SOME LIES ARE HARD TO TAKE.
THIS IS JUST A QUICK NOTE.

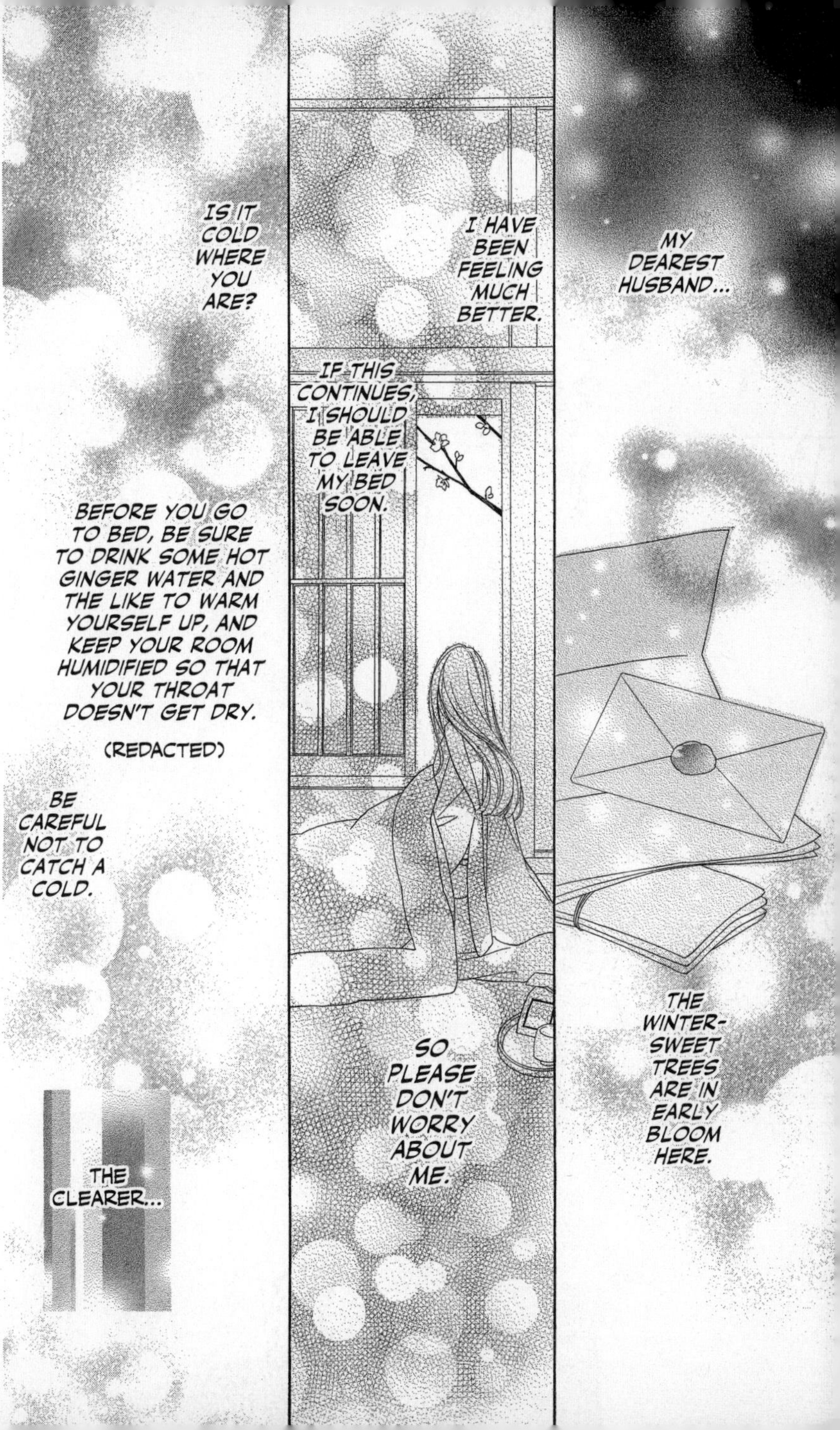
MY DEAREST HUSBAND...
THE WINTER-SWEET TREES ARE IN EARLY BLOOM HERE.
I HAVE BEEN FEELING MUCH BETTER.
IF THIS CONTINUES, I SHOULD BE ABLE TO LEAVE MY BED SOON.
SO PLEASE DON'T WORRY ABOUT ME.
IS IT COLD WHERE YOU ARE?
BEFORE YOU GO TO BED, BE SURE TO DRINK SOME HOT GINGER WATER AND THE LIKE TO WARM YOURSELF UP, AND KEEP YOUR ROOM HUMIDIFIED SO THAT YOUR THROAT DOESN'T GET DRY.
(REDACTED)
BE CAREFUL NOT TO CATCH A COLD.
THE CLEARER...

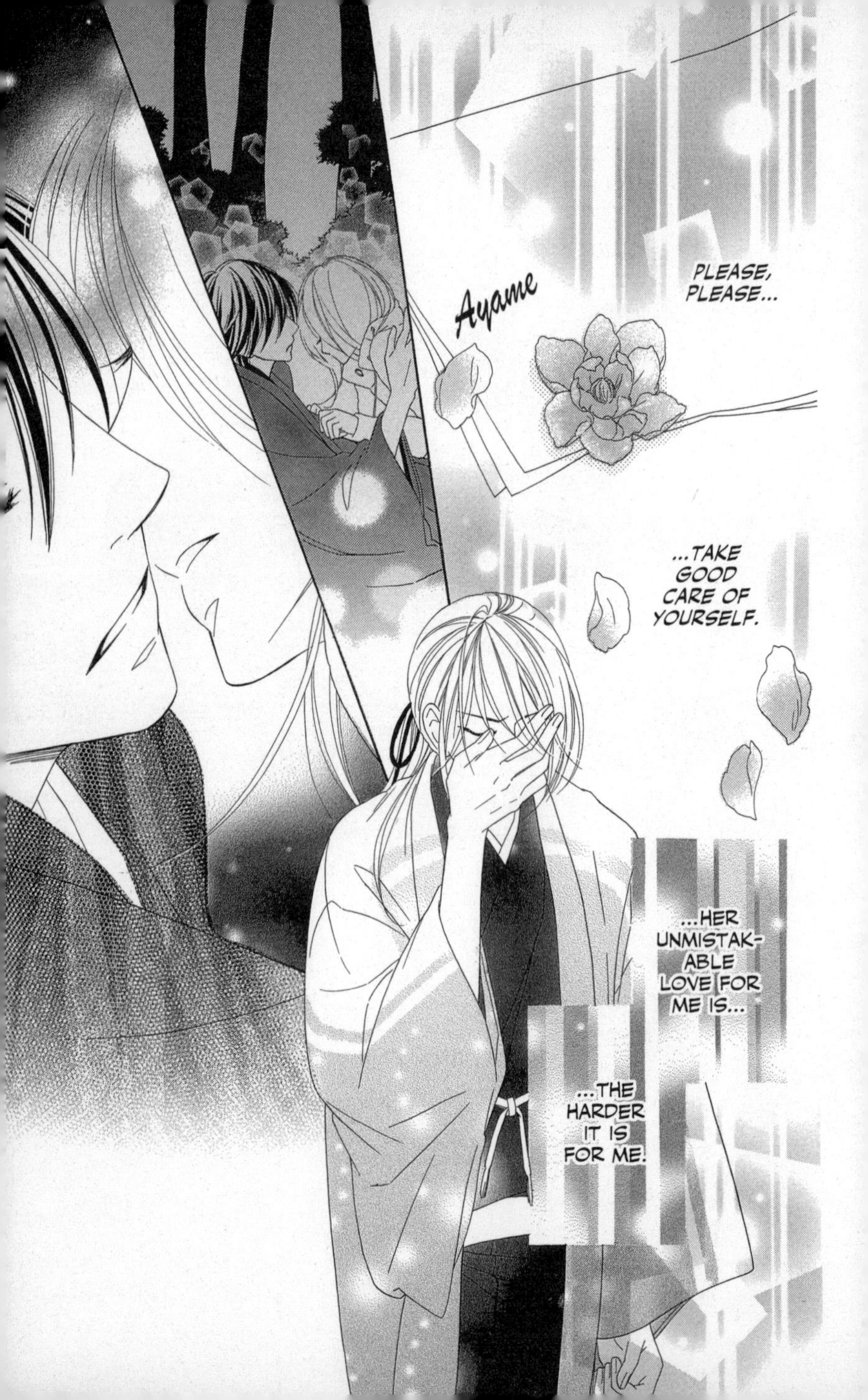
PLEASE, PLEASE...
Ayame
...TAKE GOOD CARE OF YOURSELF.
...HER UNMISTAK-ABLE LOVE FOR ME IS...
...THE HARDER IT IS FOR ME.

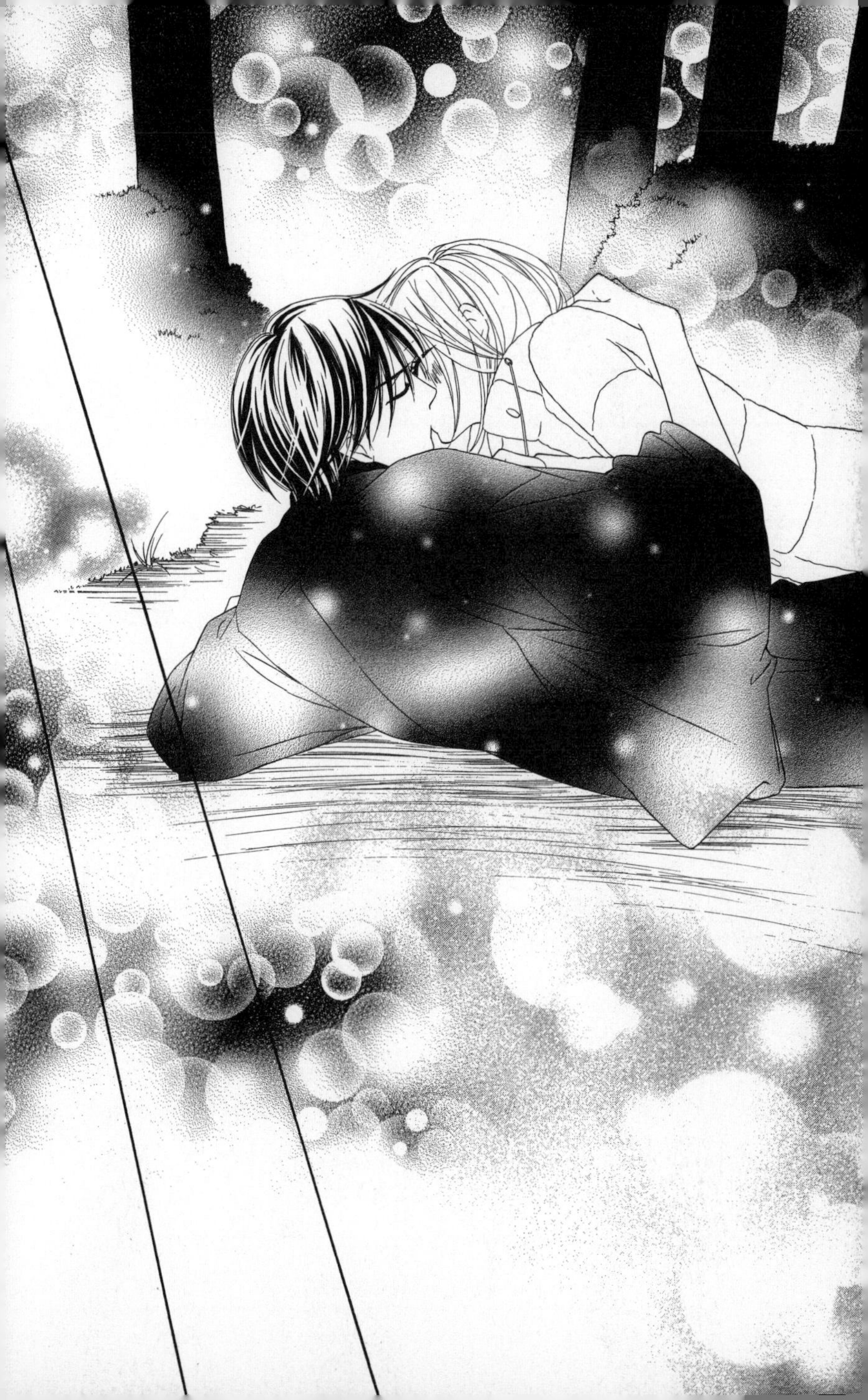

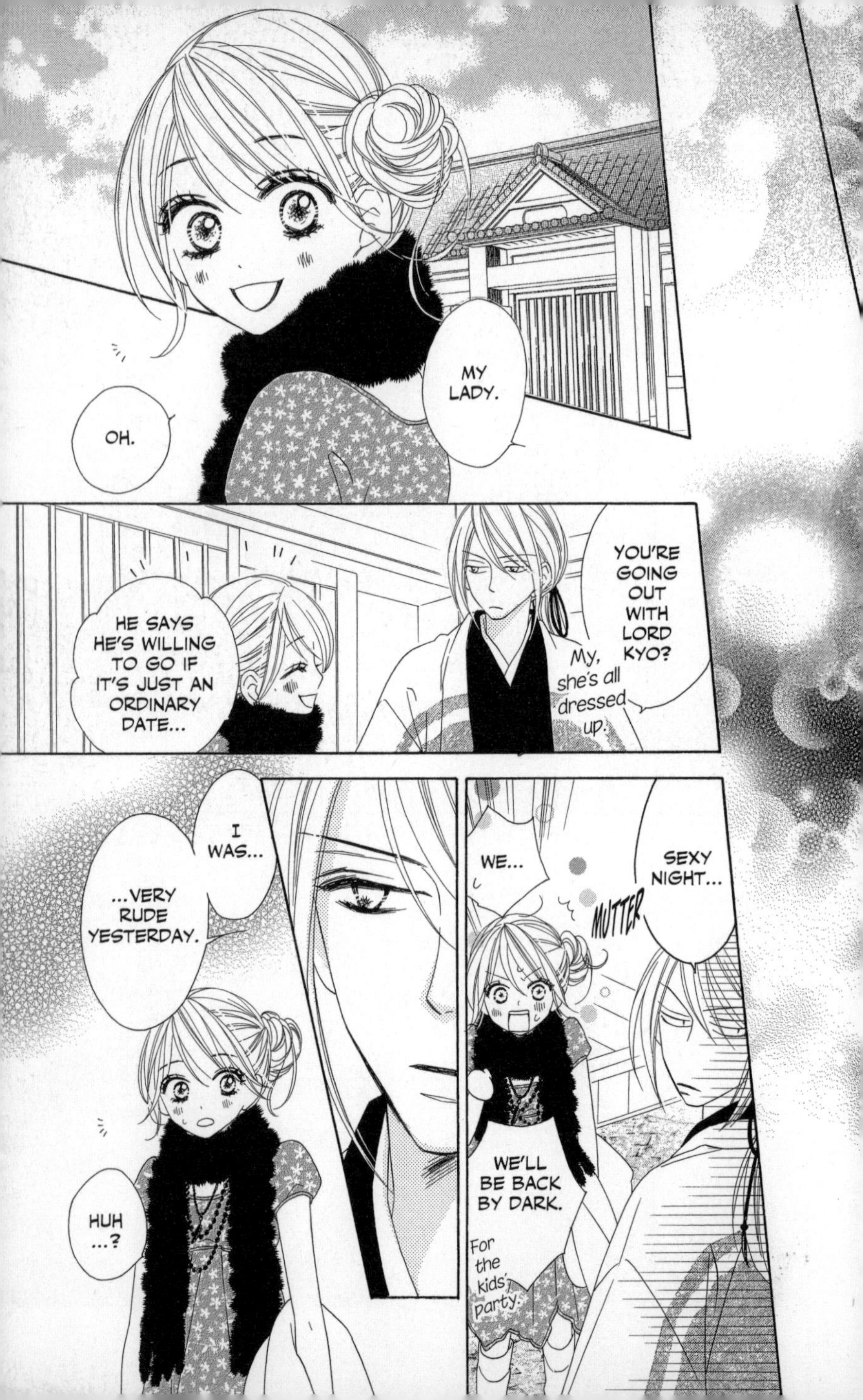
MY LADY.
OH.
YOU'RE GOING OUT WITH LORD KYO?
My, she's all dressed up.
HE SAYS HE'S WILLING TO GO IF IT'S JUST AN ORDINARY DATE...
SEXY NIGHT...
MUTTER
WE...
WE'LL BE BACK BY DARK.
For the kids' party.
I WAS...
...VERY RUDE YESTERDAY.
HUH ...?

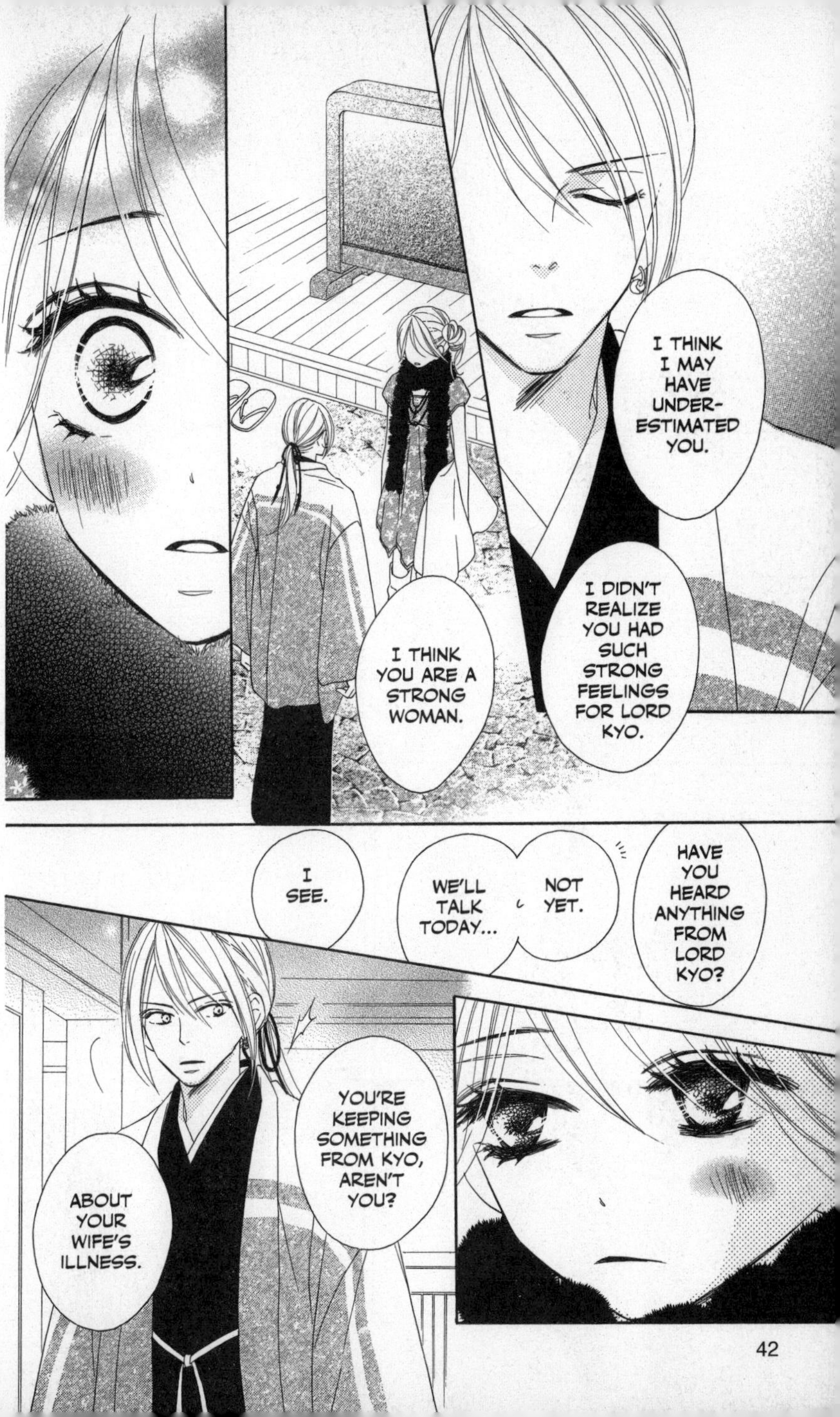
I THINK I MAY HAVE UNDER-ESTIMATED YOU.
I DIDN'T REALIZE YOU HAD SUCH STRONG FEELINGS FOR LORD KYO.
I THINK YOU ARE A STRONG WOMAN.
HAVE YOU HEARD ANYTHING FROM LORD KYO?
NOT YET.
WE'LL TALK TODAY...
I SEE.
YOU'RE KEEPING SOMETHING FROM KYO, AREN'T YOU?
ABOUT YOUR WIFE'S ILLNESS.

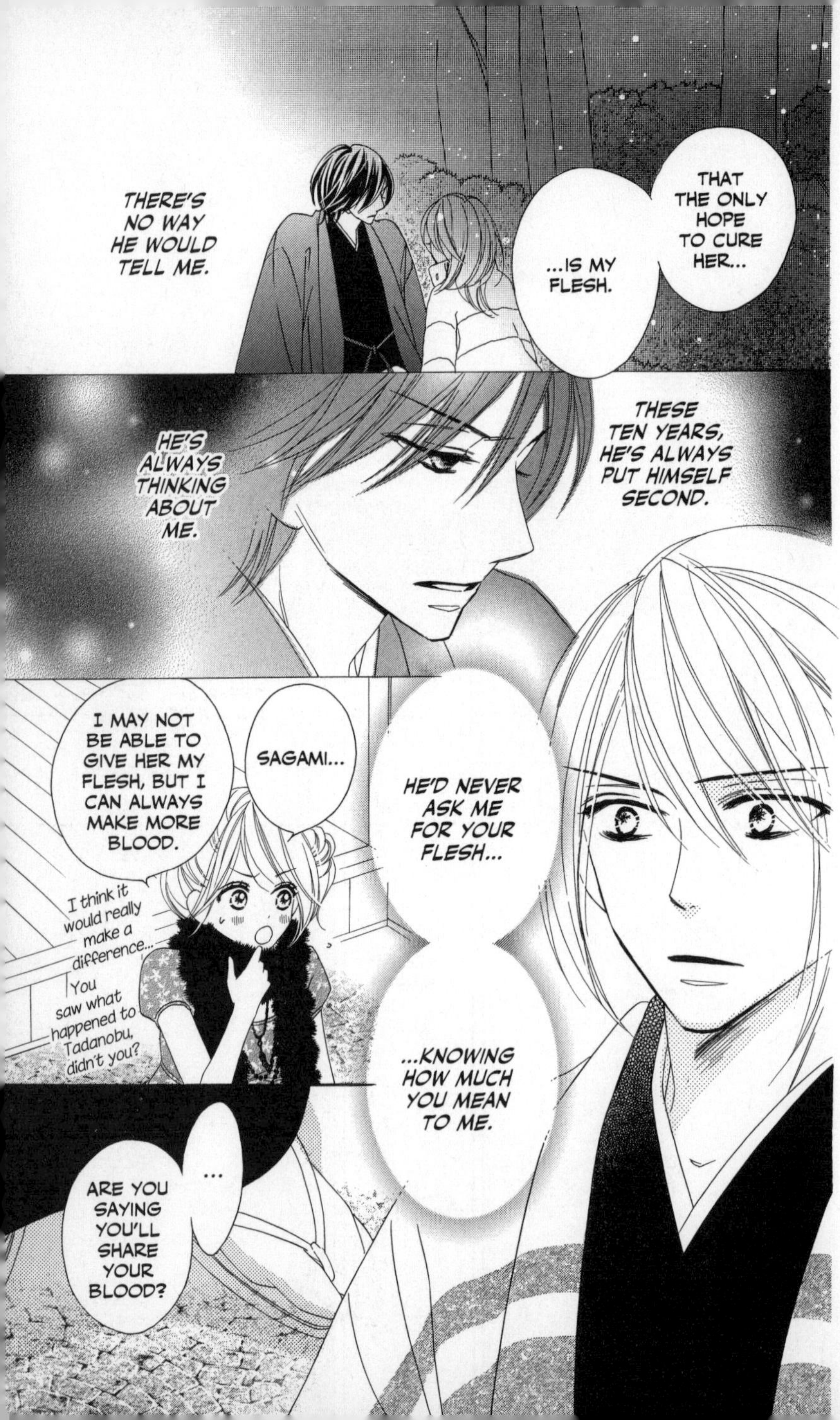
THAT THE ONLY HOPE TO CURE HER...
...IS MY FLESH.
THERE'S NO WAY HE WOULD TELL ME.
THESE TEN YEARS, HE'S ALWAYS PUT HIMSELF SECOND.
HE'S ALWAYS THINKING ABOUT ME.
HE'D NEVER ASK ME FOR YOUR FLESH...
...KNOWING HOW MUCH YOU MEAN TO ME.
SAGAMI...
I MAY NOT BE ABLE TO GIVE HER MY FLESH, BUT I CAN ALWAYS MAKE MORE BLOOD.
I think it would really make a difference...
You saw what happened to Tadanobu, didn't you?
...
ARE YOU SAYING YOU'LL SHARE YOUR BLOOD?

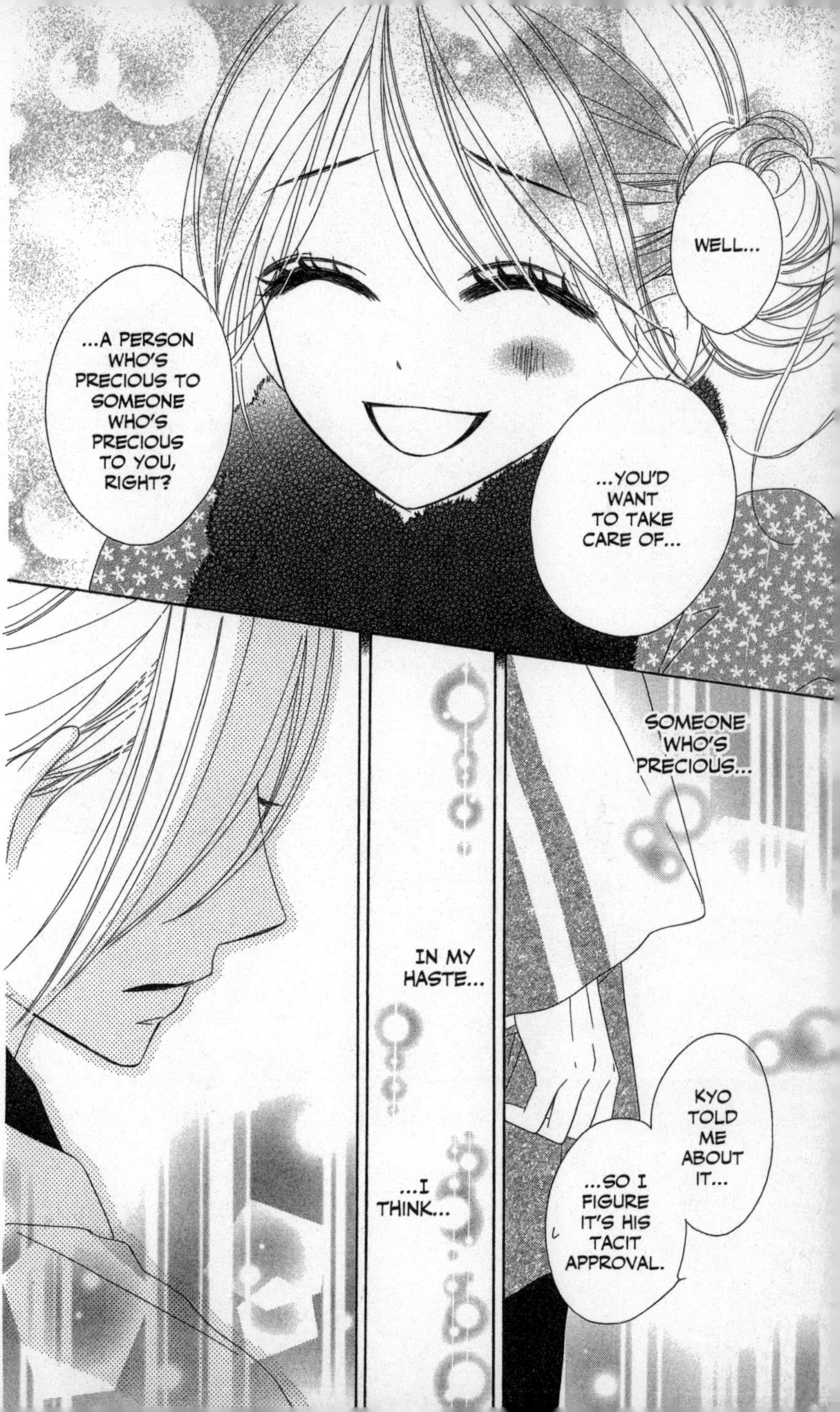
WELL...
...YOU'D WANT TO TAKE CARE OF...
...A PERSON WHO'S PRECIOUS TO SOMEONE WHO'S PRECIOUS TO YOU, RIGHT?
SOMEONE WHO'S PRECIOUS...
KYO TOLD ME ABOUT IT...
...SO I FIGURE IT'S HIS TACIT APPROVAL.
IN MY HASTE...
...I THINK...

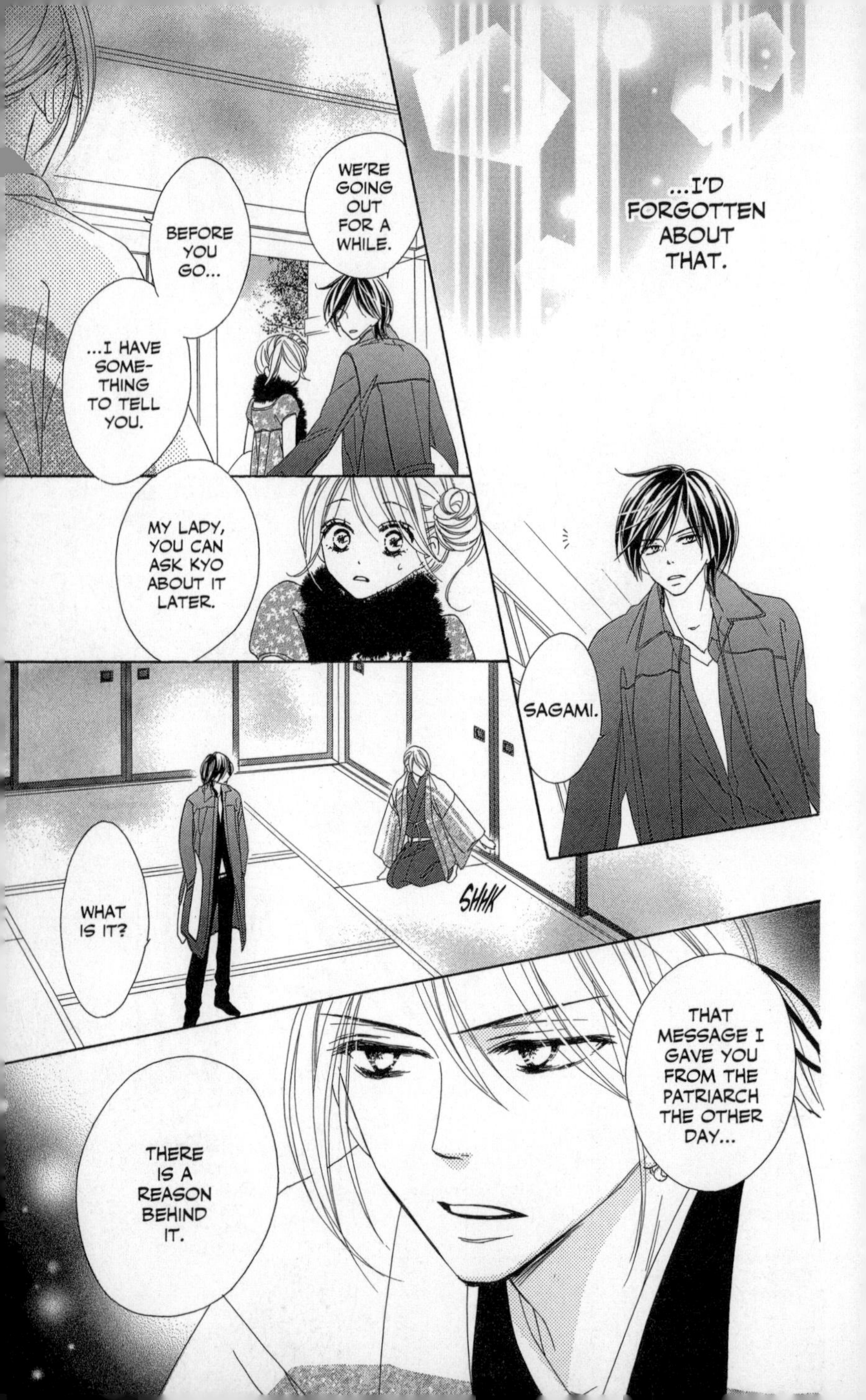
...I'D FORGOTTEN ABOUT THAT.
WE'RE GOING OUT FOR A WHILE.
BEFORE YOU GO...
...I HAVE SOME-THING TO TELL YOU.
SAGAMI.
MY LADY, YOU CAN ASK KYO ABOUT IT LATER.
WHAT IS IT?
SHHK
THAT MESSAGE I GAVE YOU FROM THE PATRIARCH THE OTHER DAY...
THERE IS A REASON BEHIND IT.

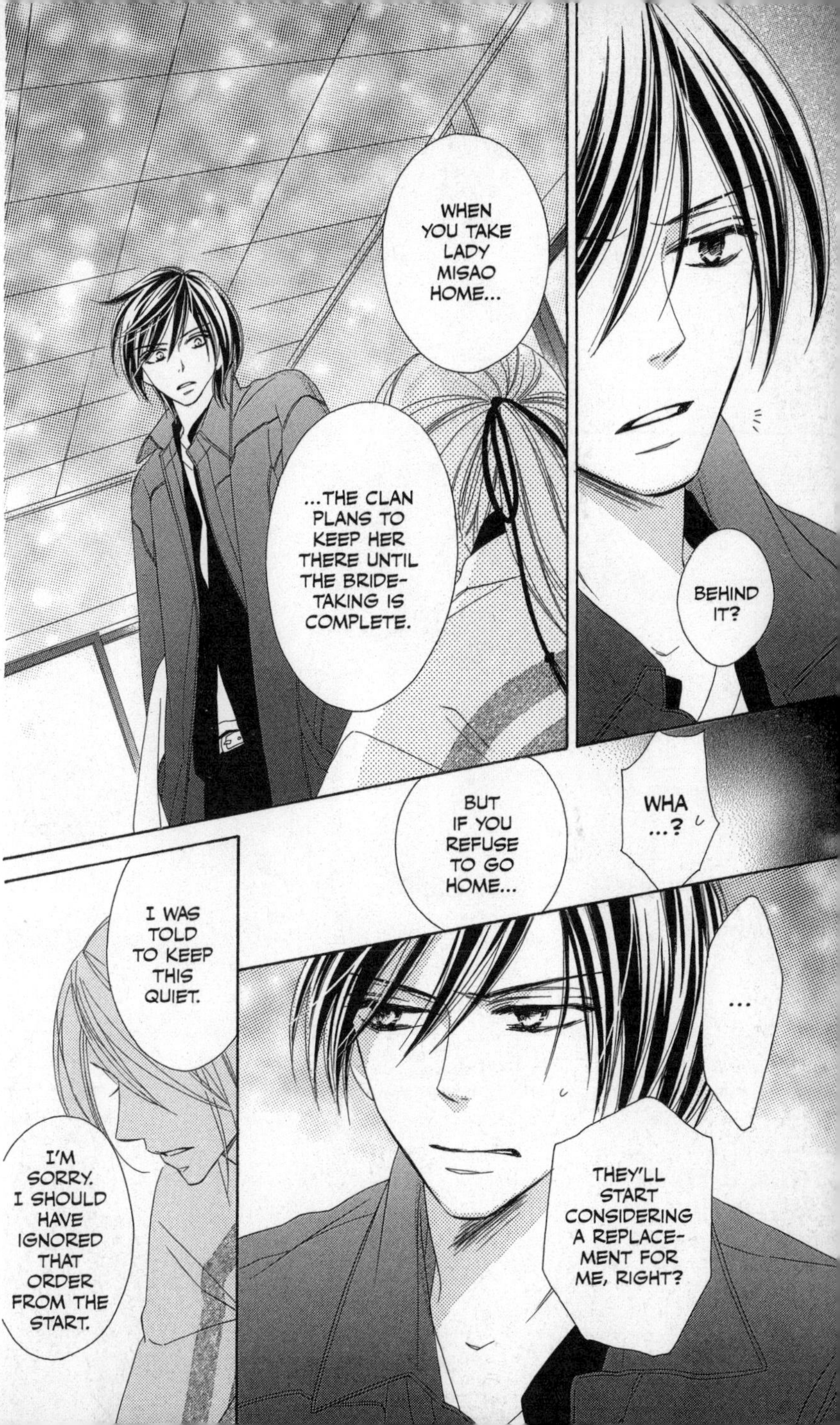
BEHIND IT?
WHEN YOU TAKE LADY MISAO HOME...
...THE CLAN PLANS TO KEEP HER THERE UNTIL THE BRIDE-TAKING IS COMPLETE.
WHA ...?
BUT IF YOU REFUSE TO GO HOME...
...
THEY'LL START CONSIDERING A REPLACE-MENT FOR ME, RIGHT?
I WAS TOLD TO KEEP THIS QUIET.
I'M SORRY. I SHOULD HAVE IGNORED THAT ORDER FROM THE START.

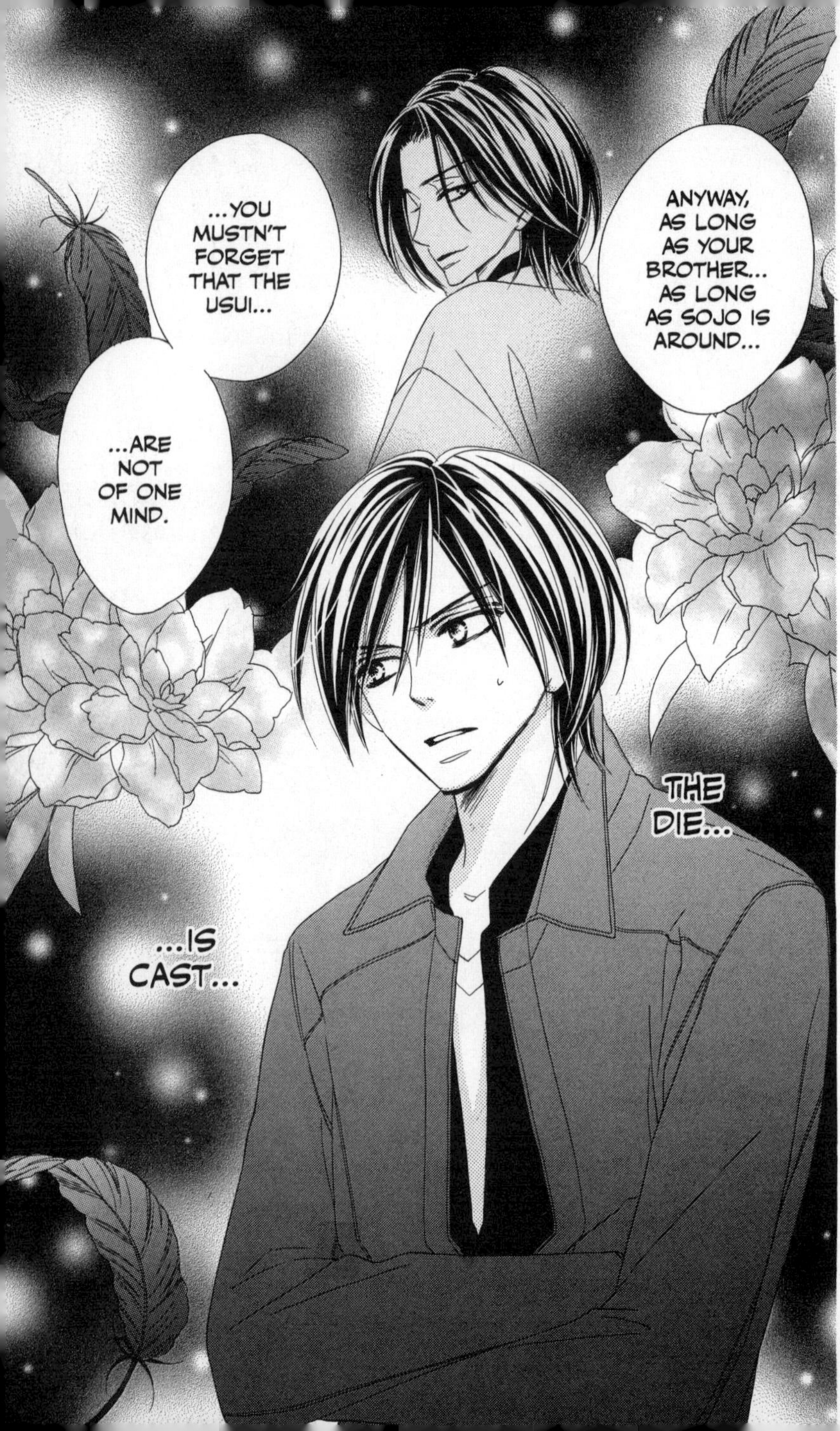
ANYWAY, AS LONG AS YOUR BROTHER... AS LONG AS SOJO IS AROUND...
...YOU MUSTN'T FORGET THAT THE USUI...
...ARE NOT OF ONE MIND.
THE DIE...
...IS CAST...

Illustration Request Number Six

"These three should say this like they were childhood friends."

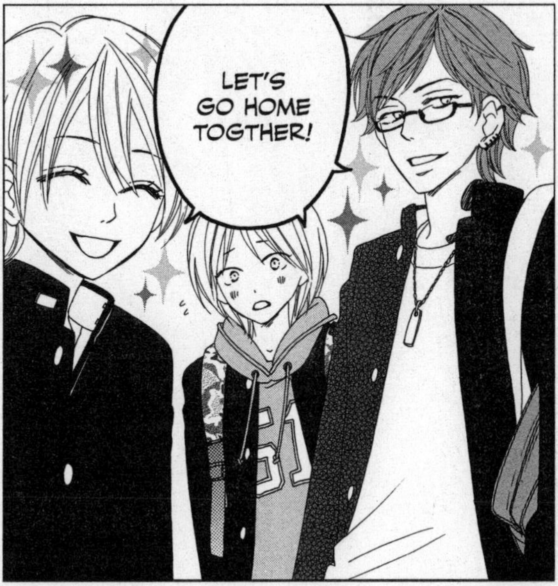
LET'S GO HOME TOGTHER!

Perhaps because I always draw them in Japanese clothing, I get a lot of requests to dress them in Western clothing or uniforms.

I guess I can understand that.

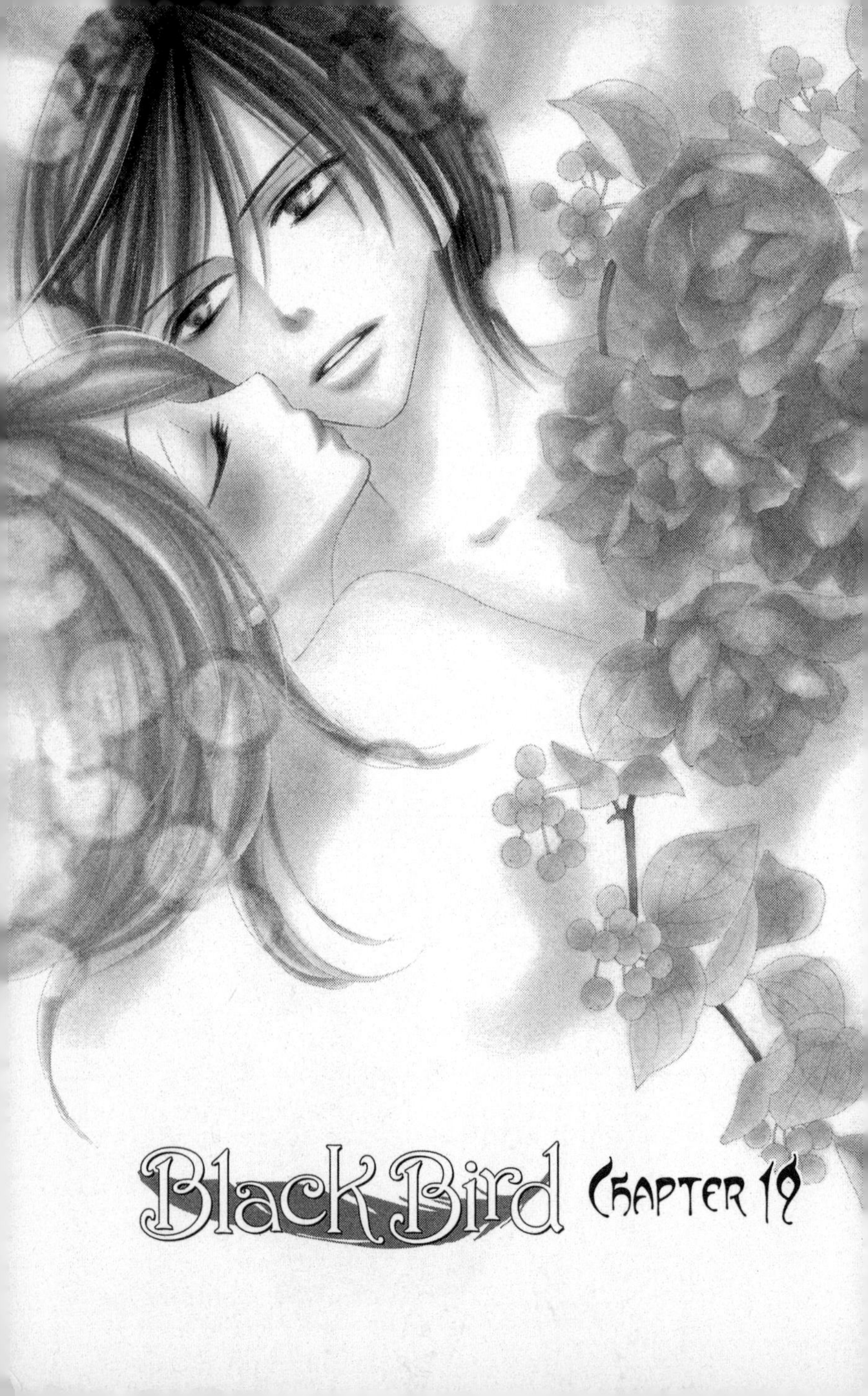
Black Bird
Chapter 19

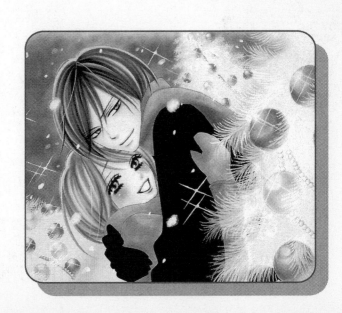

I HAD IT WRONG.
IT'S NOT THAT THE CLAN LEADER ***CAN*** MAKE ME HIS BRIDE...
...IT'S THAT HE ***MUST***...

To tell you the truth, I often forget to draw in the ring that Misao gave Kyo... If you should happen to find a panel like that, I wish you'd think of it as a "Find the Errors" game that I have provided for your enjoyment!! There are also panels with missing earrings or ones where the bloody clothes from the previous frame have been bleached clean... And the reason why Kyo's mansion looks a little different each time it appears is that it belongs to demons!!

It's just too much trouble to draw this...
...

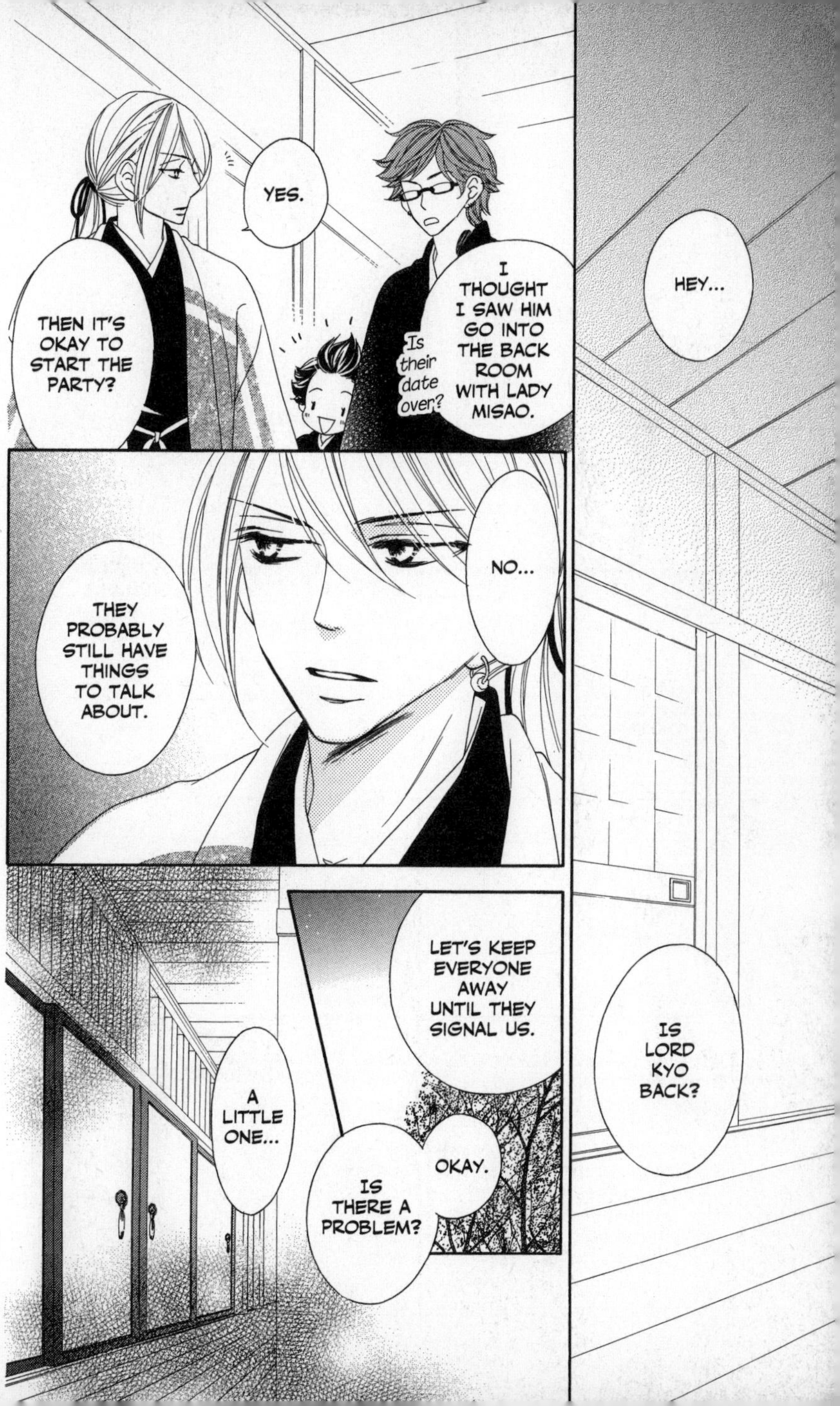
HEY...
IS LORD KYO BACK?
YES.
I THOUGHT I SAW HIM GO INTO THE BACK ROOM WITH LADY MISAO.
Is their date over?
THEN IT'S OKAY TO START THE PARTY?
NO...
THEY PROBABLY STILL HAVE THINGS TO TALK ABOUT.
LET'S KEEP EVERYONE AWAY UNTIL THEY SIGNAL US.
OKAY.
IS THERE A PROBLEM?
A LITTLE ONE...

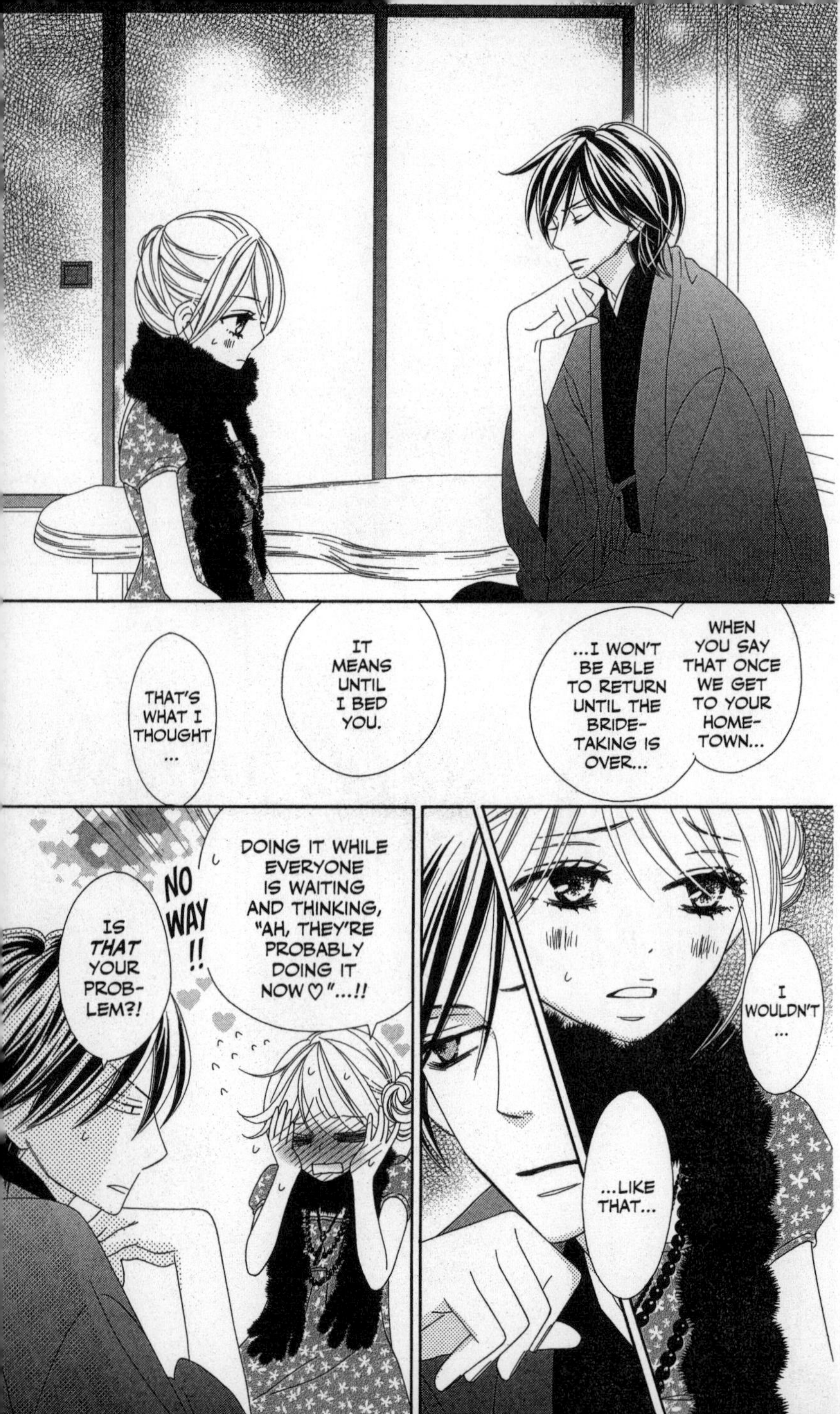
WHEN YOU SAY THAT ONCE WE GET TO YOUR HOME-TOWN...
...I WON'T BE ABLE TO RETURN UNTIL THE BRIDE-TAKING IS OVER...
IT MEANS UNTIL I BED YOU.
THAT'S WHAT I THOUGHT...
I WOULDN'T...
...LIKE THAT...
DOING IT WHILE EVERYONE IS WAITING AND THINKING, "AH, THEY'RE PROBABLY DOING IT NOW♡"...!!
NO WAY!!
IS *THAT* YOUR PROB-LEM?!

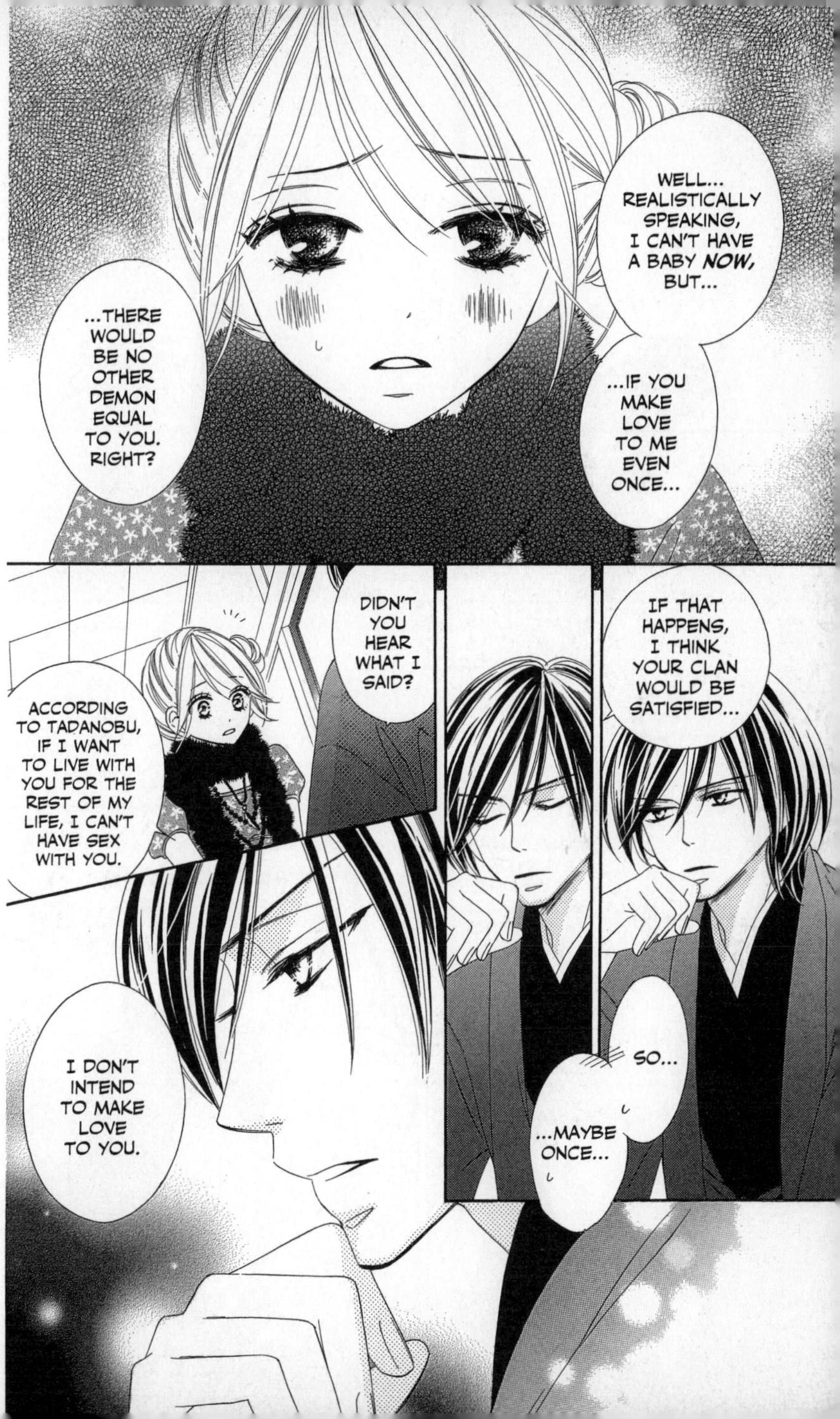
WELL... REALISTICALLY SPEAKING, I CAN'T HAVE A BABY *NOW,* BUT...
...IF YOU MAKE LOVE TO ME EVEN ONCE...
...THERE WOULD BE NO OTHER DEMON EQUAL TO YOU. RIGHT?
IF THAT HAPPENS, I THINK YOUR CLAN WOULD BE SATISFIED...
SO...
...MAYBE ONCE...
DIDN'T YOU HEAR WHAT I SAID?
ACCORDING TO TADANOBU, IF I WANT TO LIVE WITH YOU FOR THE REST OF MY LIFE, I CAN'T HAVE SEX WITH YOU.
I DON'T INTEND TO MAKE LOVE TO YOU.

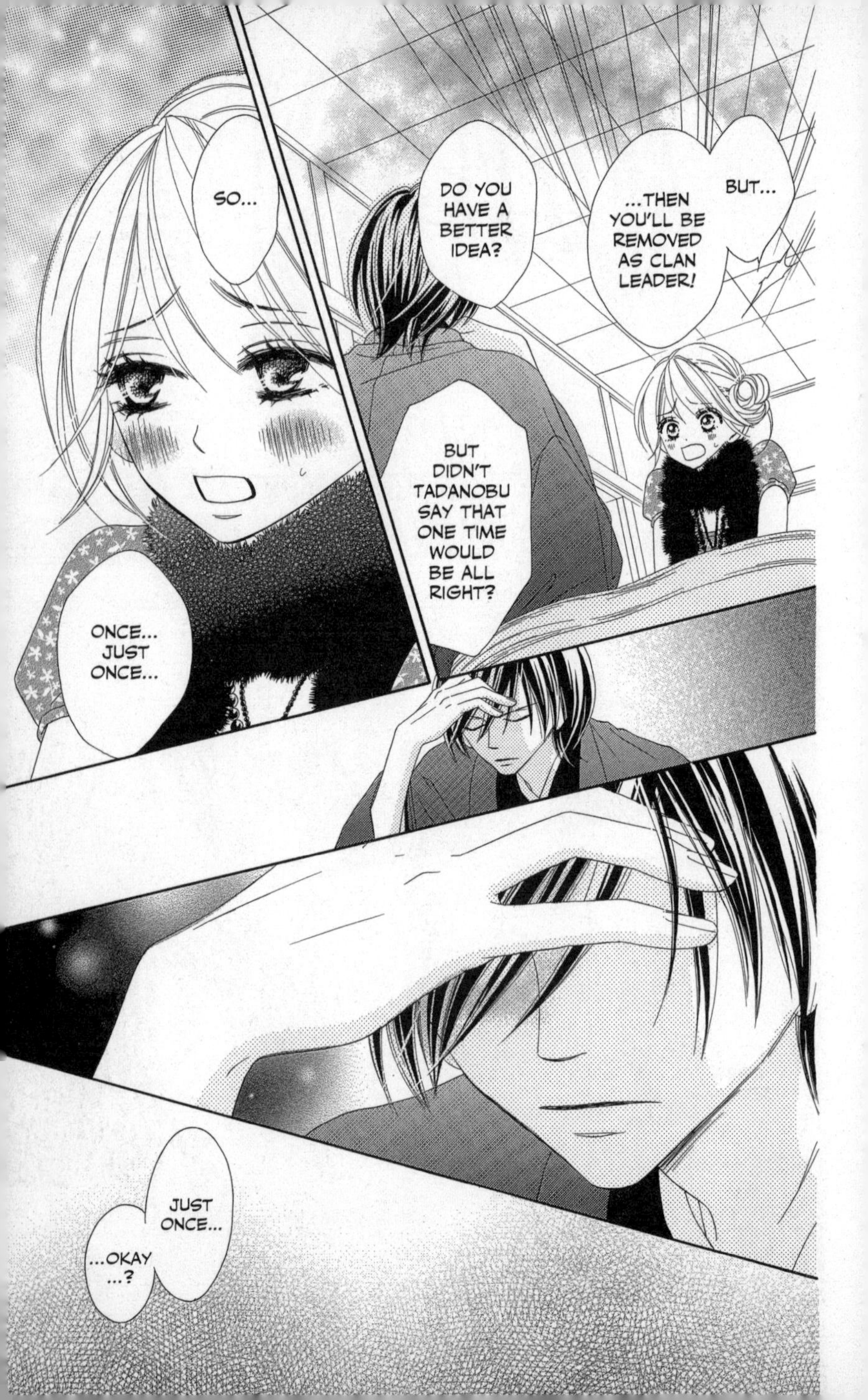
BUT...
...THEN YOU'LL BE REMOVED AS CLAN LEADER!
DO YOU HAVE A BETTER IDEA?
BUT DIDN'T TADANOBU SAY THAT ONE TIME WOULD BE ALL RIGHT?
SO...
ONCE... JUST ONCE...
JUST ONCE...
...OKAY ...?

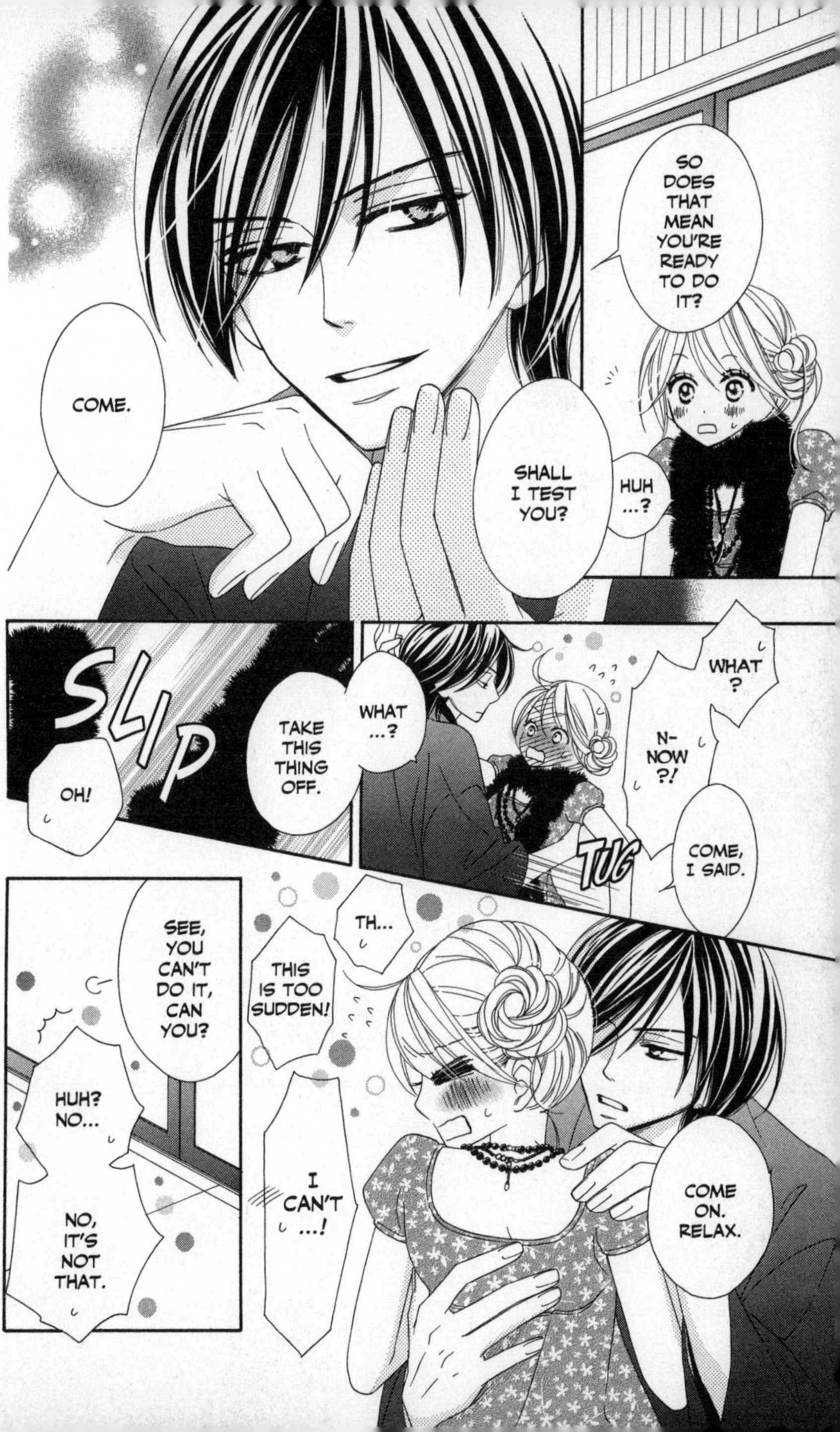
SO DOES THAT MEAN YOU'RE READY TO DO IT?
HUH ...?
SHALL I TEST YOU?
COME.
WHAT?
N-NOW?!
COME, I SAID.
TUG
WHAT ...?
TAKE THIS THING OFF.
SLIP
OH!
TH...
THIS IS TOO SUDDEN!
COME ON. RELAX.
I CAN'T ...!
SEE, YOU CAN'T DO IT, CAN YOU?
HUH? NO...
NO, IT'S NOT THAT.

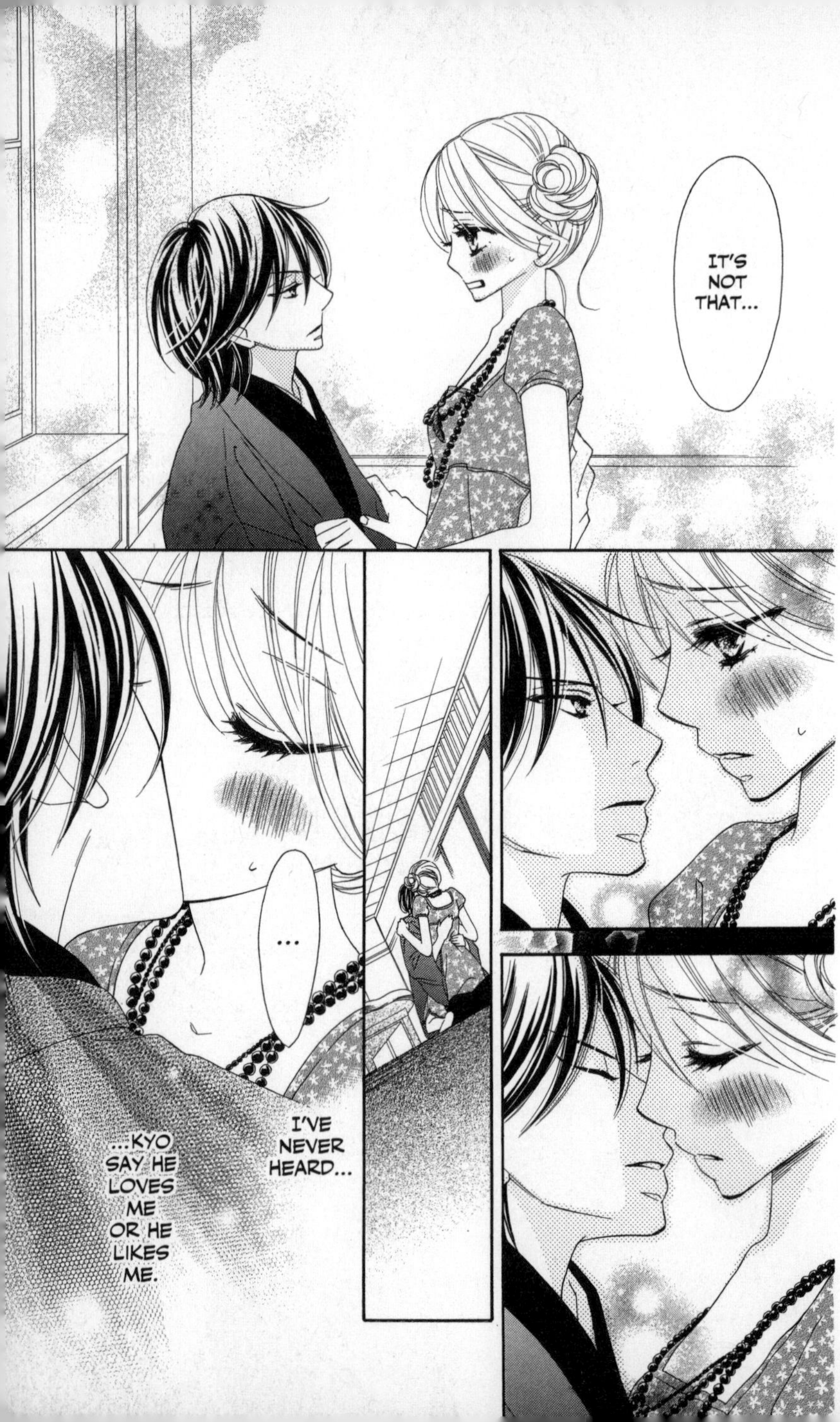
IT'S NOT THAT...
...
I'VE NEVER HEARD...
...KYO SAY HE LOVES ME OR HE LIKES ME.

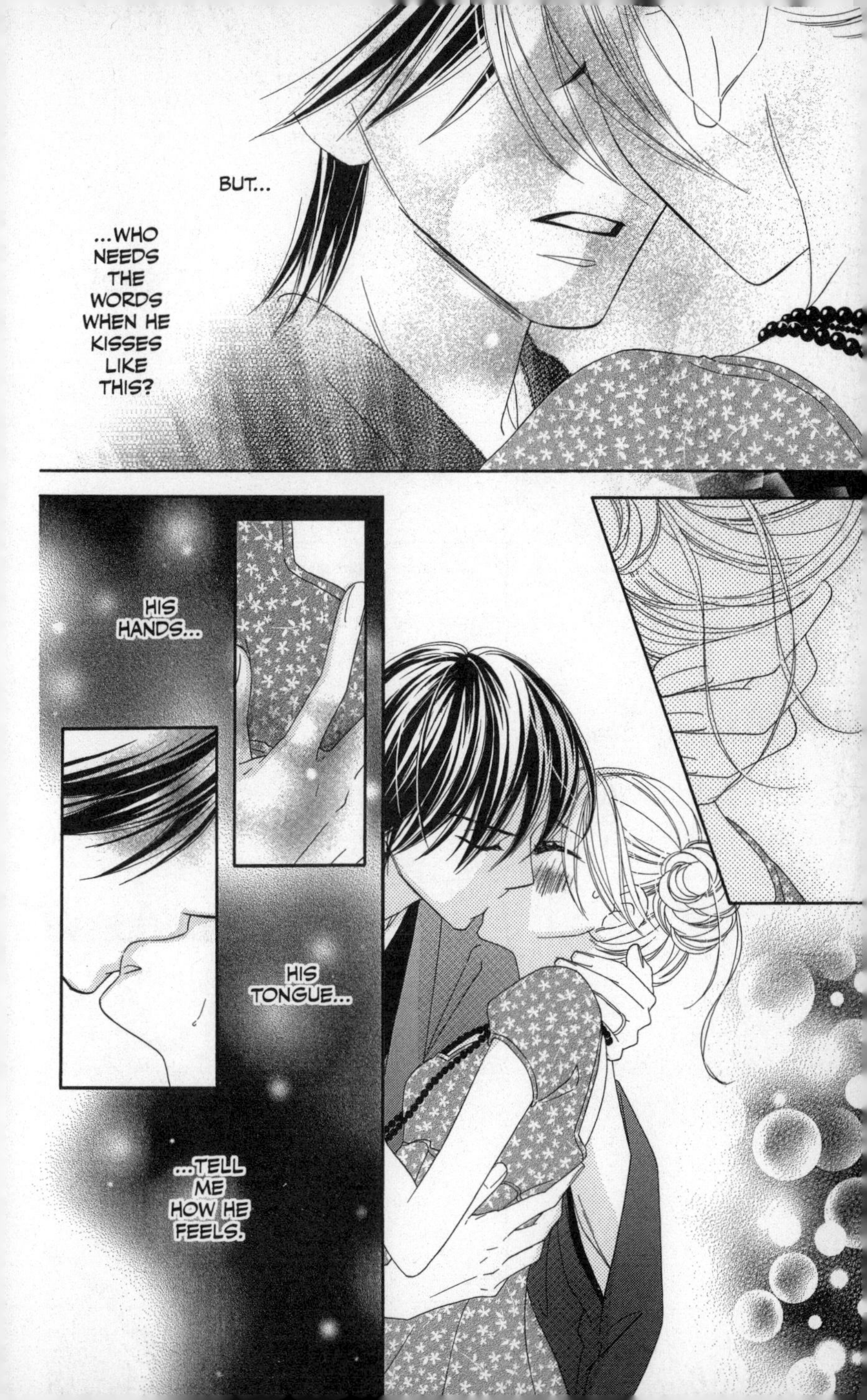
BUT...
...WHO NEEDS THE WORDS WHEN HE KISSES LIKE THIS?
HIS HANDS...
HIS TONGUE...
...TELL ME HOW HE FEELS.

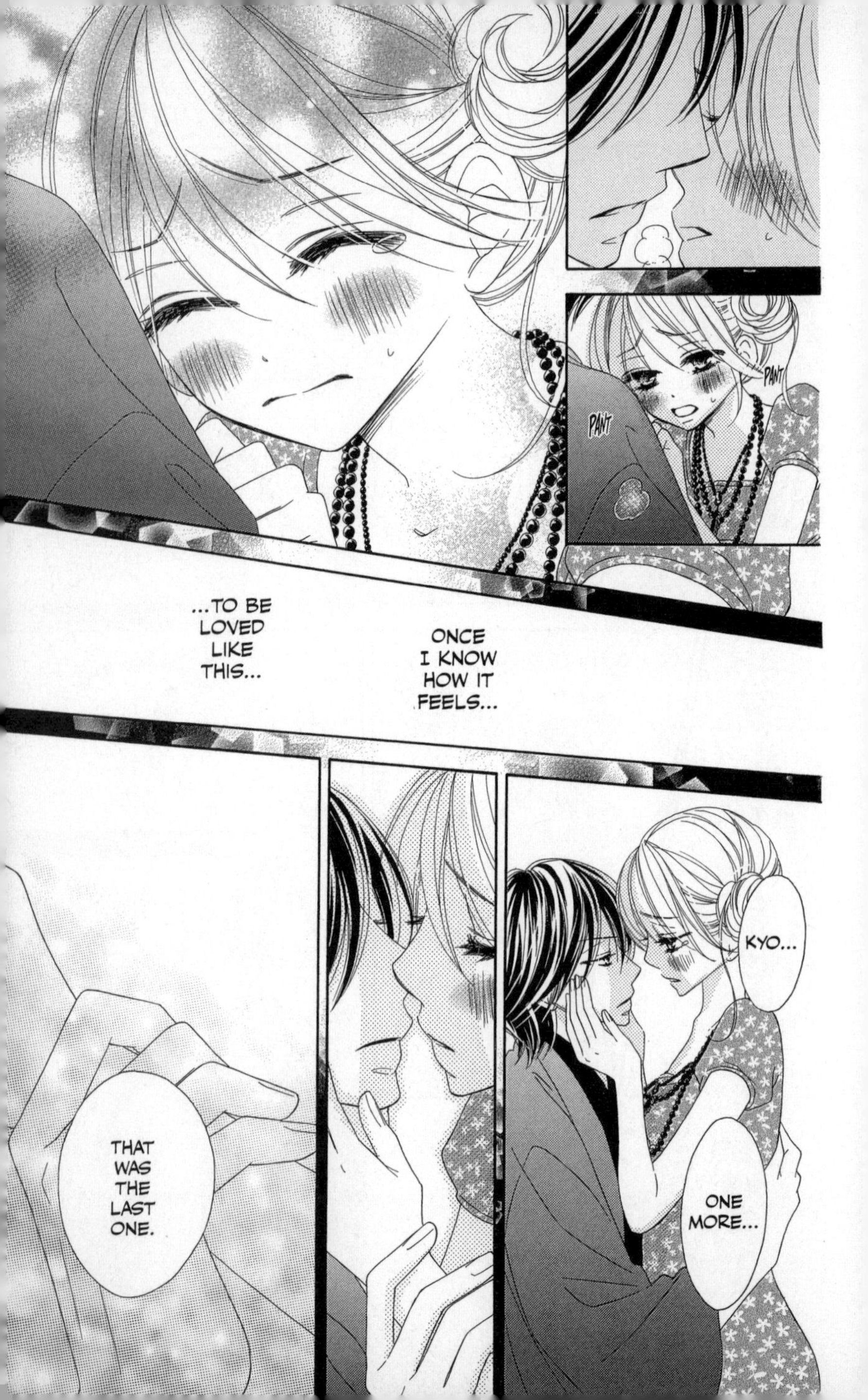
PANT
PANT
ONCE I KNOW HOW IT FEELS...
...TO BE LOVED LIKE THIS...
KYO...
ONE MORE...
THAT WAS THE LAST ONE.

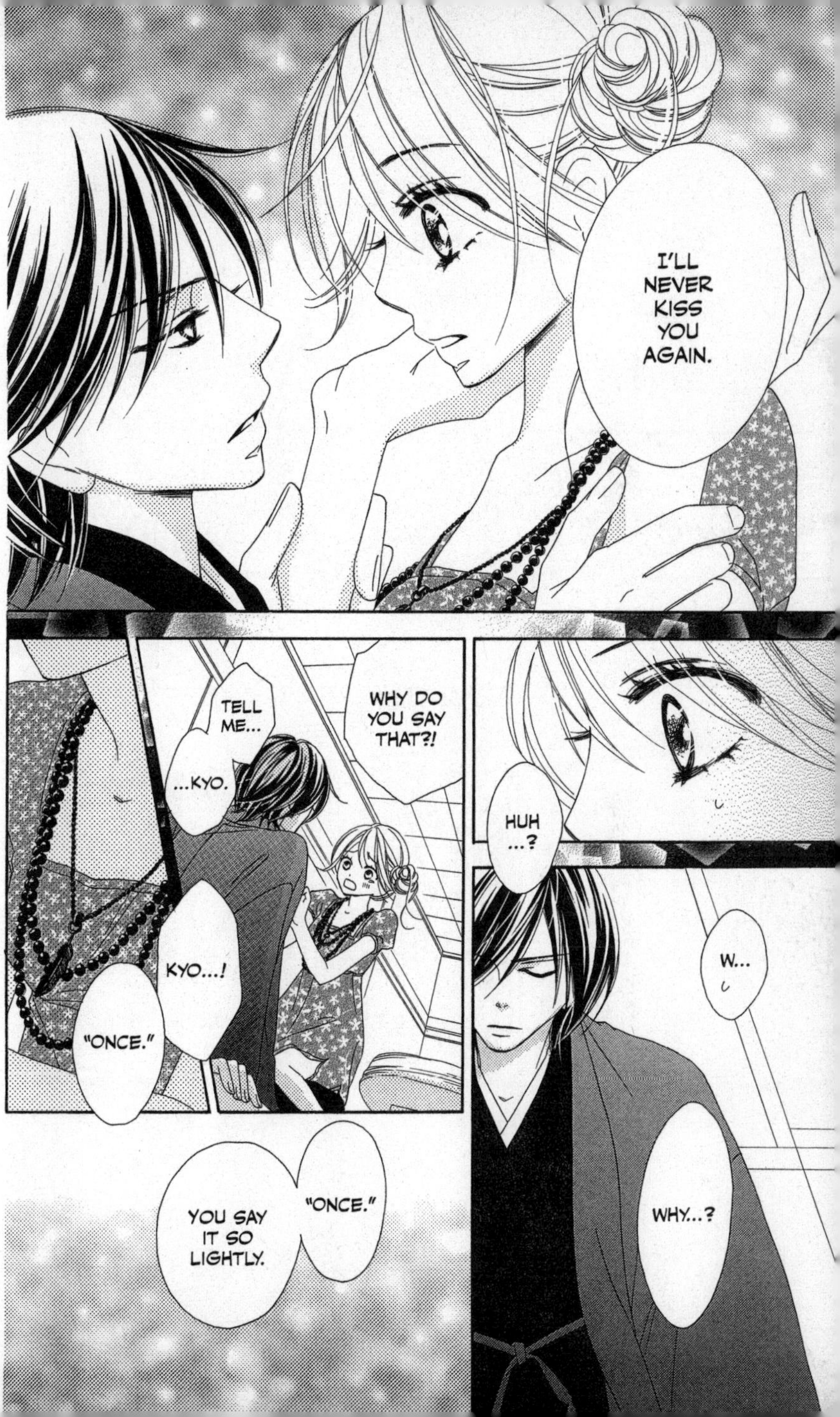
I'LL NEVER KISS YOU AGAIN.
HUH ...?
WHY DO YOU SAY THAT?!
TELL ME...
...KYO.
KYO...!
"ONCE."
W...
WHY...?
"ONCE."
YOU SAY IT SO LIGHTLY.

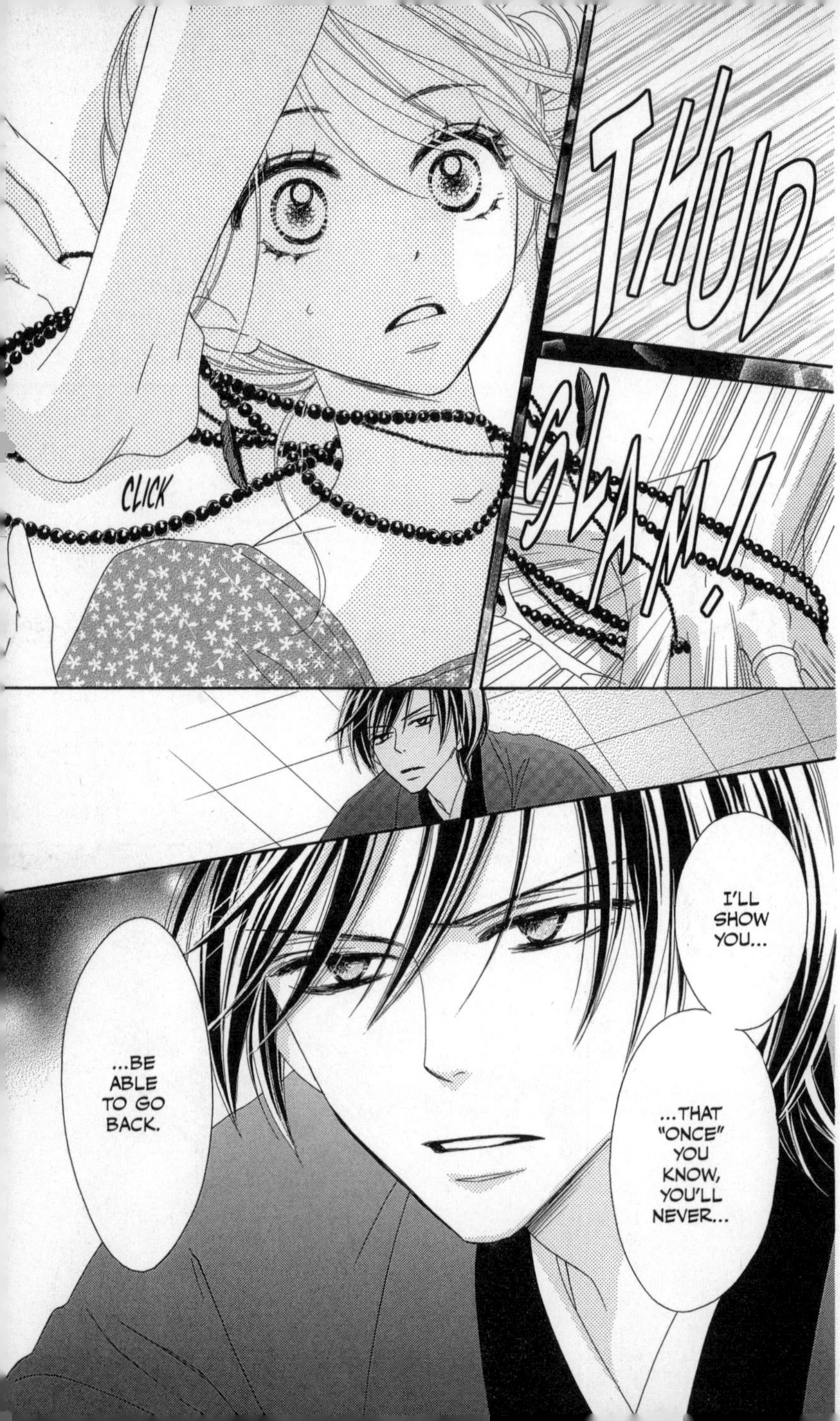
THUD
SLAM!
CLICK
I'LL SHOW YOU...
...THAT "ONCE" YOU KNOW, YOU'LL NEVER...
...BE ABLE TO GO BACK.

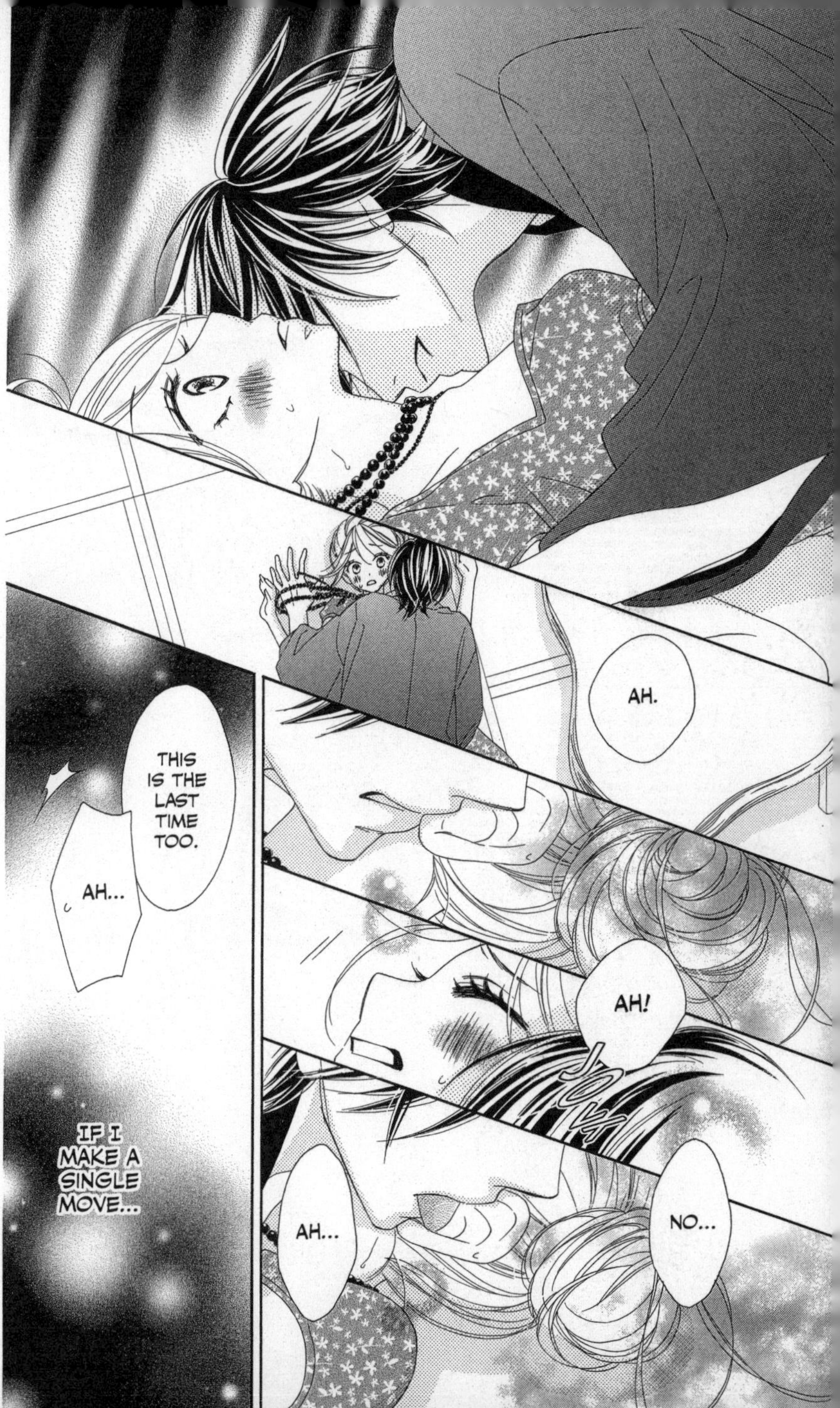
AH.
AH!
NO...
AH...
THIS IS THE LAST TIME TOO.
AH...
IF I MAKE A SINGLE MOVE...

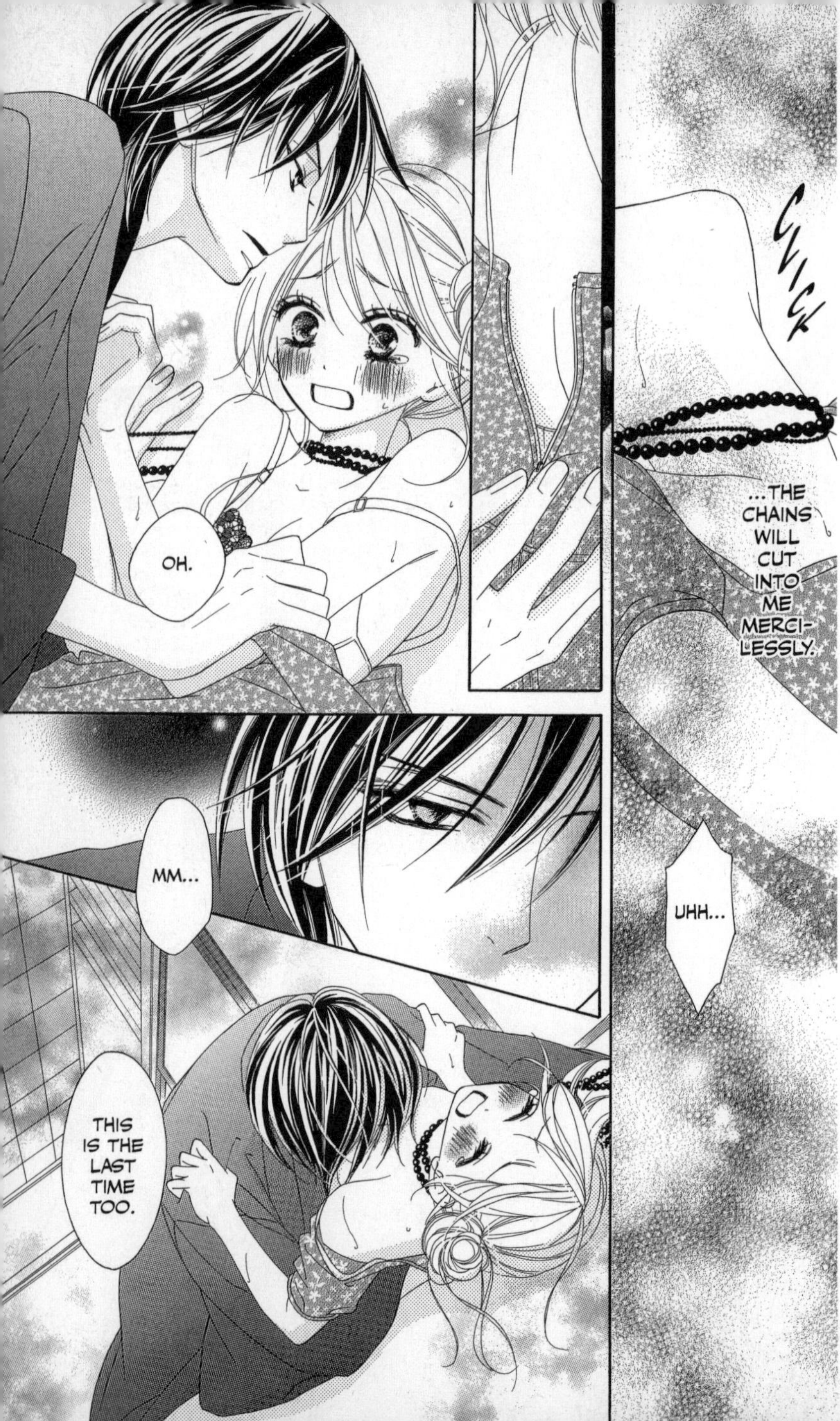
CLICK
...THE CHAINS WILL CUT INTO ME MERCI-LESSLY.
UHH...
OH.
MM...
THIS IS THE LAST TIME TOO.

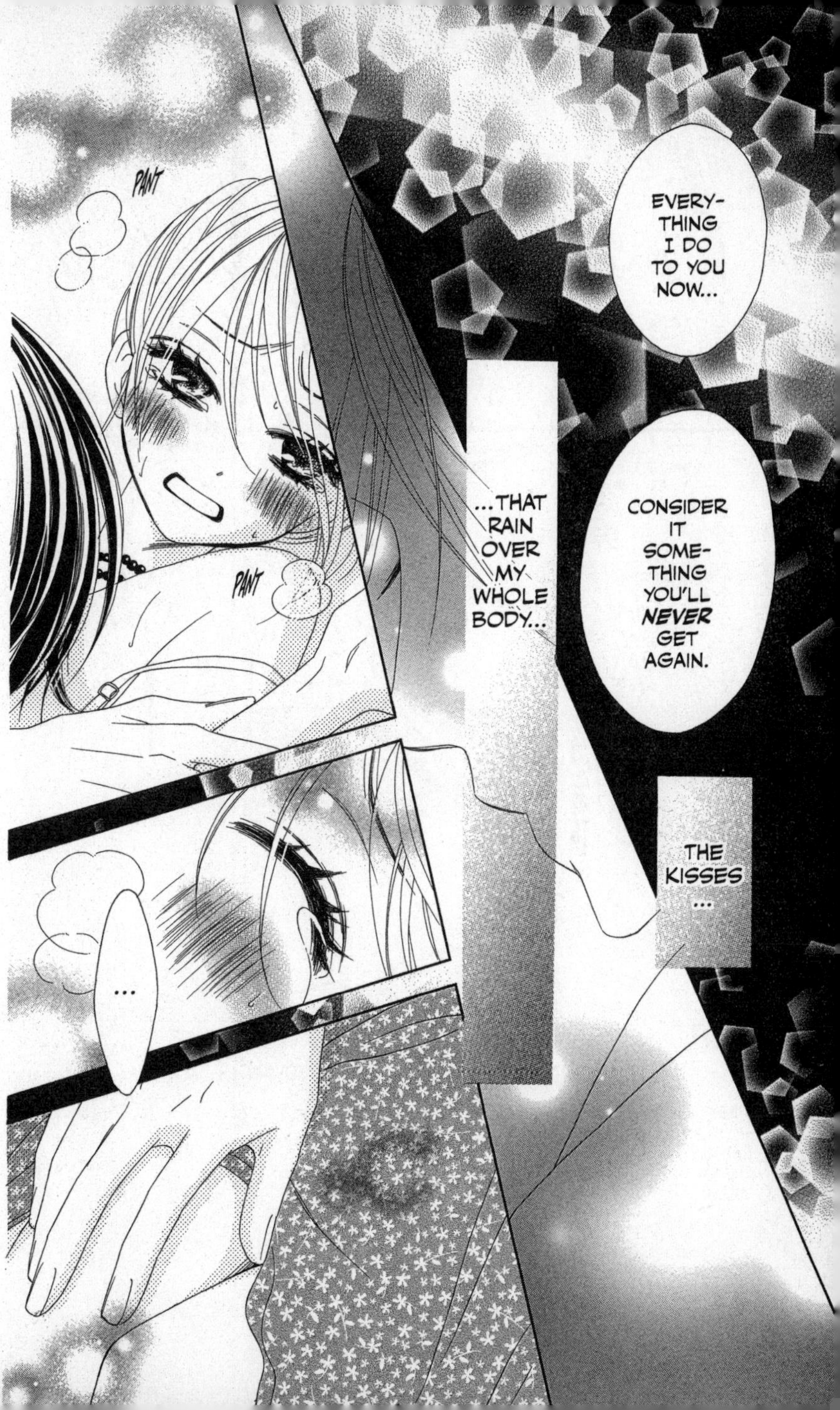
EVERYTHING I DO TO YOU NOW...
CONSIDER IT SOMETHING YOU'LL ***NEVER*** GET AGAIN.
THE KISSES...
...THAT RAIN OVER MY WHOLE BODY...
PANT
PANT
...

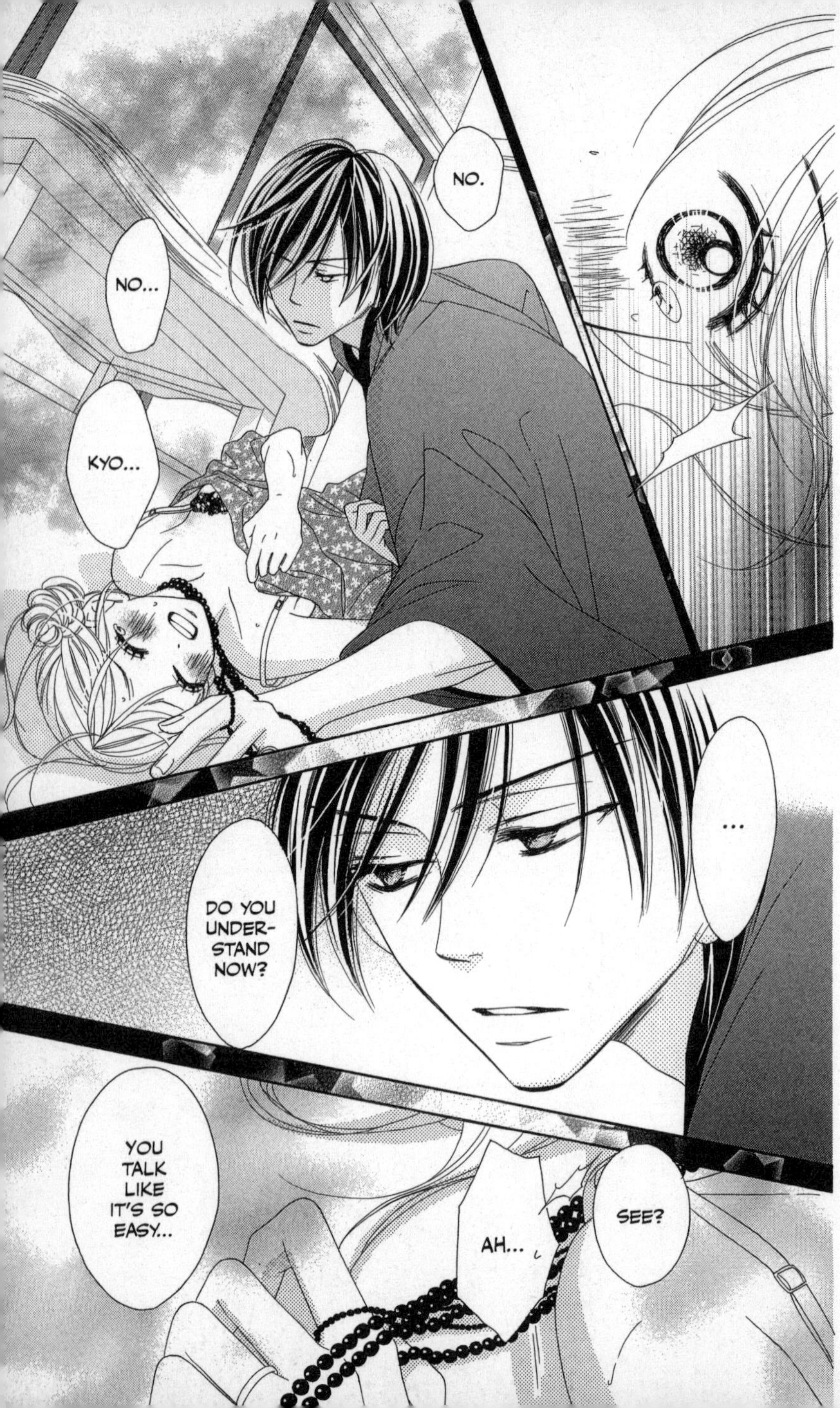
NO.
NO...
KYO...
...
DO YOU UNDER-STAND NOW?
SEE?
AH...
YOU TALK LIKE IT'S SO EASY...

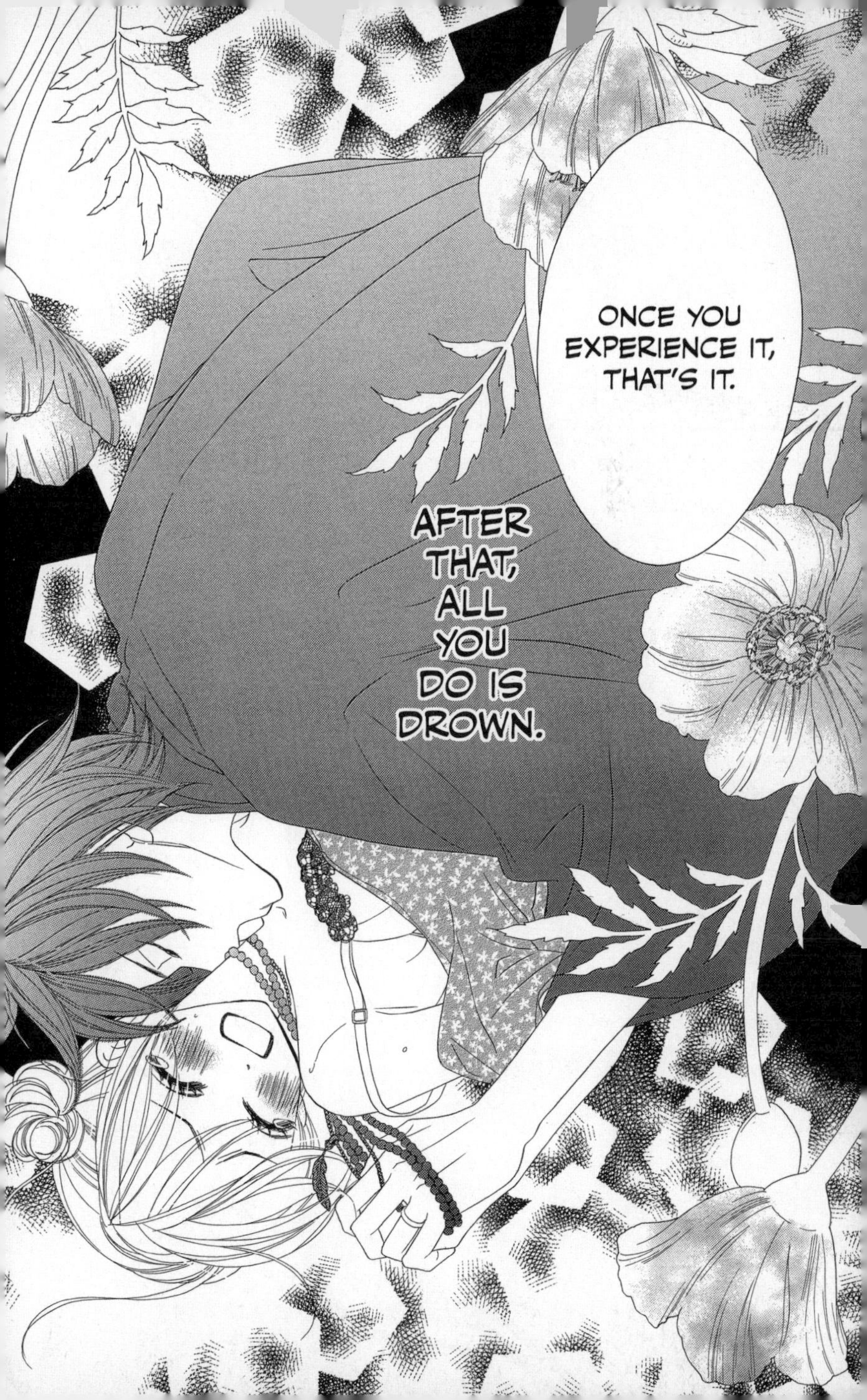
ONCE YOU EXPERIENCE IT, THAT'S IT.
AFTER THAT, ALL YOU DO IS DROWN.

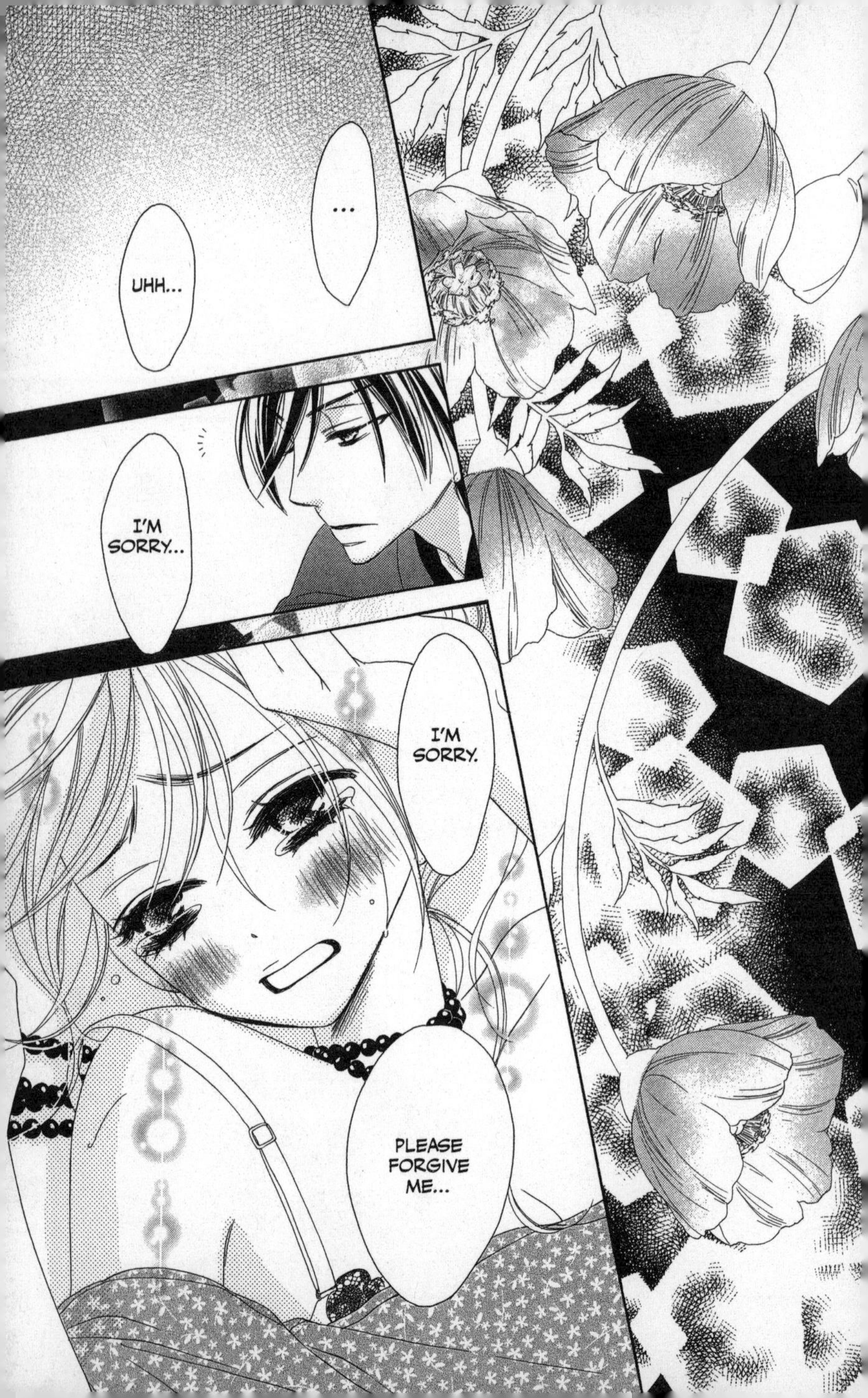
...
UHH...
I'M SORRY...
I'M SORRY.
PLEASE FORGIVE ME...

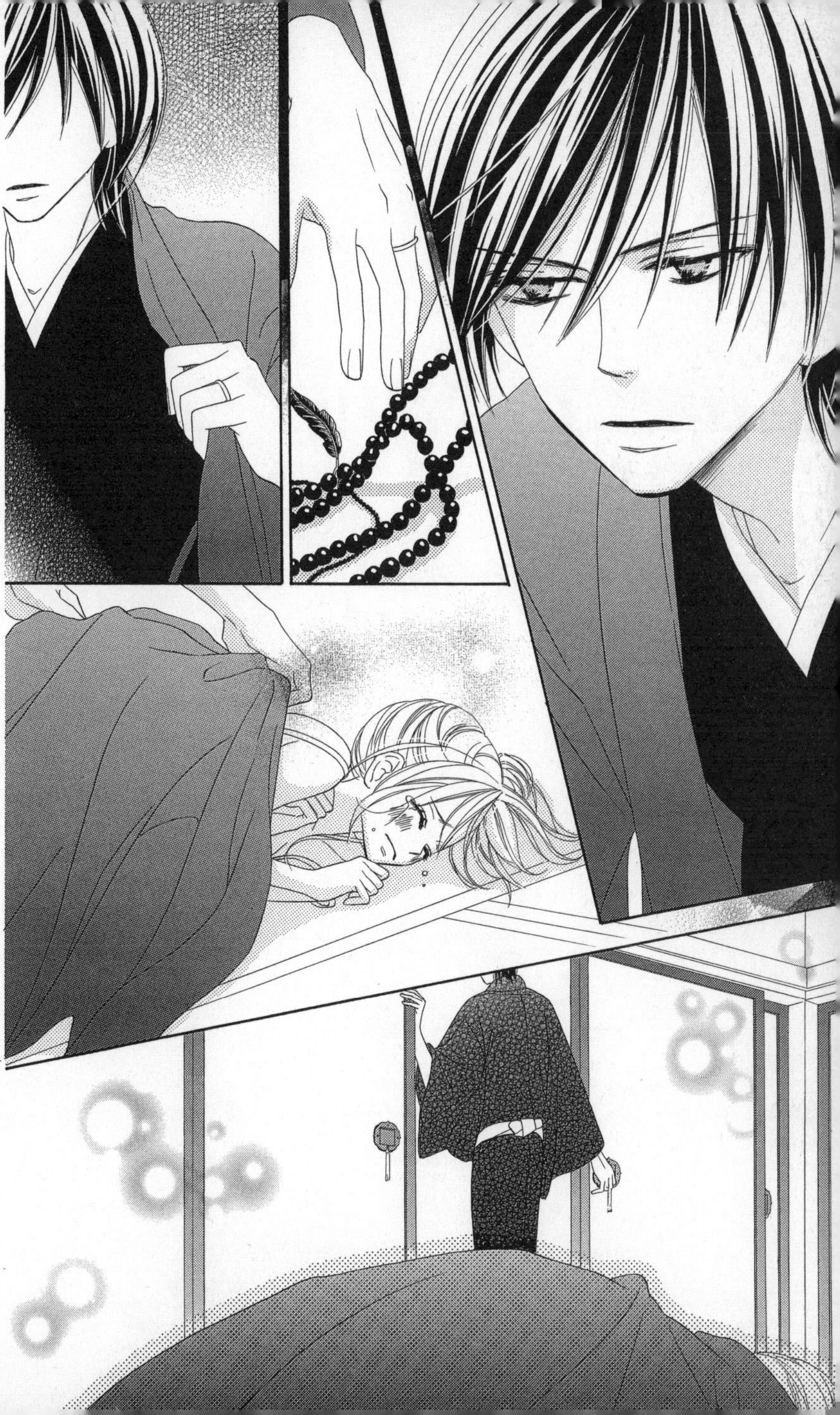

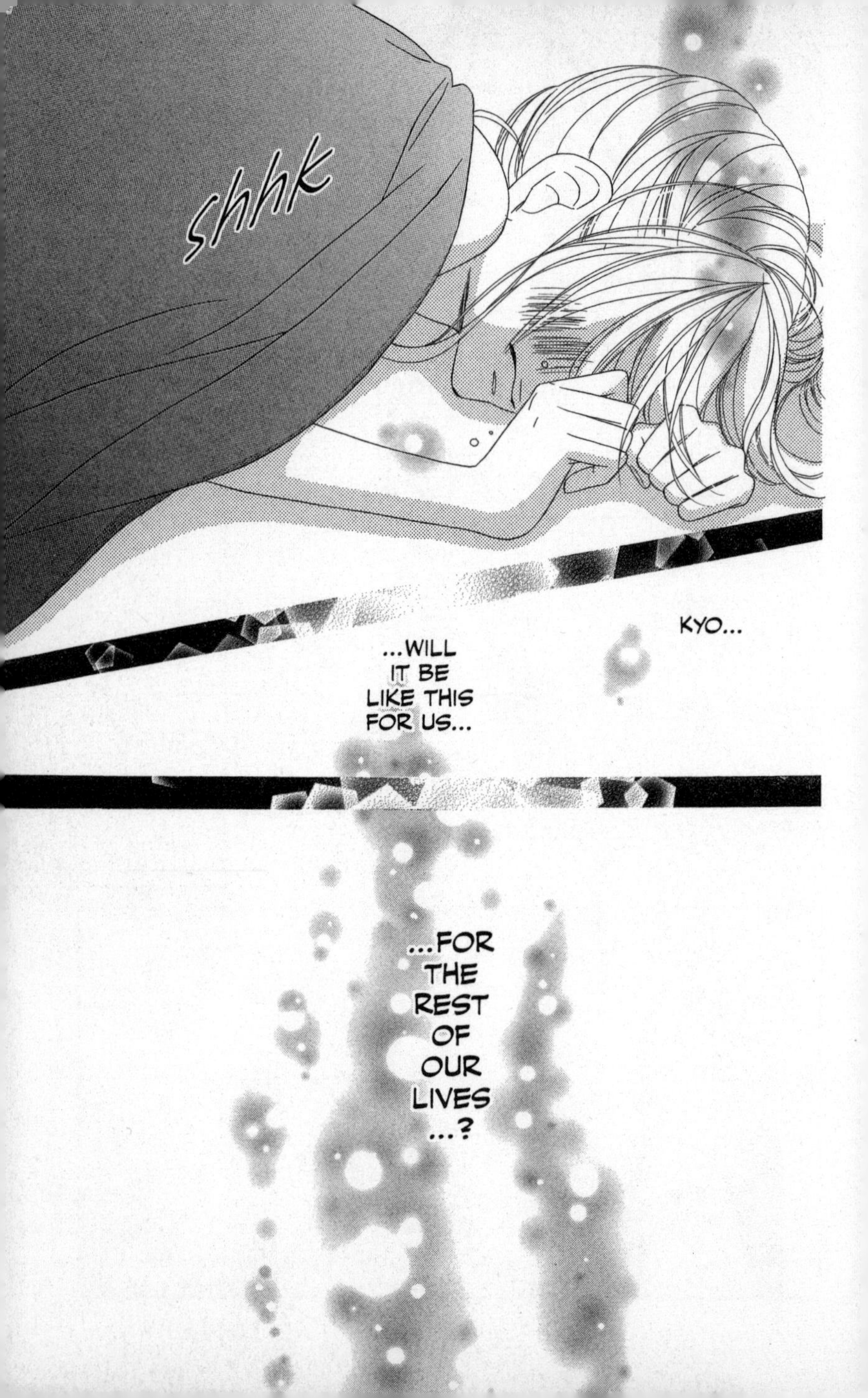
shhk
KYO...
...WILL IT BE LIKE THIS FOR US...
...FOR THE REST OF OUR LIVES ...?

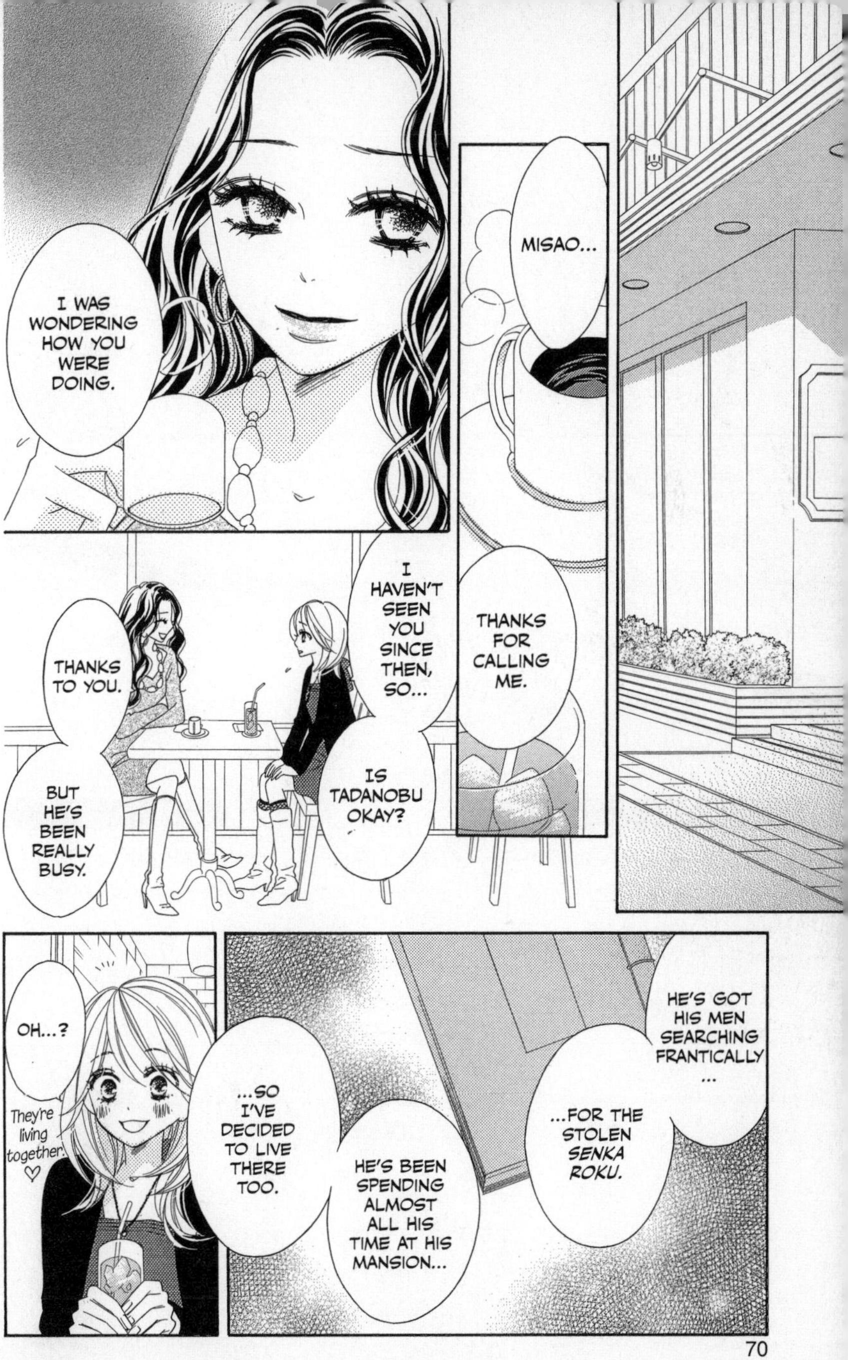
MISAO...
THANKS FOR CALLING ME.
I WAS WONDERING HOW YOU WERE DOING.
I HAVEN'T SEEN YOU SINCE THEN, SO...
IS TADANOBU OKAY?
THANKS TO YOU.
BUT HE'S BEEN REALLY BUSY.
HE'S GOT HIS MEN SEARCHING FRANTICALLY...
...FOR THE STOLEN *SENKA ROKU*.
HE'S BEEN SPENDING ALMOST ALL HIS TIME AT HIS MANSION...
...SO I'VE DECIDED TO LIVE THERE TOO.
OH...?
They're living together. ♡

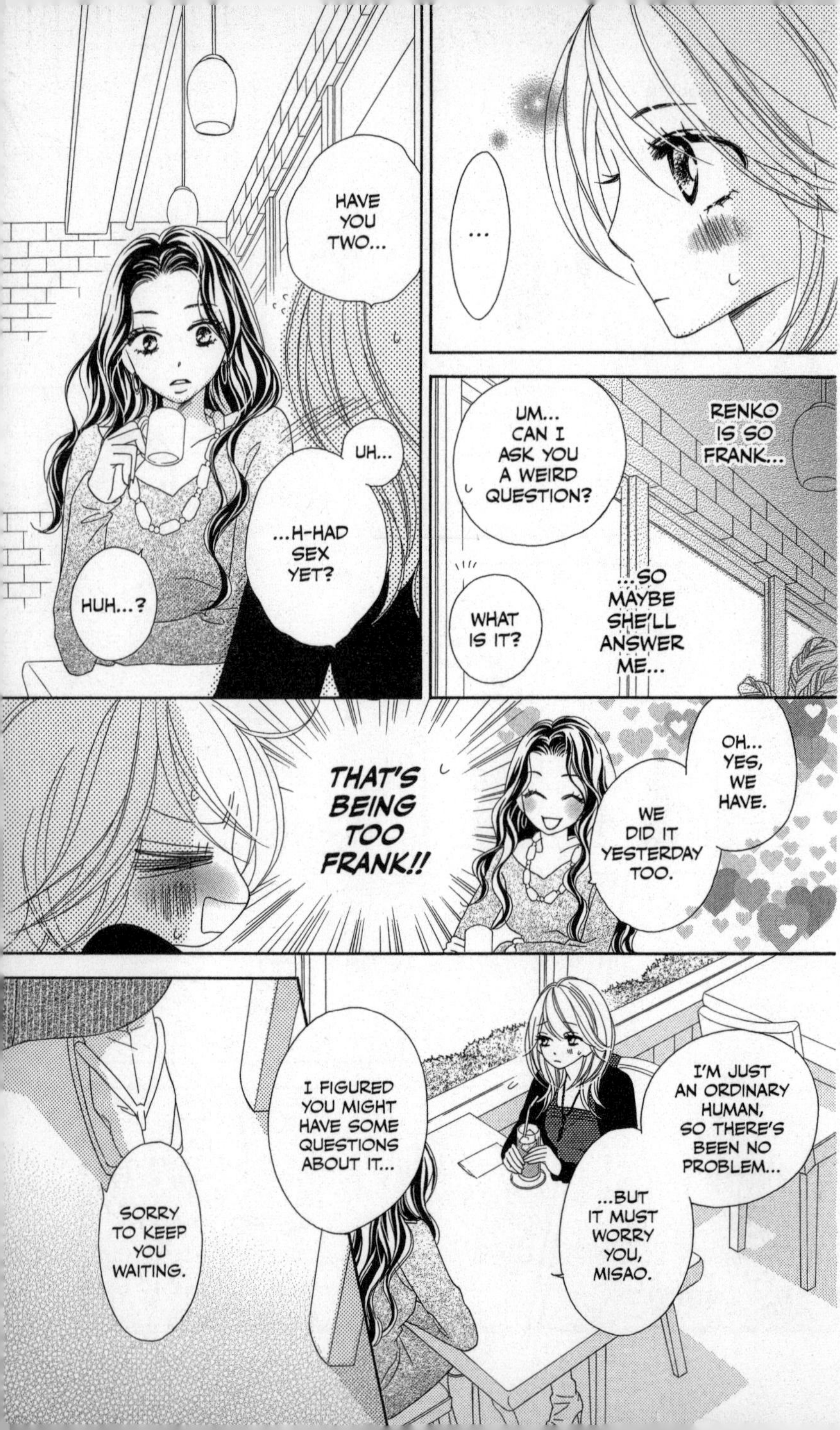
...
RENKO IS SO FRANK...
...SO MAYBE SHE'LL ANSWER ME...
UM... CAN I ASK YOU A WEIRD QUESTION?
WHAT IS IT?
HAVE YOU TWO...
UH...
...H-HAD SEX YET?
HUH...?
OH... YES, WE HAVE.
WE DID IT YESTERDAY TOO.
THAT'S BEING TOO FRANK!!
I'M JUST AN ORDINARY HUMAN, SO THERE'S BEEN NO PROBLEM...
...BUT IT MUST WORRY YOU, MISAO.
I FIGURED YOU MIGHT HAVE SOME QUESTIONS ABOUT IT...
SORRY TO KEEP YOU WAITING.

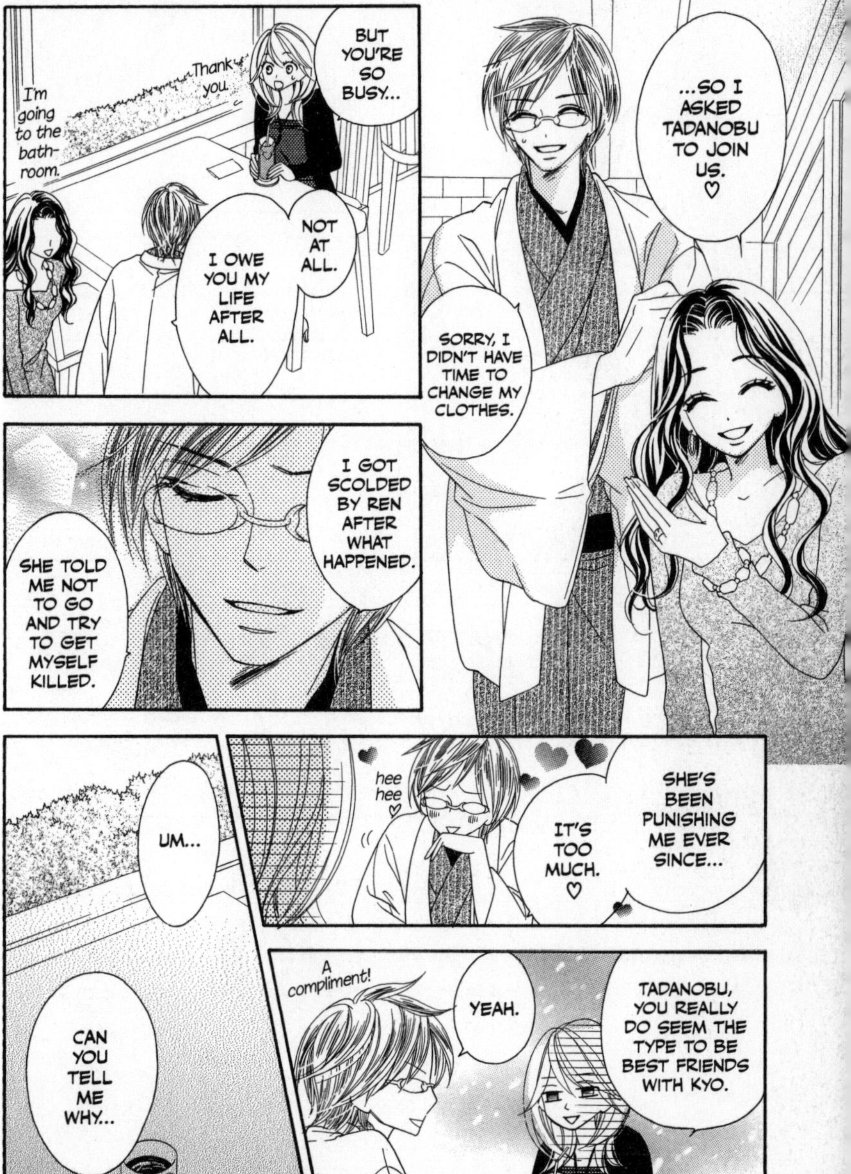
...SO I ASKED TADANOBU TO JOIN US. ♡
SORRY, I DIDN'T HAVE TIME TO CHANGE MY CLOTHES.
BUT YOU'RE SO BUSY...
Thank you.
I'm going to the bathroom.
NOT AT ALL.
I OWE YOU MY LIFE AFTER ALL.
I GOT SCOLDED BY REN AFTER WHAT HAPPENED.
SHE TOLD ME NOT TO GO AND TRY TO GET MYSELF KILLED.
SHE'S BEEN PUNISHING ME EVER SINCE...
IT'S TOO MUCH. ♡
hee hee ♡
TADANOBU, YOU REALLY DO SEEM THE TYPE TO BE BEST FRIENDS WITH KYO.
YEAH.
A compliment!
UM...
CAN YOU TELL ME WHY...

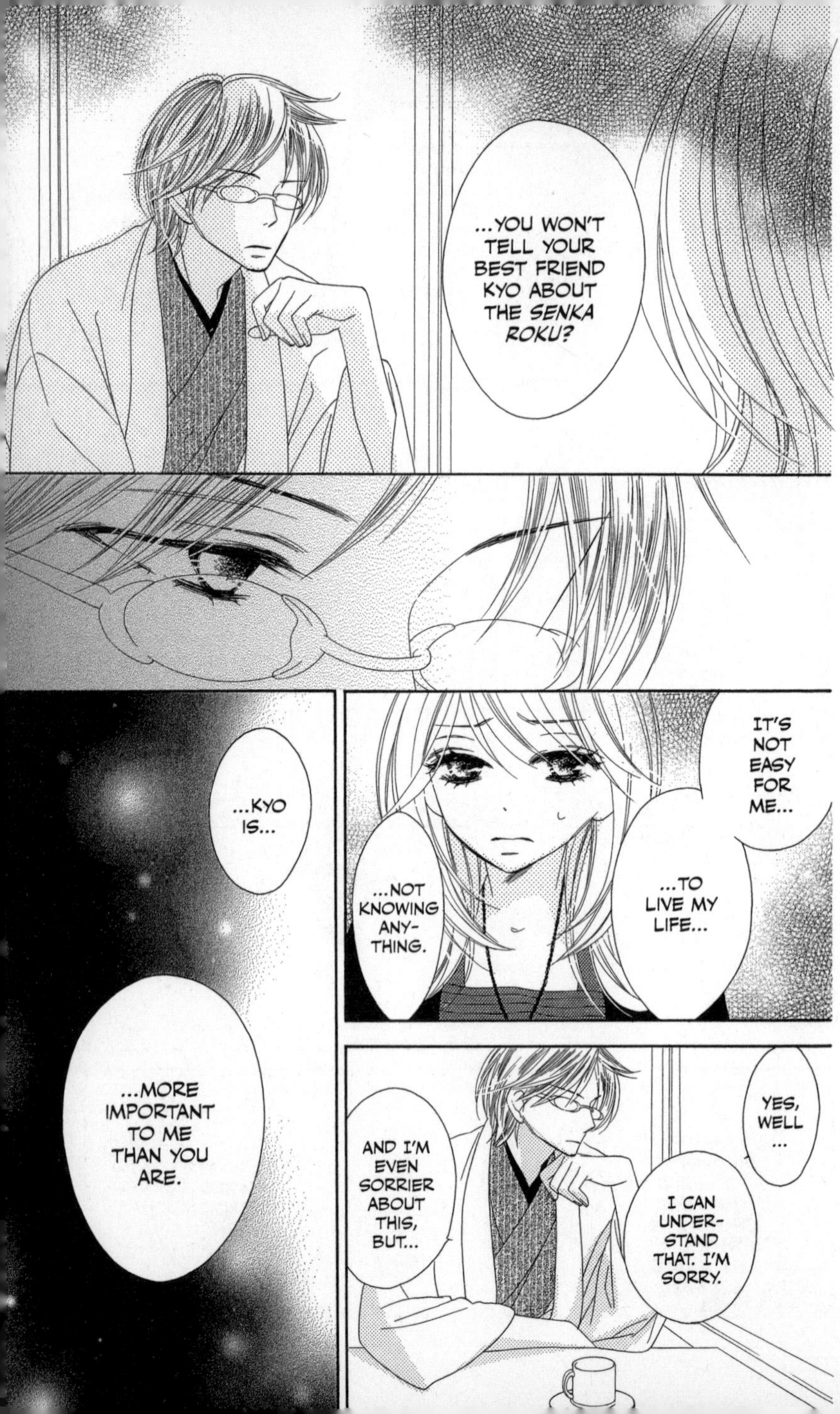
...YOU WON'T TELL YOUR BEST FRIEND KYO ABOUT THE *SENKA ROKU*?
IT'S NOT EASY FOR ME...
...TO LIVE MY LIFE...
...NOT KNOWING ANYTHING.
YES, WELL...
I CAN UNDERSTAND THAT. I'M SORRY.
AND I'M EVEN SORRIER ABOUT THIS, BUT...
...KYO IS...
...MORE IMPORTANT TO ME THAN YOU ARE.

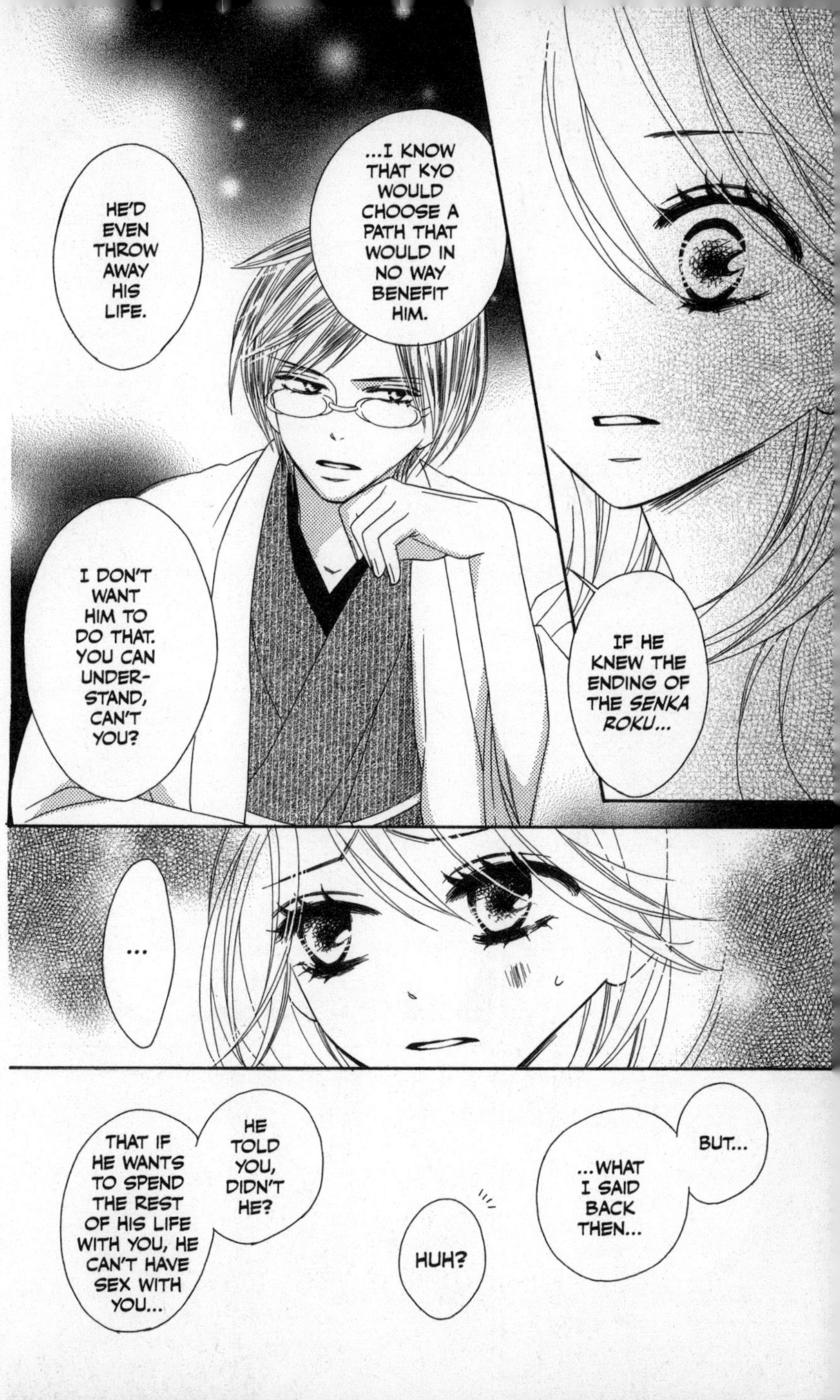
IF HE KNEW THE ENDING OF THE *SENKA ROKU*...
...I KNOW THAT KYO WOULD CHOOSE A PATH THAT WOULD IN NO WAY BENEFIT HIM.
HE'D EVEN THROW AWAY HIS LIFE.
I DON'T WANT HIM TO DO THAT. YOU CAN UNDER-STAND, CAN'T YOU?
...
BUT...
...WHAT I SAID BACK THEN...
HUH?
HE TOLD YOU, DIDN'T HE?
THAT IF HE WANTS TO SPEND THE REST OF HIS LIFE WITH YOU, HE CAN'T HAVE SEX WITH YOU...

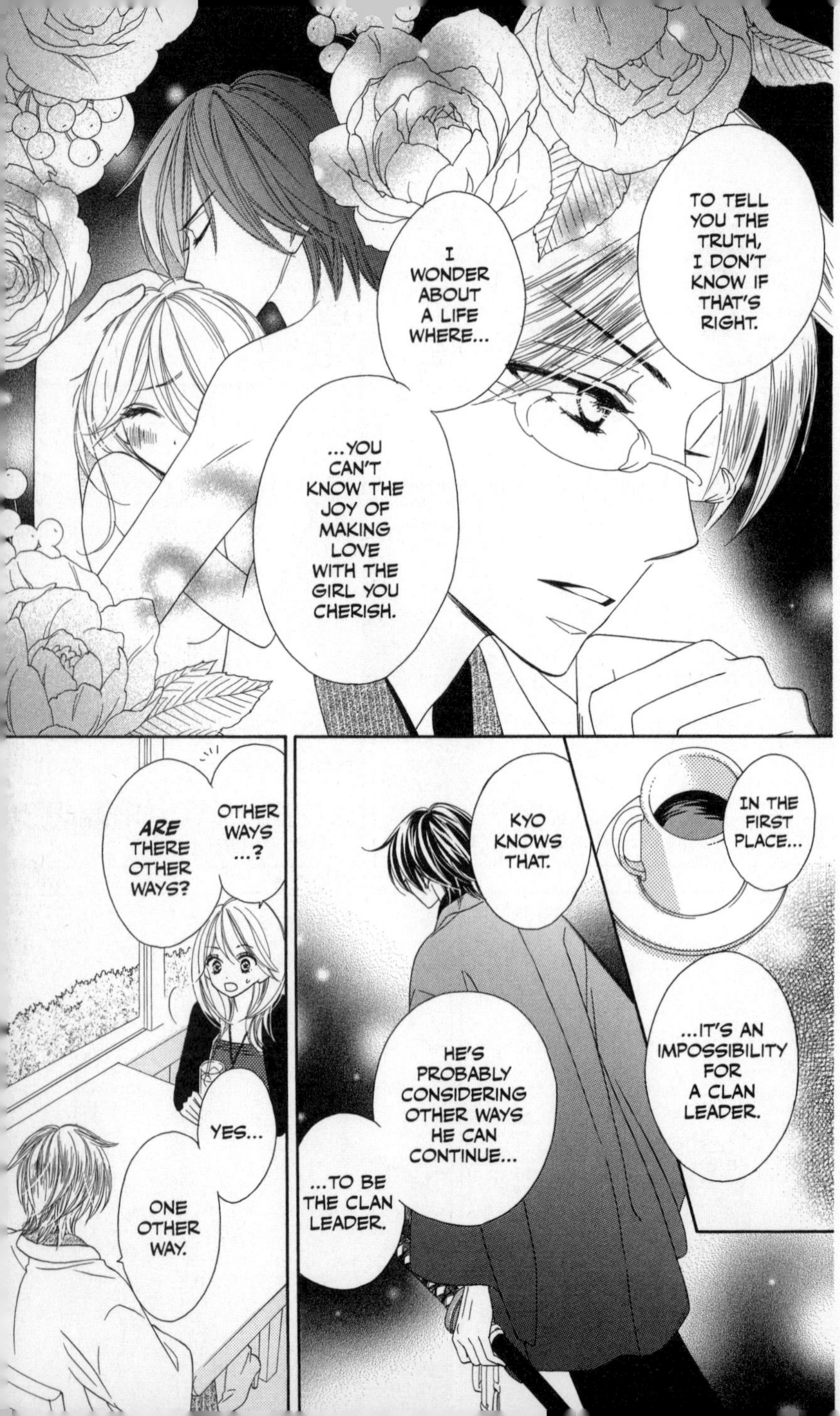
TO TELL YOU THE TRUTH, I DON'T KNOW IF THAT'S RIGHT.
I WONDER ABOUT A LIFE WHERE...
...YOU CAN'T KNOW THE JOY OF MAKING LOVE WITH THE GIRL YOU CHERISH.
IN THE FIRST PLACE...
...IT'S AN IMPOSSIBILITY FOR A CLAN LEADER.
KYO KNOWS THAT.
HE'S PROBABLY CONSIDERING OTHER WAYS HE CAN CONTINUE...
...TO BE THE CLAN LEADER.
OTHER WAYS...?
ARE THERE OTHER WAYS?
YES...
ONE OTHER WAY.

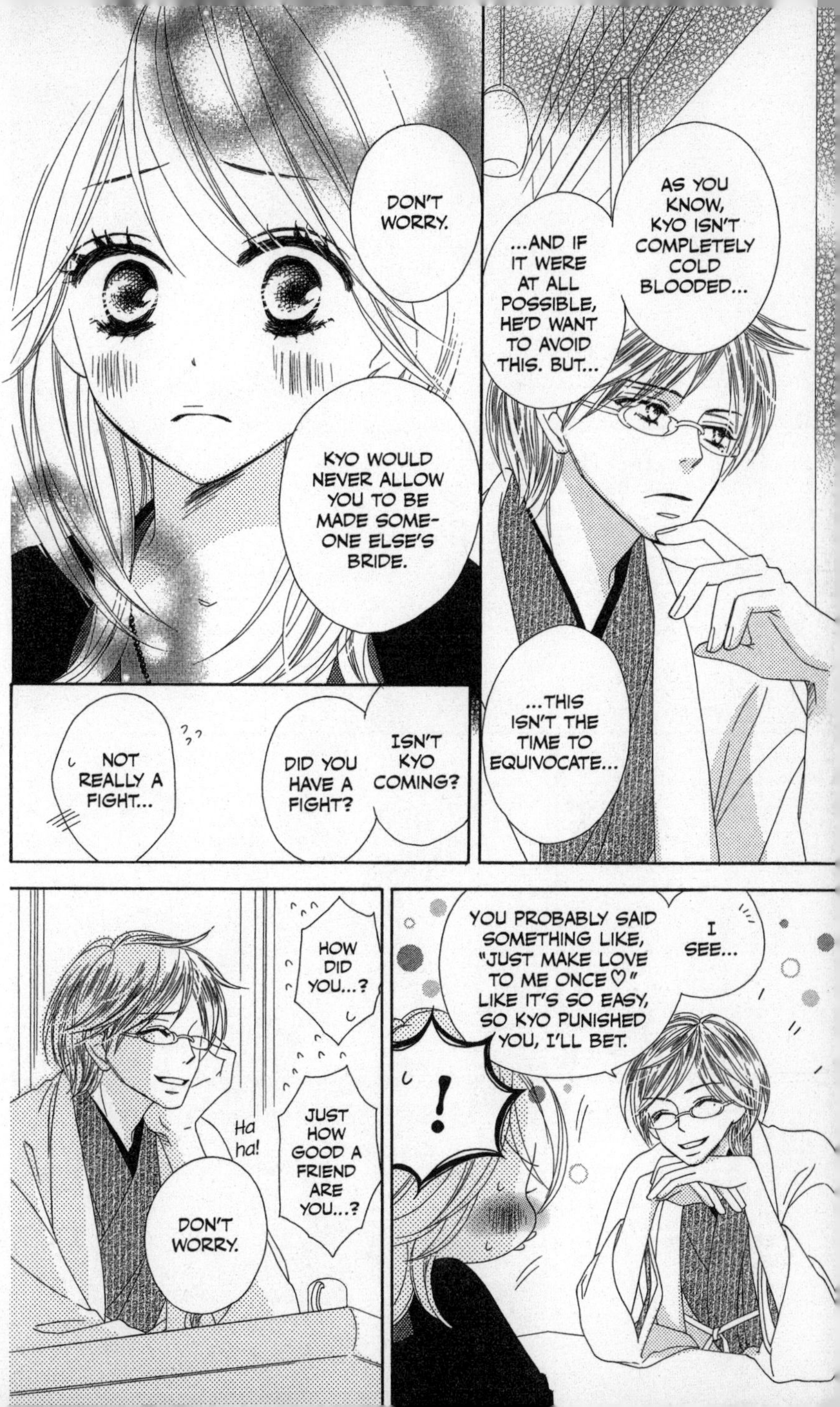
AS YOU KNOW, KYO ISN'T COMPLETELY COLD BLOODED...
...AND IF IT WERE AT ALL POSSIBLE, HE'D WANT TO AVOID THIS. BUT...
...THIS ISN'T THE TIME TO EQUIVOCATE...
DON'T WORRY.
KYO WOULD NEVER ALLOW YOU TO BE MADE SOME-ONE ELSE'S BRIDE.
ISN'T KYO COMING?
DID YOU HAVE A FIGHT?
NOT REALLY A FIGHT...
I SEE...
YOU PROBABLY SAID SOMETHING LIKE, "JUST MAKE LOVE TO ME ONCE♡" LIKE IT'S SO EASY, SO KYO PUNISHED YOU, I'LL BET.
!
HOW DID YOU...?
JUST HOW GOOD A FRIEND ARE YOU...?
Ha ha!
DON'T WORRY.

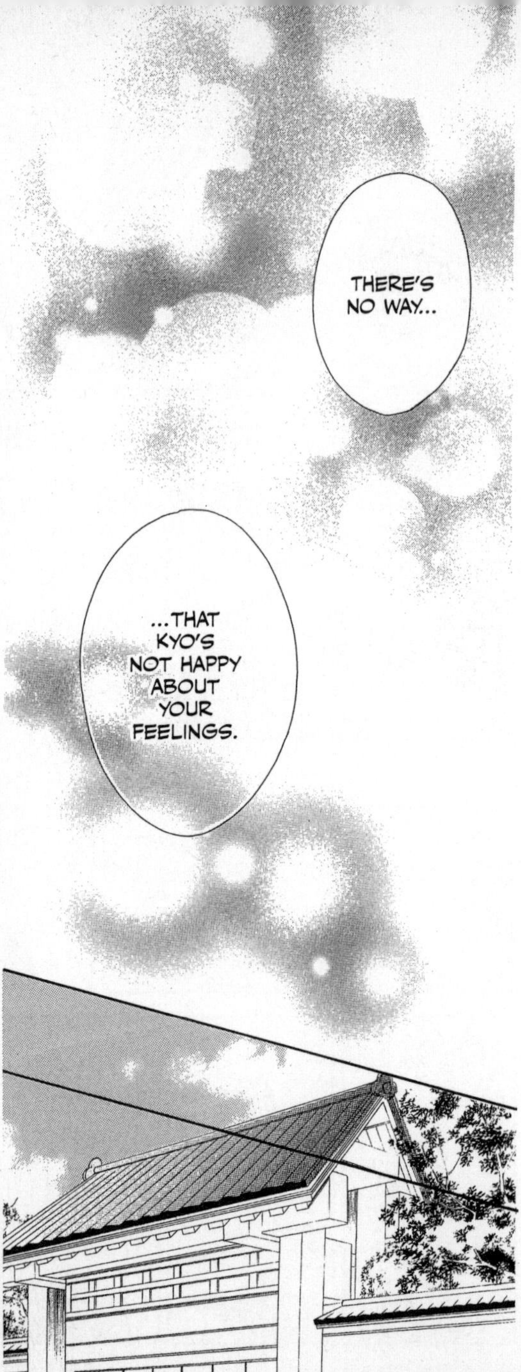
THERE'S NO WAY...
...THAT KYO'S NOT HAPPY ABOUT YOUR FEELINGS.

Character Introduction

Renko Jonouchi
age: 19 height: 168 cm

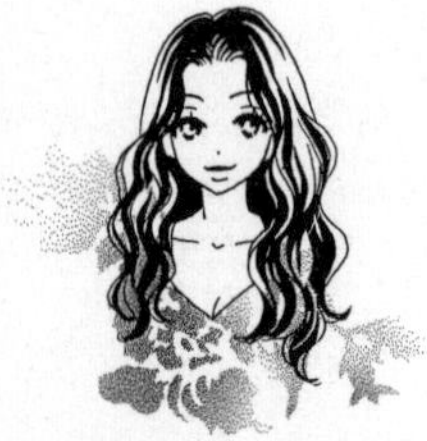

She has a name like a Japanese enka singer's. I wanted to create a girl who is in a similar position as Misao but who is her opposite in many ways.

On a previous page, Tadanobu says something that makes him sound like a masochist. But actually, it's Renko who is the extreme masochist, and she, along with extreme sadist Tadanobu, have learned the allure of the other side...

What in the world am I saying?!

By the way, the study of folklore is actually not the study of demons.

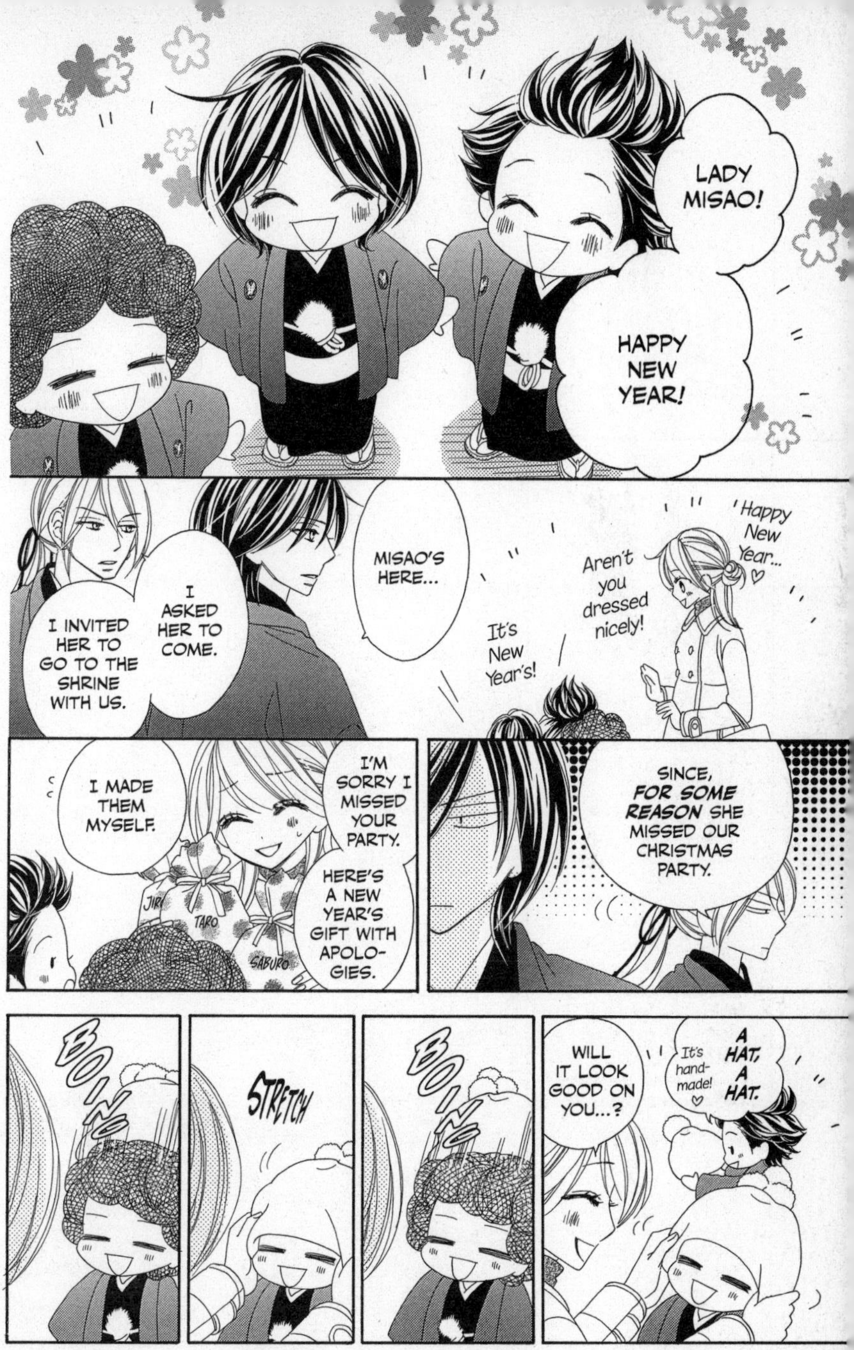

LADY MISAO!
HAPPY NEW YEAR!
Happy New Year... ♥
Aren't you dressed nicely!
It's New Year's!
MISAO'S HERE...
I ASKED HER TO COME.
I INVITED HER TO GO TO THE SHRINE WITH US.
SINCE, *FOR SOME REASON* SHE MISSED OUR CHRISTMAS PARTY.
I'M SORRY I MISSED YOUR PARTY.
HERE'S A NEW YEAR'S GIFT WITH APOLOGIES.
I MADE THEM MYSELF.
TARO
SABURO
A HAT, A HAT.
It's hand-made! ♡
WILL IT LOOK GOOD ON YOU...?
BOING
STRETCH
BOING

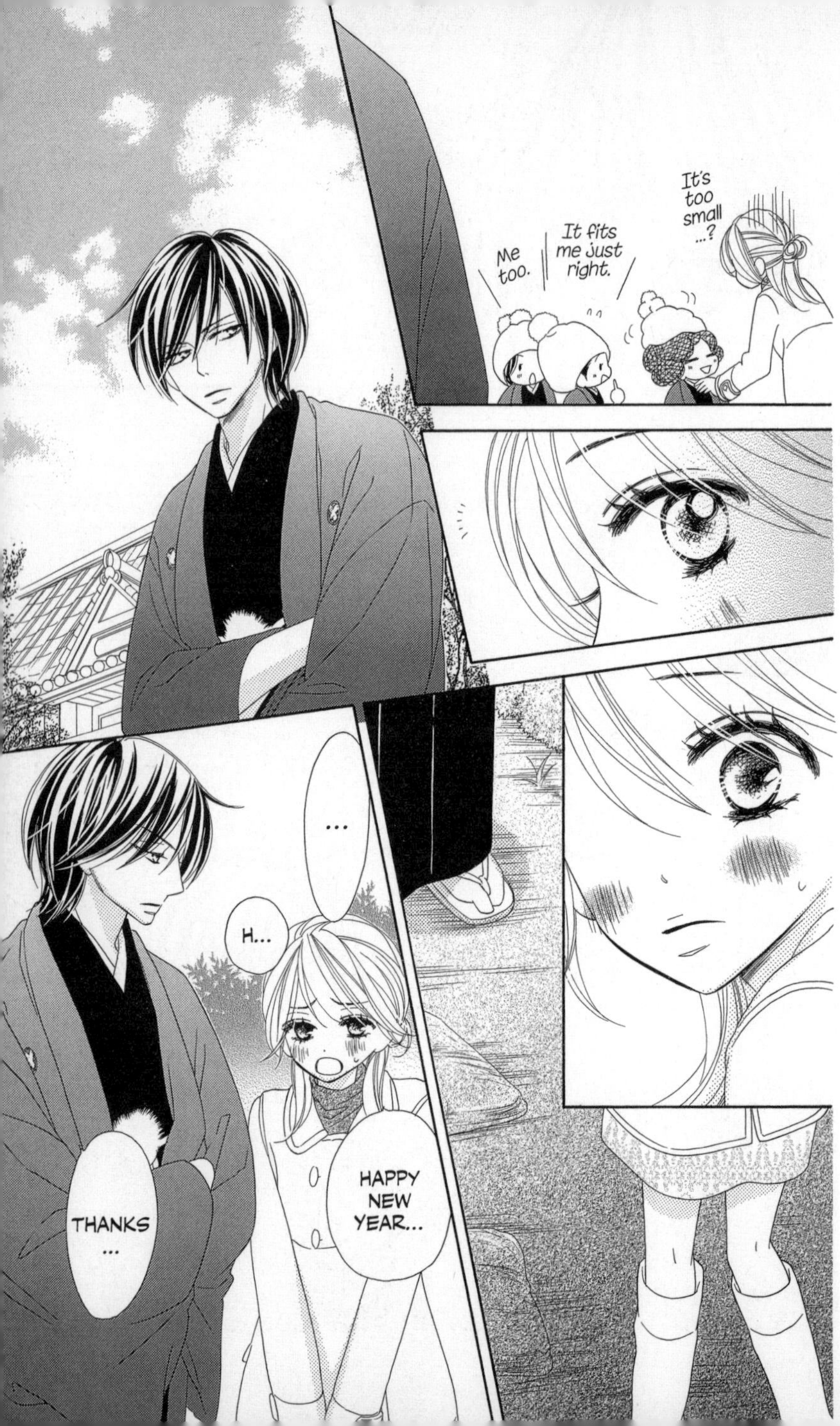
It's too small ...?
It fits me just right.
Me too.
...
H...
HAPPY NEW YEAR...
THANKS ...

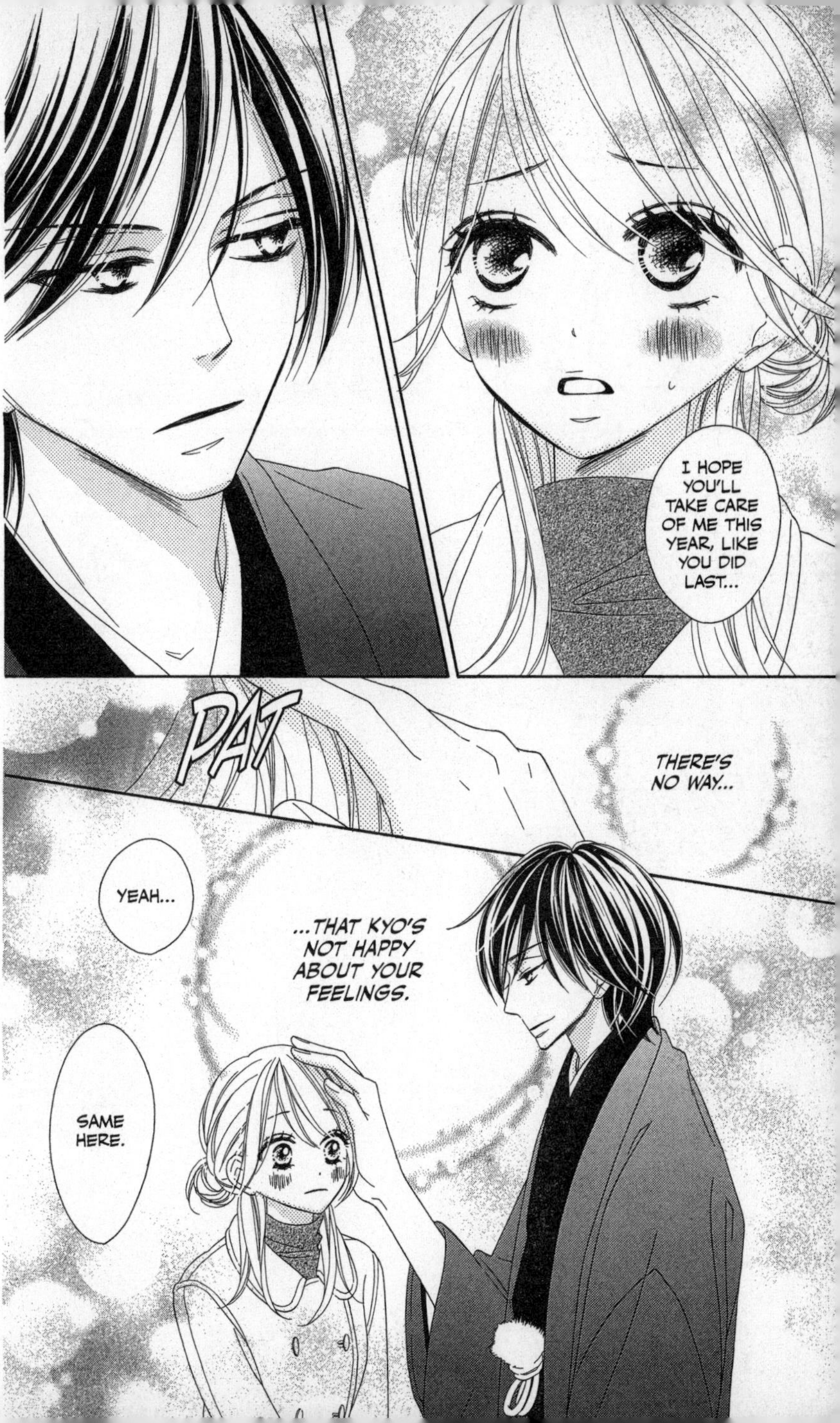
I HOPE YOU'LL TAKE CARE OF ME THIS YEAR, LIKE YOU DID LAST...
PAT
THERE'S NO WAY...
...THAT KYO'S NOT HAPPY ABOUT YOUR FEELINGS.
YEAH...
SAME HERE.

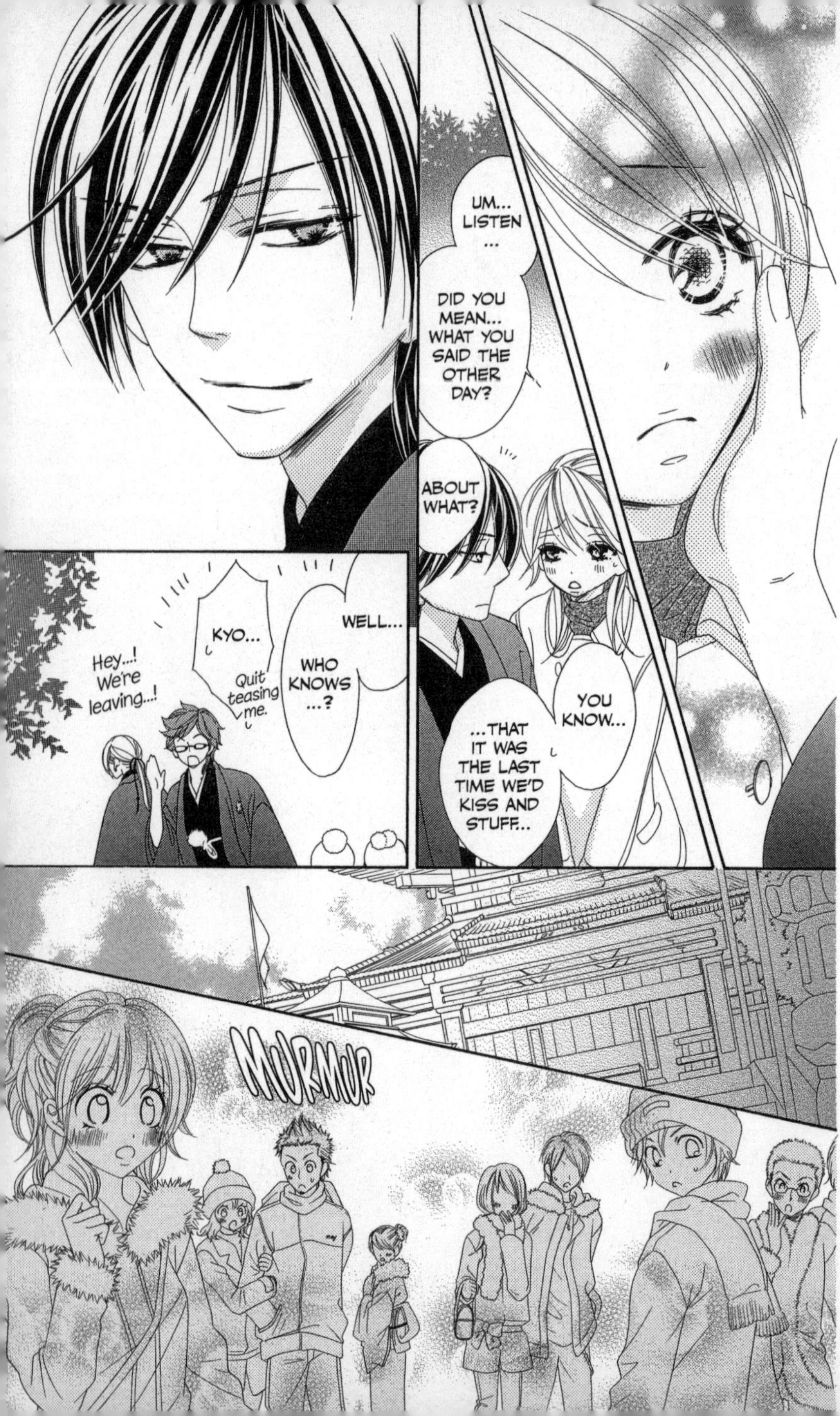
UM... LISTEN ...
DID YOU MEAN... WHAT YOU SAID THE OTHER DAY?
ABOUT WHAT?
YOU KNOW...
...THAT IT WAS THE LAST TIME WE'D KISS AND STUFF...
WELL...
WHO KNOWS ...?
KYO...
Quit teasing me.
Hey...! We're leaving...!
MURMUR

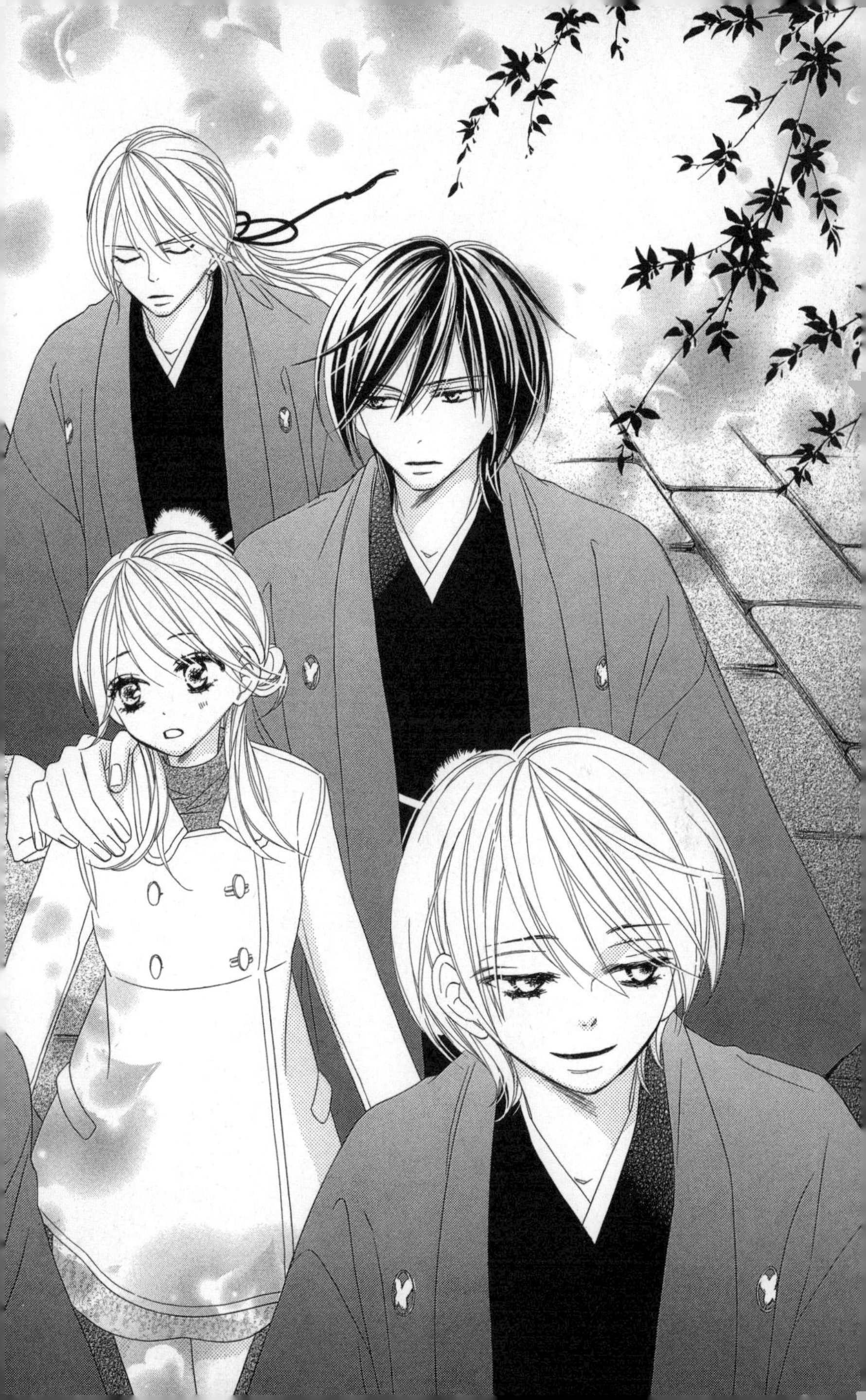

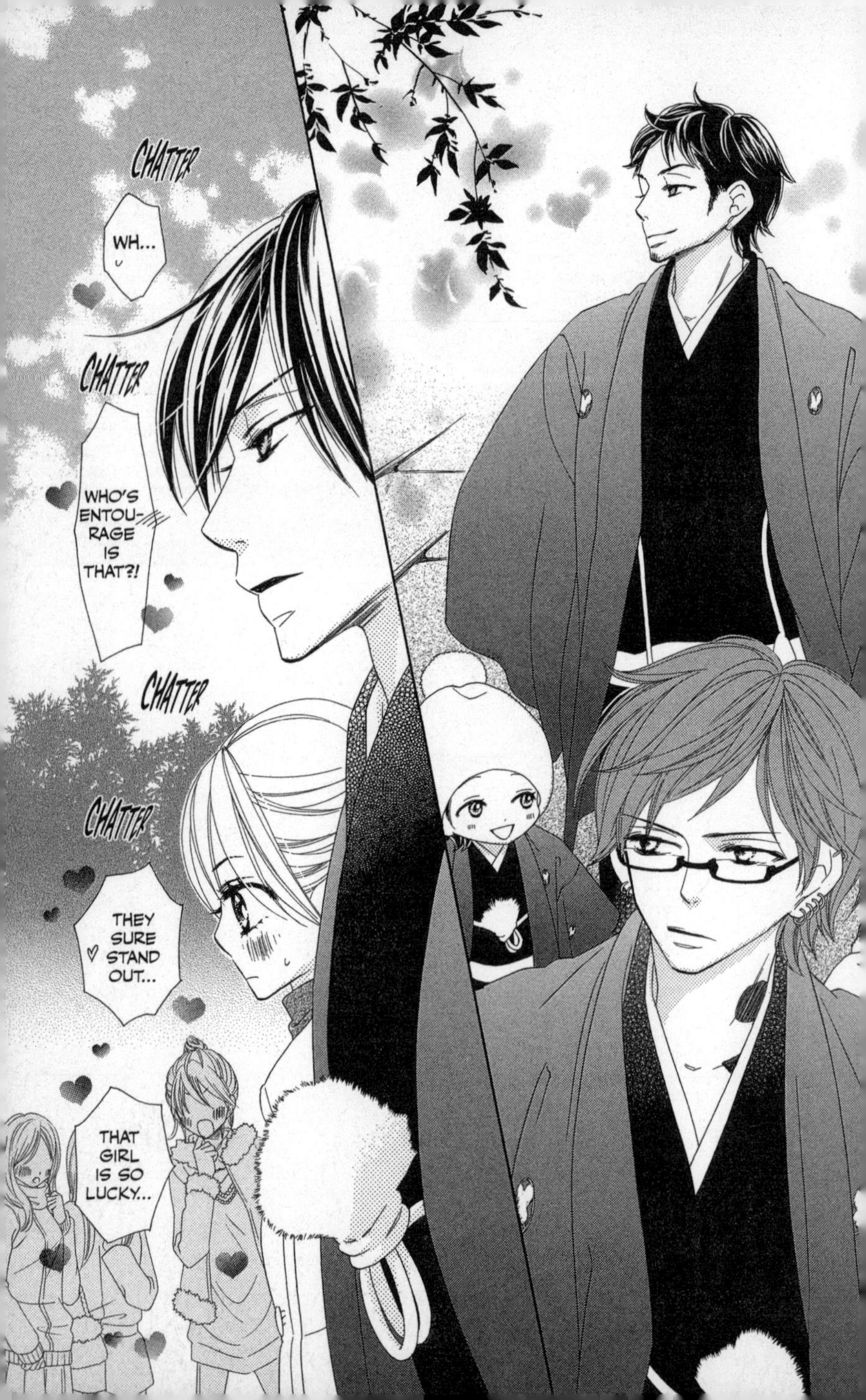
CHATTER
WH...
CHATTER
WHO'S ENTOURAGE IS THAT?!
CHATTER
CHATTER
THEY SURE STAND OUT... ♡
THAT GIRL IS SO LUCKY...

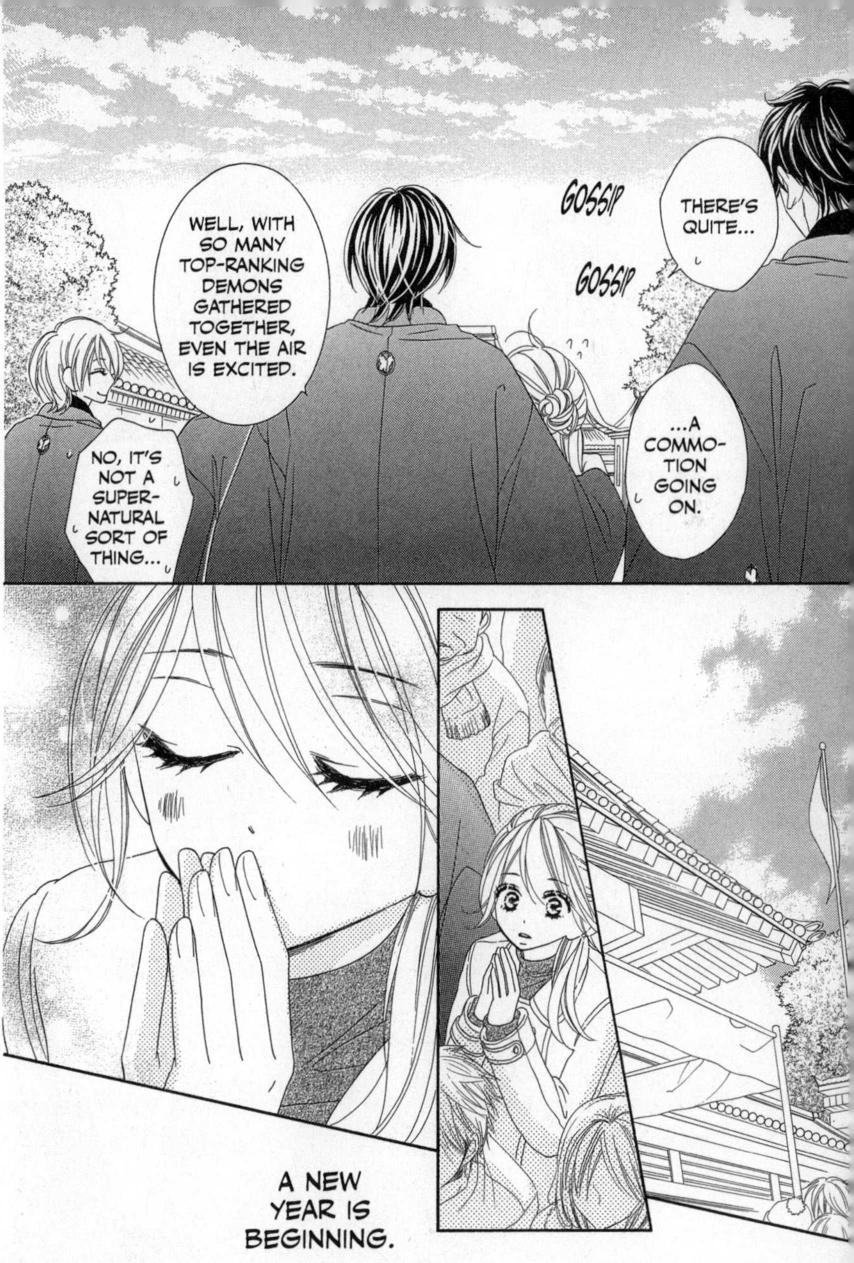
THERE'S QUITE...
GOSSIP
GOSSIP
...A COMMOTION GOING ON.
WELL, WITH SO MANY TOP-RANKING DEMONS GATHERED TOGETHER, EVEN THE AIR IS EXCITED.
NO, IT'S NOT A SUPERNATURAL SORT OF THING...
A NEW YEAR IS BEGINNING.

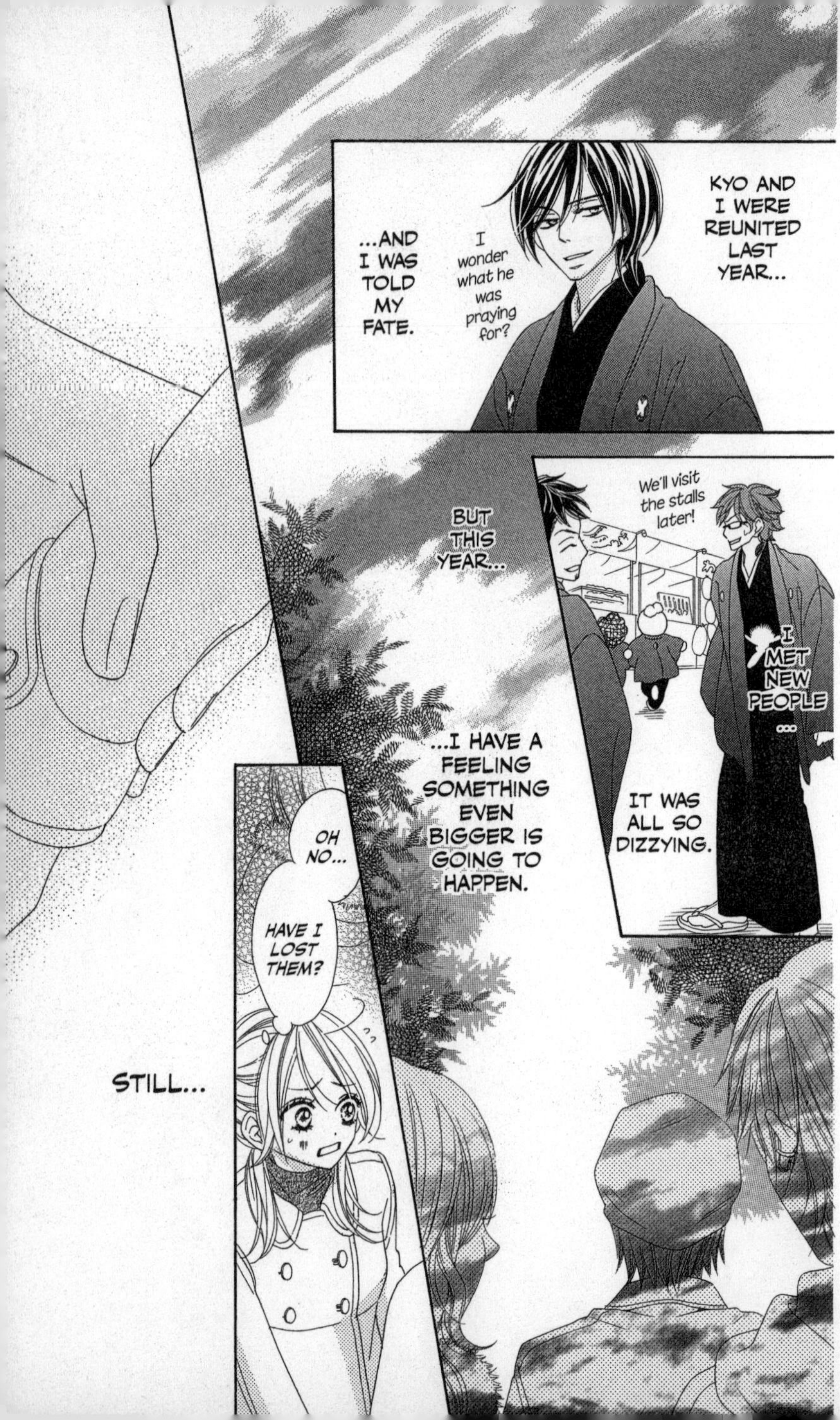
KYO AND I WERE REUNITED LAST YEAR...
I wonder what he was praying for?
...AND I WAS TOLD MY FATE.
We'll visit the stalls later!
I MET NEW PEOPLE...
IT WAS ALL SO DIZZYING.
BUT THIS YEAR...
...I HAVE A FEELING SOMETHING EVEN BIGGER IS GOING TO HAPPEN.
OH NO...
HAVE I LOST THEM?
STILL...

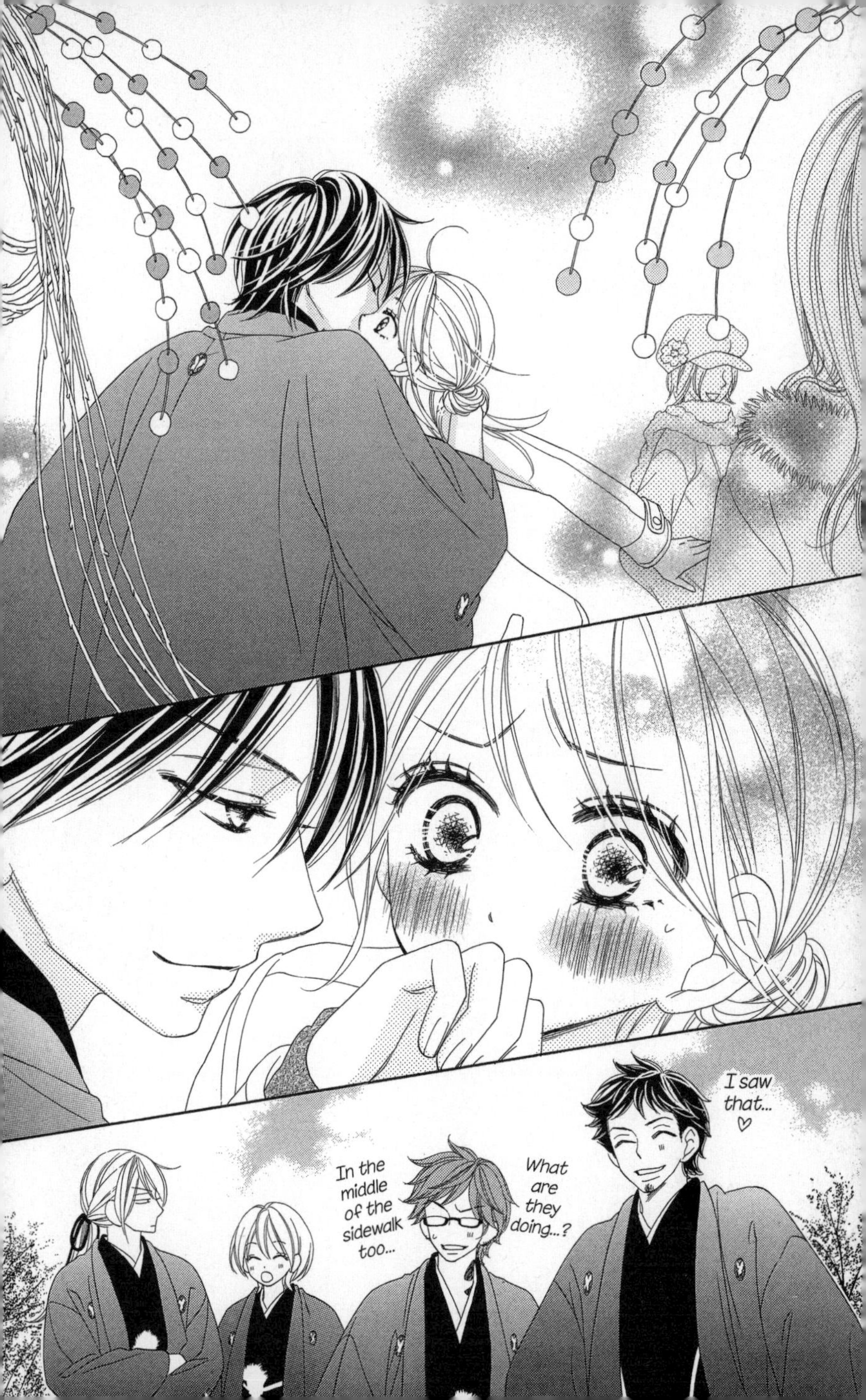
I saw that... ♥
What are they doing...?
In the middle of the sidewalk too...

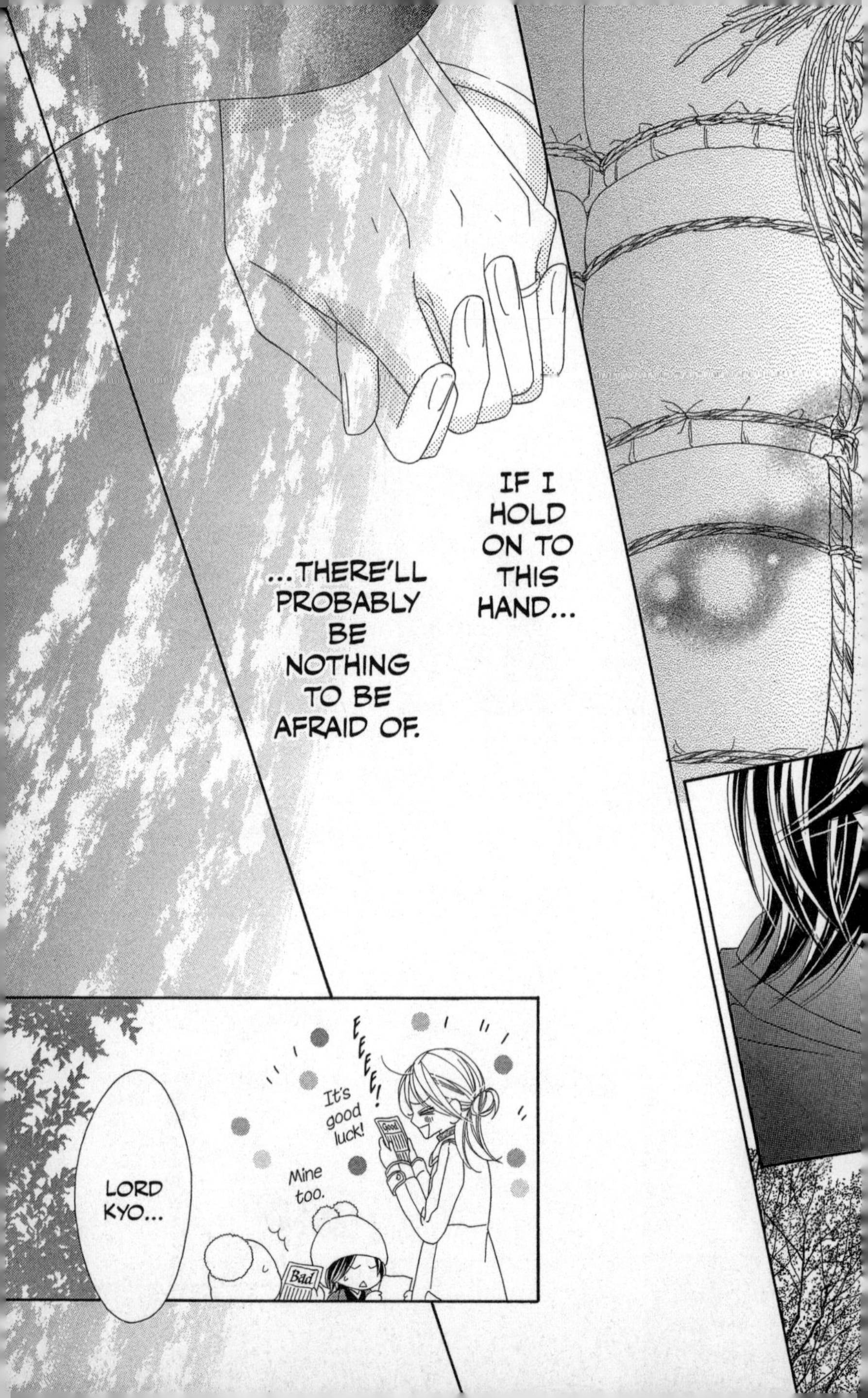
IF I HOLD ON TO THIS HAND...
...THERE'LL PROBABLY BE NOTHING TO BE AFRAID OF.
EEEE!
It's good luck!
Good
Mine too.
Bad
LORD KYO...

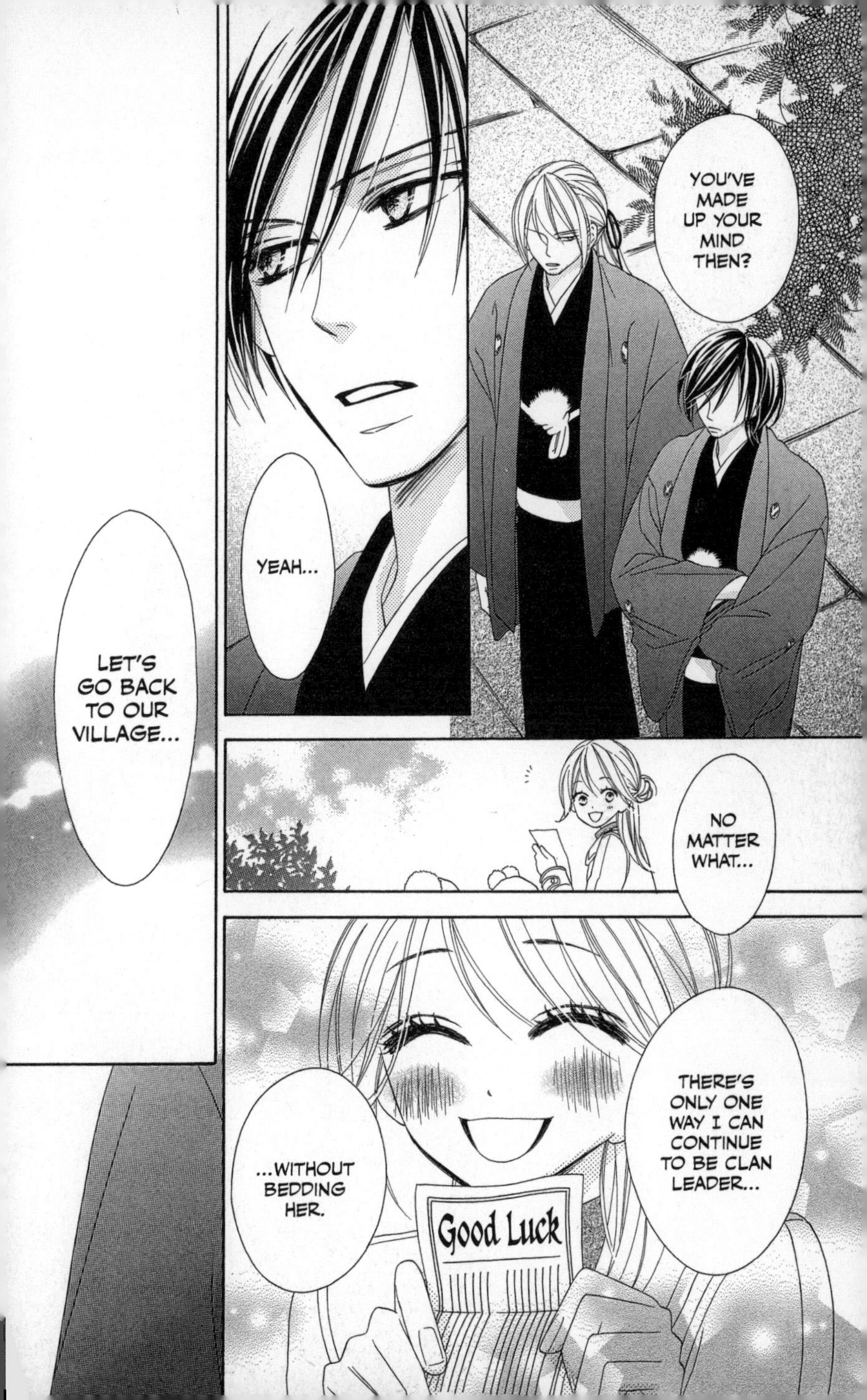
YOU'VE MADE UP YOUR MIND THEN?
YEAH...
LET'S GO BACK TO OUR VILLAGE...
NO MATTER WHAT...
THERE'S ONLY ONE WAY I CAN CONTINUE TO BE CLAN LEADER...
...WITHOUT BEDDING HER.
Good Luck

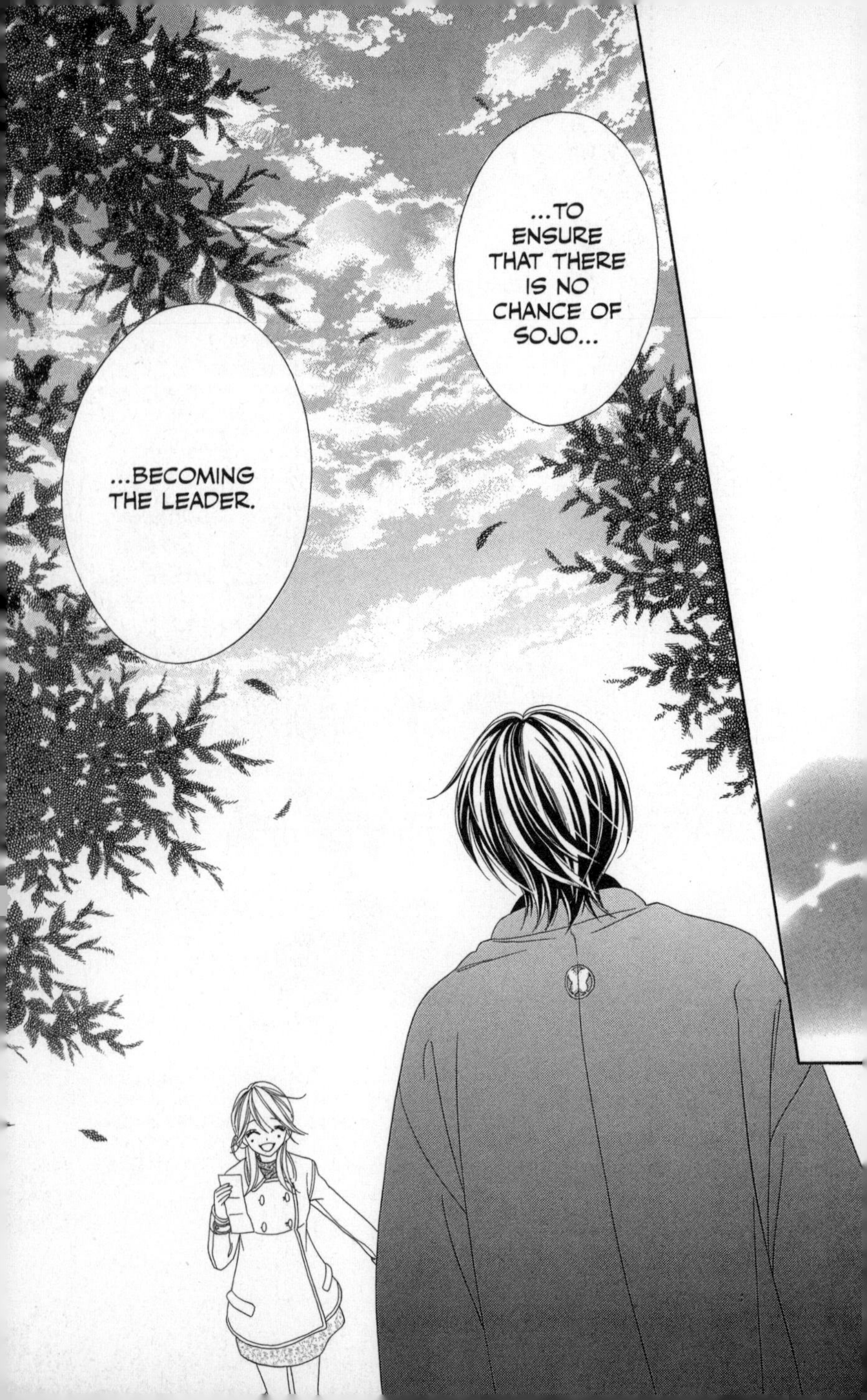
...TO ENSURE THAT THERE IS NO CHANCE OF SOJO...
...BECOMING THE LEADER.

Illustration Request Number Seven

"Kyo's Sexual Harassment
Private After-School Lessons"

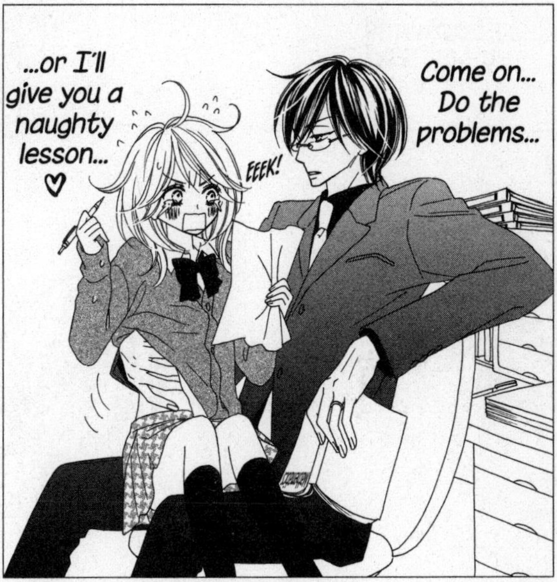
Come on... Do the problems...
...or I'll give you a naughty lesson... ♥
EEEK!

Lately, Kyo has been very good in the story,
so I haven't been able to draw too many pictures like this...

This is the way Kyo should be!

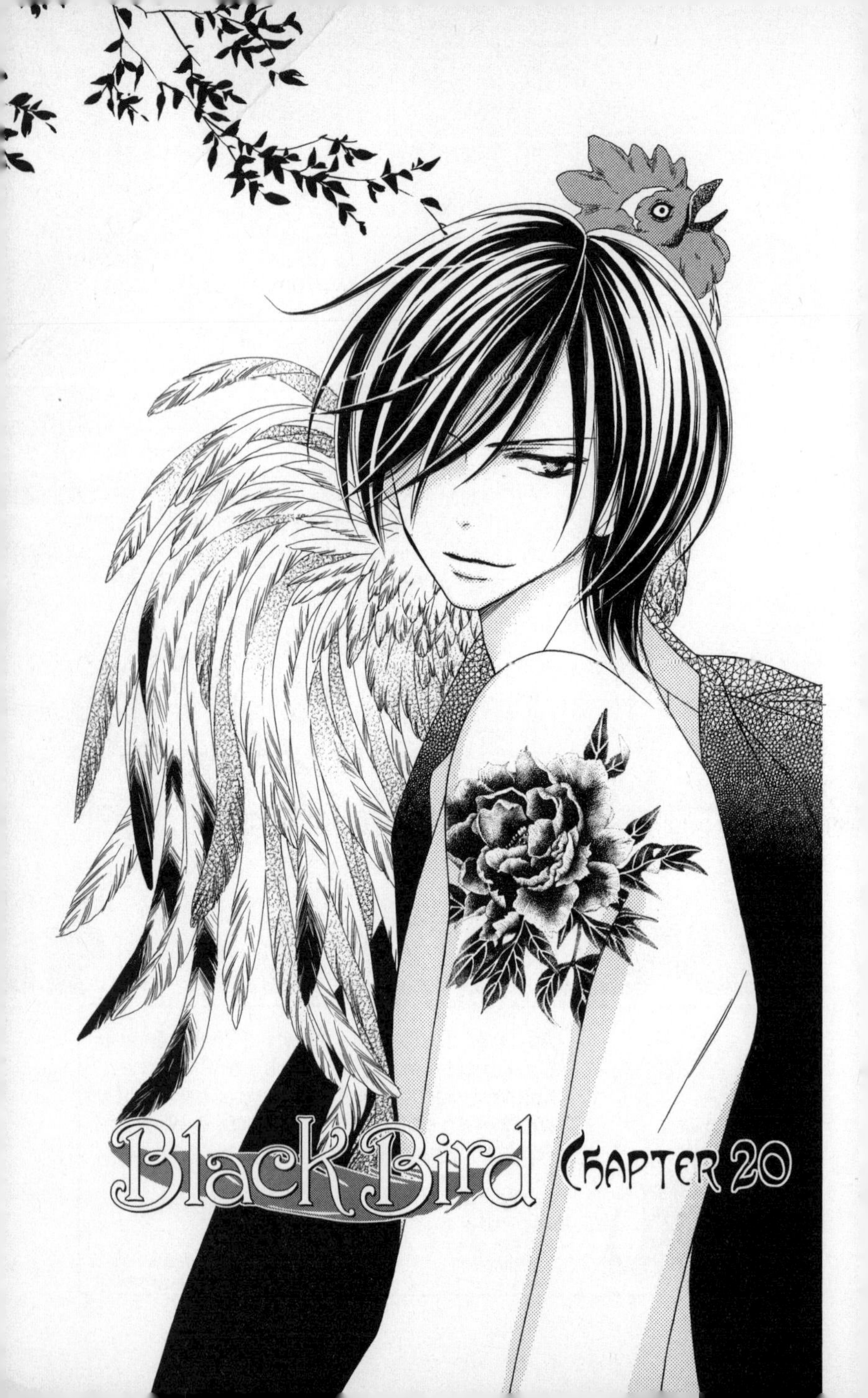
Black Bird
Chapter 20

IF A DEMON...
...DRINKS MY BLOOD HE IS GRANTED A LONG LIFE.
IF HE EATS MY FLESH, HE GAINS ETERNAL YOUTH.
IF HE MAKES ME HIS BRIDE, HIS CLAN WILL PROSPER...
I AM THE SENKA MAIDEN.

SOB

As a rule, I, Sakurakouji, write Zenki's lines in the Kansai dialect, but since I'm from the Kanto region, when I'm unsure, I ask a native speaker to edit it. (But at times, I will go for the tempo of the line rather than for authenticity...) I am very grateful! ♡

Truly, this manga is the result of the support of all sorts of people...*

*This was Kansai dialect in the Japanese version!

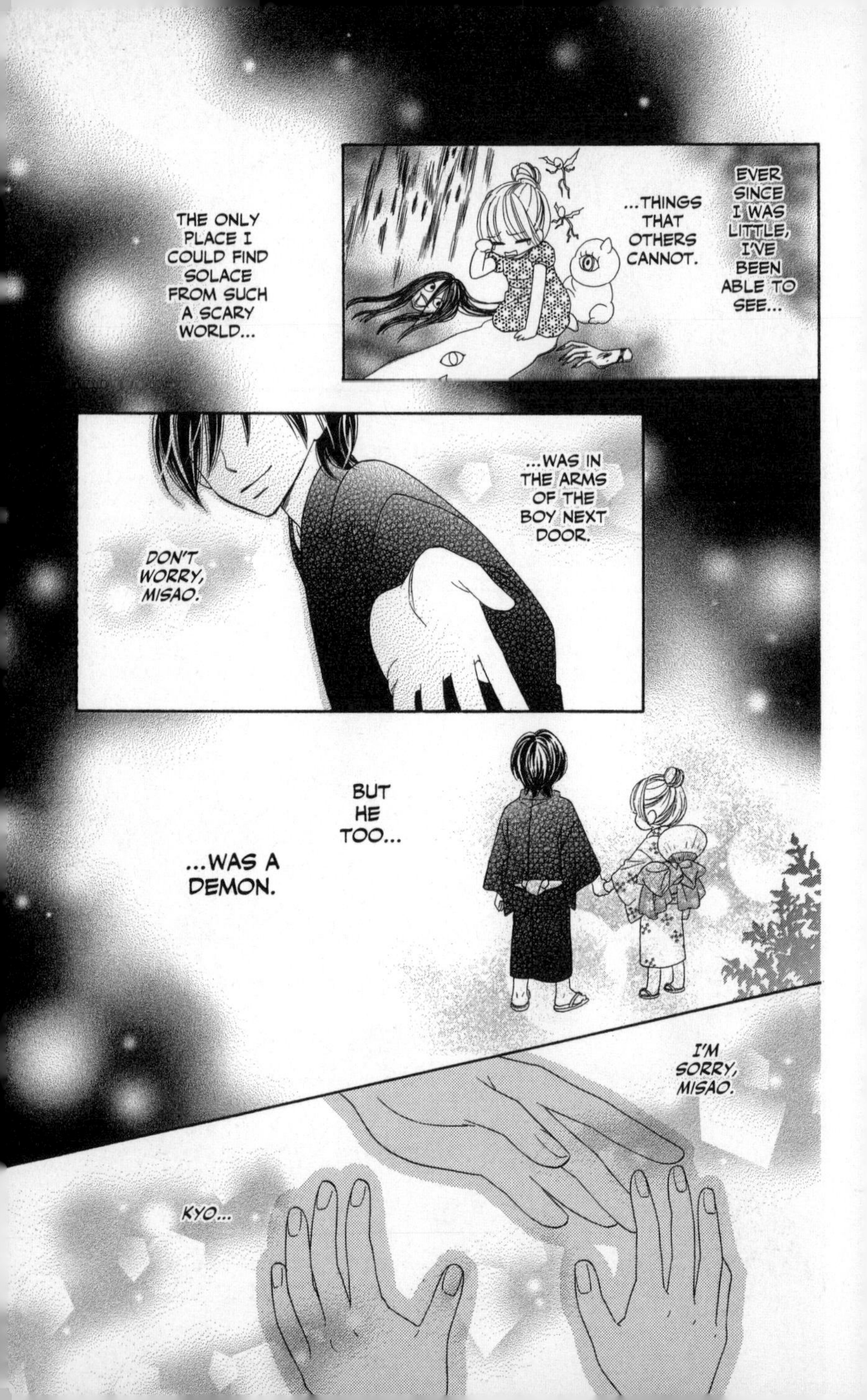
EVER SINCE I WAS LITTLE, I'VE BEEN ABLE TO SEE...
...THINGS THAT OTHERS CANNOT.
THE ONLY PLACE I COULD FIND SOLACE FROM SUCH A SCARY WORLD...
...WAS IN THE ARMS OF THE BOY NEXT DOOR.
DON'T WORRY, MISAO.
BUT HE TOO...
...WAS A DEMON.
I'M SORRY, MISAO.
KYO...

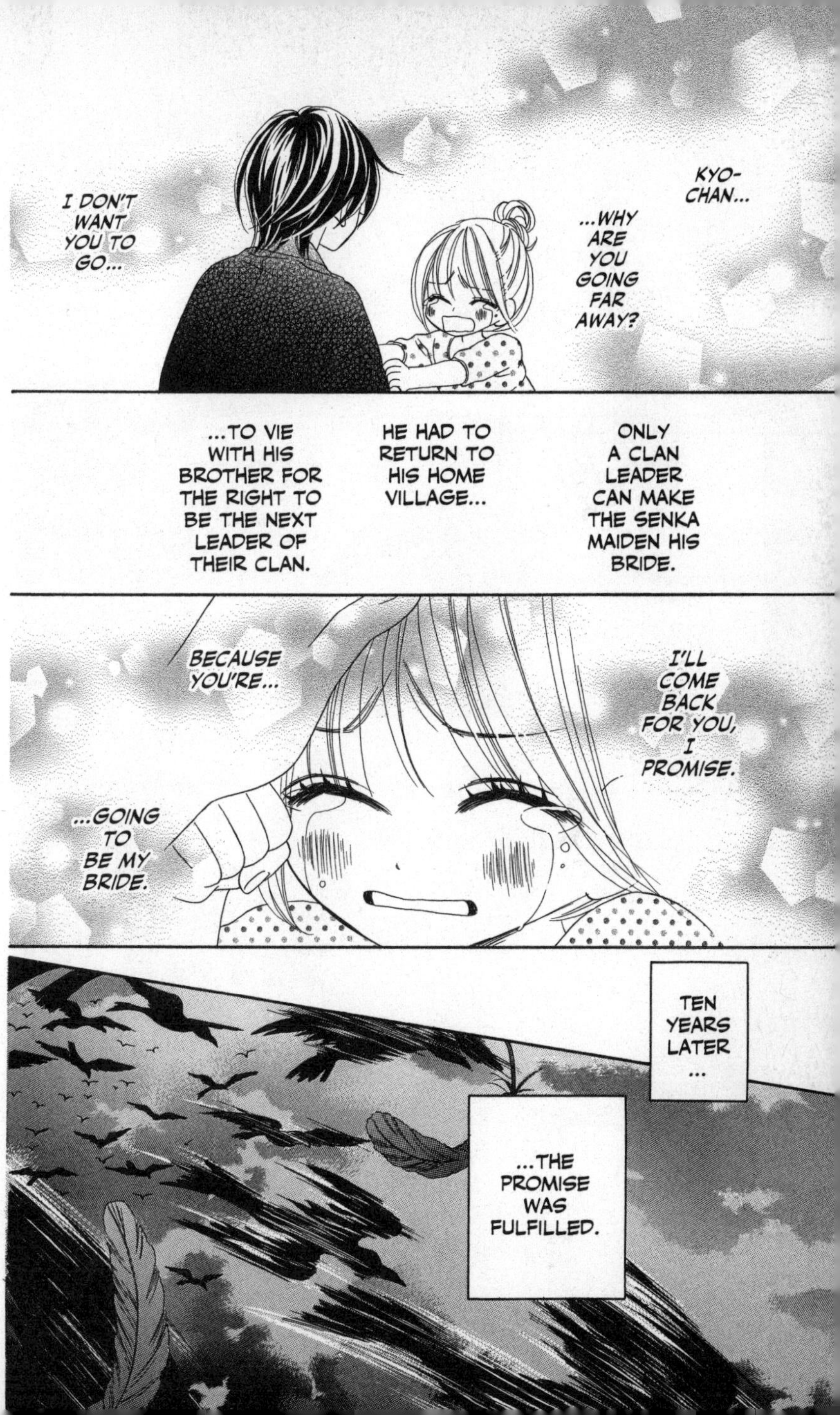
KYO-CHAN...
...WHY ARE YOU GOING FAR AWAY?
I DON'T WANT YOU TO GO...
ONLY A CLAN LEADER CAN MAKE THE SENKA MAIDEN HIS BRIDE.
HE HAD TO RETURN TO HIS HOME VILLAGE...
...TO VIE WITH HIS BROTHER FOR THE RIGHT TO BE THE NEXT LEADER OF THEIR CLAN.
I'LL COME BACK FOR YOU, I PROMISE.
BECAUSE YOU'RE...
...GOING TO BE MY BRIDE.
TEN YEARS LATER...
...THE PROMISE WAS FULFILLED.

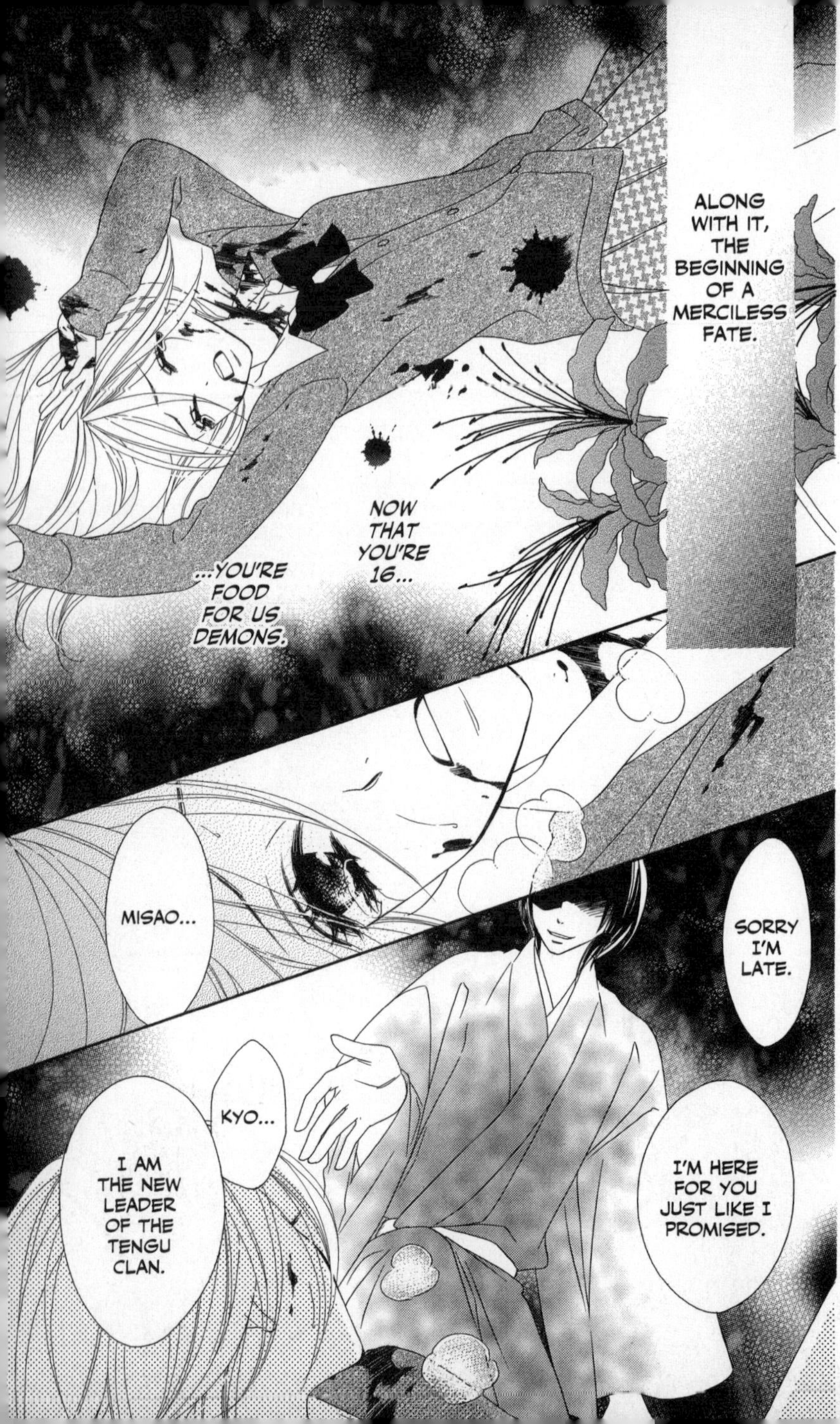
ALONG WITH IT, THE BEGINNING OF A MERCILESS FATE.
NOW THAT YOU'RE 16...
...YOU'RE FOOD FOR US DEMONS.
MISAO...
SORRY I'M LATE.
I'M HERE FOR YOU JUST LIKE I PROMISED.
KYO...
I AM THE NEW LEADER OF THE TENGU CLAN.

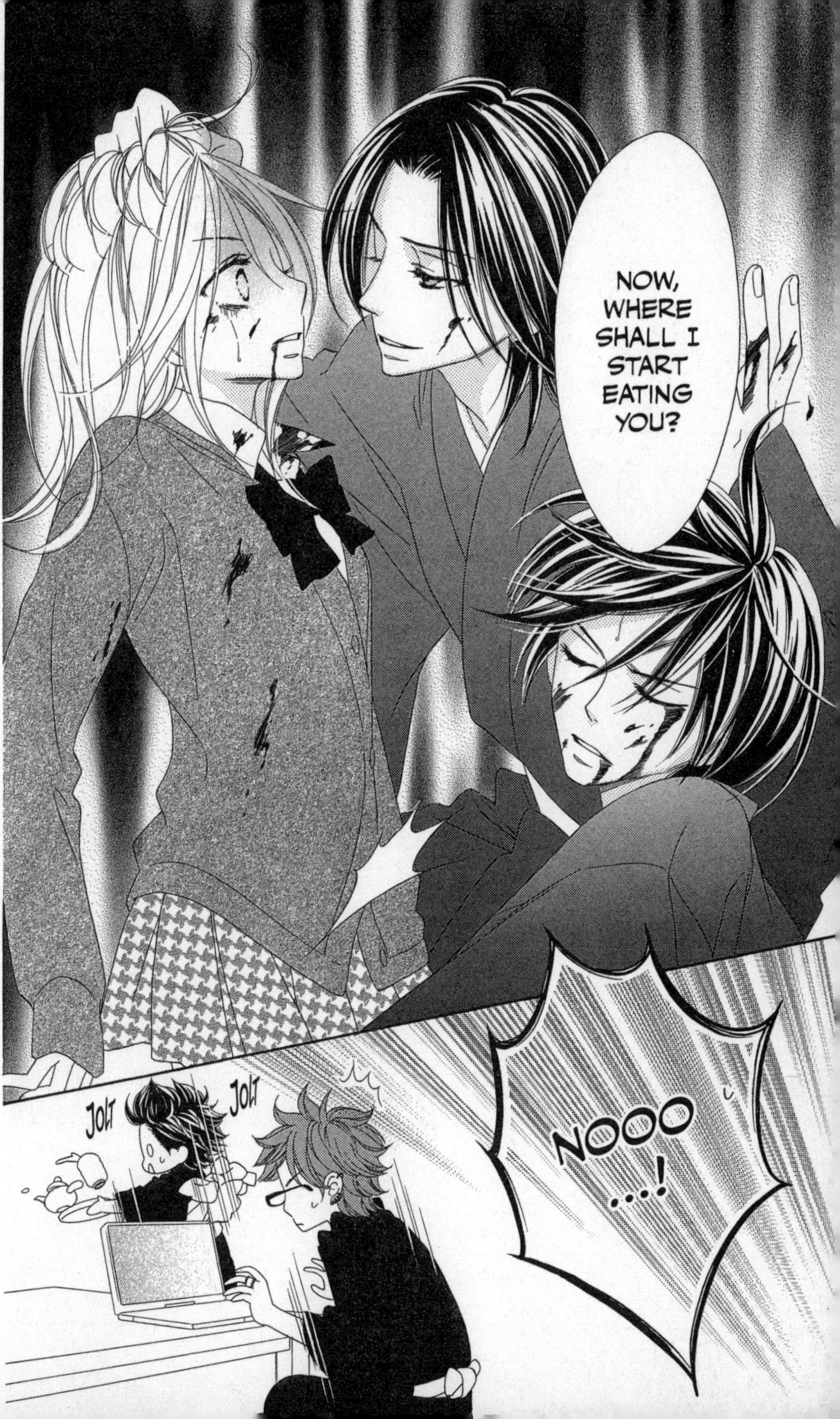
NOW, WHERE SHALL I START EATING YOU?
NOOO ...!
JOLT
JOLT

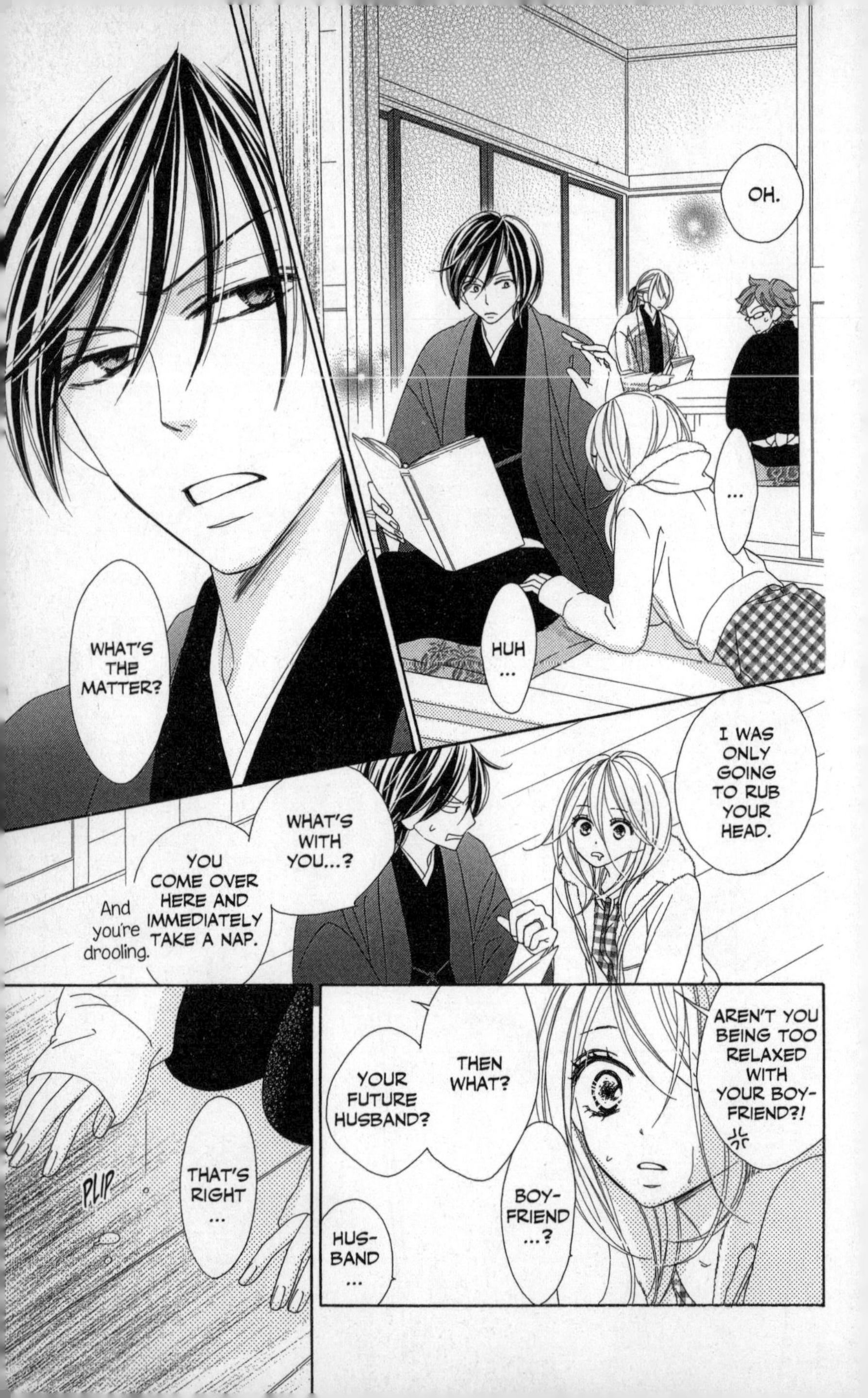
OH.
...
HUH ...
WHAT'S THE MATTER?
I WAS ONLY GOING TO RUB YOUR HEAD.
WHAT'S WITH YOU...?
YOU COME OVER HERE AND IMMEDIATELY TAKE A NAP.
And you're drooling.
AREN'T YOU BEING TOO RELAXED WITH YOUR BOY-FRIEND?!
THEN WHAT?
YOUR FUTURE HUSBAND?
BOY-FRIEND ...?
HUS-BAND ...
THAT'S RIGHT ...
PLIP

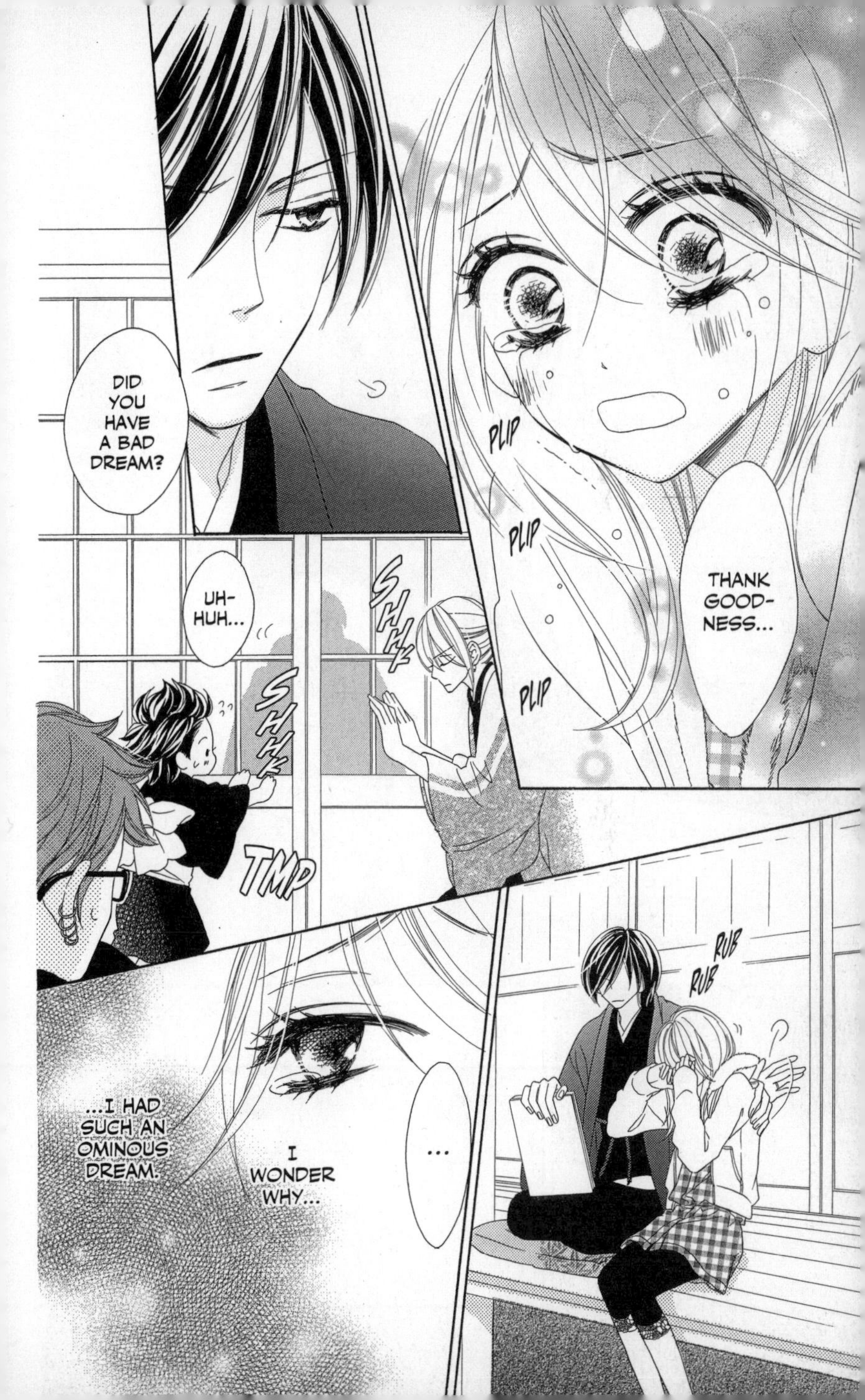
PLIP
PLIP
PLIP
THANK GOODNESS...
DID YOU HAVE A BAD DREAM?
SHHK
UH-HUH...
SHHK
TMP
RUB RUB
...
I WONDER WHY...
...I HAD SUCH AN OMINOUS DREAM.

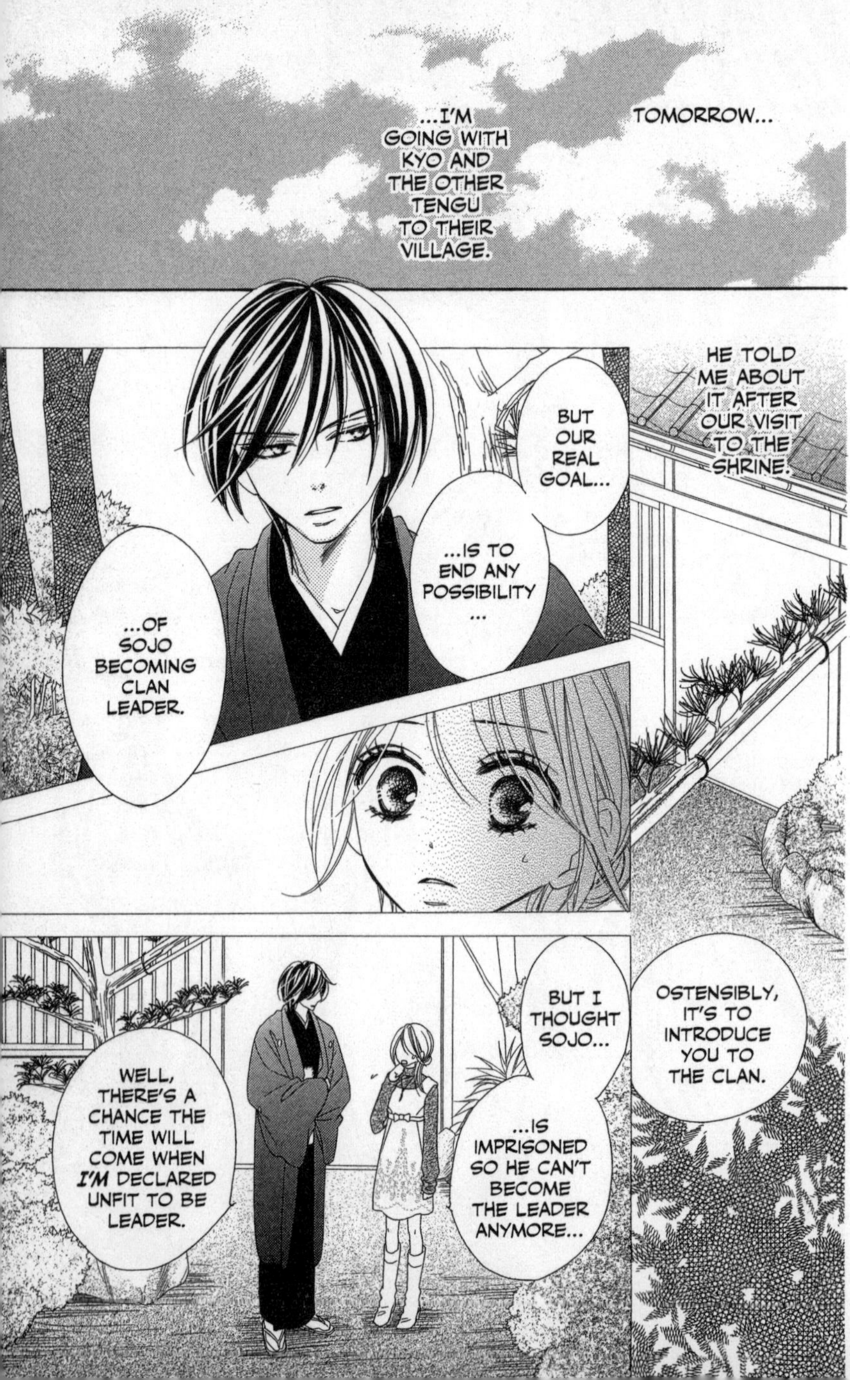
TOMORROW...
...I'M GOING WITH KYO AND THE OTHER TENGU TO THEIR VILLAGE.
HE TOLD ME ABOUT IT AFTER OUR VISIT TO THE SHRINE.
OSTENSIBLY, IT'S TO INTRODUCE YOU TO THE CLAN.
BUT OUR REAL GOAL...
...IS TO END ANY POSSIBILITY ...
...OF SOJO BECOMING CLAN LEADER.
BUT I THOUGHT SOJO...
...IS IMPRISONED SO HE CAN'T BECOME THE LEADER ANYMORE...
WELL, THERE'S A CHANCE THE TIME WILL COME WHEN *I'M* DECLARED UNFIT TO BE LEADER.

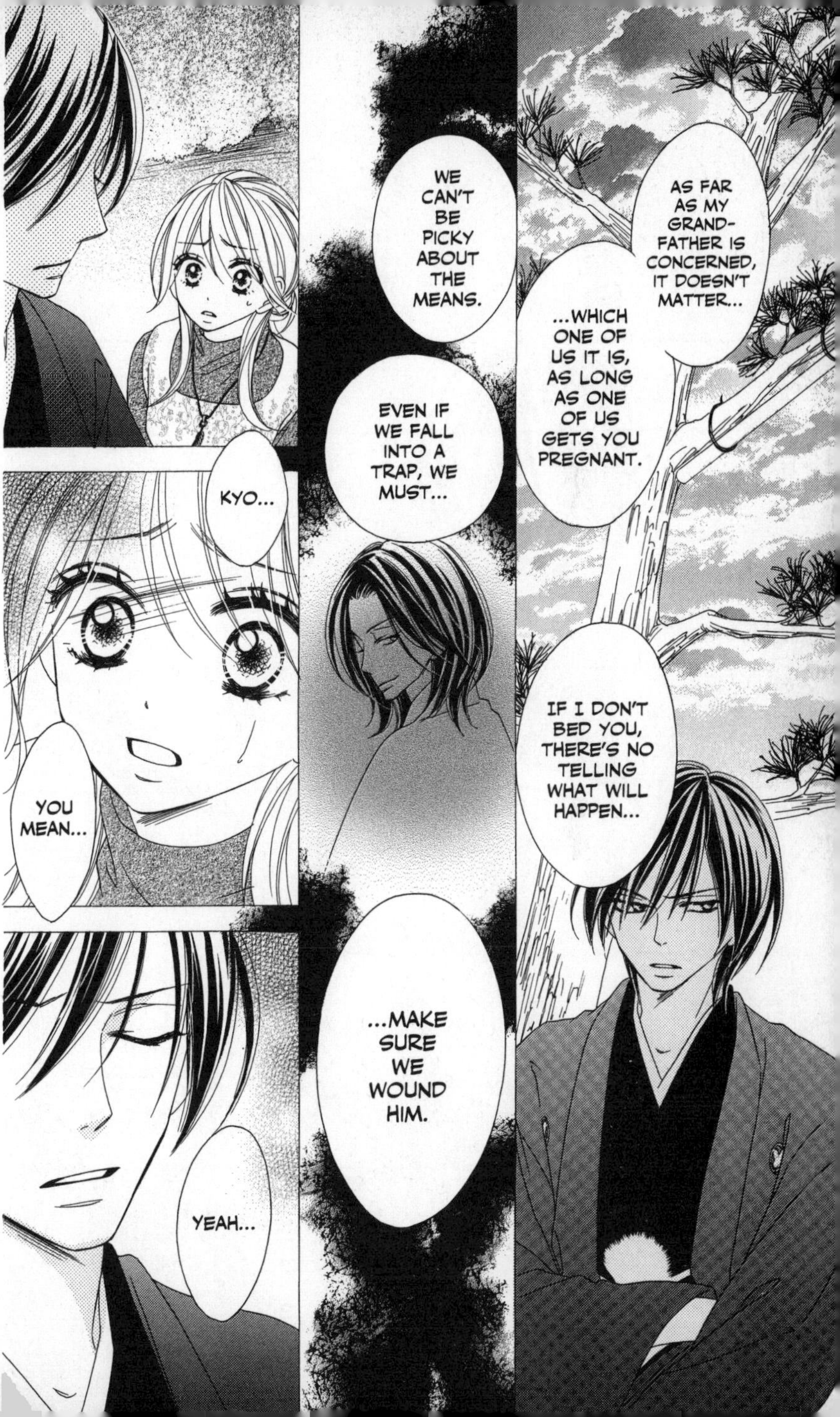
AS FAR AS MY GRAND-FATHER IS CONCERNED, IT DOESN'T MATTER...
...WHICH ONE OF US IT IS, AS LONG AS ONE OF US GETS YOU PREGNANT.
IF I DON'T BED YOU, THERE'S NO TELLING WHAT WILL HAPPEN...
WE CAN'T BE PICKY ABOUT THE MEANS.
EVEN IF WE FALL INTO A TRAP, WE MUST...
...MAKE SURE WE WOUND HIM.
KYO...
YOU MEAN...
YEAH...

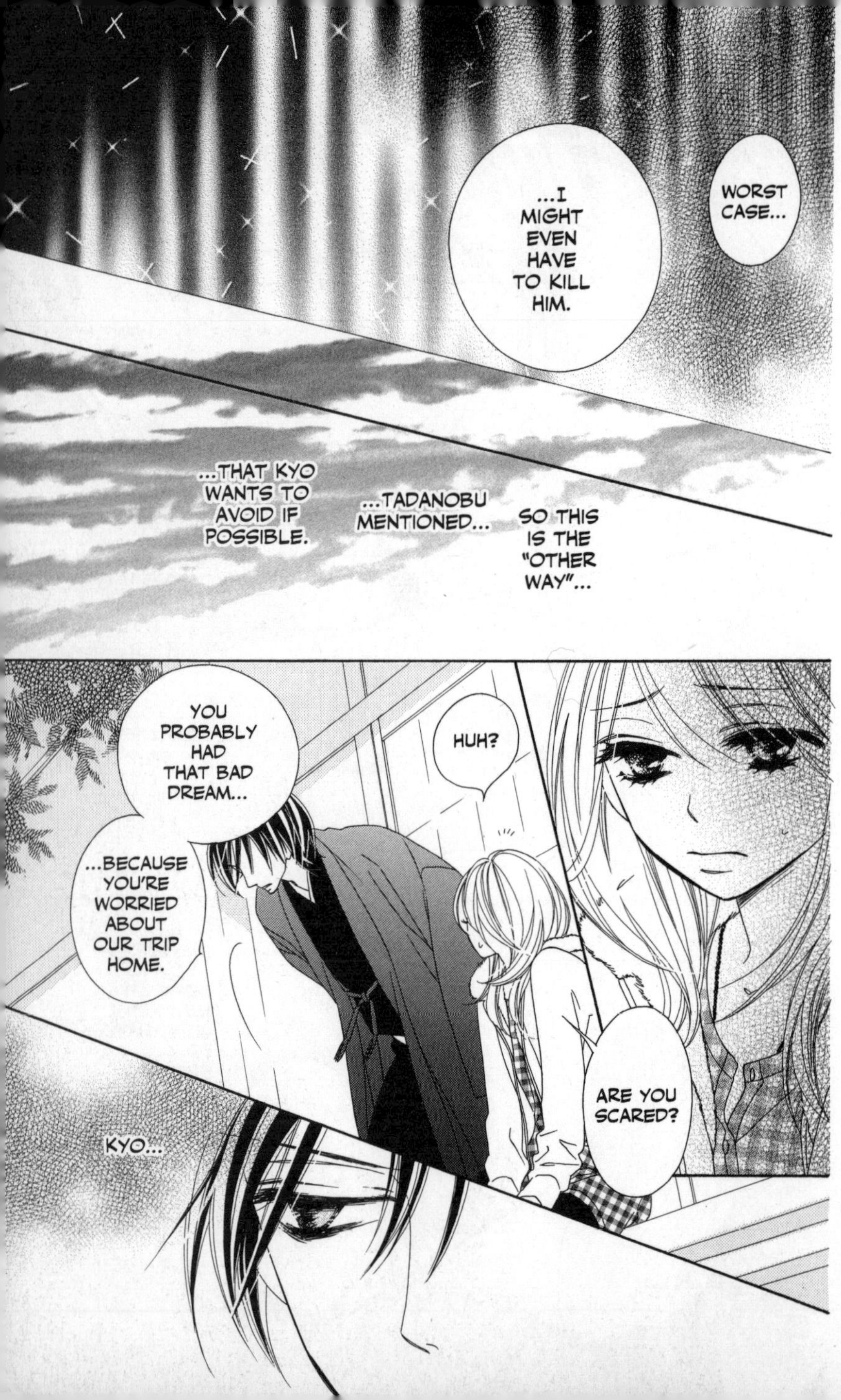
WORST CASE...
...I MIGHT EVEN HAVE TO KILL HIM.
SO THIS IS THE "OTHER WAY"...
...TADANOBU MENTIONED...
...THAT KYO WANTS TO AVOID IF POSSIBLE.
YOU PROBABLY HAD THAT BAD DREAM...
...BECAUSE YOU'RE WORRIED ABOUT OUR TRIP HOME.
HUH?
ARE YOU SCARED?
KYO...

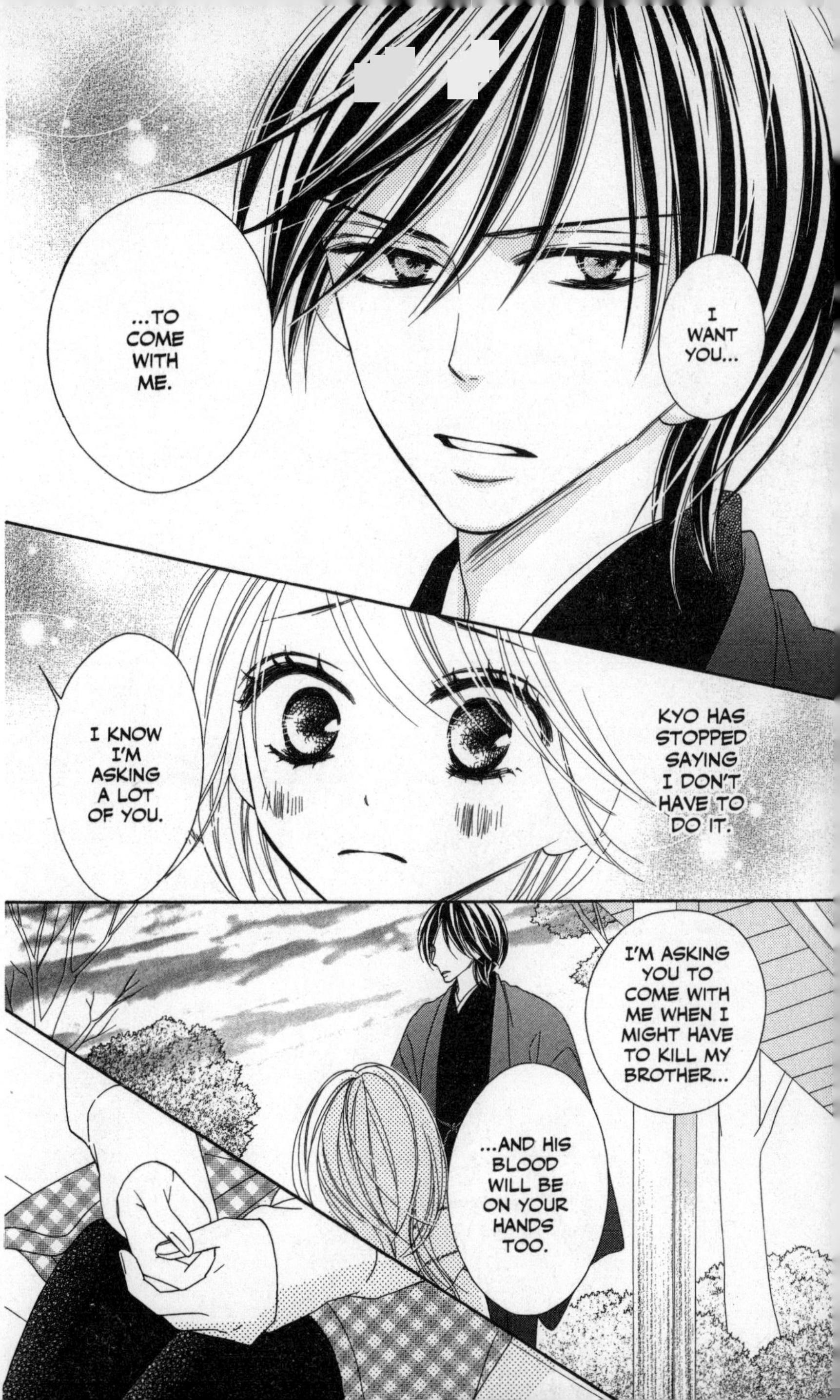
I WANT YOU...
...TO COME WITH ME.
KYO HAS STOPPED SAYING I DON'T HAVE TO DO IT.
I KNOW I'M ASKING A LOT OF YOU.
I'M ASKING YOU TO COME WITH ME WHEN I MIGHT HAVE TO KILL MY BROTHER...
...AND HIS BLOOD WILL BE ON YOUR HANDS TOO.

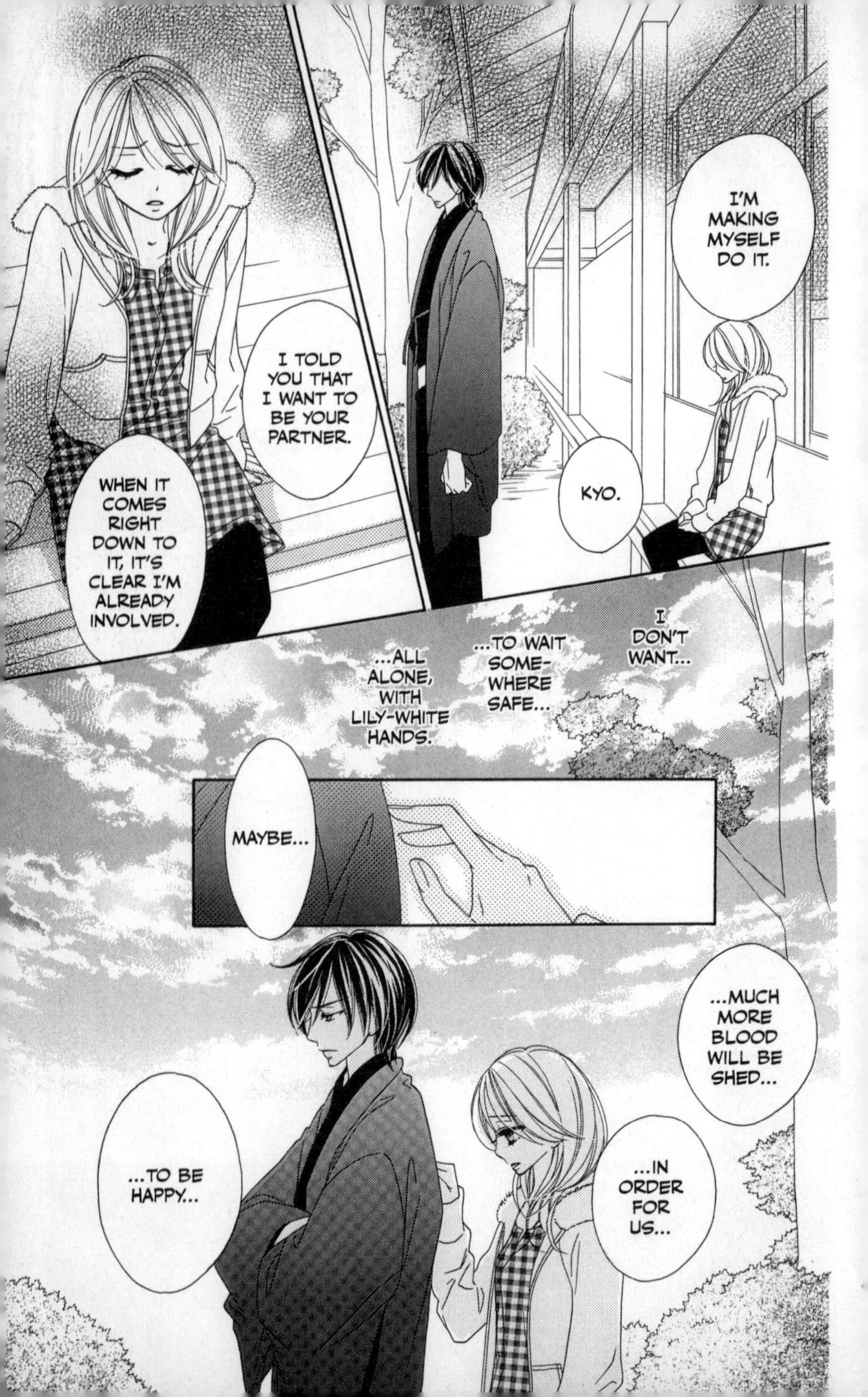
I'M MAKING MYSELF DO IT.
KYO.
I TOLD YOU THAT I WANT TO BE YOUR PARTNER.
WHEN IT COMES RIGHT DOWN TO IT, IT'S CLEAR I'M ALREADY INVOLVED.
I DON'T WANT...
...TO WAIT SOME-WHERE SAFE...
...ALL ALONE, WITH LILY-WHITE HANDS.
MAYBE...
...MUCH MORE BLOOD WILL BE SHED...
...IN ORDER FOR US...
...TO BE HAPPY...

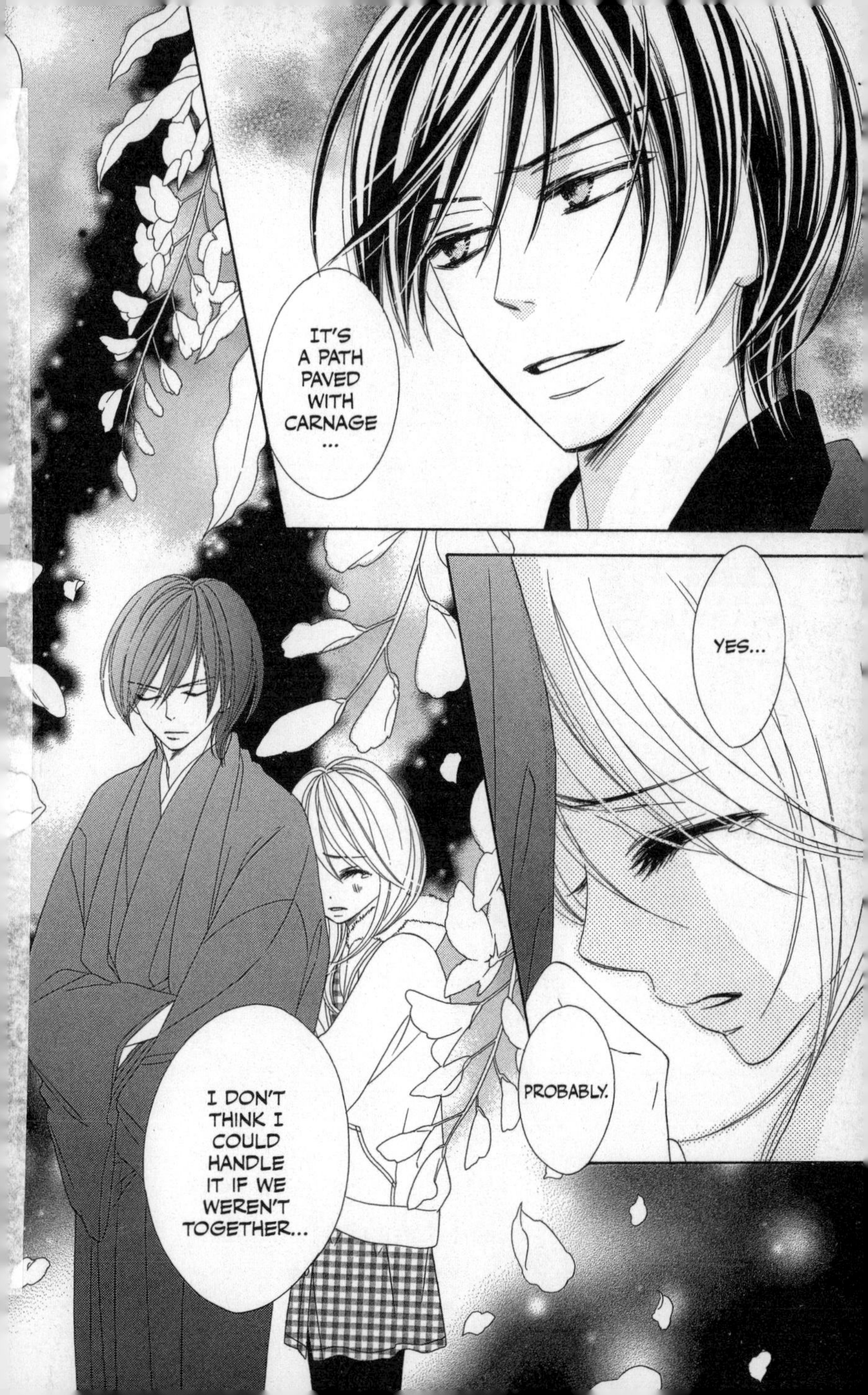
IT'S A PATH PAVED WITH CARNAGE...
YES...
PROBABLY.
I DON'T THINK I COULD HANDLE IT IF WE WEREN'T TOGETHER...

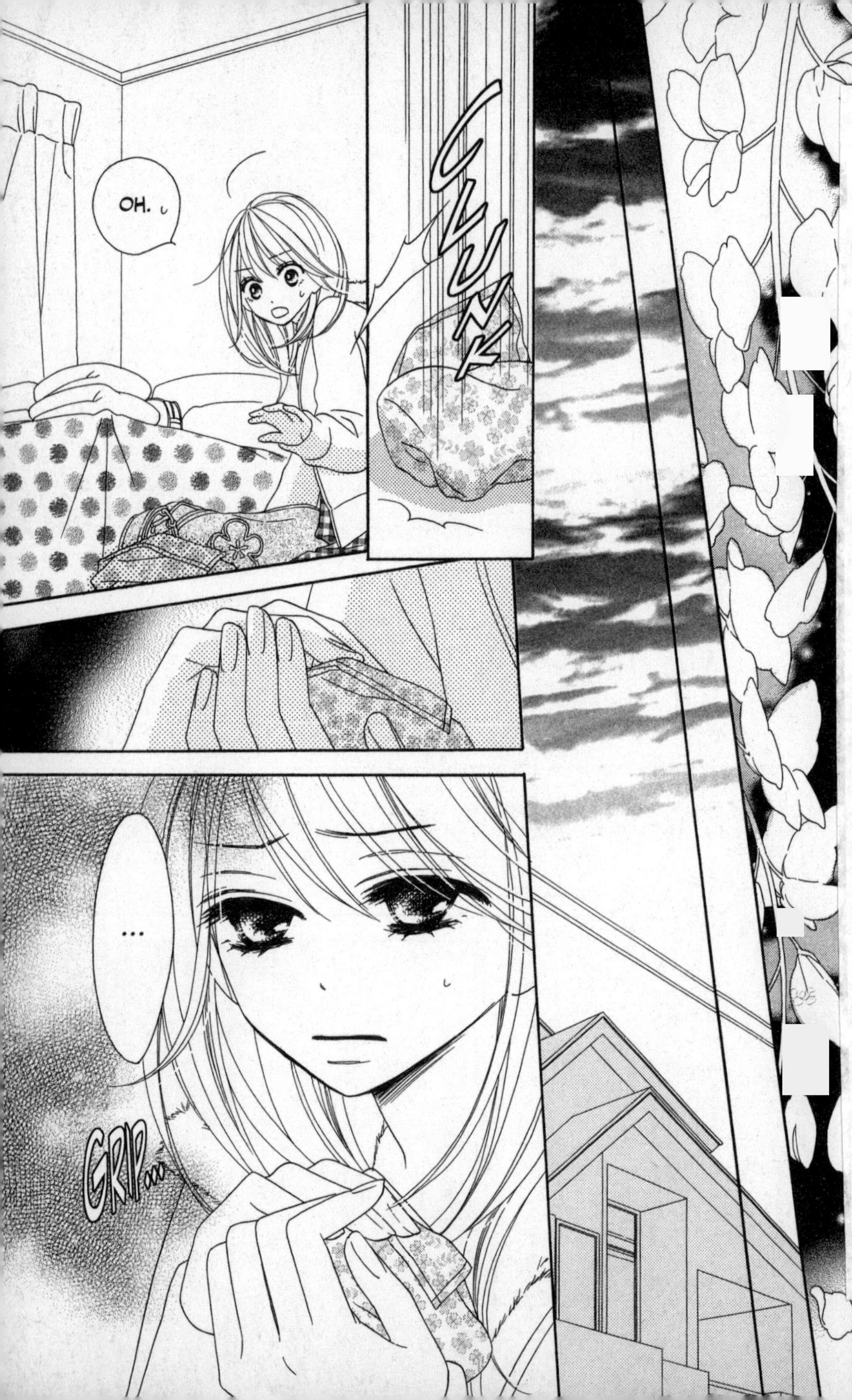
CLUNK
OH.
...
GRIP...

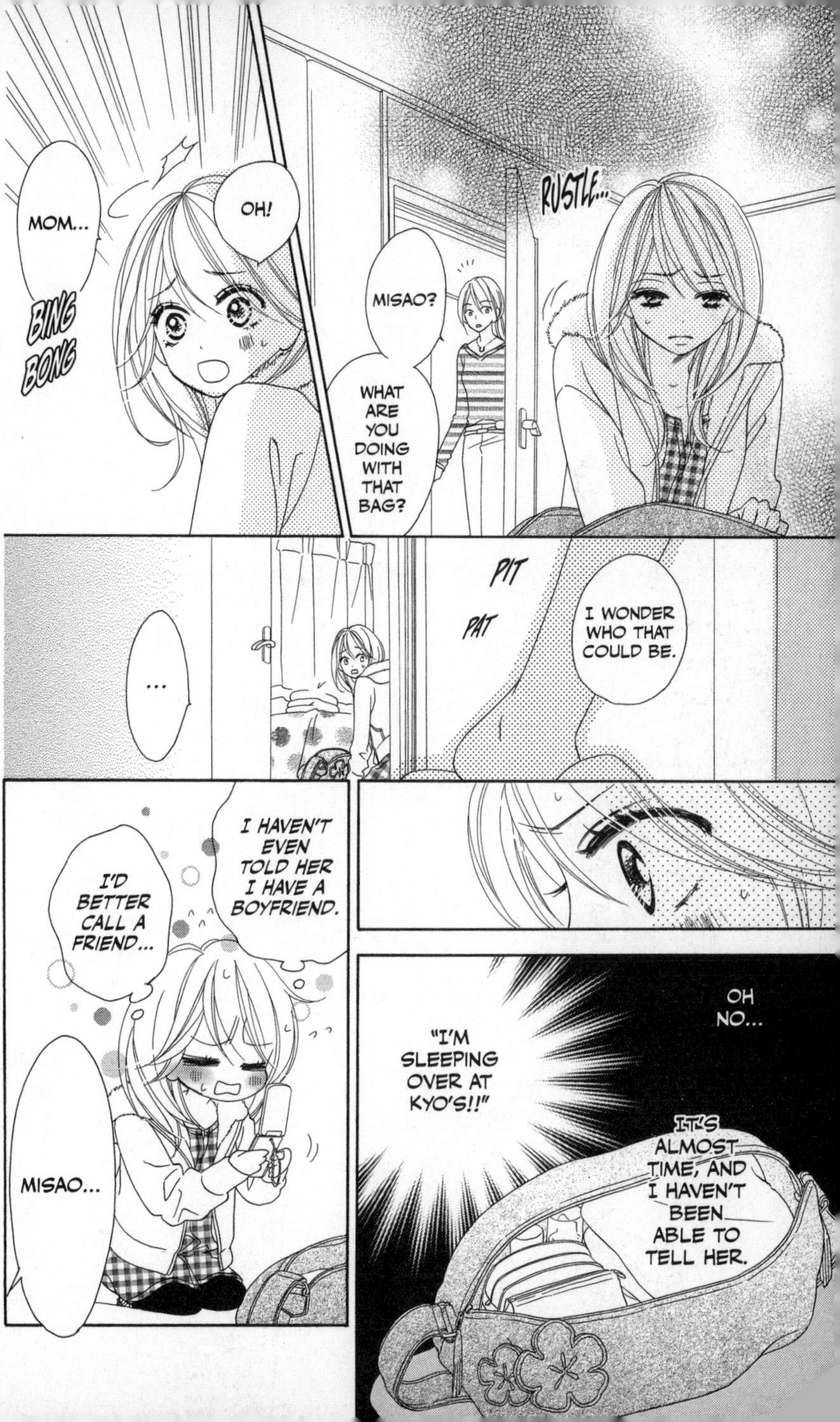
RUSTLE...
MISAO?
WHAT ARE YOU DOING WITH THAT BAG?
OH!
MOM...
BING BONG
PIT
PAT
I WONDER WHO THAT COULD BE.
...
OH NO...
"I'M SLEEPING OVER AT KYO'S!!"
IT'S ALMOST TIME, AND I HAVEN'T BEEN ABLE TO TELL HER.
I HAVEN'T EVEN TOLD HER I HAVE A BOYFRIEND.
I'D BETTER CALL A FRIEND...
MISAO...

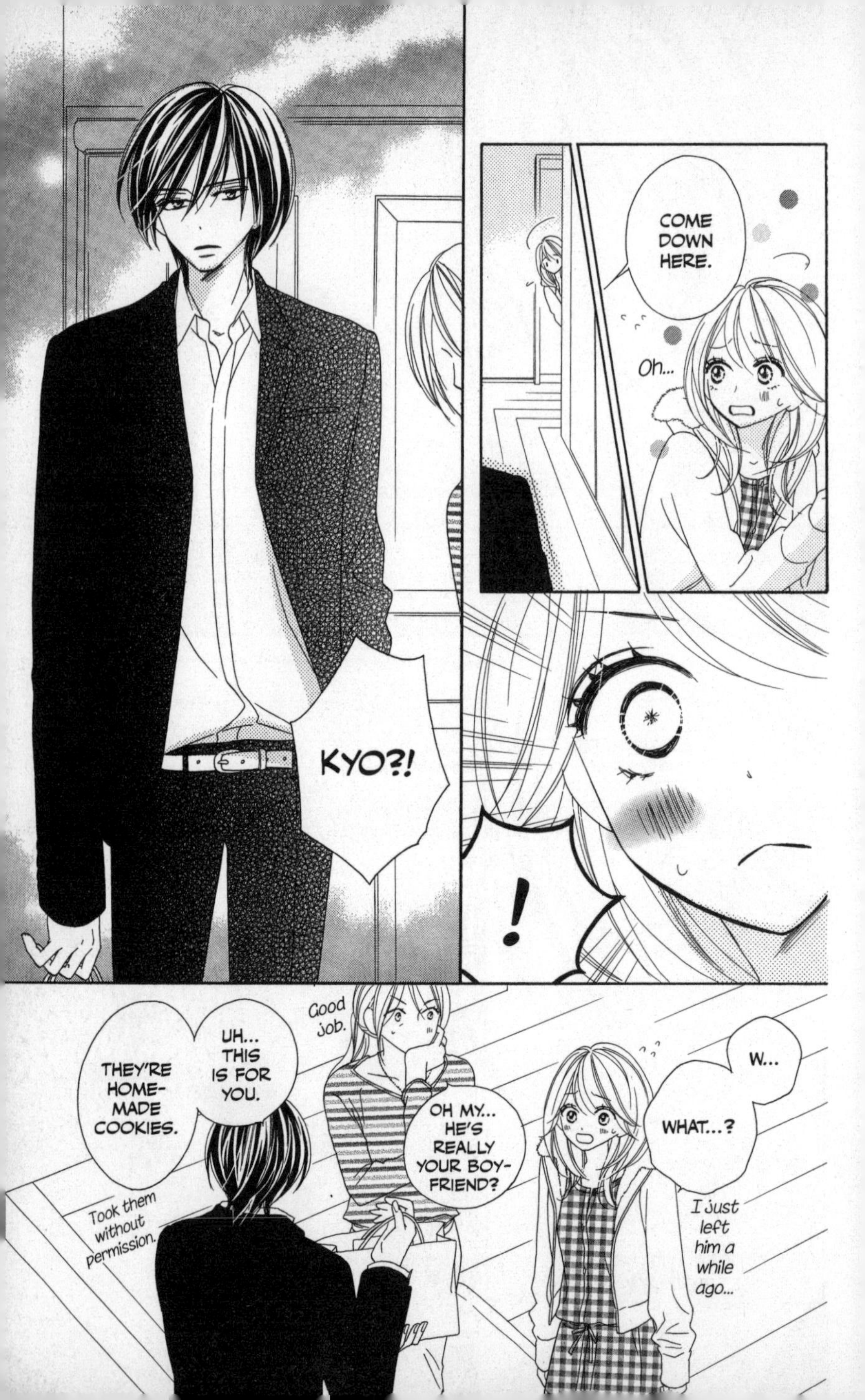
COME DOWN HERE.
Oh...
!
KYO?!
W...
WHAT...?
I just left him a while ago...
OH MY... HE'S REALLY YOUR BOY-FRIEND?
Good job.
UH... THIS IS FOR YOU.
THEY'RE HOME-MADE COOKIES.
Took them without permission.

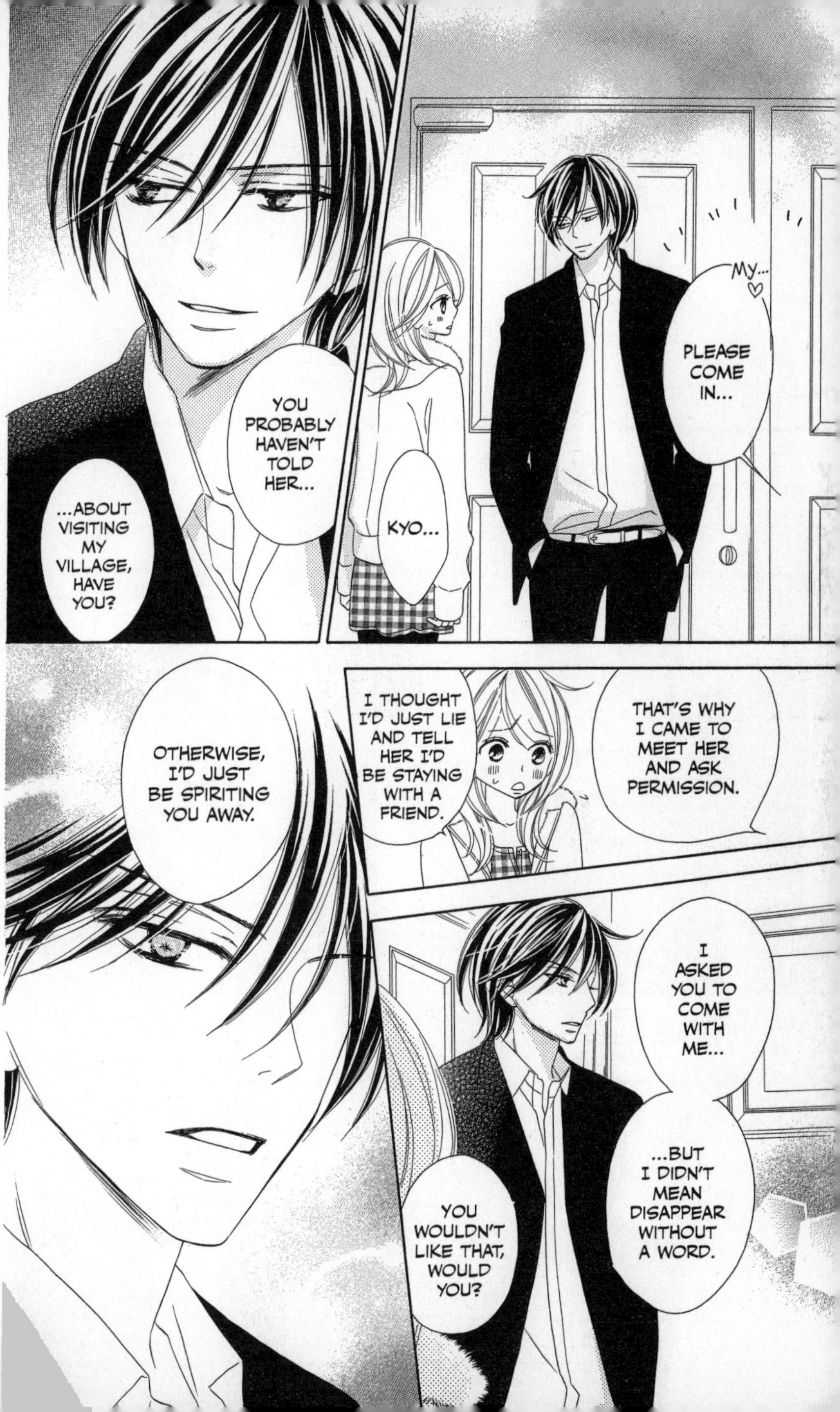
My...♡
PLEASE COME IN...
KYO...
YOU PROBABLY HAVEN'T TOLD HER...
...ABOUT VISITING MY VILLAGE, HAVE YOU?
THAT'S WHY I CAME TO MEET HER AND ASK PERMISSION.
I THOUGHT I'D JUST LIE AND TELL HER I'D BE STAYING WITH A FRIEND.
I ASKED YOU TO COME WITH ME...
...BUT I DIDN'T MEAN DISAPPEAR WITHOUT A WORD.
YOU WOULDN'T LIKE THAT, WOULD YOU?
OTHERWISE, I'D JUST BE SPIRITING YOU AWAY.

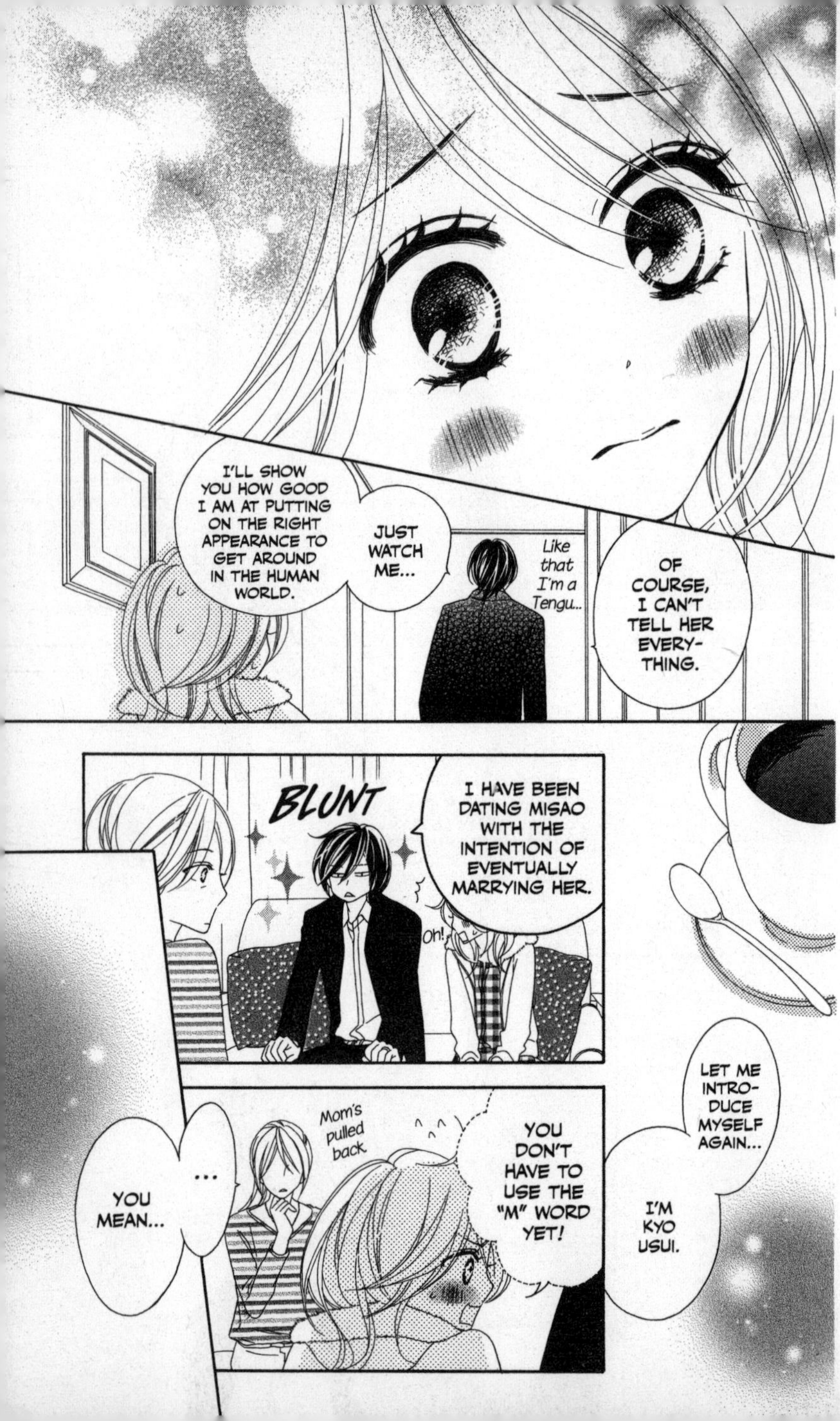
OF COURSE, I CAN'T TELL HER EVERYTHING.
Like that I'm a Tengu...
JUST WATCH ME...
I'LL SHOW YOU HOW GOOD I AM AT PUTTING ON THE RIGHT APPEARANCE TO GET AROUND IN THE HUMAN WORLD.
LET ME INTRODUCE MYSELF AGAIN...
I'M KYO USUI.
I HAVE BEEN DATING MISAO WITH THE INTENTION OF EVENTUALLY MARRYING HER.
BLUNT
Oh!
YOU DON'T HAVE TO USE THE "M" WORD YET!
Mom's pulled back
...
YOU MEAN...

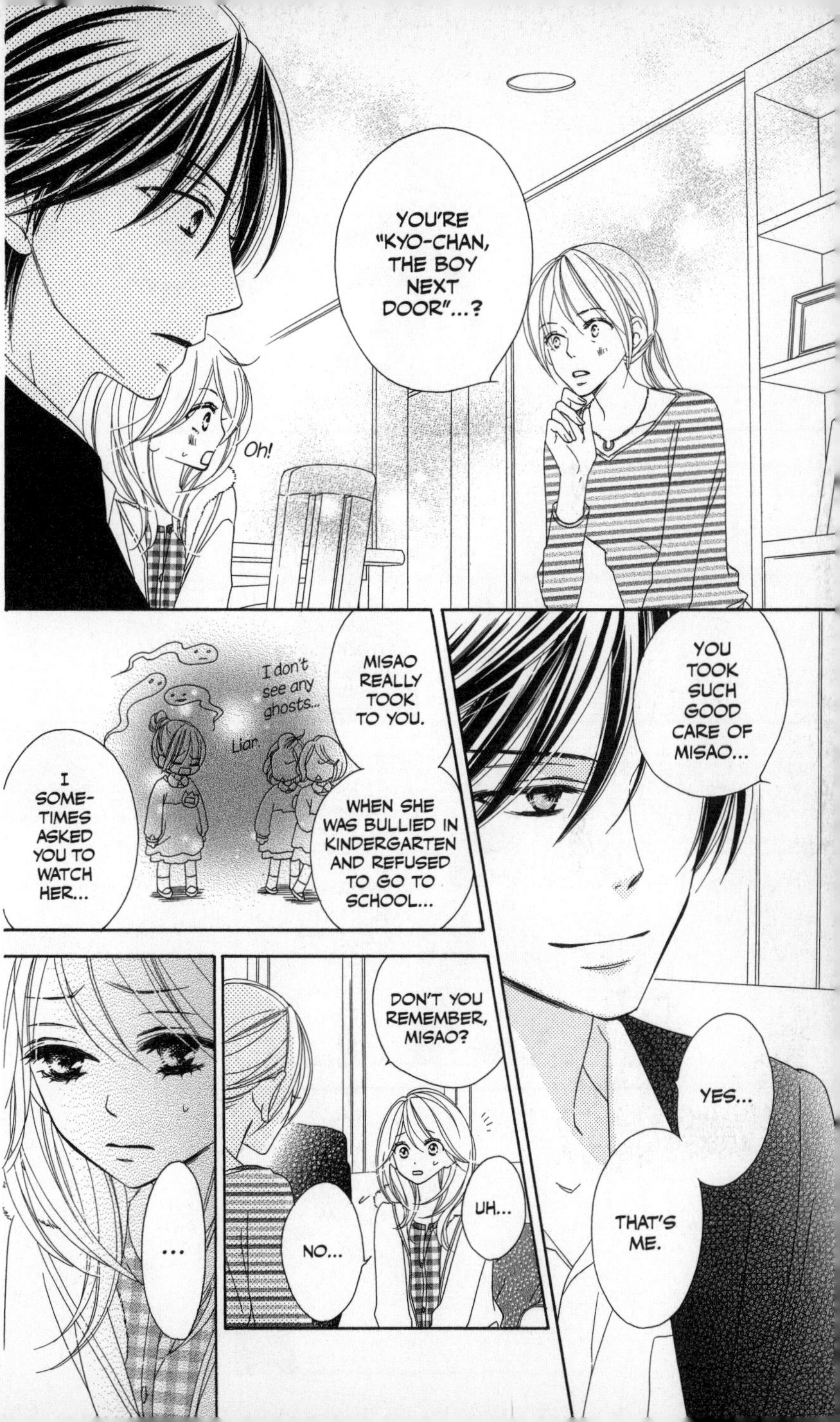
YOU'RE "KYO-CHAN, THE BOY NEXT DOOR"...?
Oh!
YOU TOOK SUCH GOOD CARE OF MISAO...
YES...
THAT'S ME.
MISAO REALLY TOOK TO YOU.
WHEN SHE WAS BULLIED IN KINDERGARTEN AND REFUSED TO GO TO SCHOOL...
I don't see any ghosts...
Liar.
I SOMETIMES ASKED YOU TO WATCH HER...
DON'T YOU REMEMBER, MISAO?
UH...
NO...
...

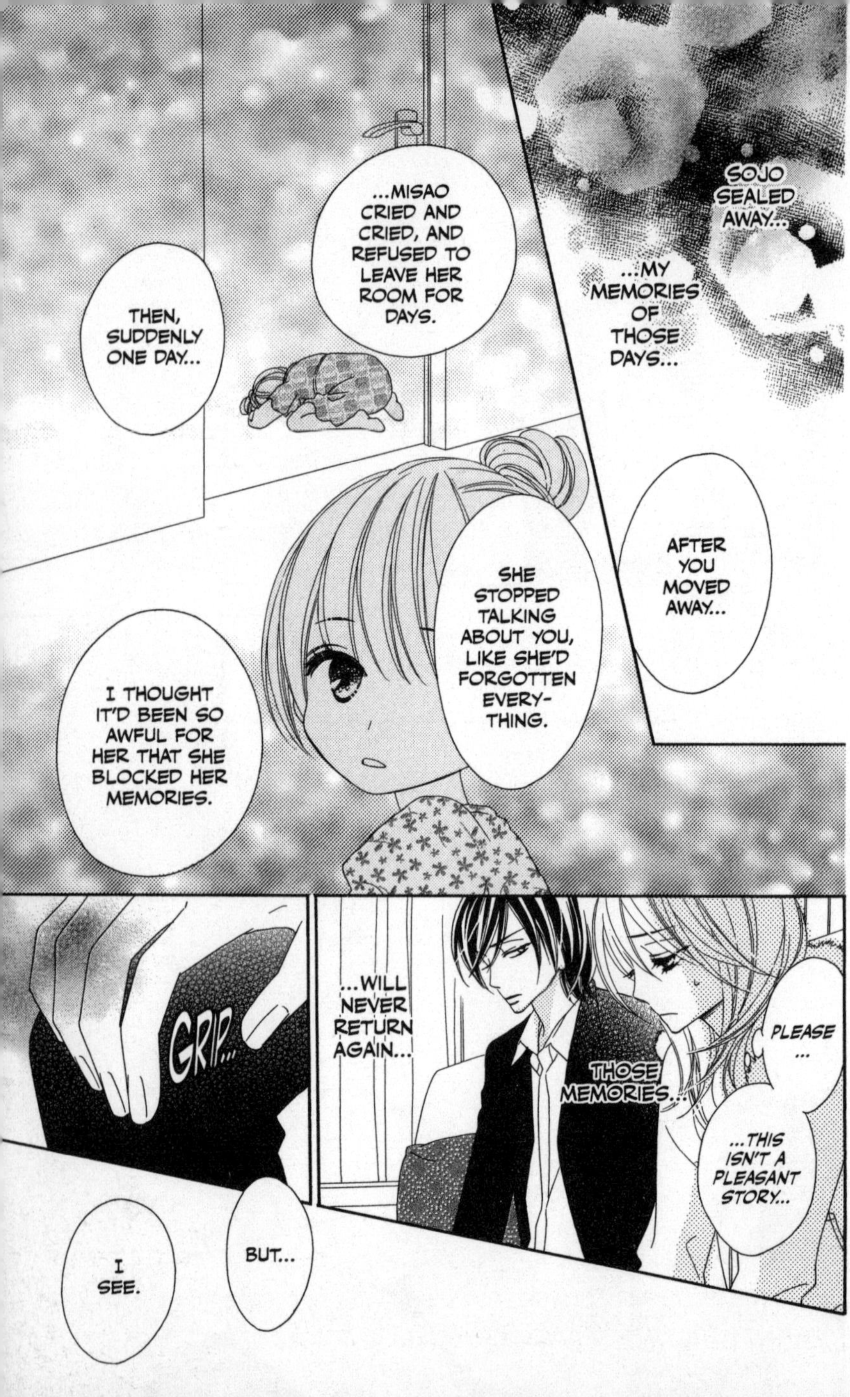
SOJO SEALED AWAY...
...MY MEMORIES OF THOSE DAYS...
AFTER YOU MOVED AWAY...
...MISAO CRIED AND CRIED, AND REFUSED TO LEAVE HER ROOM FOR DAYS.
THEN, SUDDENLY ONE DAY...
SHE STOPPED TALKING ABOUT YOU, LIKE SHE'D FORGOTTEN EVERY-THING.
I THOUGHT IT'D BEEN SO AWFUL FOR HER THAT SHE BLOCKED HER MEMORIES.
PLEASE...
...THIS ISN'T A PLEASANT STORY...
THOSE MEMORIES...
...WILL NEVER RETURN AGAIN...
GRIP...
BUT...
I SEE.

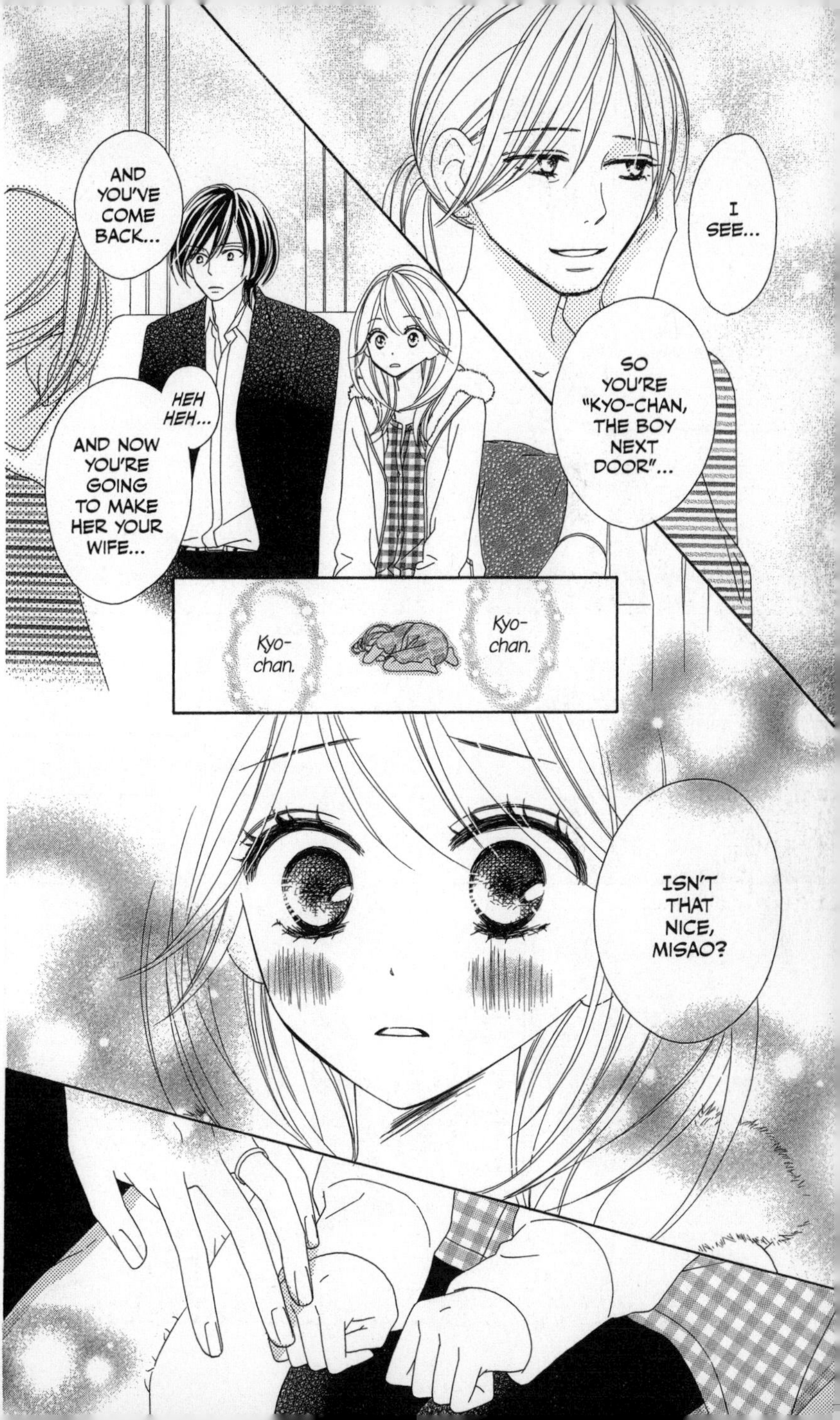
I SEE...
SO YOU'RE "KYO-CHAN, THE BOY NEXT DOOR"...
AND YOU'VE COME BACK...
HEH HEH...
AND NOW YOU'RE GOING TO MAKE HER YOUR WIFE...
Kyo-chan.
Kyo-chan.
ISN'T THAT NICE, MISAO?

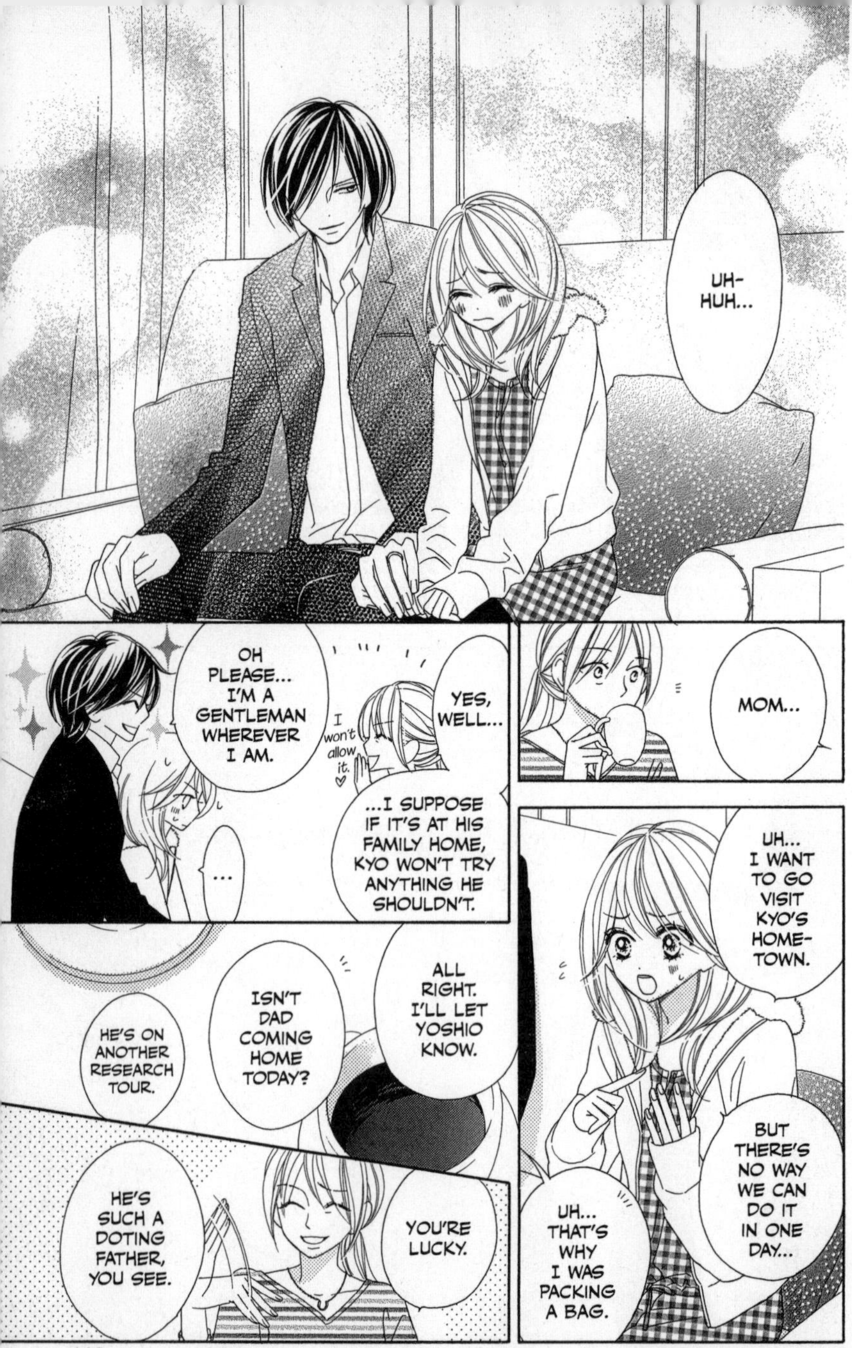
UH-HUH...
MOM...
UH... I WANT TO GO VISIT KYO'S HOMETOWN.
BUT THERE'S NO WAY WE CAN DO IT IN ONE DAY...
UH... THAT'S WHY I WAS PACKING A BAG.
YES, WELL...
I won't allow it. ♡
...I SUPPOSE IF IT'S AT HIS FAMILY HOME, KYO WON'T TRY ANYTHING HE SHOULDN'T.
OH PLEASE... I'M A GENTLEMAN WHEREVER I AM.
...
ALL RIGHT. I'LL LET YOSHIO KNOW.
ISN'T DAD COMING HOME TODAY?
HE'S ON ANOTHER RESEARCH TOUR.
YOU'RE LUCKY.
HE'S SUCH A DOTING FATHER, YOU SEE.

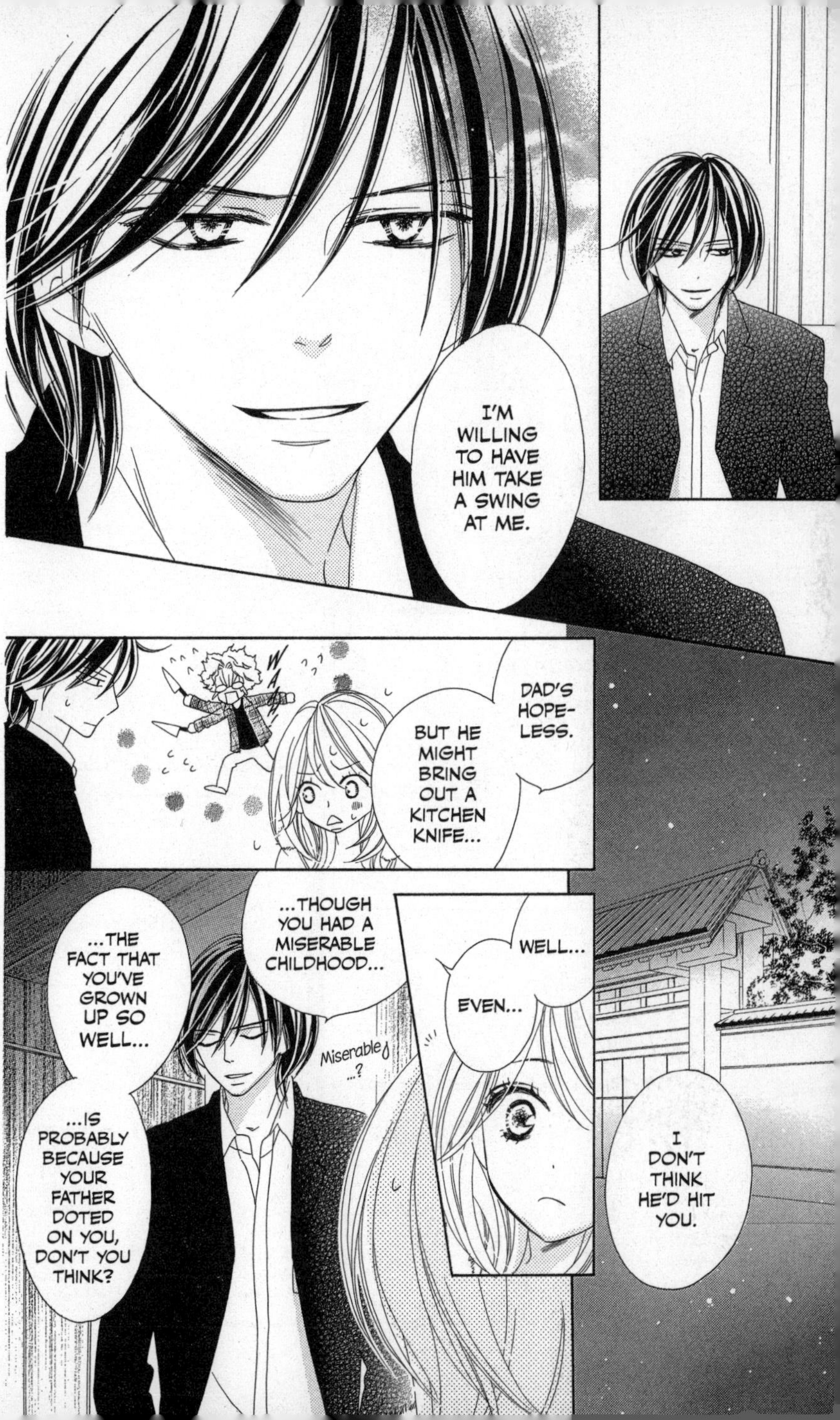
I'M WILLING TO HAVE HIM TAKE A SWING AT ME.
DAD'S HOPE-LESS.
BUT HE MIGHT BRING OUT A KITCHEN KNIFE...
I DON'T THINK HE'D HIT YOU.
WELL...
EVEN...
...THOUGH YOU HAD A MISERABLE CHILDHOOD...
Miserable ...?
...THE FACT THAT YOU'VE GROWN UP SO WELL...
...IS PROBABLY BECAUSE YOUR FATHER DOTED ON YOU, DON'T YOU THINK?

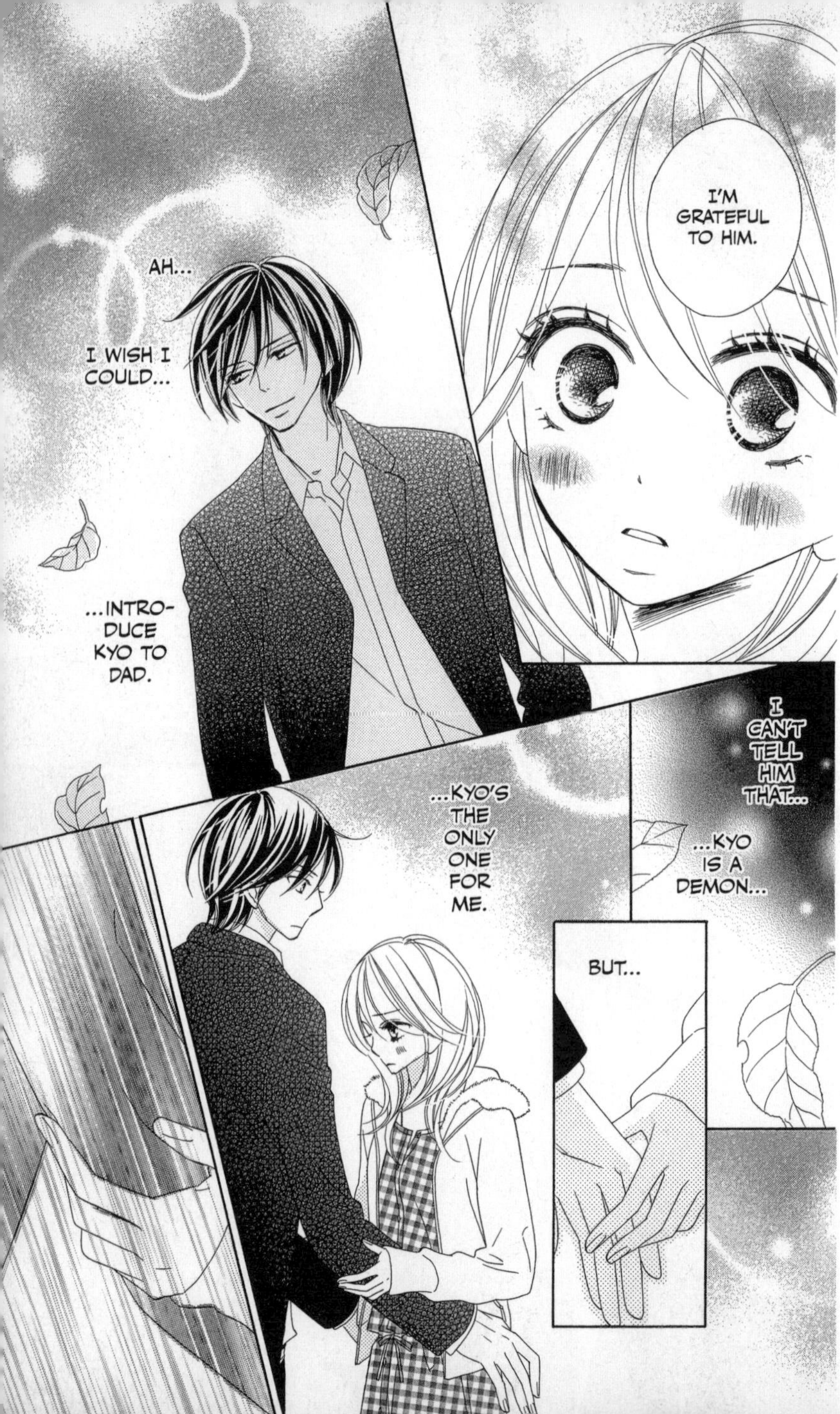
I'M GRATEFUL TO HIM.
AH...
I WISH I COULD...
...INTRO-DUCE KYO TO DAD.
I CAN'T TELL HIM THAT...
...KYO IS A DEMON...
BUT...
...KYO'S THE ONLY ONE FOR ME.

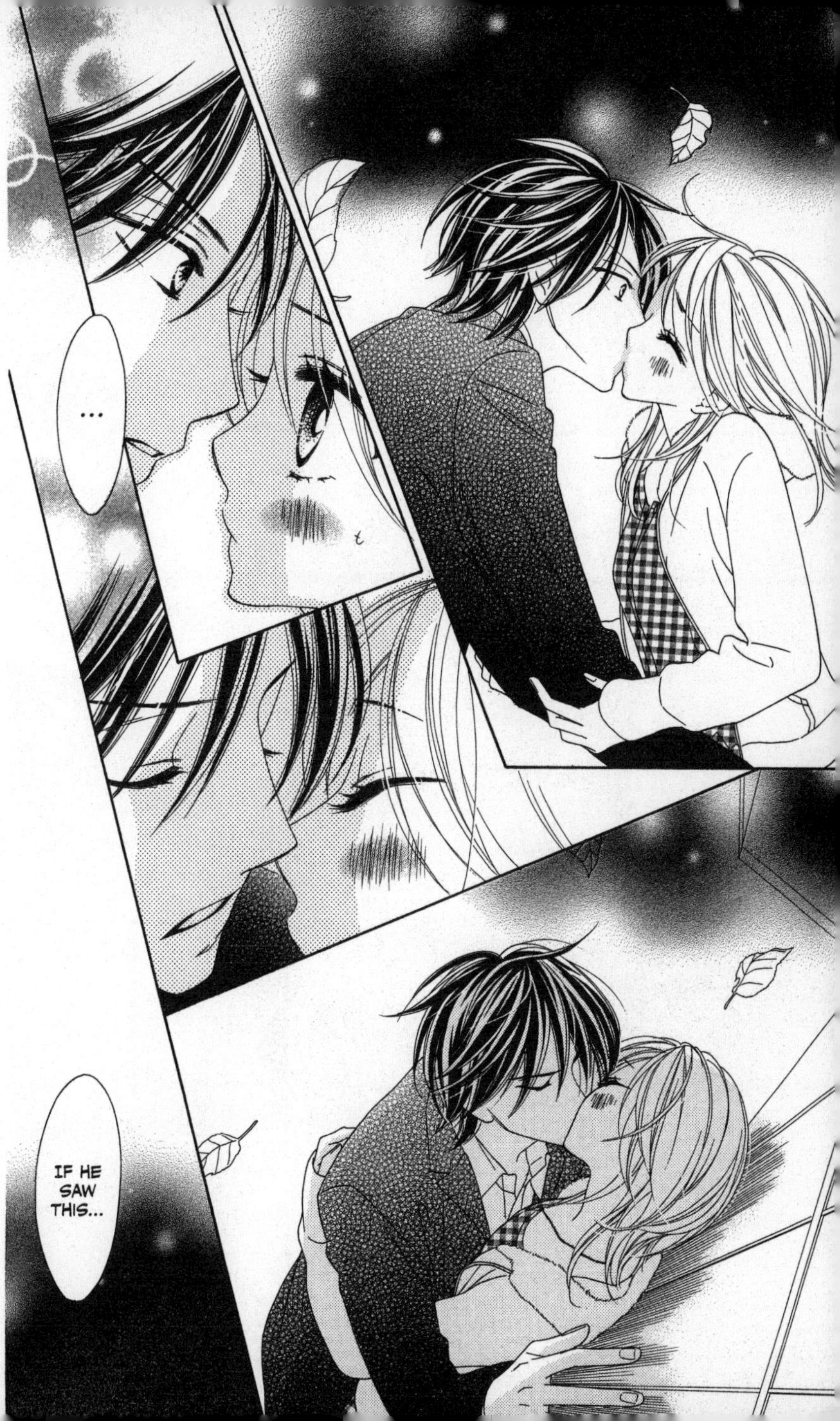
...
IF HE SAW THIS...

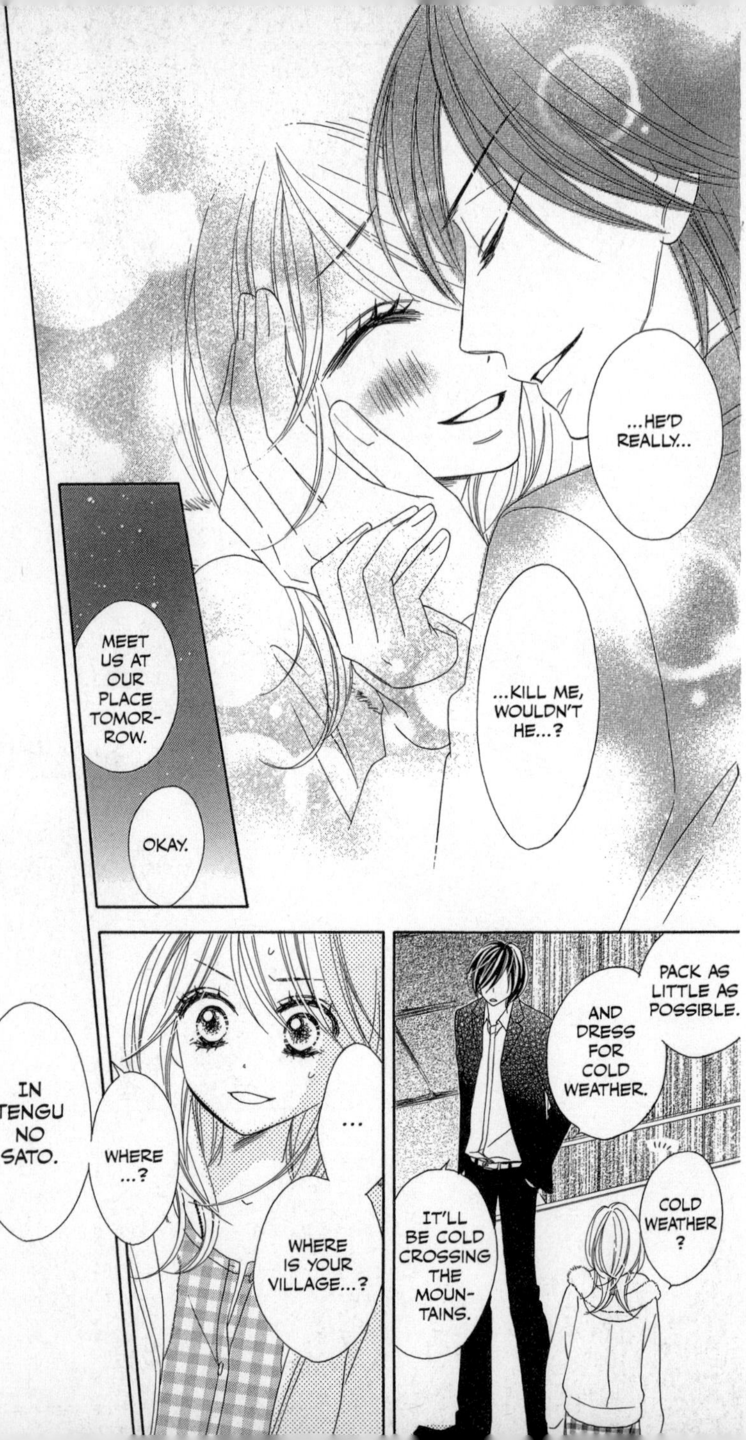
...HE'D REALLY...
...KILL ME, WOULDN'T HE...?
MEET US AT OUR PLACE TOMORROW.
OKAY.
PACK AS LITTLE AS POSSIBLE.
AND DRESS FOR COLD WEATHER.
COLD WEATHER?
IT'LL BE COLD CROSSING THE MOUNTAINS.
...
WHERE IS YOUR VILLAGE...?
WHERE ...?
IN TENGU NO SATO.

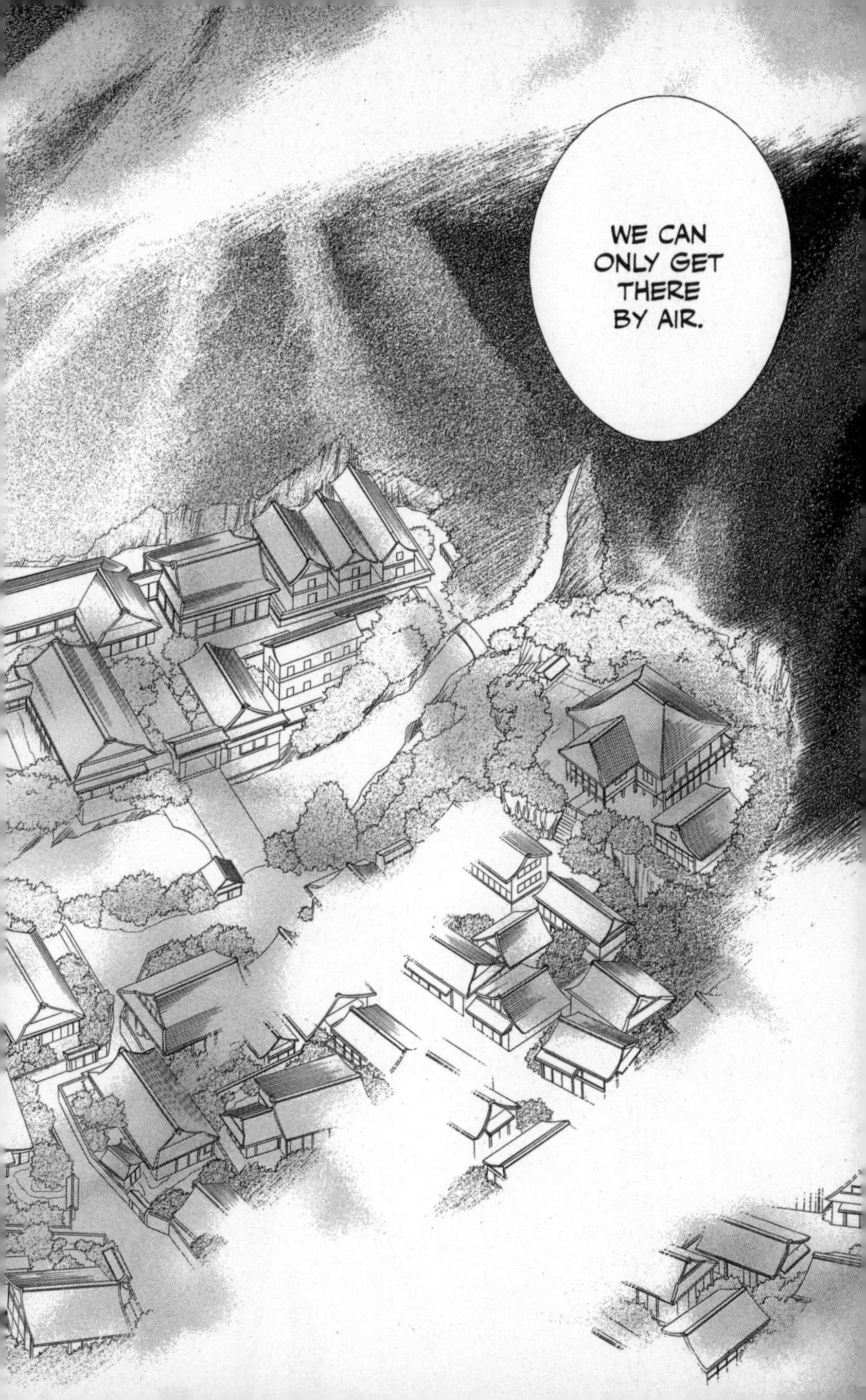
WE CAN ONLY GET THERE BY AIR.

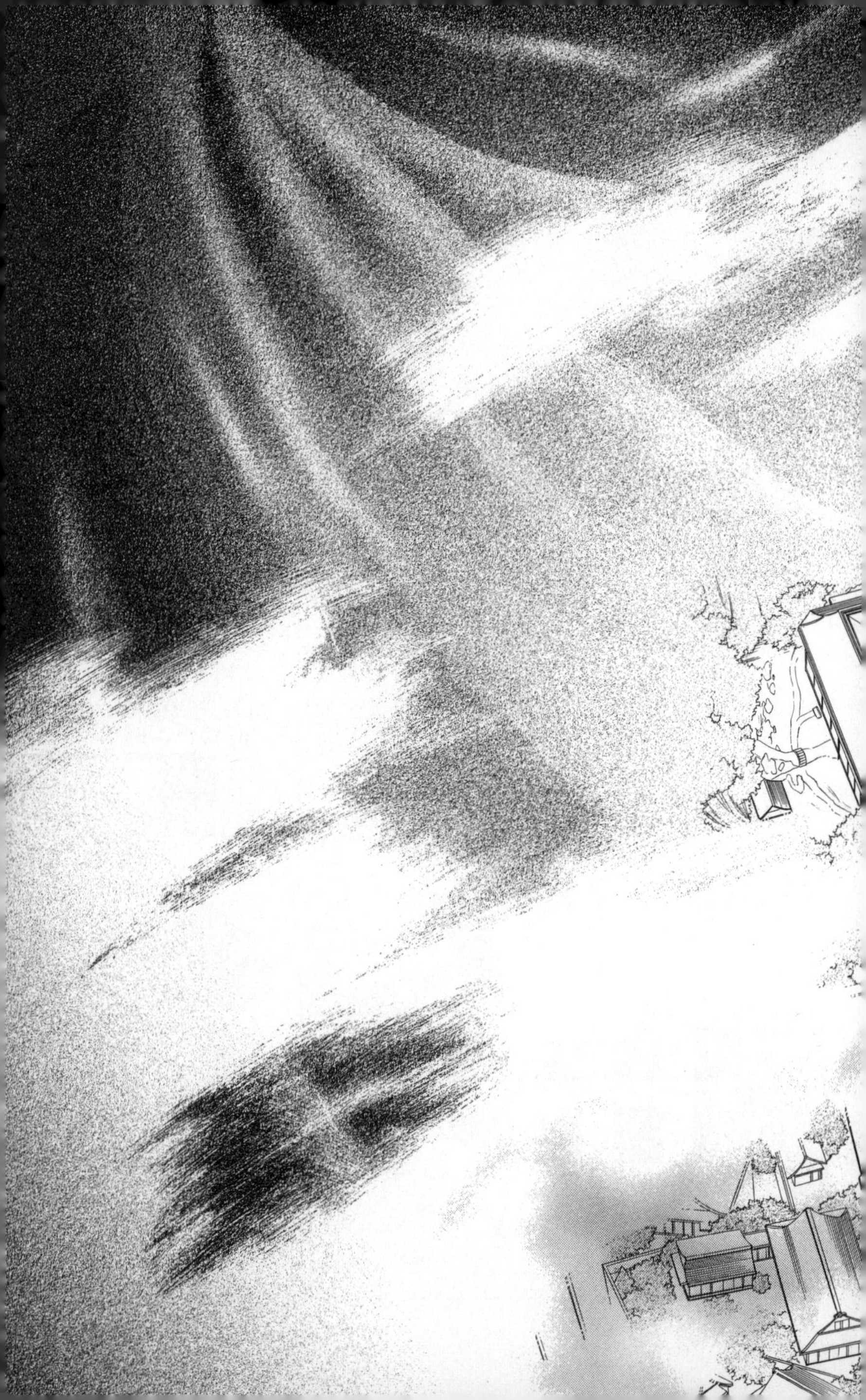

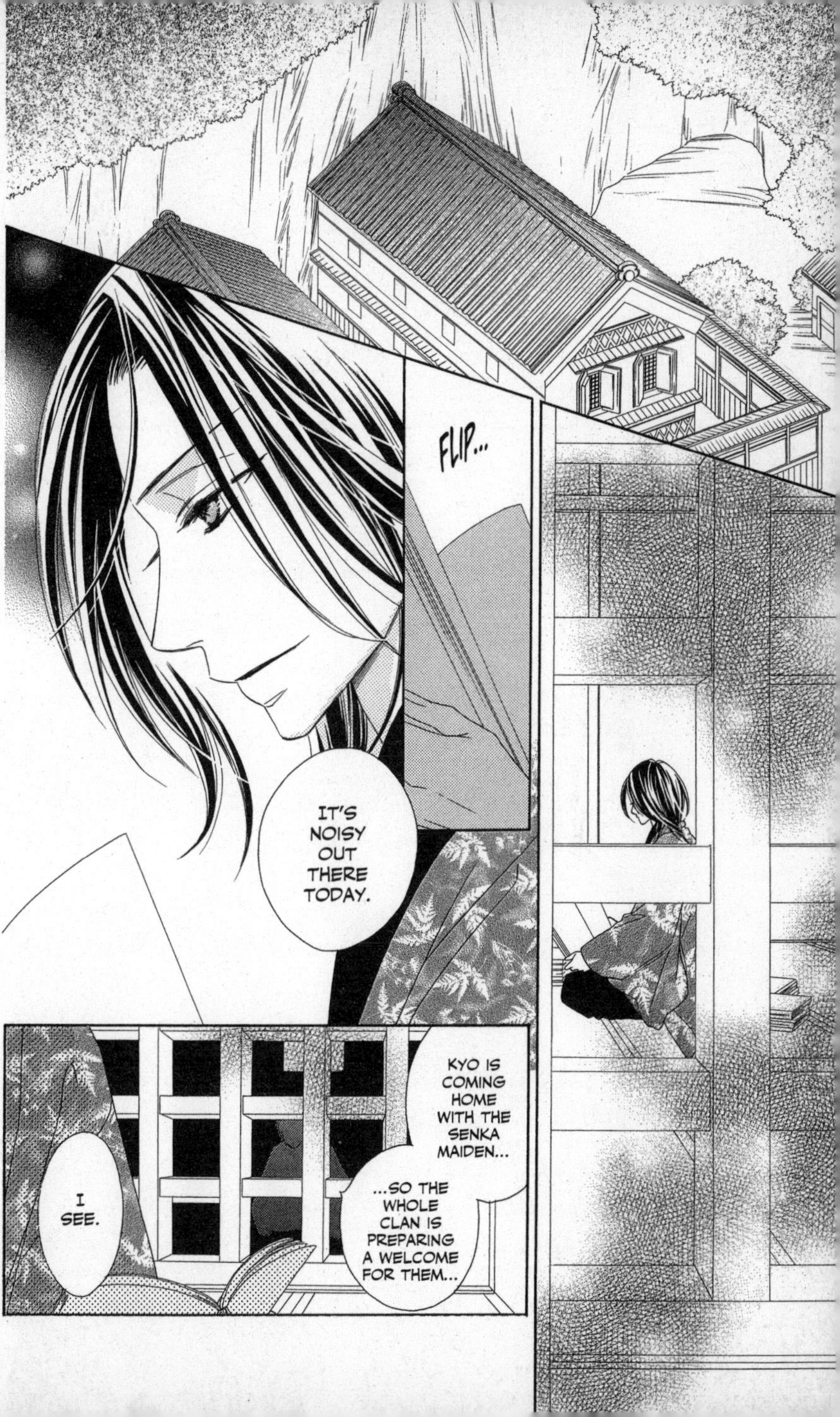
FLIP...
IT'S NOISY OUT THERE TODAY.
KYO IS COMING HOME WITH THE SENKA MAIDEN...
...SO THE WHOLE CLAN IS PREPARING A WELCOME FOR THEM...
I SEE.

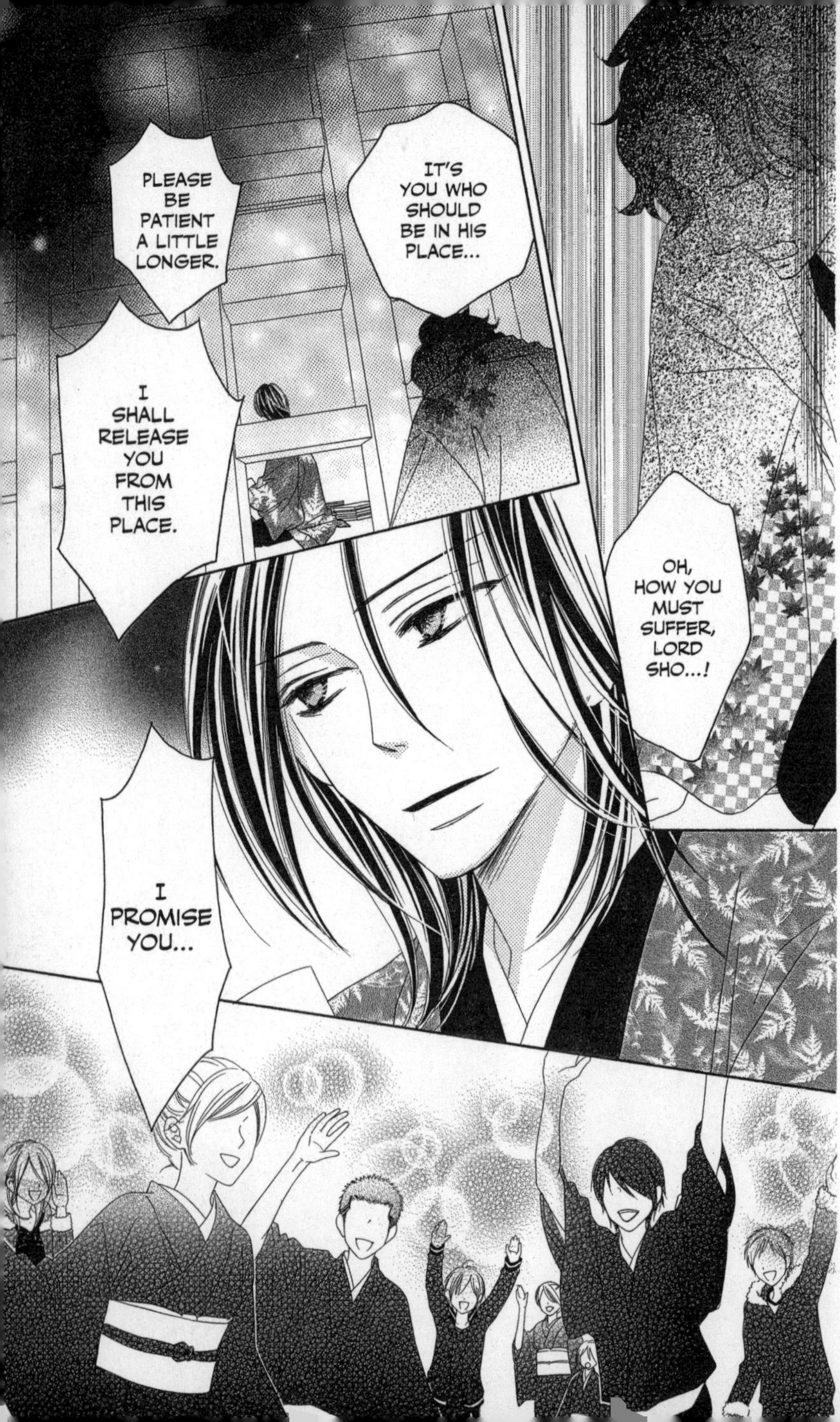
OH, HOW YOU MUST SUFFER, LORD SHO...!
IT'S YOU WHO SHOULD BE IN HIS PLACE...
PLEASE BE PATIENT A LITTLE LONGER.
I SHALL RELEASE YOU FROM THIS PLACE.
I PROMISE YOU...

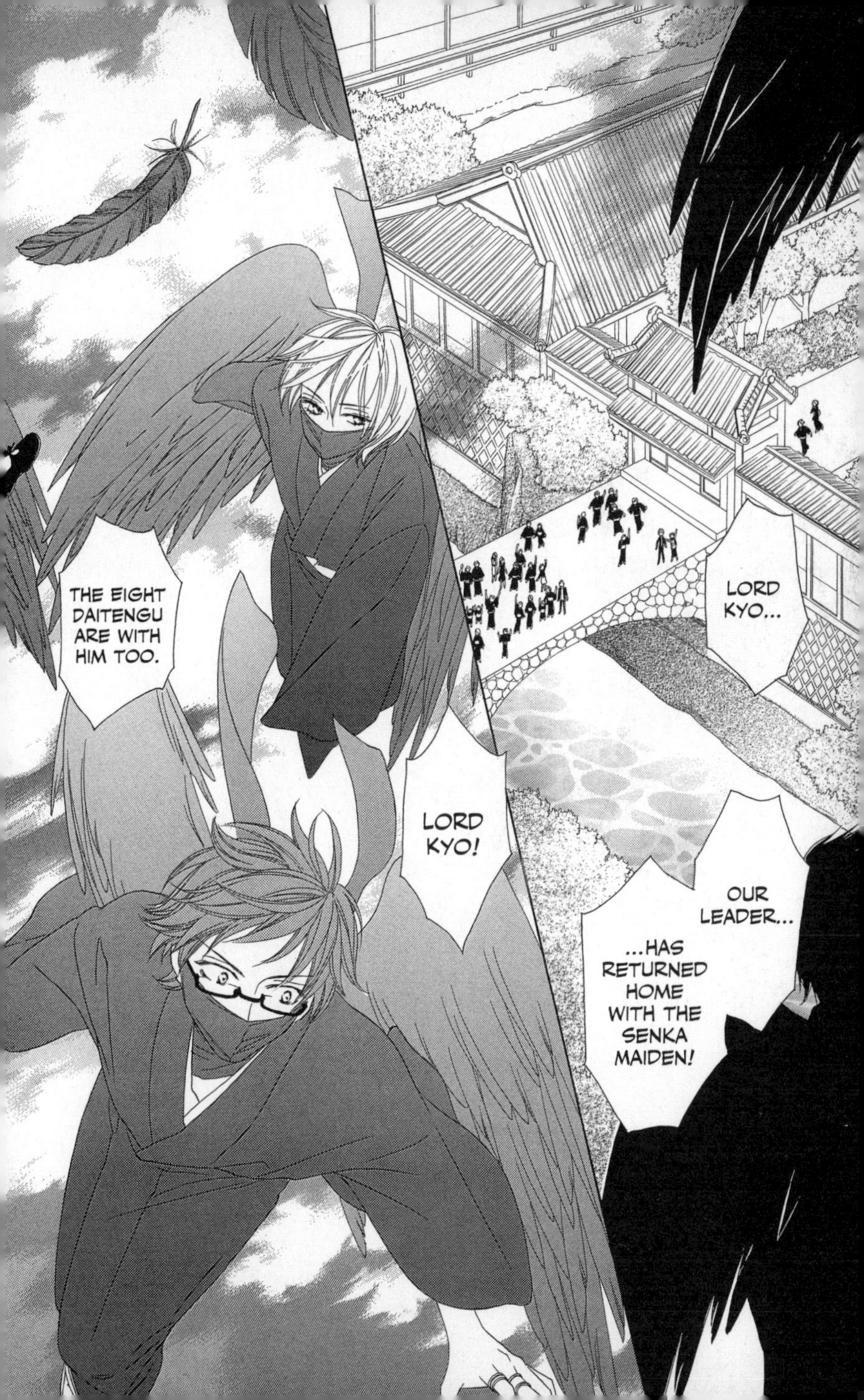
LORD KYO...
OUR LEADER...
...HAS RETURNED HOME WITH THE SENKA MAIDEN!
THE EIGHT DAITENGU ARE WITH HIM TOO.
LORD KYO!

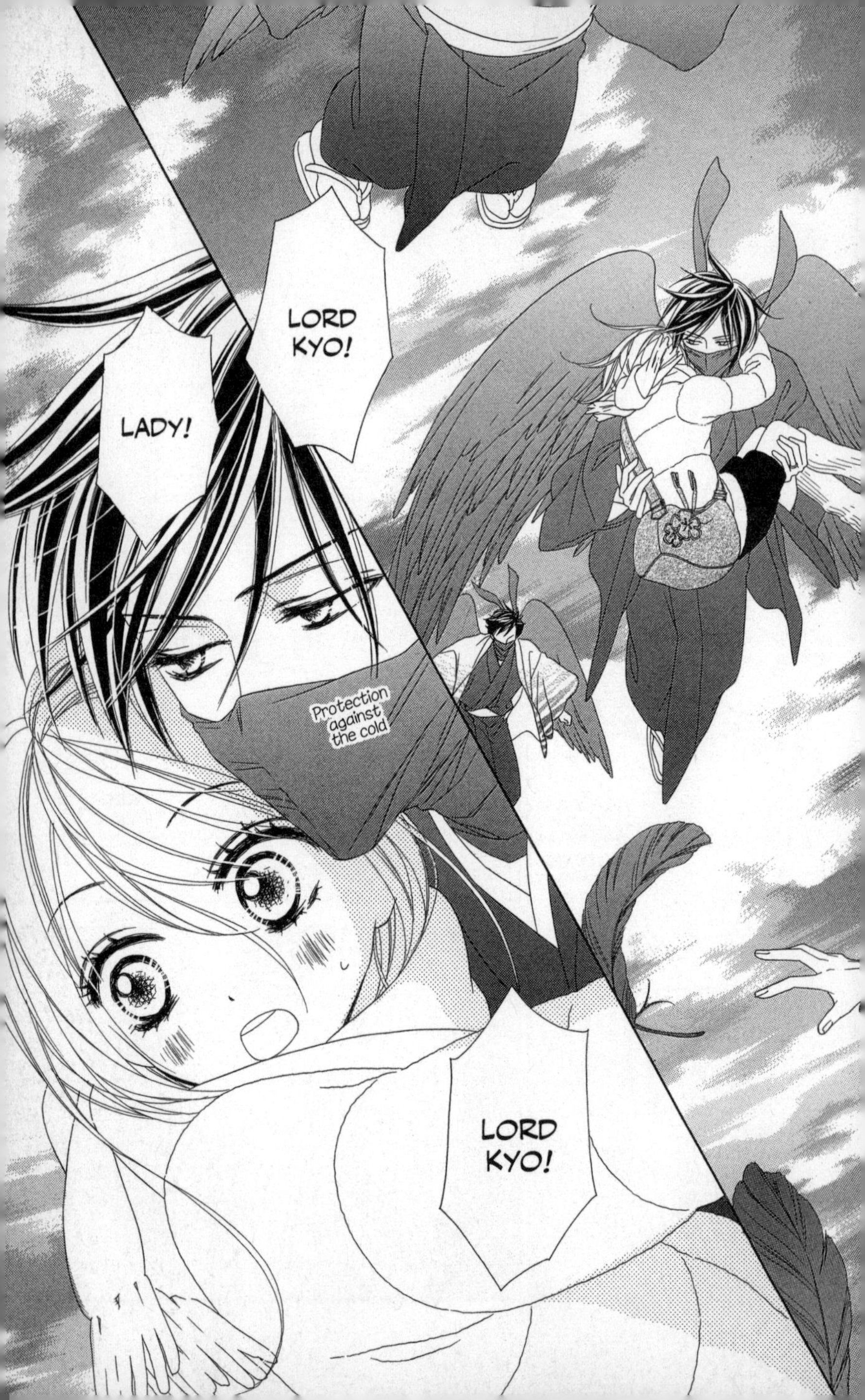
LORD KYO!
LADY!
Protection against the cold
LORD KYO!

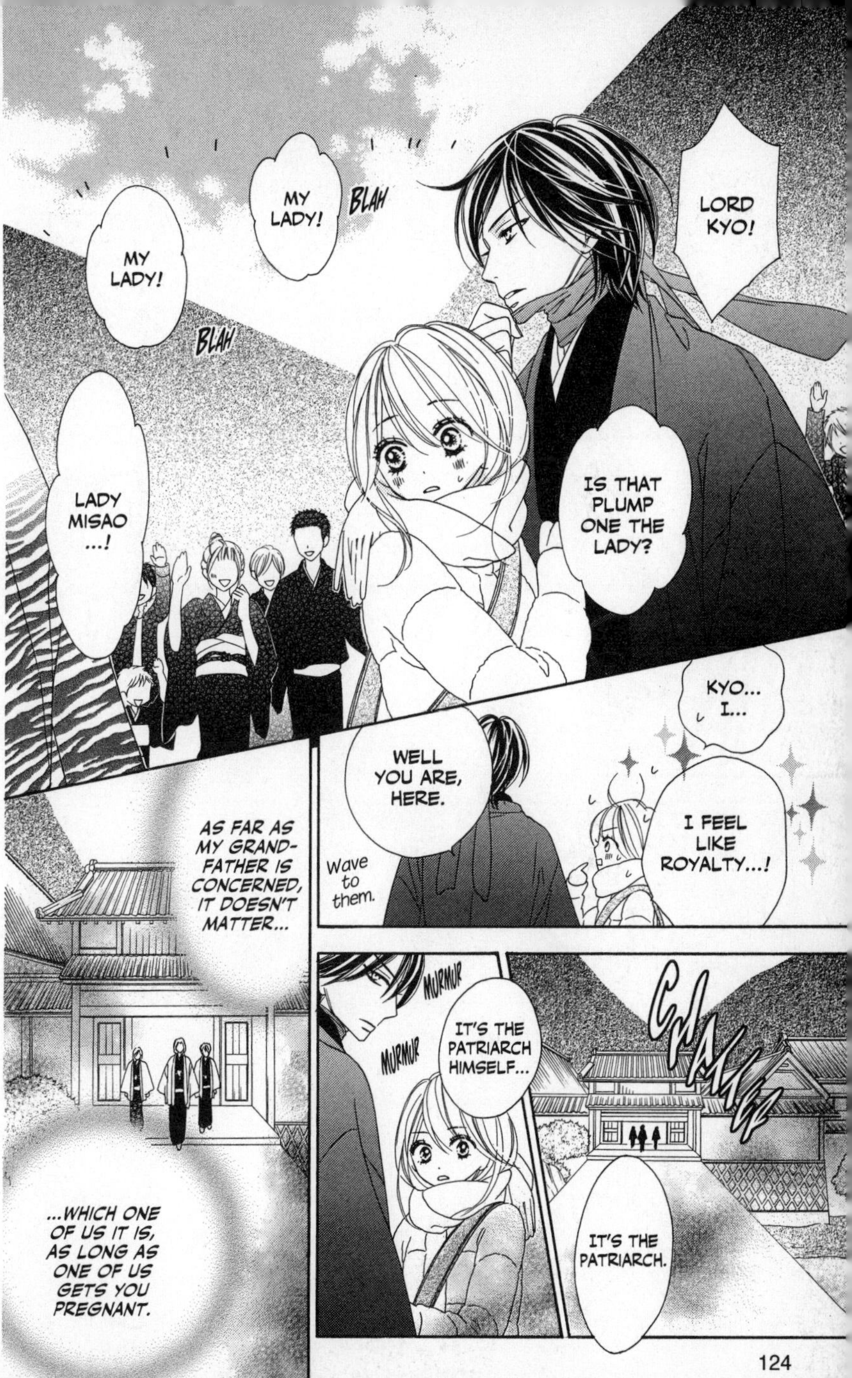
LORD KYO!
IS THAT PLUMP ONE THE LADY?
MY LADY!
BLAH
MY LADY!
BLAH
LADY MISAO ...!
KYO... I...
I FEEL LIKE ROYALTY...!
WELL YOU ARE, HERE.
Wave to them.
IT'S THE PATRIARCH.
MURMUR
IT'S THE PATRIARCH HIMSELF...
MURMUR
AS FAR AS MY GRAND-FATHER IS CONCERNED, IT DOESN'T MATTER...
...WHICH ONE OF US IT IS, AS LONG AS ONE OF US GETS YOU PREGNANT.

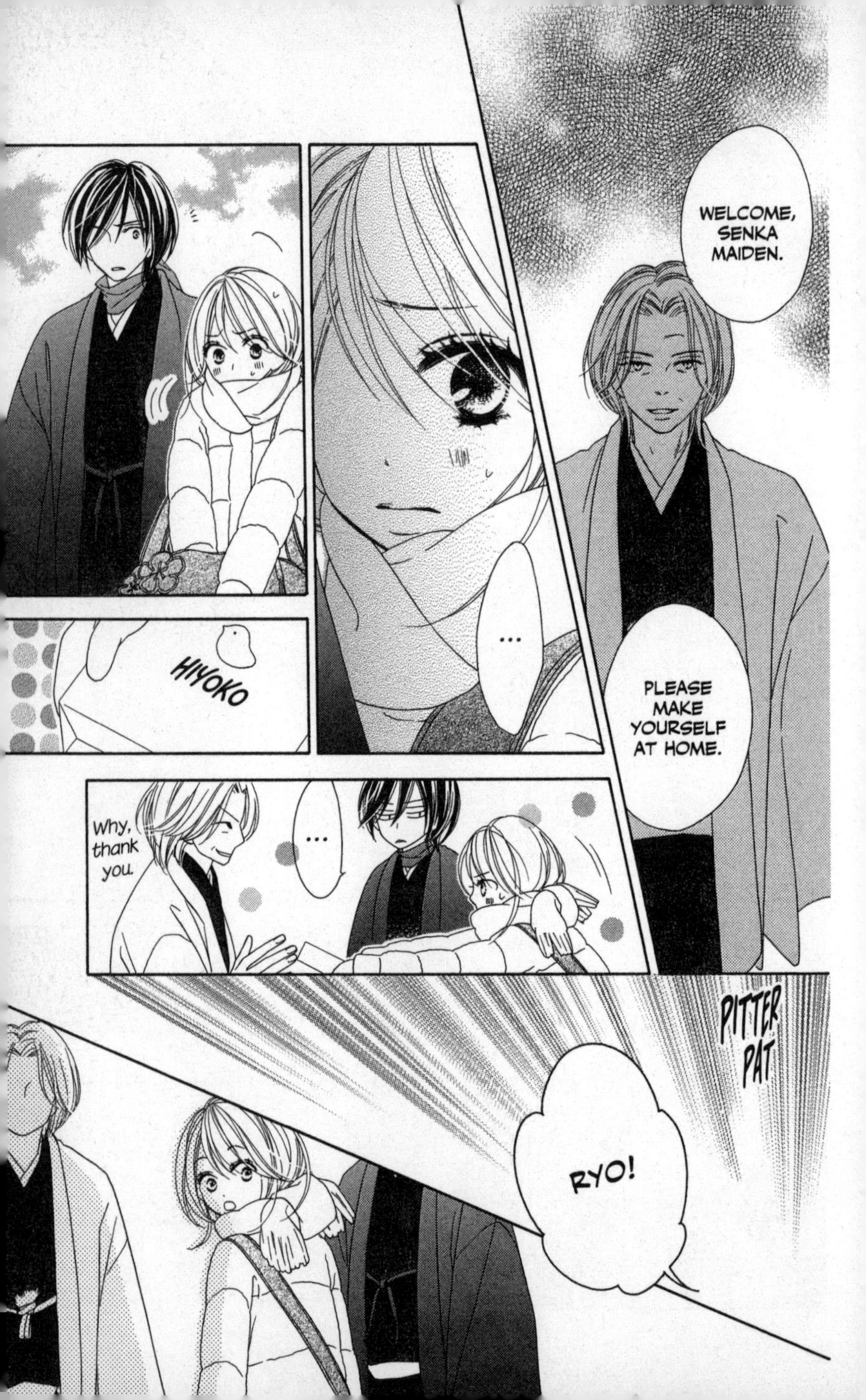
WELCOME, SENKA MAIDEN.
PLEASE MAKE YOURSELF AT HOME.
...
HIYOKO
...
Why, thank you.
PITTER PAT
RYO!

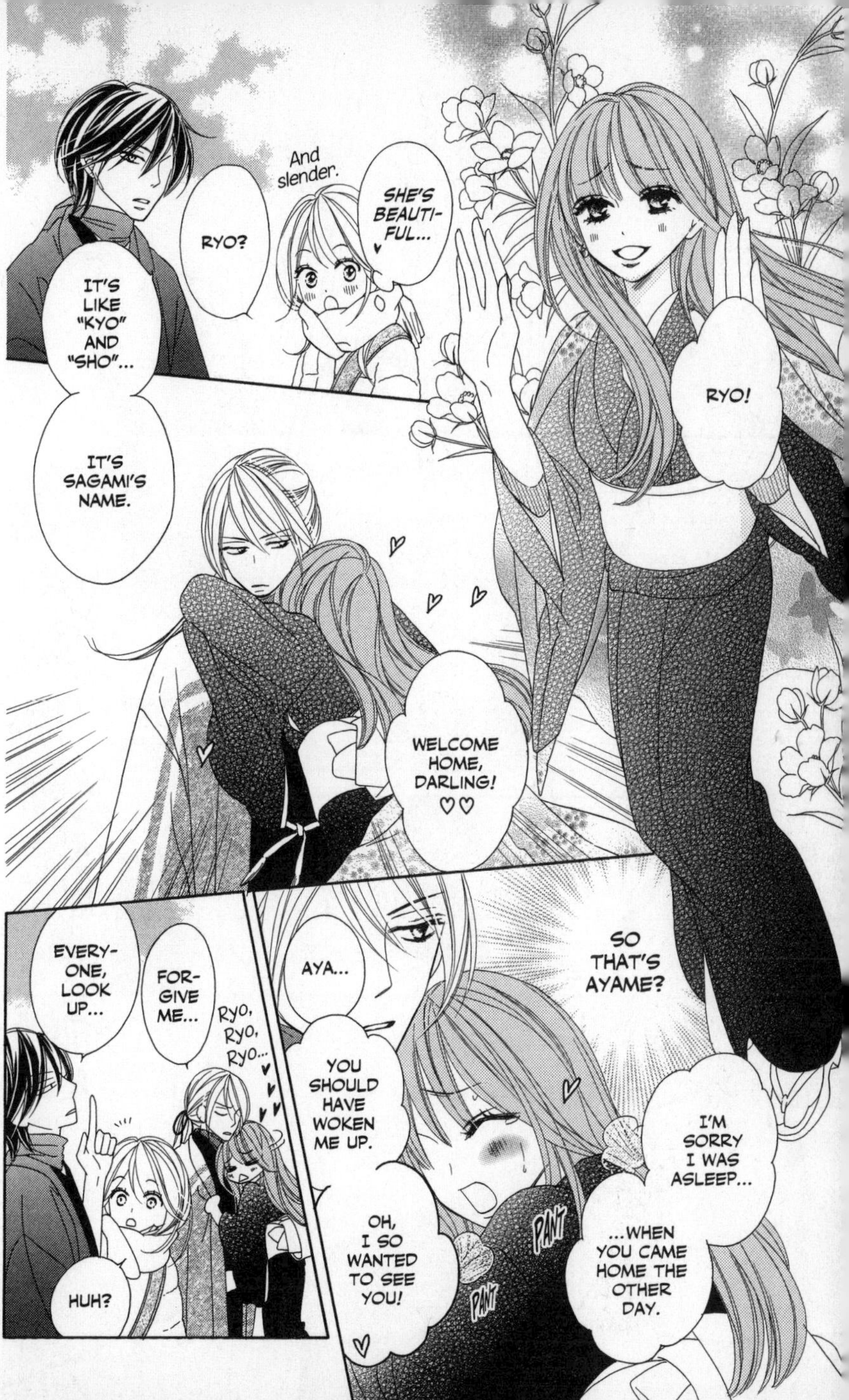
RYO!
SHE'S BEAUTIFUL...
And slender.
RYO?
IT'S LIKE "KYO" AND "SHO"...
IT'S SAGAMI'S NAME.
WELCOME HOME, DARLING!
SO THAT'S AYAME?
AYA...
I'M SORRY I WAS ASLEEP...
...WHEN YOU CAME HOME THE OTHER DAY.
YOU SHOULD HAVE WOKEN ME UP.
PANT
PANT
OH, I SO WANTED TO SEE YOU!
Ryo, Ryo, Ryo...
FORGIVE ME...
EVERYONE, LOOK UP...
HUH?

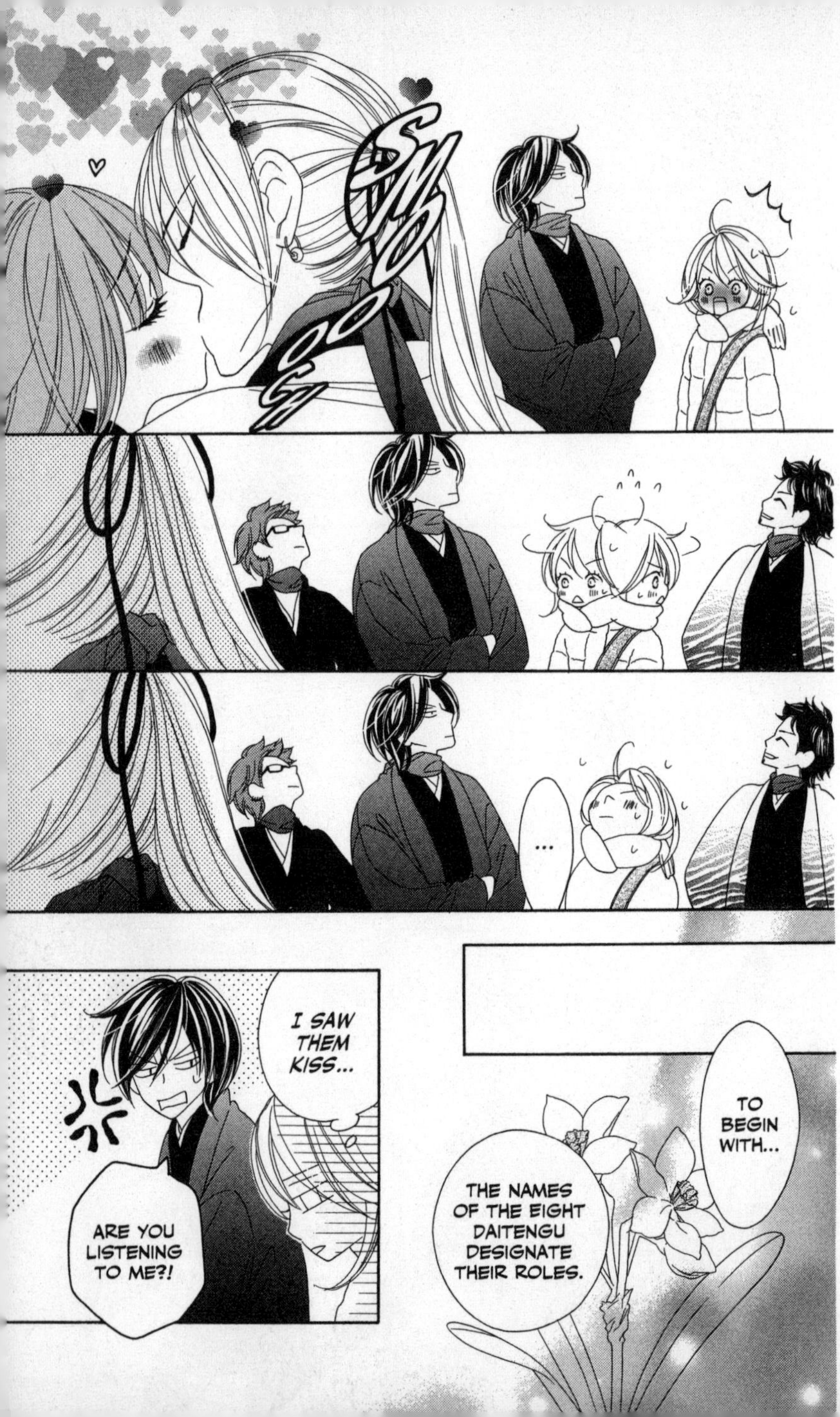
SMOOOOCH
...
TO BEGIN WITH...
THE NAMES OF THE EIGHT DAITENGU DESIGNATE THEIR ROLES.
I SAW THEM KISS...
ARE YOU LISTENING TO ME?!

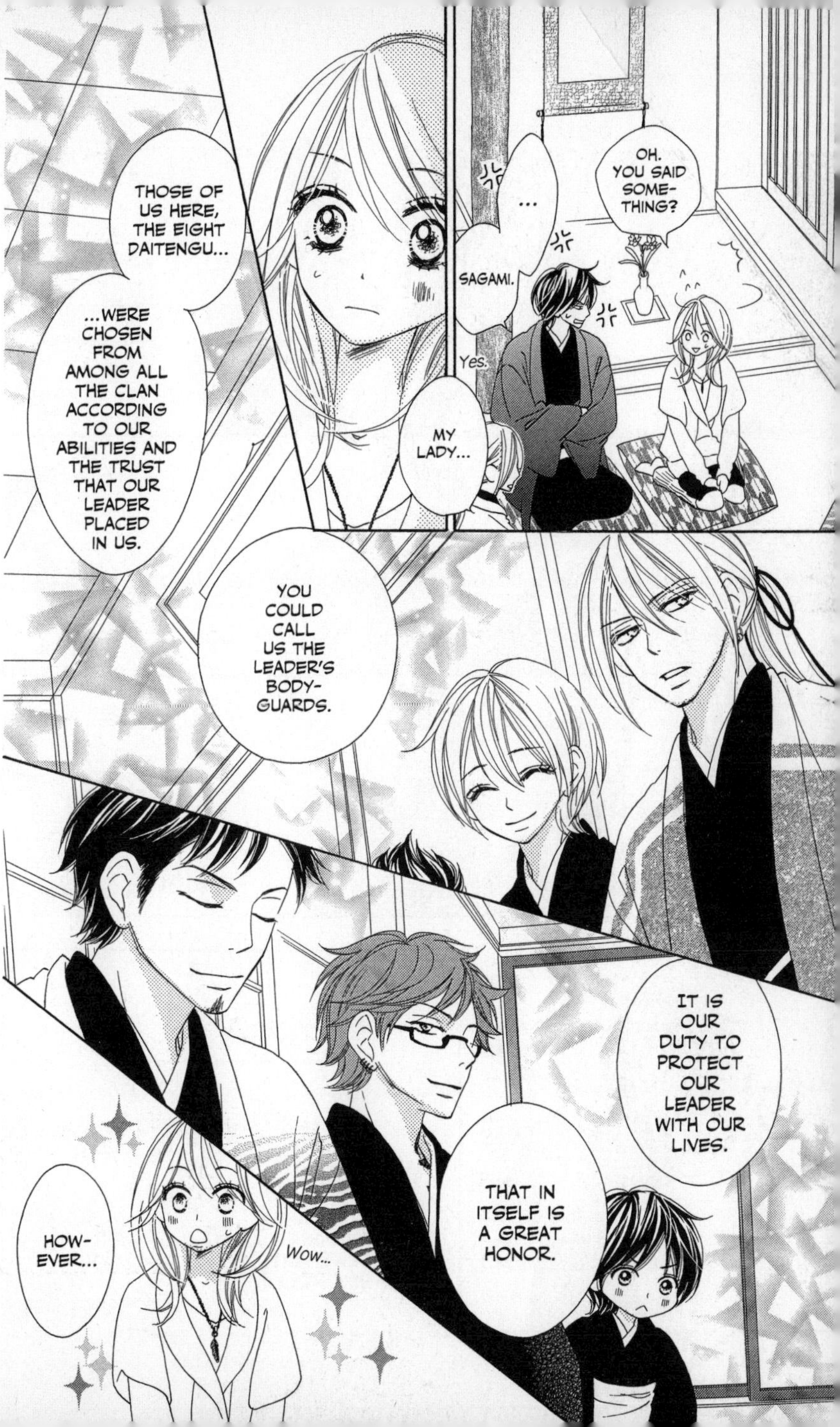
OH. YOU SAID SOME-THING?
...
SAGAMI.
Yes.
MY LADY...
THOSE OF US HERE, THE EIGHT DAITENGU...
...WERE CHOSEN FROM AMONG ALL THE CLAN ACCORDING TO OUR ABILITIES AND THE TRUST THAT OUR LEADER PLACED IN US.
YOU COULD CALL US THE LEADER'S BODY-GUARDS.
IT IS OUR DUTY TO PROTECT OUR LEADER WITH OUR LIVES.
THAT IN ITSELF IS A GREAT HONOR.
Wow...
HOW-EVER...

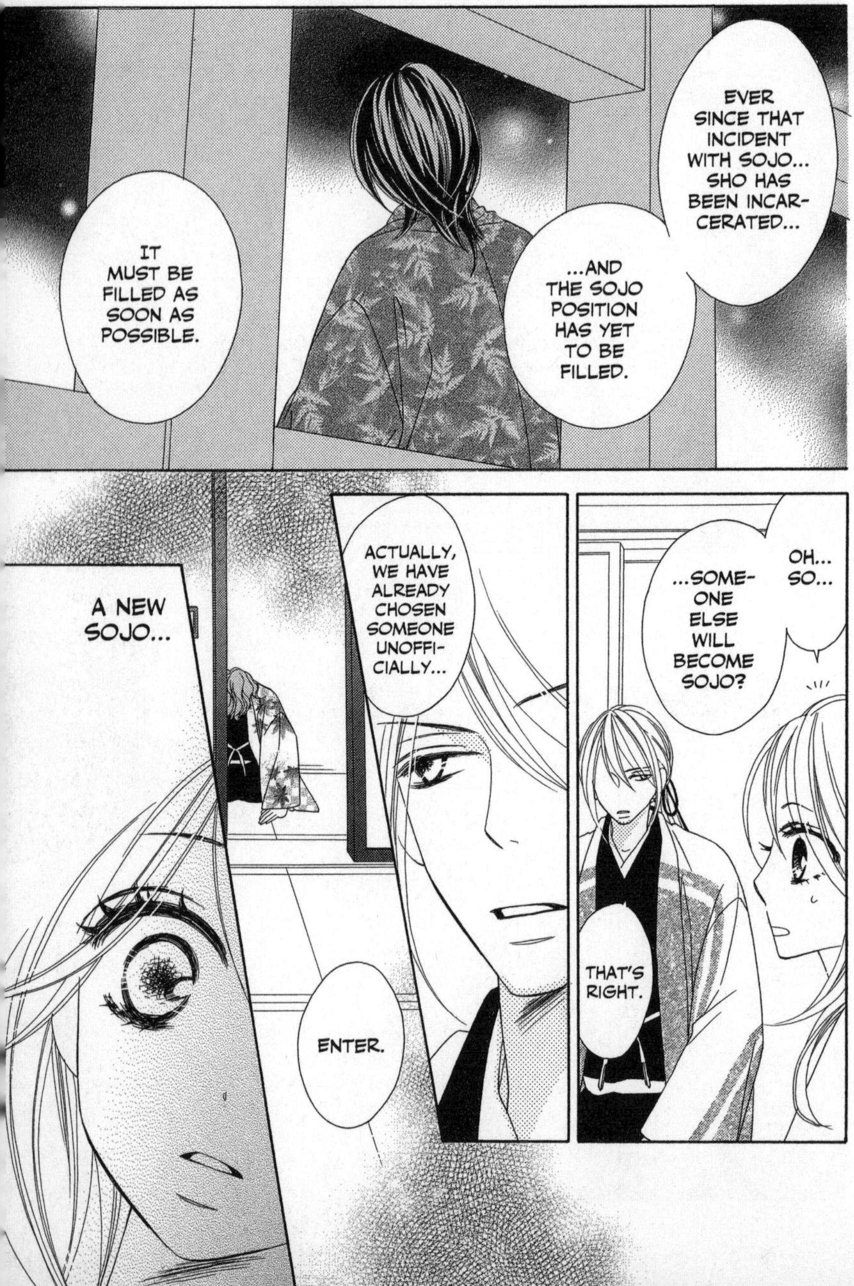
EVER SINCE THAT INCIDENT WITH SOJO... SHO HAS BEEN INCARCERATED...
...AND THE SOJO POSITION HAS YET TO BE FILLED.
IT MUST BE FILLED AS SOON AS POSSIBLE.
OH... SO...
...SOMEONE ELSE WILL BECOME SOJO?
THAT'S RIGHT.
ACTUALLY, WE HAVE ALREADY CHOSEN SOMEONE UNOFFICIALLY...
ENTER.
A NEW SOJO...

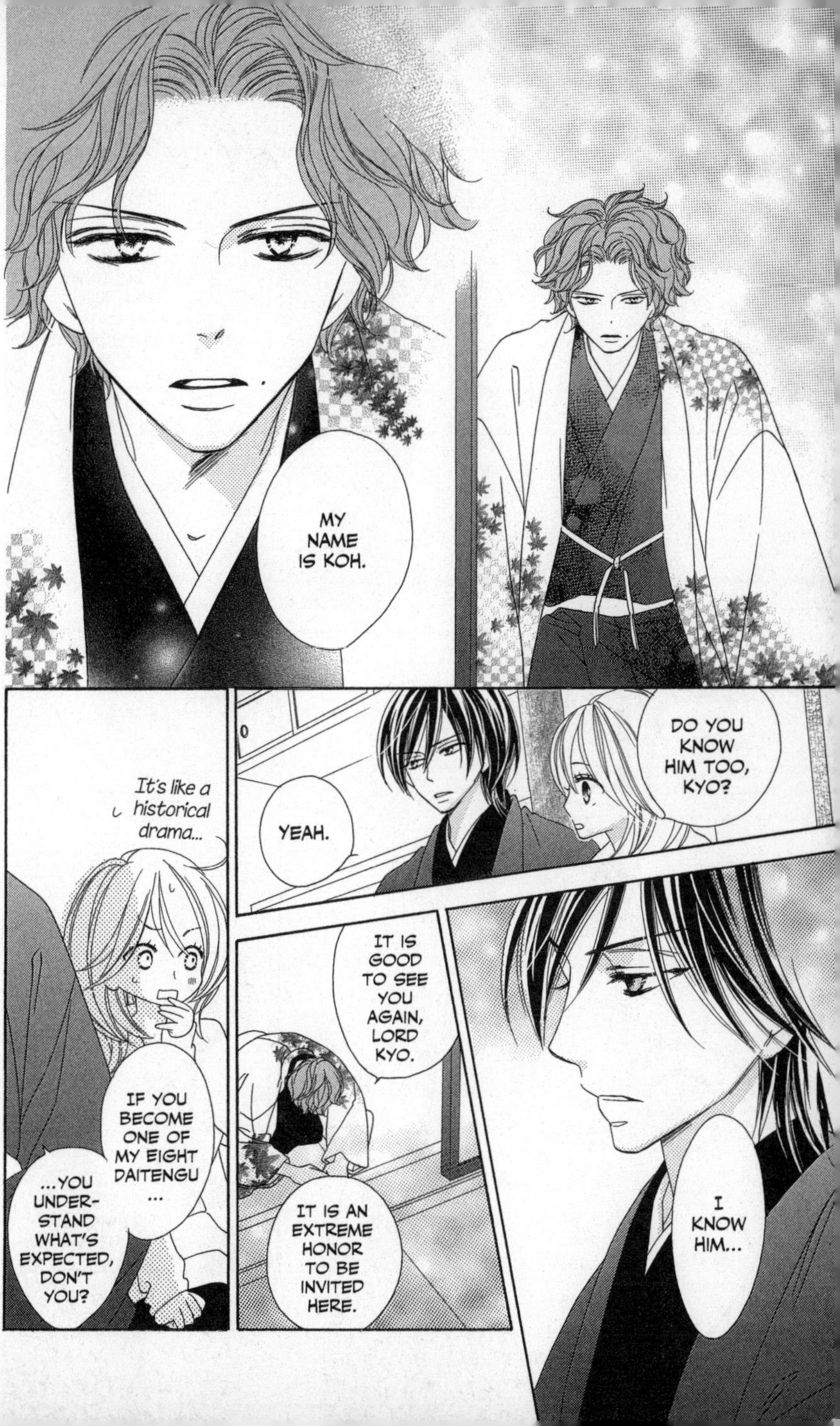
MY NAME IS KOH.
DO YOU KNOW HIM TOO, KYO?
YEAH.
I KNOW HIM...
IT IS GOOD TO SEE YOU AGAIN, LORD KYO.
IT IS AN EXTREME HONOR TO BE INVITED HERE.
It's like a historical drama...
IF YOU BECOME ONE OF MY EIGHT DAITENGU ...
...YOU UNDERSTAND WHAT'S EXPECTED, DON'T YOU?

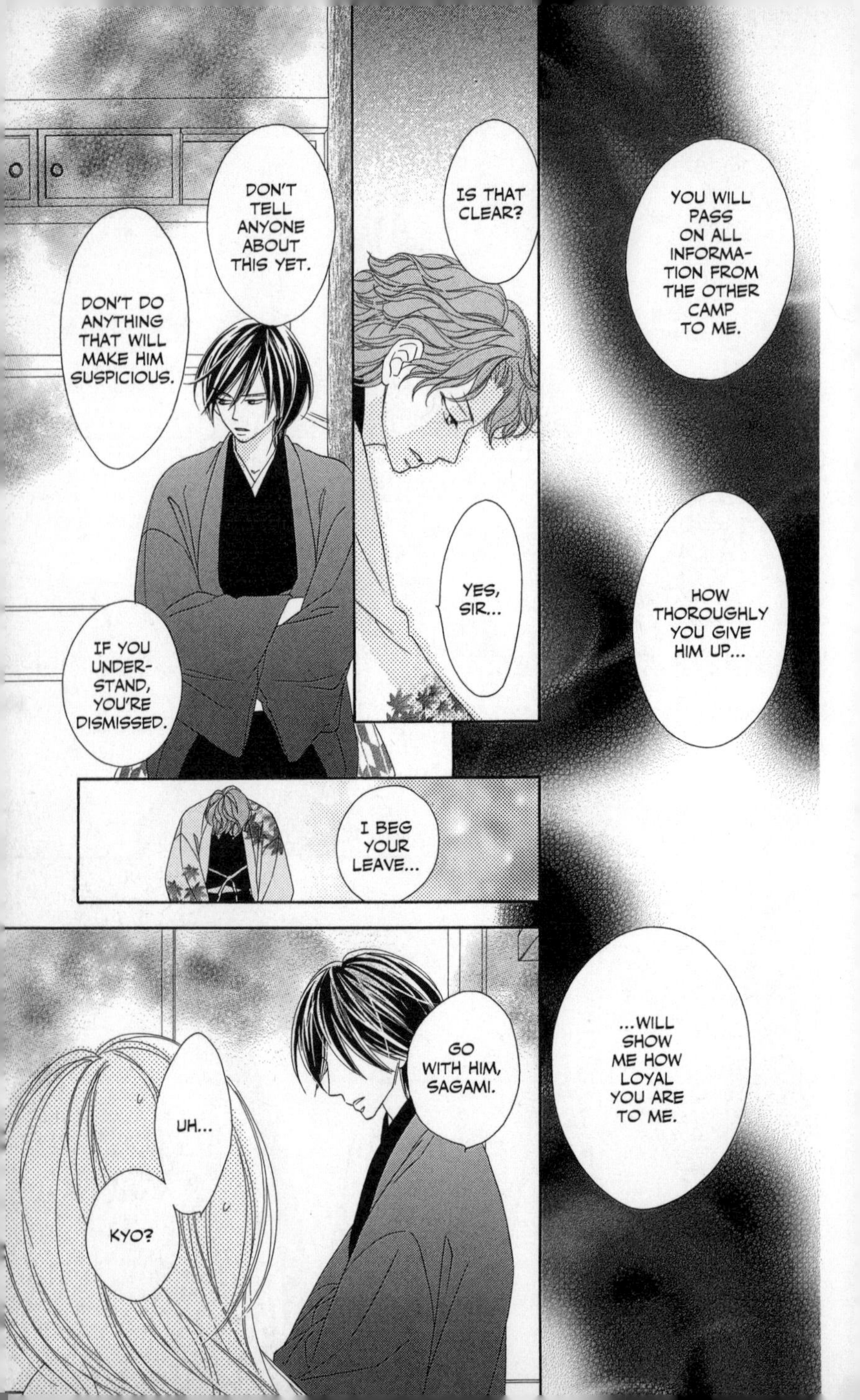
YOU WILL PASS ON ALL INFORMATION FROM THE OTHER CAMP TO ME.
HOW THOROUGHLY YOU GIVE HIM UP...
...WILL SHOW ME HOW LOYAL YOU ARE TO ME.
IS THAT CLEAR?
YES, SIR...
DON'T TELL ANYONE ABOUT THIS YET.
DON'T DO ANYTHING THAT WILL MAKE HIM SUSPICIOUS.
IF YOU UNDERSTAND, YOU'RE DISMISSED.
I BEG YOUR LEAVE...
GO WITH HIM, SAGAMI.
UH...
KYO?

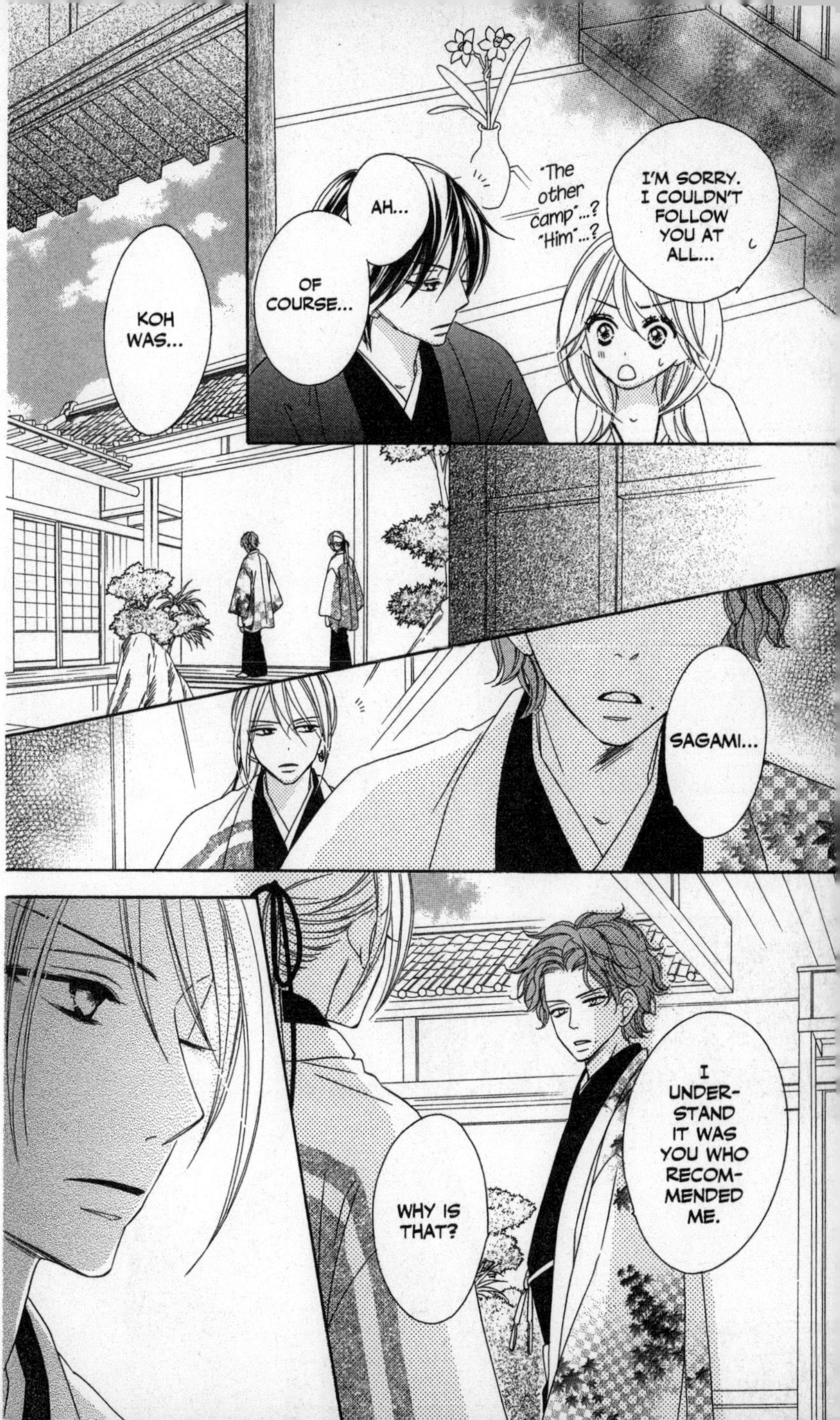
I'M SORRY. I COULDN'T FOLLOW YOU AT ALL...
"The other camp"...? "Him"...?
AH...
OF COURSE...
KOH WAS...
SAGAMI...
I UNDER-STAND IT WAS YOU WHO RECOM-MENDED ME.
WHY IS THAT?

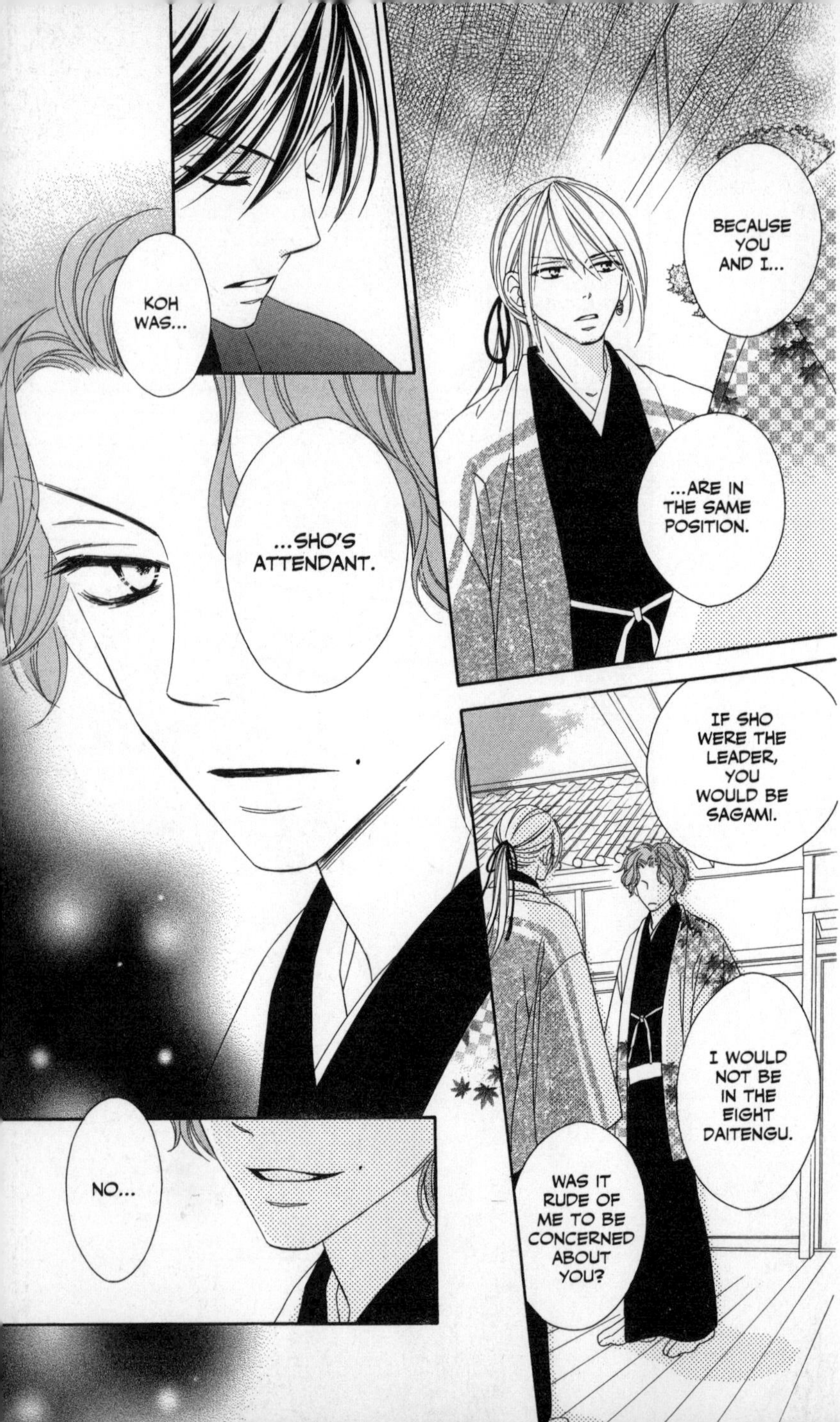
BECAUSE YOU AND I...
...ARE IN THE SAME POSITION.
KOH WAS...
...SHO'S ATTENDANT.
IF SHO WERE THE LEADER, YOU WOULD BE SAGAMI.
I WOULD NOT BE IN THE EIGHT DAITENGU.
WAS IT RUDE OF ME TO BE CONCERNED ABOUT YOU?
NO...

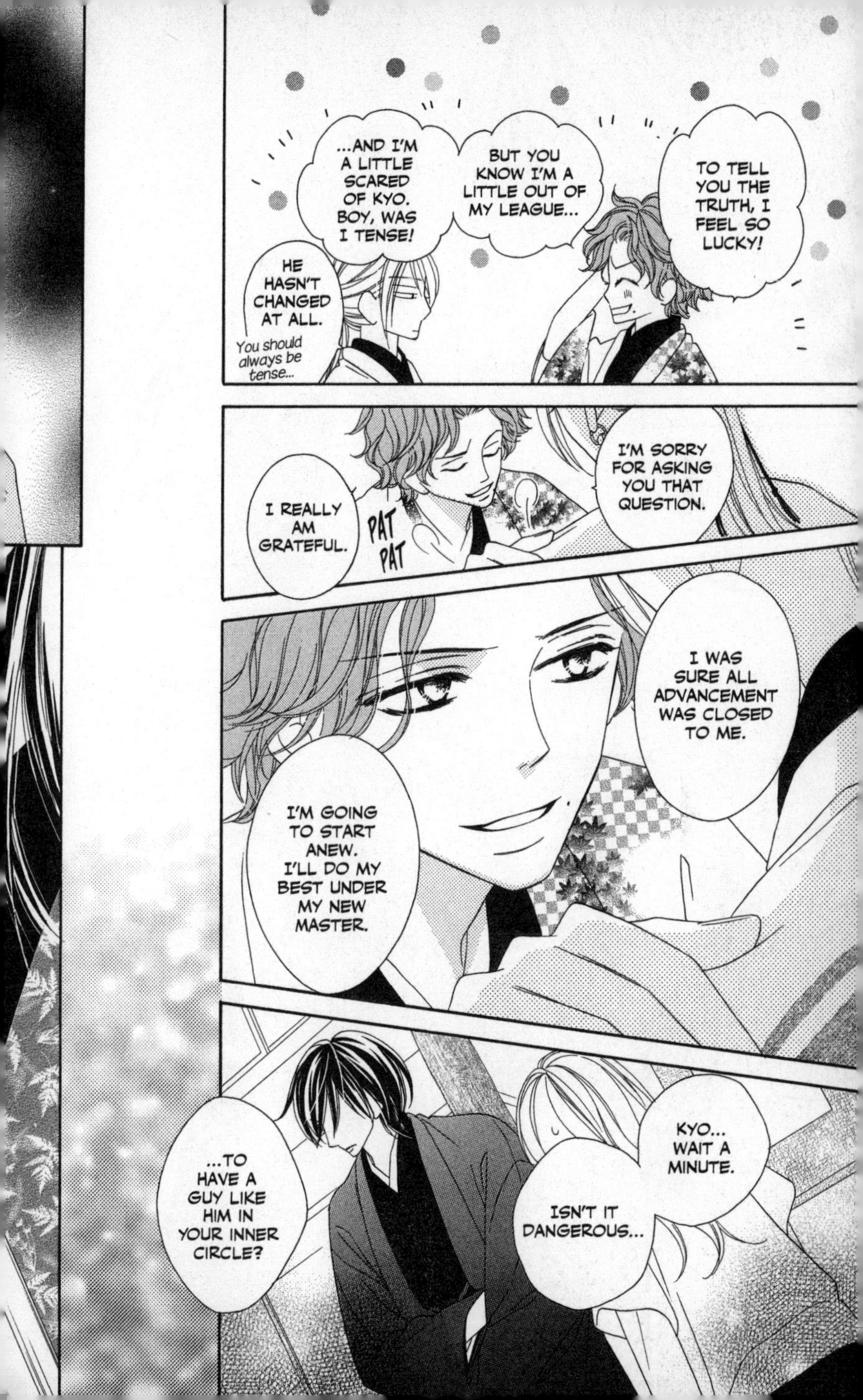
TO TELL YOU THE TRUTH, I FEEL SO LUCKY!
BUT YOU KNOW I'M A LITTLE OUT OF MY LEAGUE...
...AND I'M A LITTLE SCARED OF KYO. BOY, WAS I TENSE!
HE HASN'T CHANGED AT ALL.
You should always be tense...
I'M SORRY FOR ASKING YOU THAT QUESTION.
PAT PAT
I REALLY AM GRATEFUL.
I WAS SURE ALL ADVANCEMENT WAS CLOSED TO ME.
I'M GOING TO START ANEW. I'LL DO MY BEST UNDER MY NEW MASTER.
KYO... WAIT A MINUTE.
ISN'T IT DANGEROUS...
...TO HAVE A GUY LIKE HIM IN YOUR INNER CIRCLE?

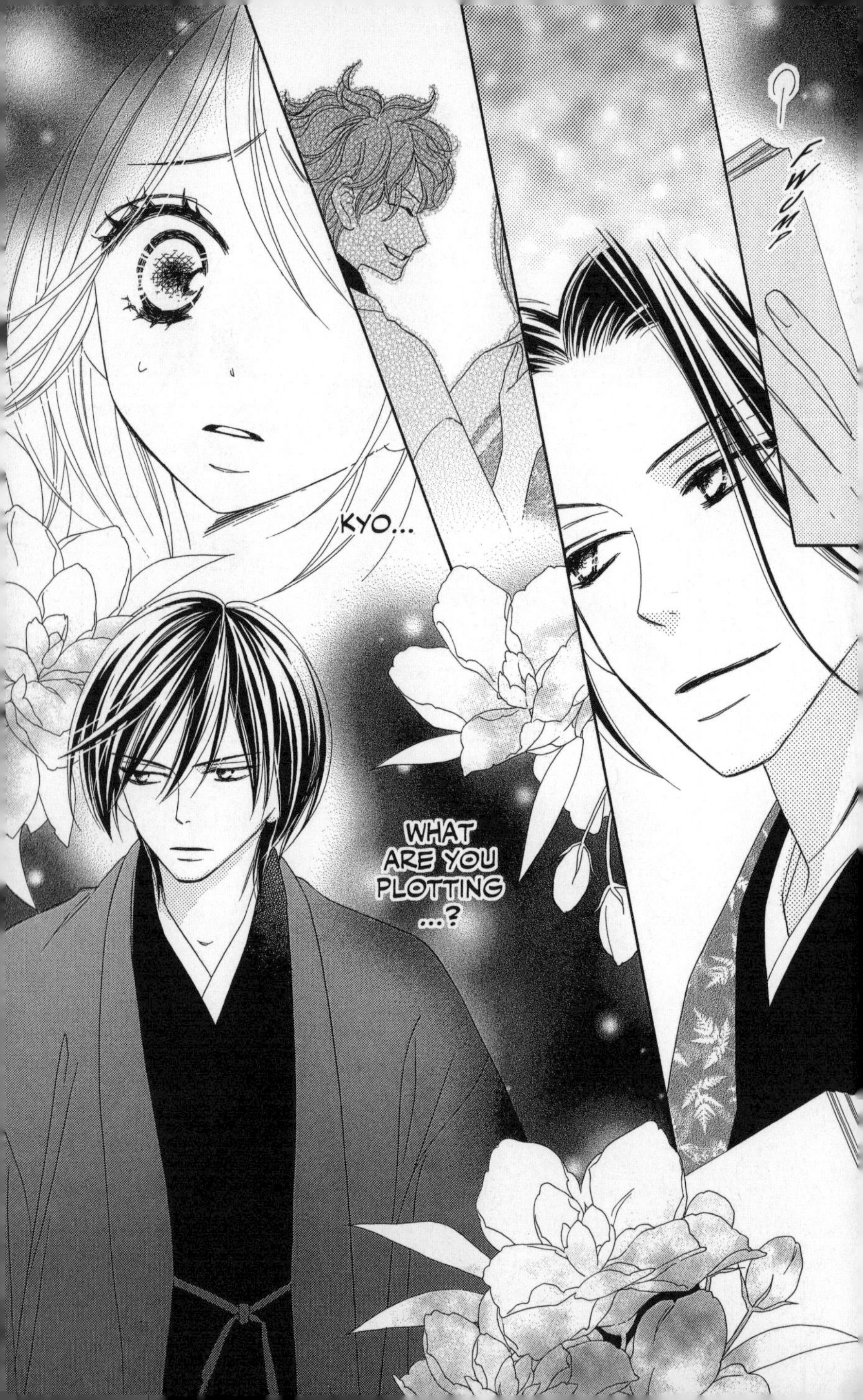
FWUMP
KYO...
WHAT ARE YOU PLOTTING ...?

♥A Day in the Life of Taro♥

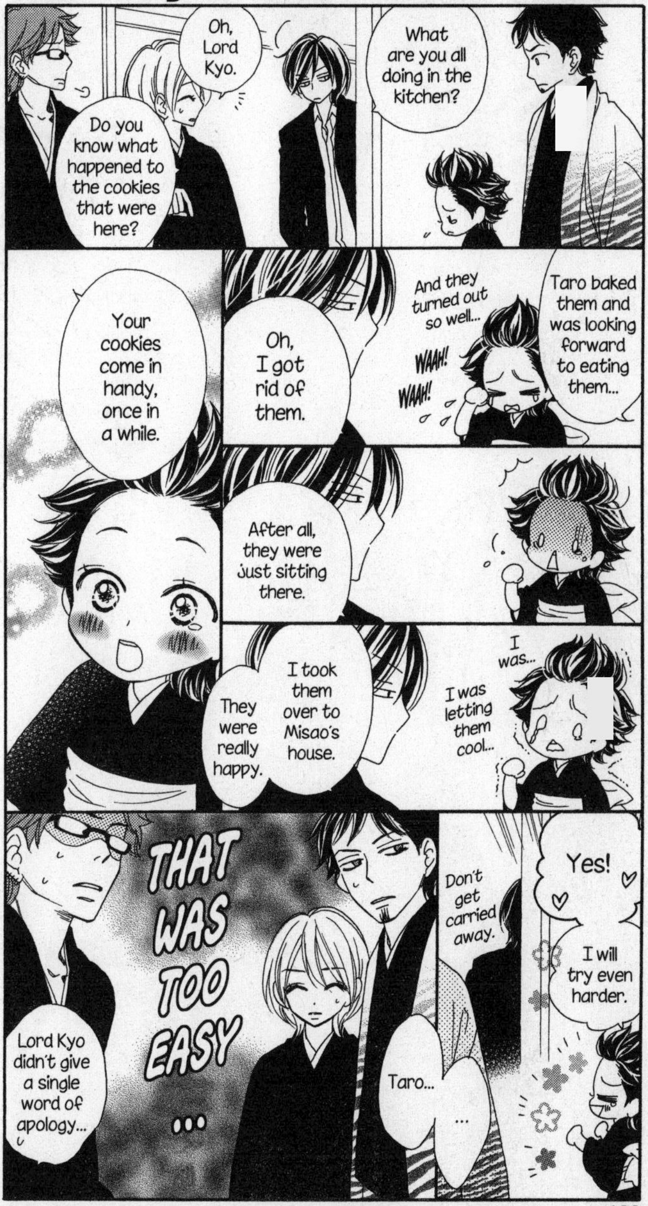
What are you all doing in the kitchen?
Oh, Lord Kyo.
Do you know what happened to the cookies that were here?
Taro baked them and was looking forward to eating them...
And they turned out so well...
WAAH!
WAAH!
Oh, I got rid of them.
After all, they were just sitting there.
I was...
I was letting them cool...
I took them over to Misao's house.
They were really happy.
Your cookies come in handy, once in a while.
Yes!
I will try even harder.
Don't get carried away.
Taro...
...
THAT WAS TOO EASY...
Lord Kyo didn't give a single word of apology...

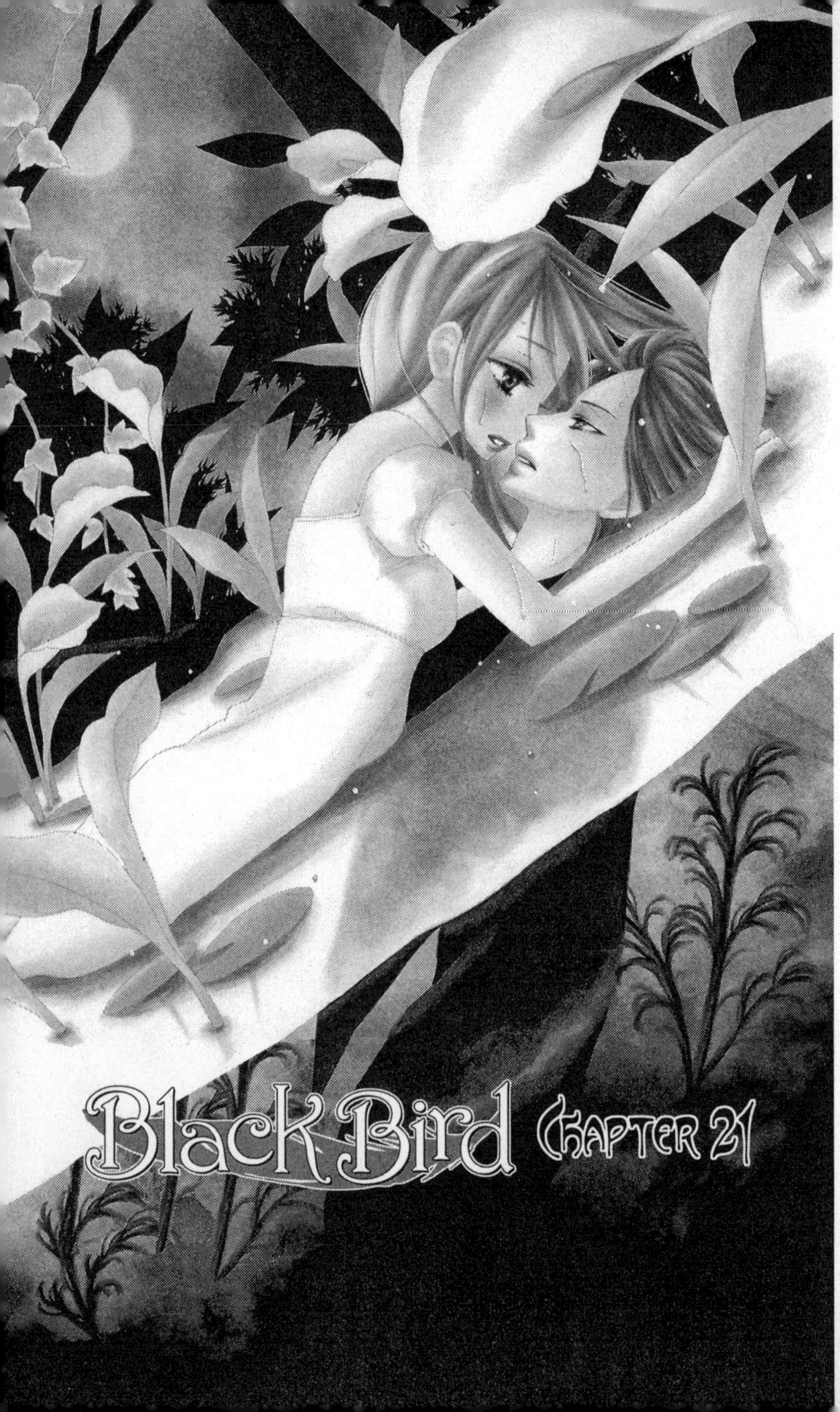
Black Bird
Chapter 21

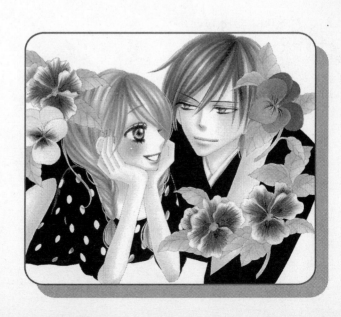

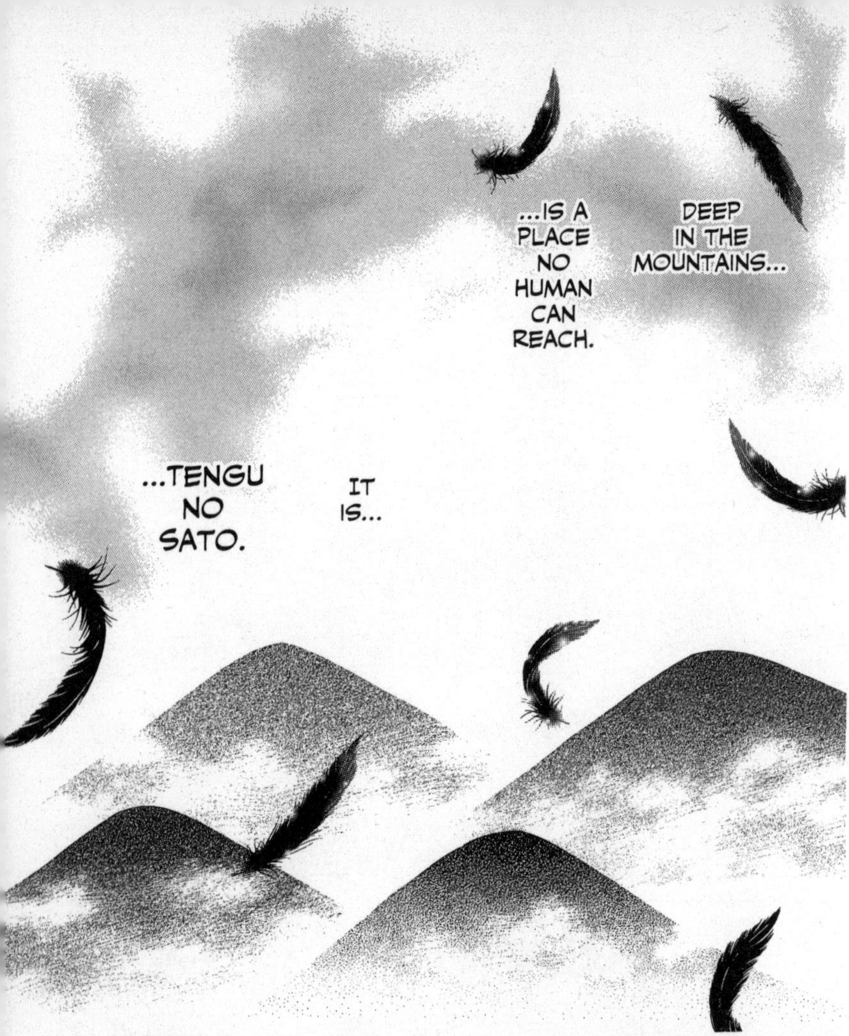
DEEP IN THE MOUNTAINS...
...IS A PLACE NO HUMAN CAN REACH.
IT IS...
...TENGU NO SATO.

I read through every piece of mail—postcards and emails—that reach me or are on my fan site.
Even if yours isn't selected, I enjoy them myself, so please continue to send them in.♡

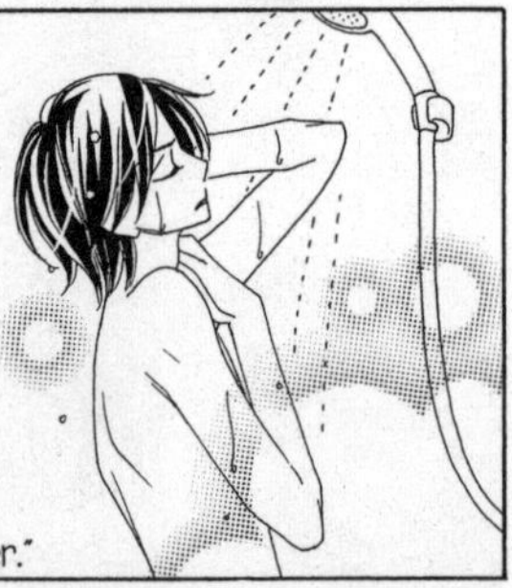

Unfortunately, this request was not selected.→ "Kyo in the shower."

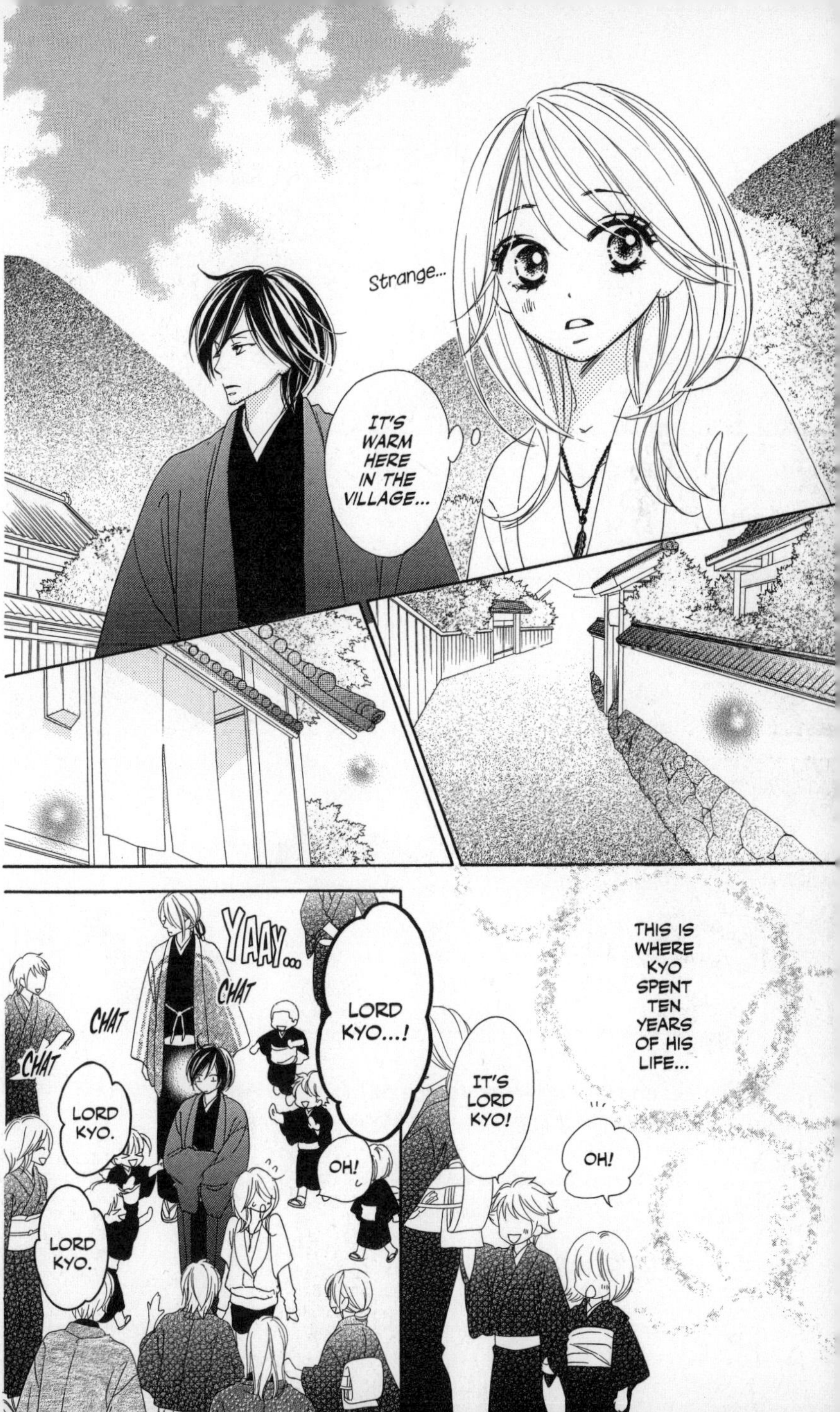
Strange...
IT'S WARM HERE IN THE VILLAGE...
THIS IS WHERE KYO SPENT TEN YEARS OF HIS LIFE...
OH!
IT'S LORD KYO!
LORD KYO...!
YAAY...
CHAT
CHAT
CHAT
OH!
LORD KYO.
LORD KYO.

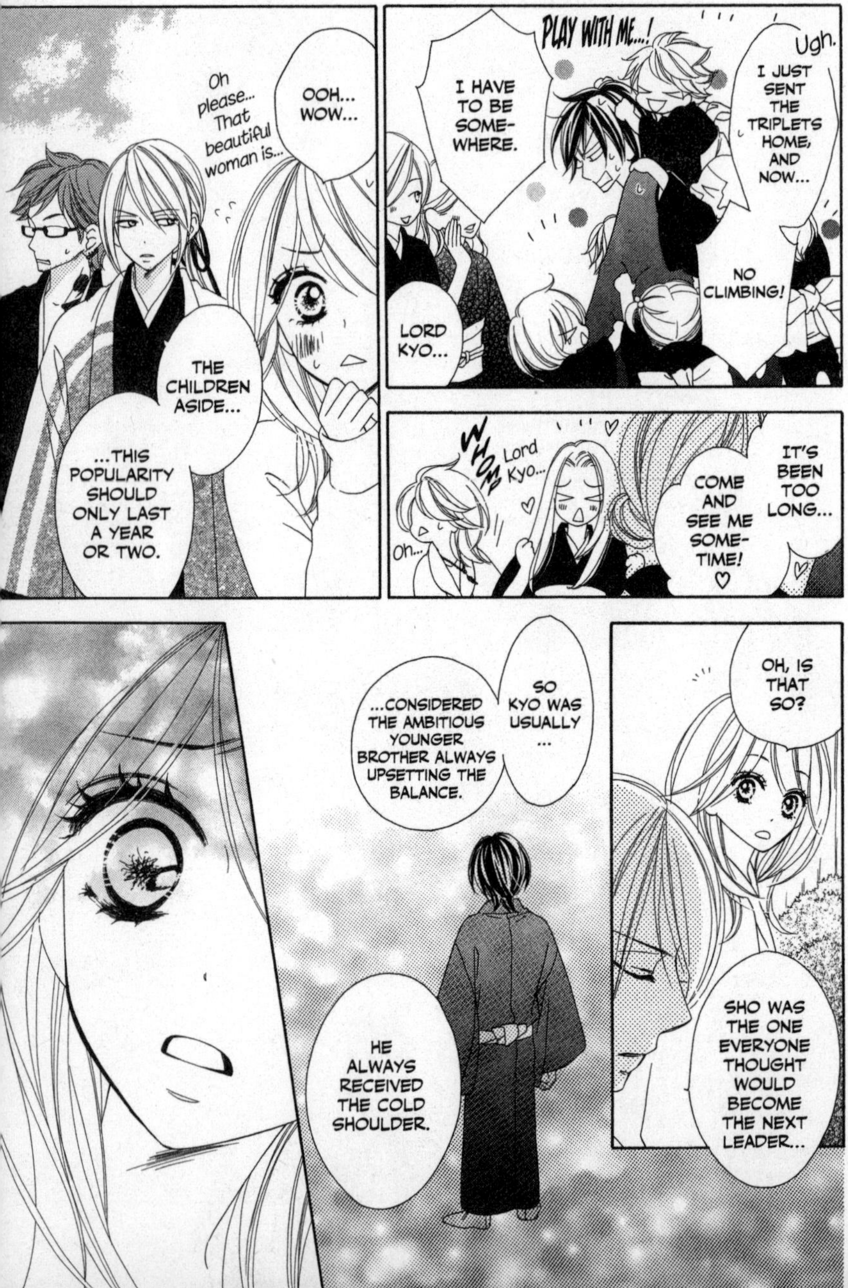
Ugh.
I JUST SENT THE TRIPLETS HOME, AND NOW...
PLAY WITH ME...!
I HAVE TO BE SOME-WHERE.
NO CLIMBING!
LORD KYO...
IT'S BEEN TOO LONG...
COME AND SEE ME SOME-TIME! ♡
Lord Kyo...
Oh...
OOH... WOW...
Oh please... That beautiful woman is...
THE CHILDREN ASIDE...
...THIS POPULARITY SHOULD ONLY LAST A YEAR OR TWO.
OH, IS THAT SO?
SHO WAS THE ONE EVERYONE THOUGHT WOULD BECOME THE NEXT LEADER...
SO KYO WAS USUALLY...
...CONSIDERED THE AMBITIOUS YOUNGER BROTHER ALWAYS UPSETTING THE BALANCE.
HE ALWAYS RECEIVED THE COLD SHOULDER.

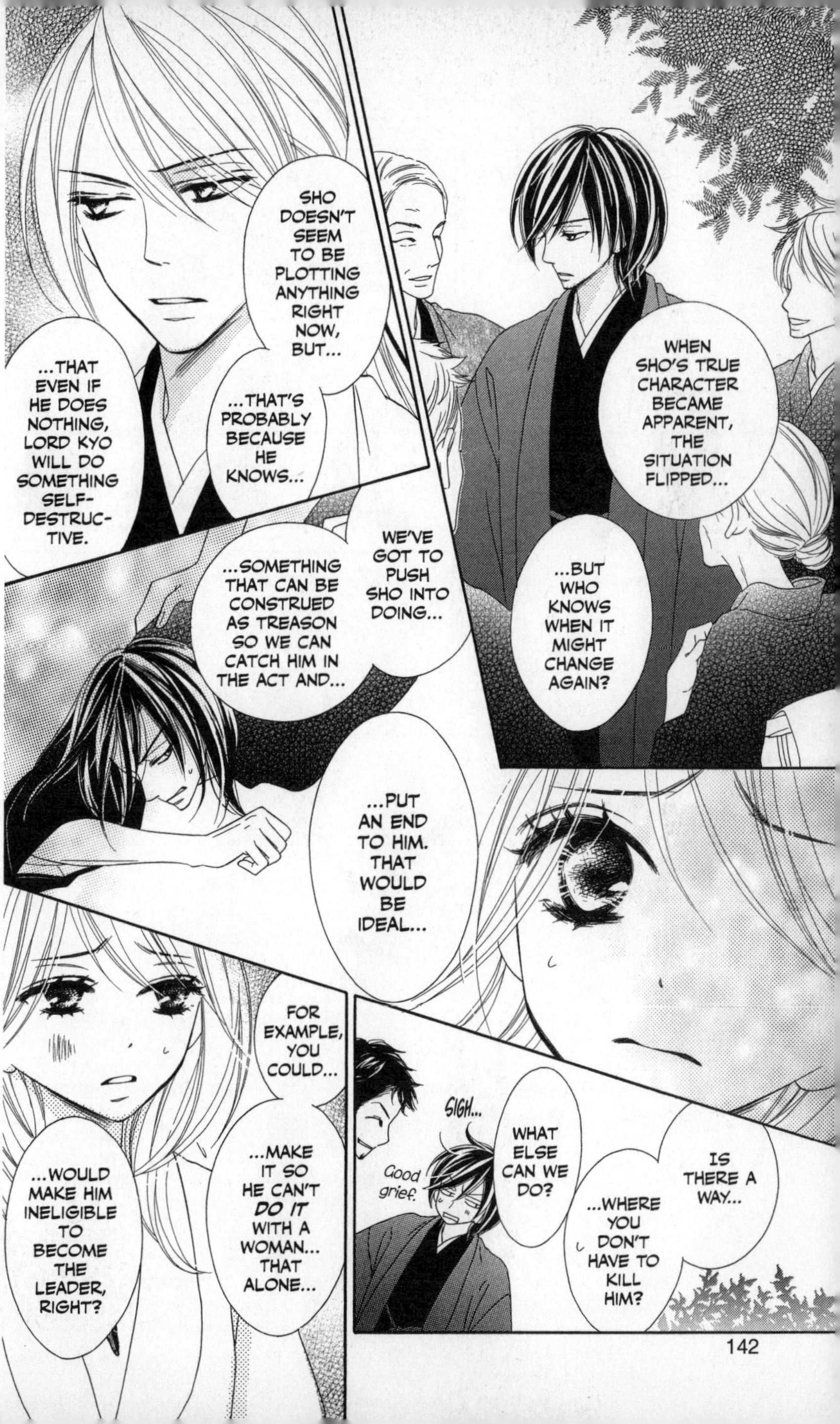
WHEN SHO'S TRUE CHARACTER BECAME APPARENT, THE SITUATION FLIPPED...
...BUT WHO KNOWS WHEN IT MIGHT CHANGE AGAIN?
SHO DOESN'T SEEM TO BE PLOTTING ANYTHING RIGHT NOW, BUT...
...THAT'S PROBABLY BECAUSE HE KNOWS...
...THAT EVEN IF HE DOES NOTHING, LORD KYO WILL DO SOMETHING SELF-DESTRUCTIVE.
WE'VE GOT TO PUSH SHO INTO DOING...
...SOMETHING THAT CAN BE CONSTRUED AS TREASON SO WE CAN CATCH HIM IN THE ACT AND...
...PUT AN END TO HIM. THAT WOULD BE IDEAL...
IS THERE A WAY...
...WHERE YOU DON'T HAVE TO KILL HIM?
WHAT ELSE CAN WE DO?
SIGH...
Good grief.
FOR EXAMPLE, YOU COULD...
...MAKE IT SO HE CAN'T *DO IT* WITH A WOMAN... THAT ALONE...
...WOULD MAKE HIM INELIGIBLE TO BECOME THE LEADER, RIGHT?

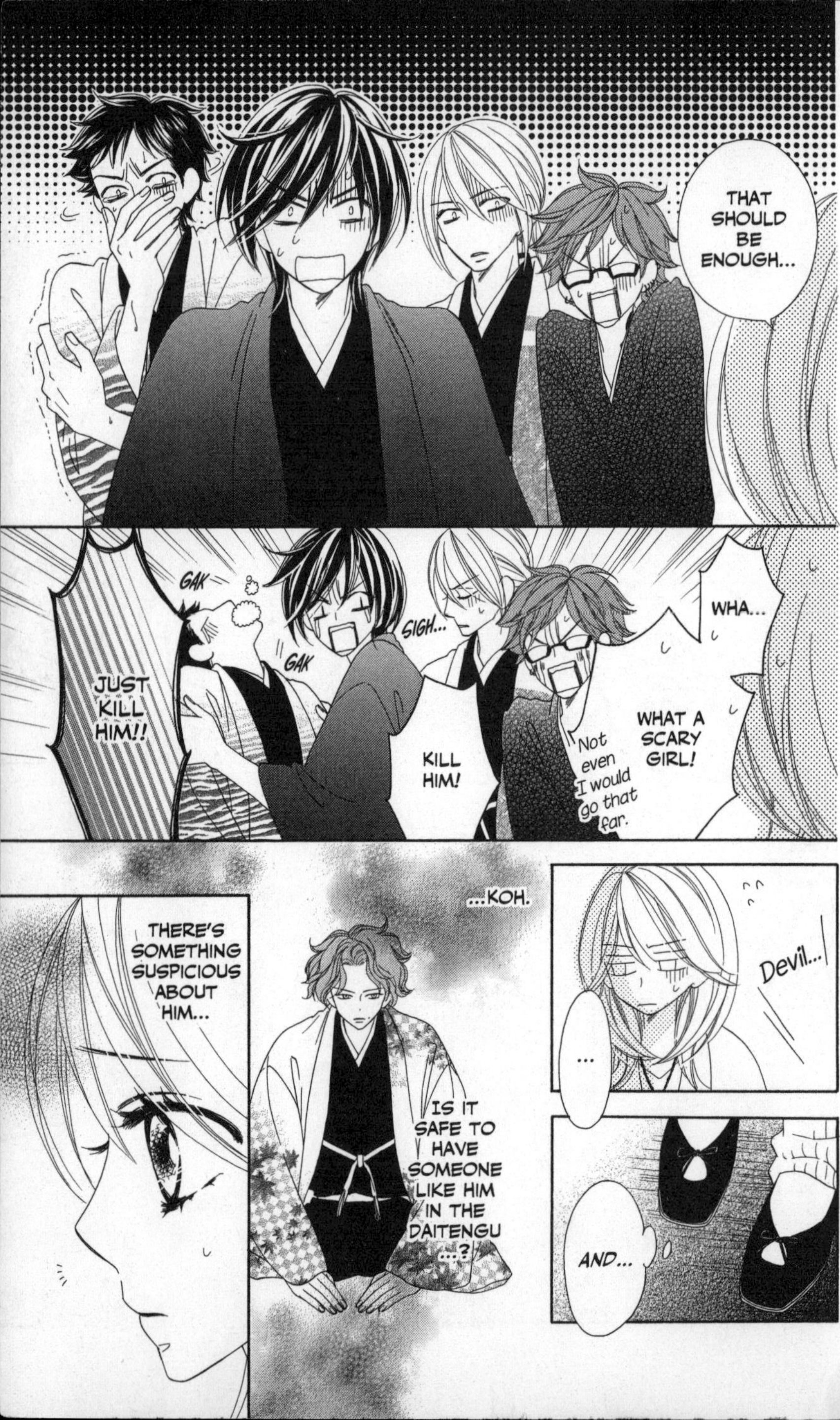
THAT SHOULD BE ENOUGH...
WHA...
WHAT A SCARY GIRL!
Not even I would go that far.
SIGH...
KILL HIM!
GAK
GAK
JUST KILL HIM!!
Devil...
...
AND...
...KOH.
IS IT SAFE TO HAVE SOMEONE LIKE HIM IN THE DAITENGU ...?
THERE'S SOMETHING SUSPICIOUS ABOUT HIM...

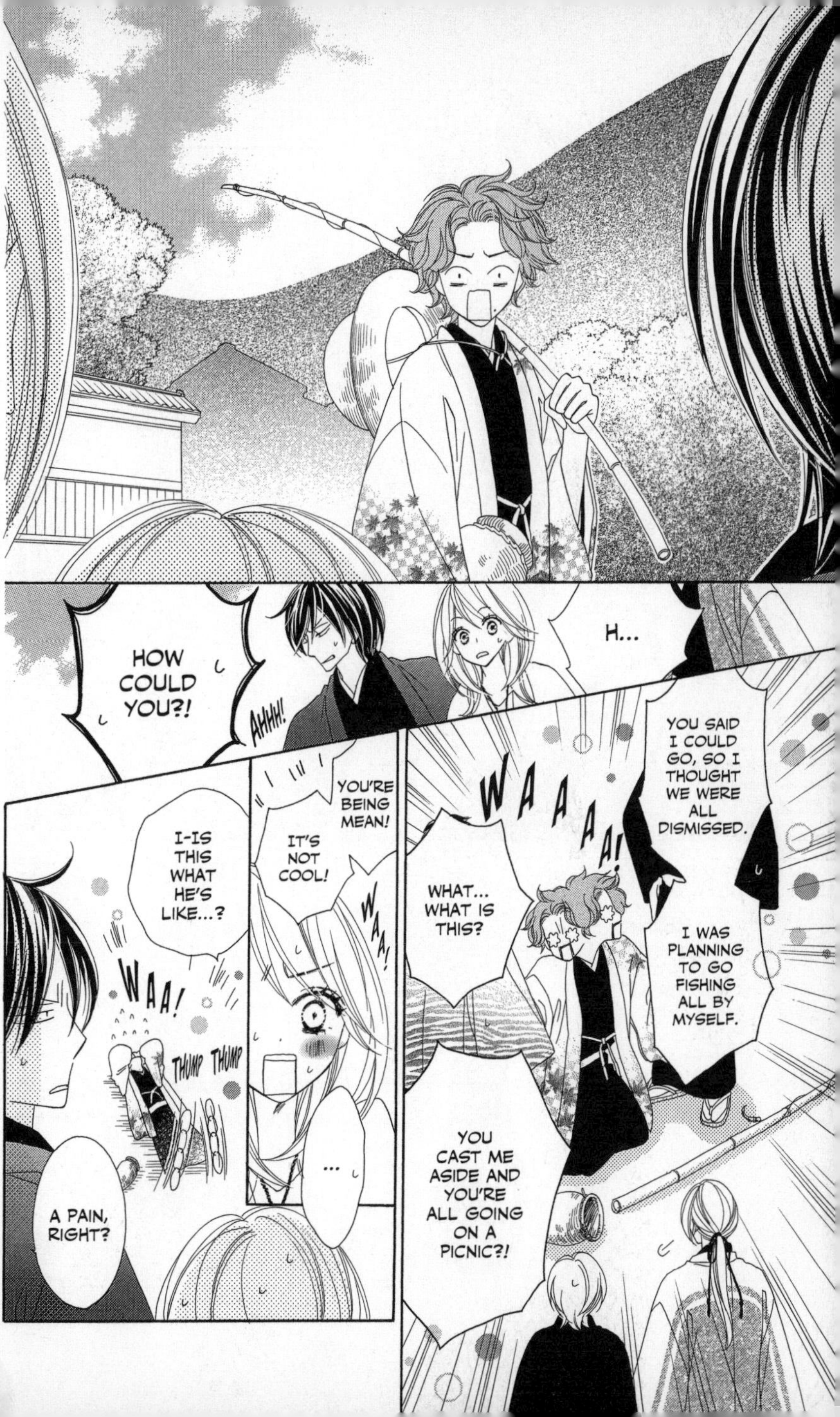
H...
HOW COULD YOU?!
AHHH!
YOU SAID I COULD GO, SO I THOUGHT WE WERE ALL DISMISSED.
WAAAAA!
I WAS PLANNING TO GO FISHING ALL BY MYSELF.
WHAT... WHAT IS THIS?
YOU CAST ME ASIDE AND YOU'RE ALL GOING ON A PICNIC?!
YOU'RE BEING MEAN!
IT'S NOT COOL!
WAAA!
...
I-IS THIS WHAT HE'S LIKE...?
WAA!
THUMP THUMP
A PAIN, RIGHT?

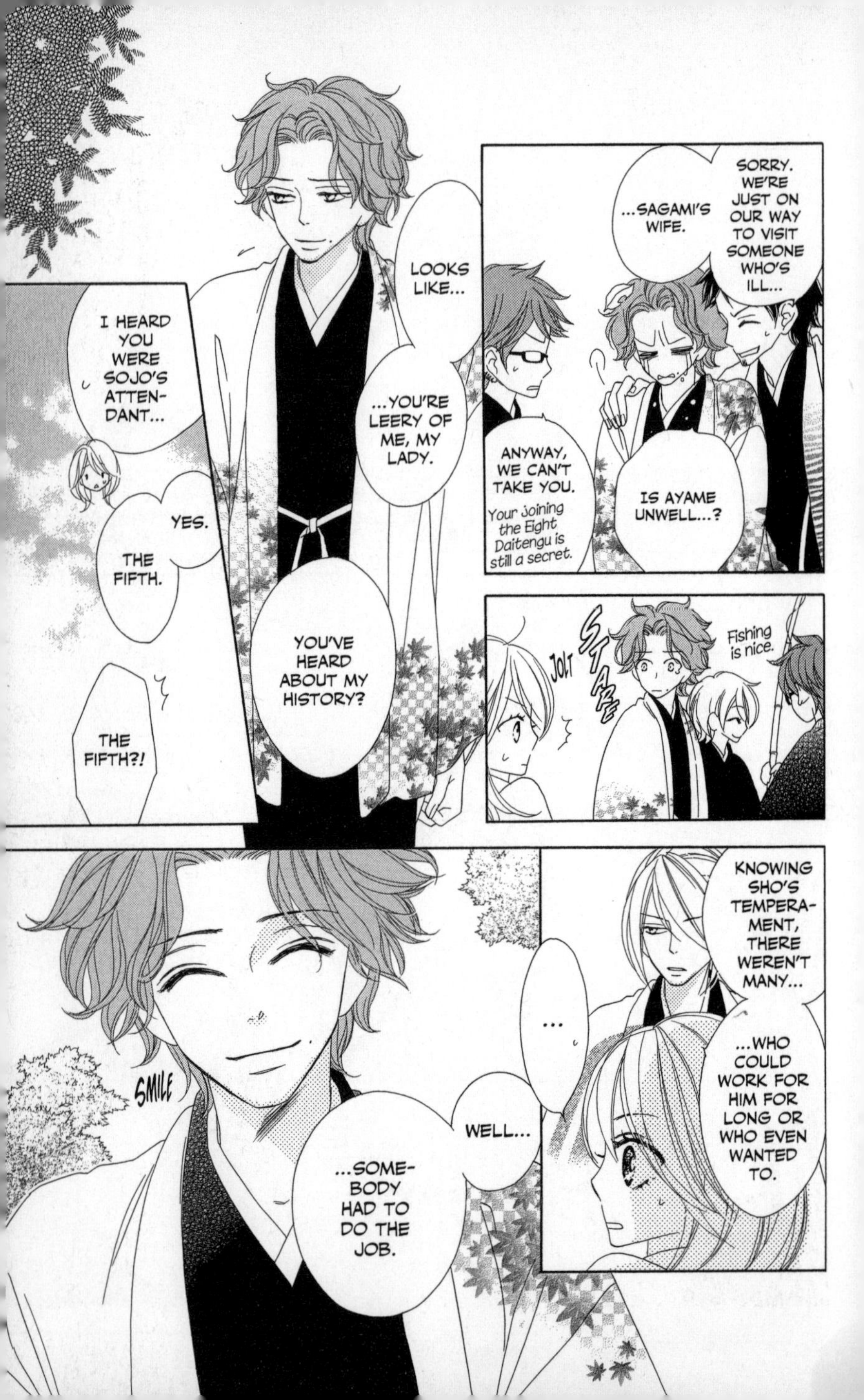
SORRY. WE'RE JUST ON OUR WAY TO VISIT SOMEONE WHO'S ILL...
...SAGAMI'S WIFE.
IS AYAME UNWELL...?
ANYWAY, WE CAN'T TAKE YOU.
Your joining the Eight Daitengu is still a secret.
Fishing is nice.
STARE
JOLT
LOOKS LIKE...
...YOU'RE LEERY OF ME, MY LADY.
YOU'VE HEARD ABOUT MY HISTORY?
I HEARD YOU WERE SOJO'S ATTEN-DANT...
YES.
THE FIFTH.
THE FIFTH?!
KNOWING SHO'S TEMPERA-MENT, THERE WEREN'T MANY...
...WHO COULD WORK FOR HIM FOR LONG OR WHO EVEN WANTED TO.
...
WELL...
...SOME-BODY HAD TO DO THE JOB.
SMILE

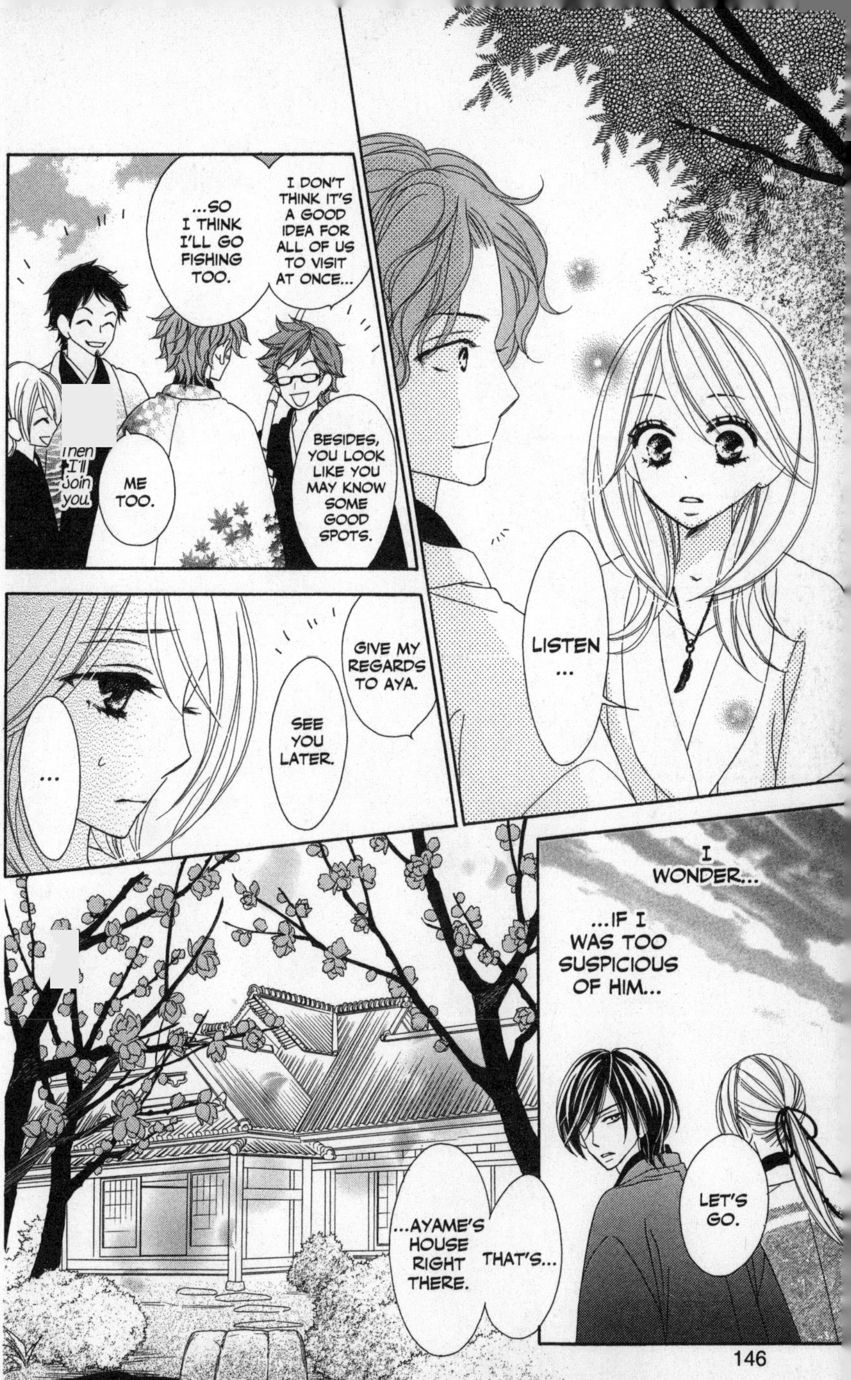
LISTEN ...
I DON'T THINK IT'S A GOOD IDEA FOR ALL OF US TO VISIT AT ONCE...
...SO I THINK I'LL GO FISHING TOO.
BESIDES, YOU LOOK LIKE YOU MAY KNOW SOME GOOD SPOTS.
ME TOO.
Then I'll join you.
GIVE MY REGARDS TO AYA.
SEE YOU LATER.
...
I WONDER...
...IF I WAS TOO SUSPICIOUS OF HIM...
LET'S GO.
THAT'S...
...AYAME'S HOUSE RIGHT THERE.

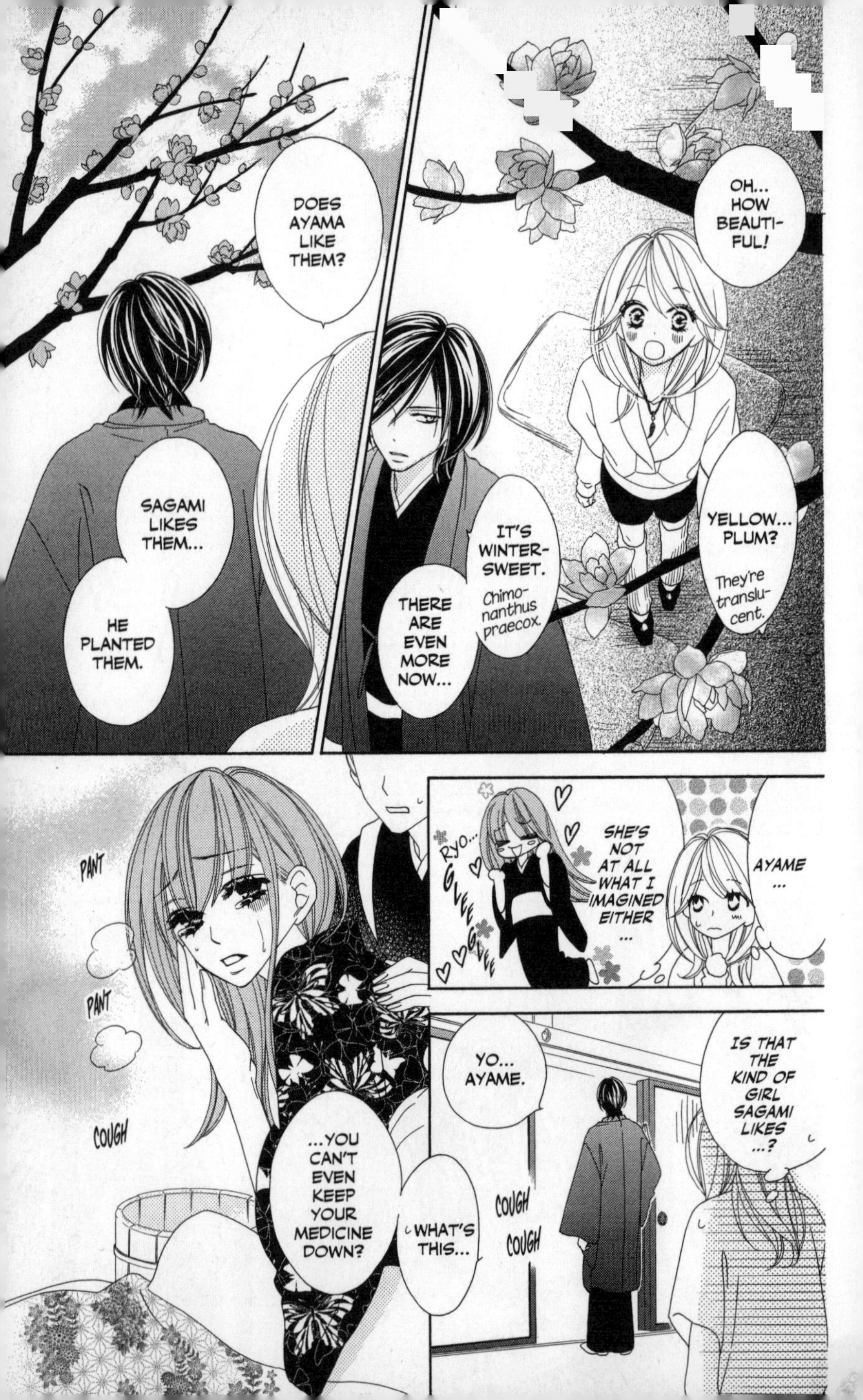
OH... HOW BEAUTIFUL!
YELLOW... PLUM?
They're translucent.
IT'S WINTERSWEET.
Chimonanthus praecox.
THERE ARE EVEN MORE NOW...
DOES AYAMA LIKE THEM?
SAGAMI LIKES THEM...
HE PLANTED THEM.
AYAME ...
SHE'S NOT AT ALL WHAT I IMAGINED EITHER ...
RYO...
IS THAT THE KIND OF GIRL SAGAMI LIKES ...?
YO... AYAME.
COUGH
COUGH
PANT
PANT
WHAT'S THIS...
...YOU CAN'T EVEN KEEP YOUR MEDICINE DOWN?
COUGH

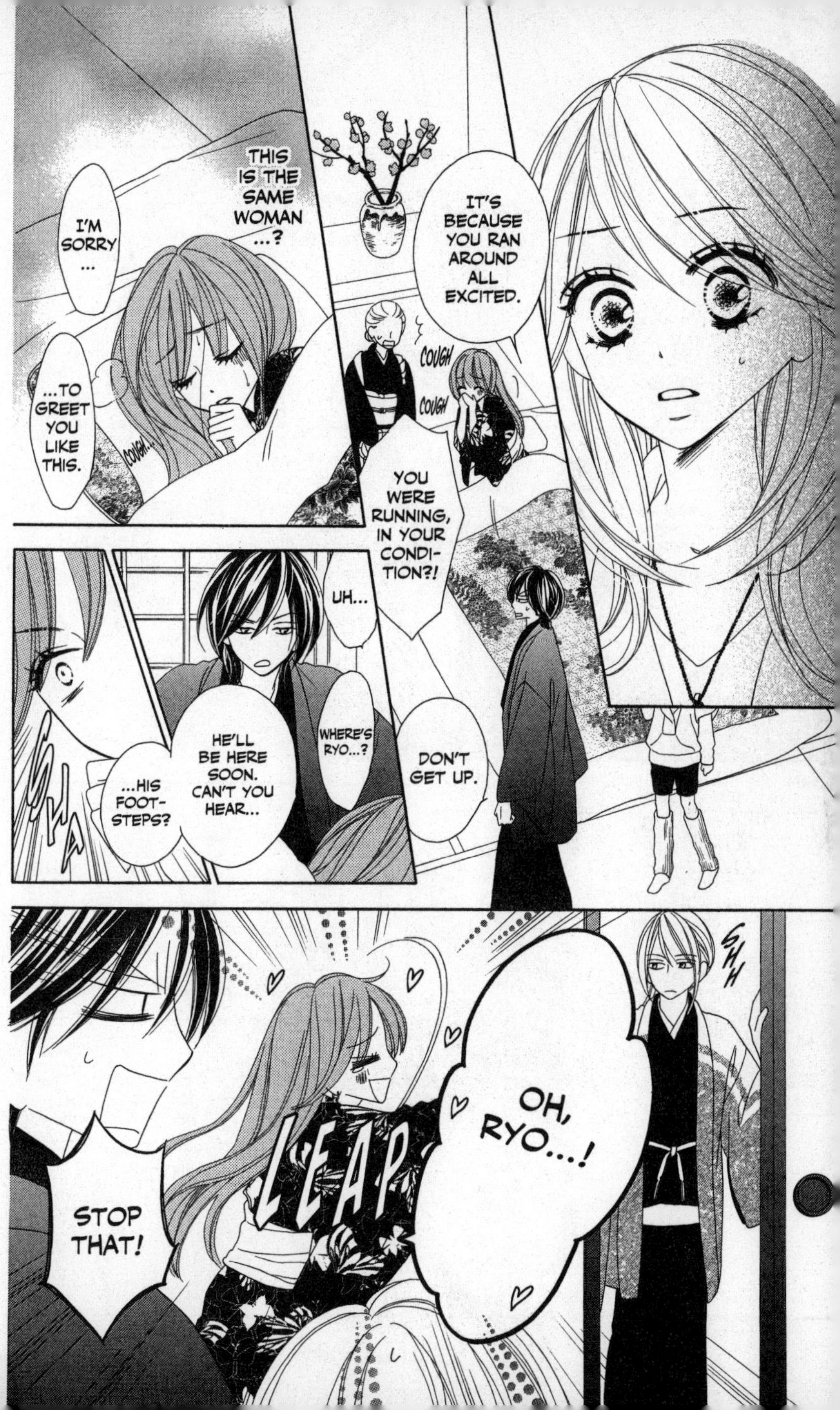
IT'S BECAUSE YOU RAN AROUND ALL EXCITED.
COUGH
COUGH
THIS IS THE SAME WOMAN ...?
I'M SORRY ...
...TO GREET YOU LIKE THIS.
COUGH...
YOU WERE RUNNING, IN YOUR CONDI-TION?!
UH...
DON'T GET UP.
WHERE'S RYO...?
HE'LL BE HERE SOON. CAN'T YOU HEAR...
...HIS FOOT-STEPS?
SHH
OH, RYO...!
LEAP
STOP THAT!

AYAME...

THERE IS JUST ONE REASON THAT I HAD LORD KYO AND LADY MISAO COME HERE.

YOU'LL BE VOMITING ORGANS SOON!

SCOOTCH

SCOOTCH

RYO!

RYO!

IT IS THE SAME WOMAN...

IT IS SO THAT YOU CAN RECEIVE LADY MISAO'S BLOOD TO CURE YOU.

...I MUST DECLINE.

SIGH...

BUT...

Scared

I TOLD YOU ABOUT IT IN MY LETTER.

YES...

IT'S GRATIFYING...

SHE'S ABOUT TO DIE.

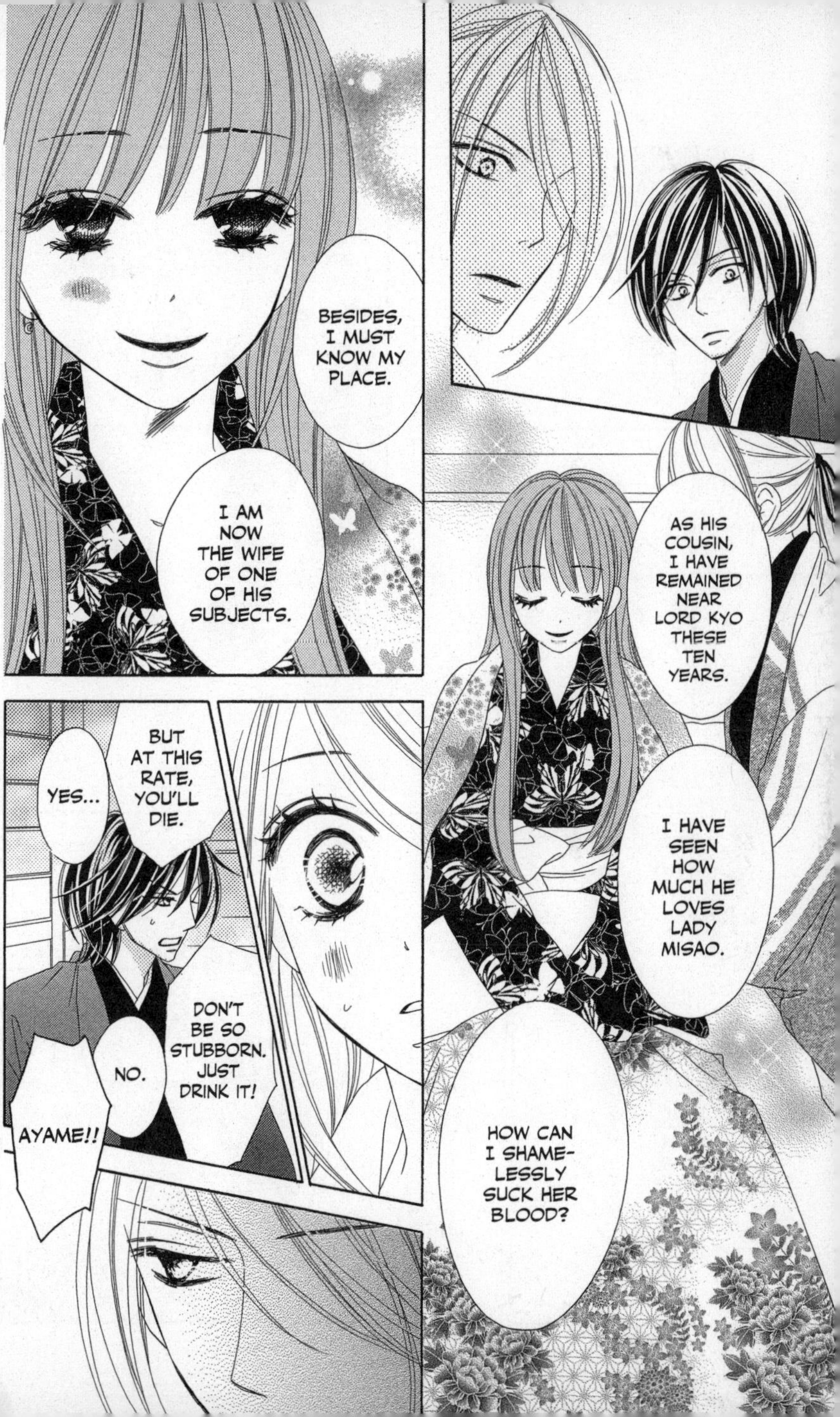
AS HIS COUSIN, I HAVE REMAINED NEAR LORD KYO THESE TEN YEARS.
I HAVE SEEN HOW MUCH HE LOVES LADY MISAO.
HOW CAN I SHAMELESSLY SUCK HER BLOOD?
BESIDES, I MUST KNOW MY PLACE.
I AM NOW THE WIFE OF ONE OF HIS SUBJECTS.
BUT AT THIS RATE, YOU'LL DIE.
YES...
DON'T BE SO STUBBORN. JUST DRINK IT!
NO.
AYAME!!

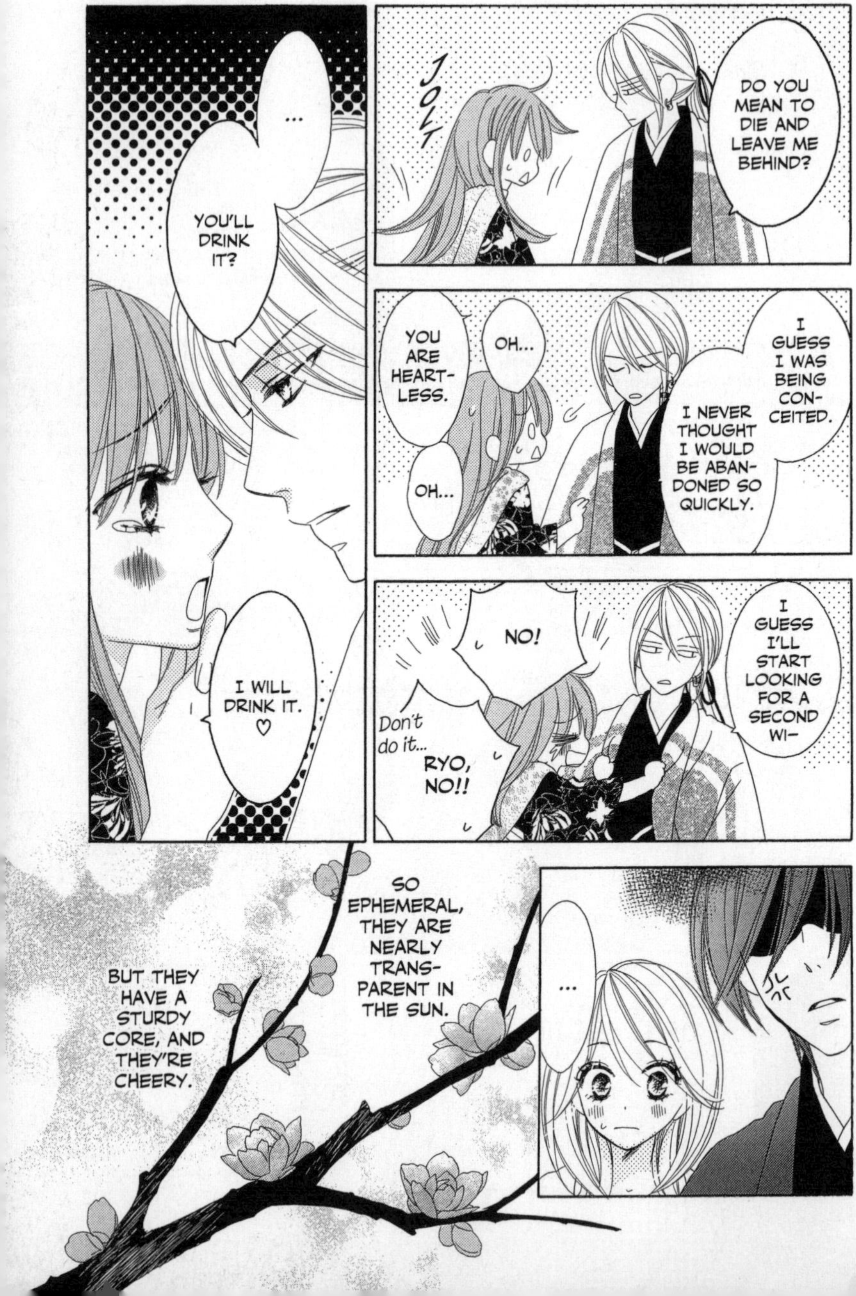
DO YOU MEAN TO DIE AND LEAVE ME BEHIND?
JOLT
I GUESS I WAS BEING CONCEITED.
I NEVER THOUGHT I WOULD BE ABANDONED SO QUICKLY.
OH...
YOU ARE HEARTLESS.
OH...
I GUESS I'LL START LOOKING FOR A SECOND WI—
NO!
RYO, NO!!
Don't do it...
...
YOU'LL DRINK IT?
I WILL DRINK IT. ♡
...
SO EPHEMERAL, THEY ARE NEARLY TRANSPARENT IN THE SUN.
BUT THEY HAVE A STURDY CORE, AND THEY'RE CHEERY.

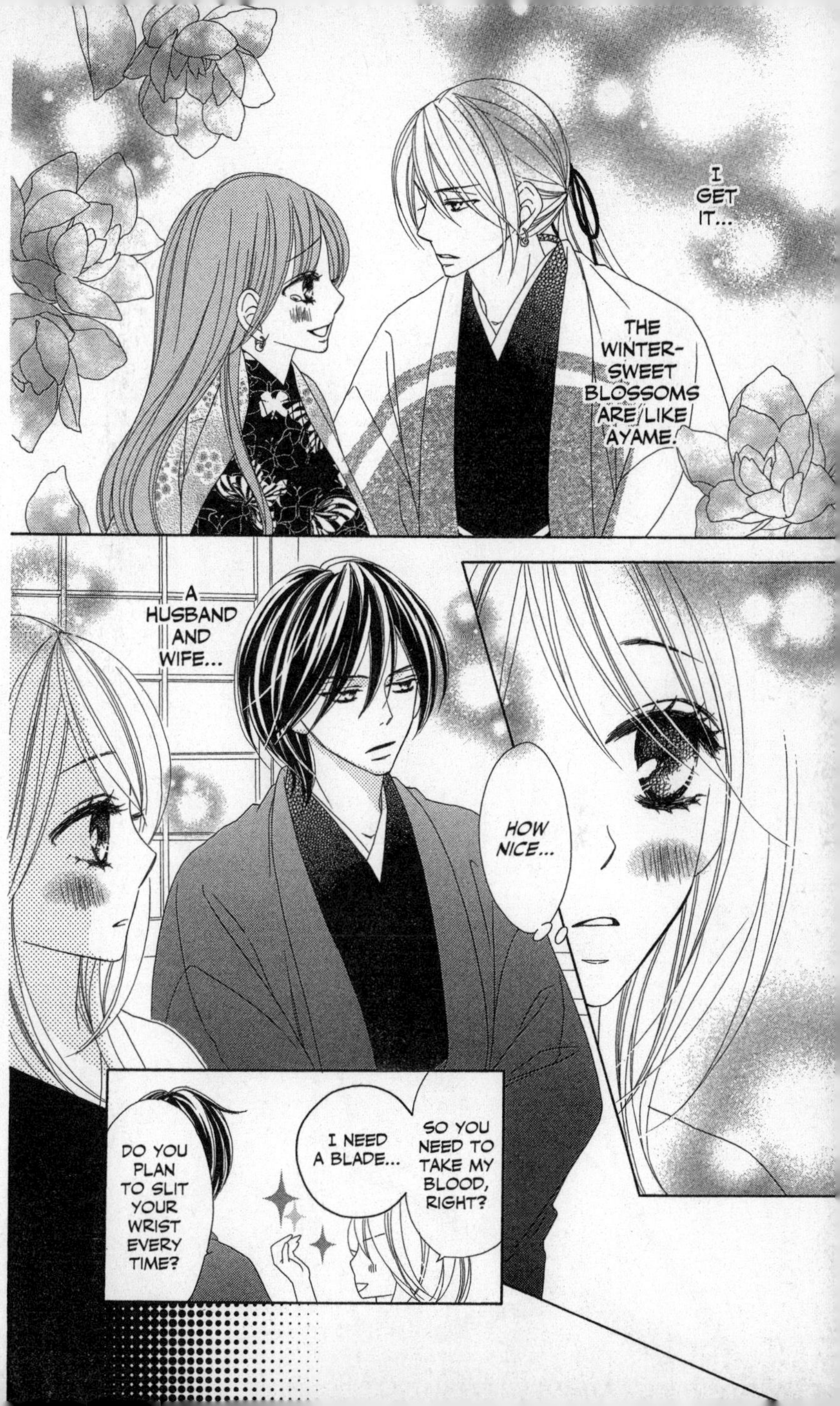
I GET IT...
THE WINTER-SWEET BLOSSOMS ARE LIKE AYAME.
HOW NICE...
A HUSBAND AND WIFE...
SO YOU NEED TO TAKE MY BLOOD, RIGHT?
I NEED A BLADE...
DO YOU PLAN TO SLIT YOUR WRIST EVERY TIME?

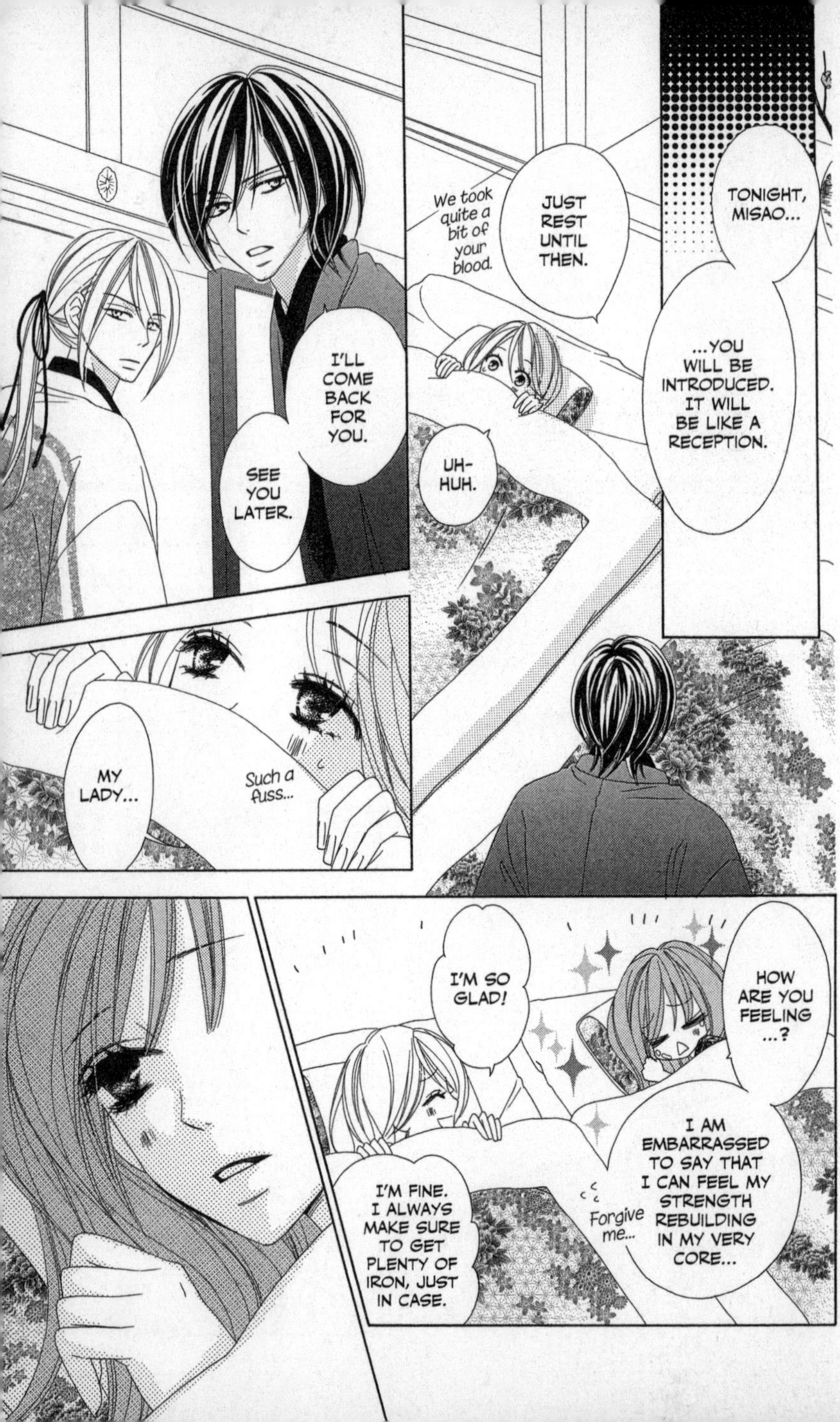
TONIGHT, MISAO...
...YOU WILL BE INTRODUCED. IT WILL BE LIKE A RECEPTION.
JUST REST UNTIL THEN.
We took quite a bit of your blood.
UH-HUH.
I'LL COME BACK FOR YOU.
SEE YOU LATER.
MY LADY...
Such a fuss...
HOW ARE YOU FEELING ...?
I'M SO GLAD!
I AM EMBARRASSED TO SAY THAT I CAN FEEL MY STRENGTH REBUILDING IN MY VERY CORE...
Forgive me...
I'M FINE. I ALWAYS MAKE SURE TO GET PLENTY OF IRON, JUST IN CASE.

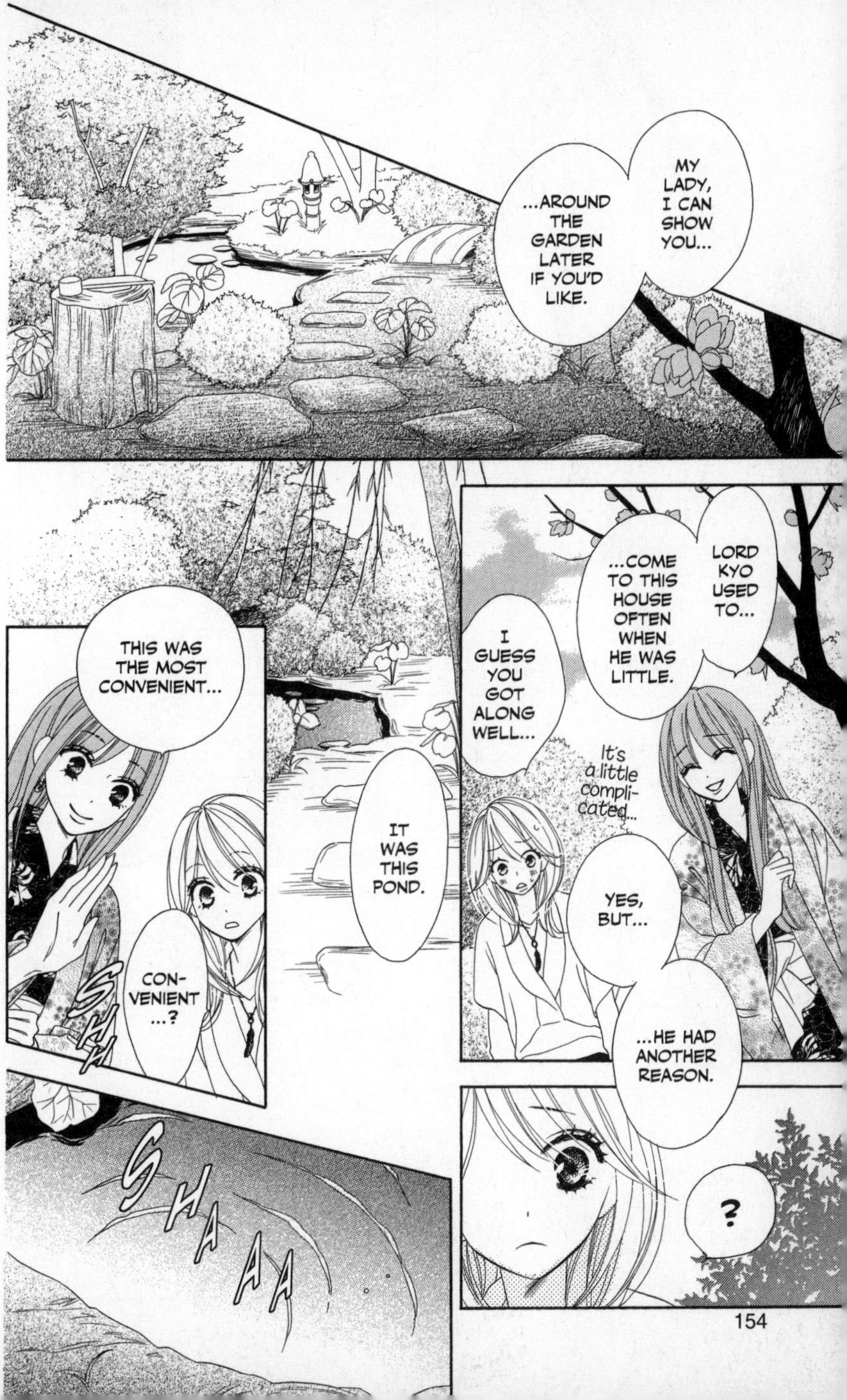
MY LADY, I CAN SHOW YOU...
...AROUND THE GARDEN LATER IF YOU'D LIKE.
LORD KYO USED TO...
...COME TO THIS HOUSE OFTEN WHEN HE WAS LITTLE.
I GUESS YOU GOT ALONG WELL...
It's a little compli-cated...
YES, BUT...
...HE HAD ANOTHER REASON.
?
IT WAS THIS POND.
THIS WAS THE MOST CONVENIENT...
CON-VENIENT...?
SHH
SHAAA

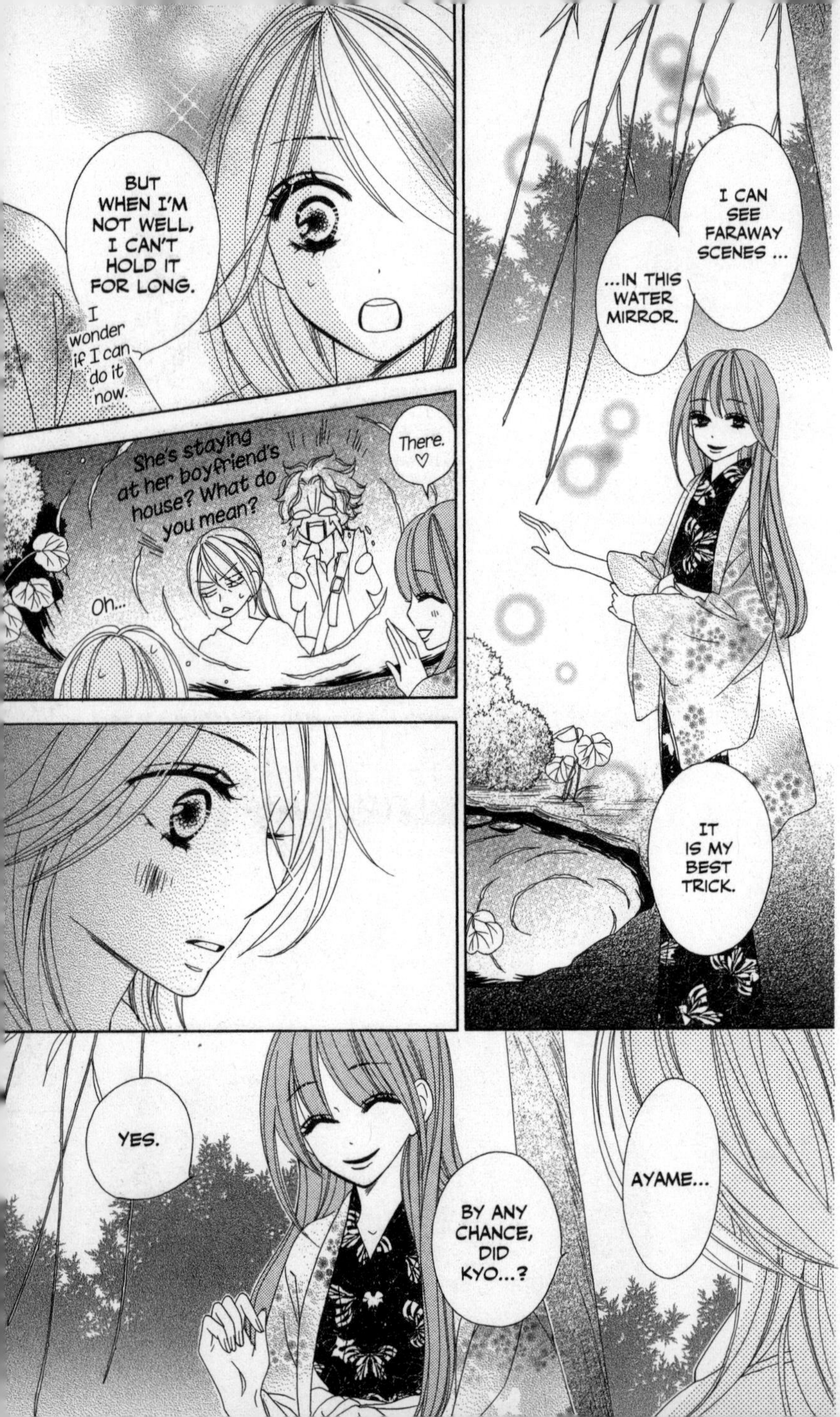
I CAN SEE FARAWAY SCENES ...
...IN THIS WATER MIRROR.
IT IS MY BEST TRICK.
BUT WHEN I'M NOT WELL, I CAN'T HOLD IT FOR LONG.
I wonder if I can do it now.
There. ♥
She's staying at her boyfriend's house? What do you mean?
Oh...
AYAME...
BY ANY CHANCE, DID KYO...?
YES.

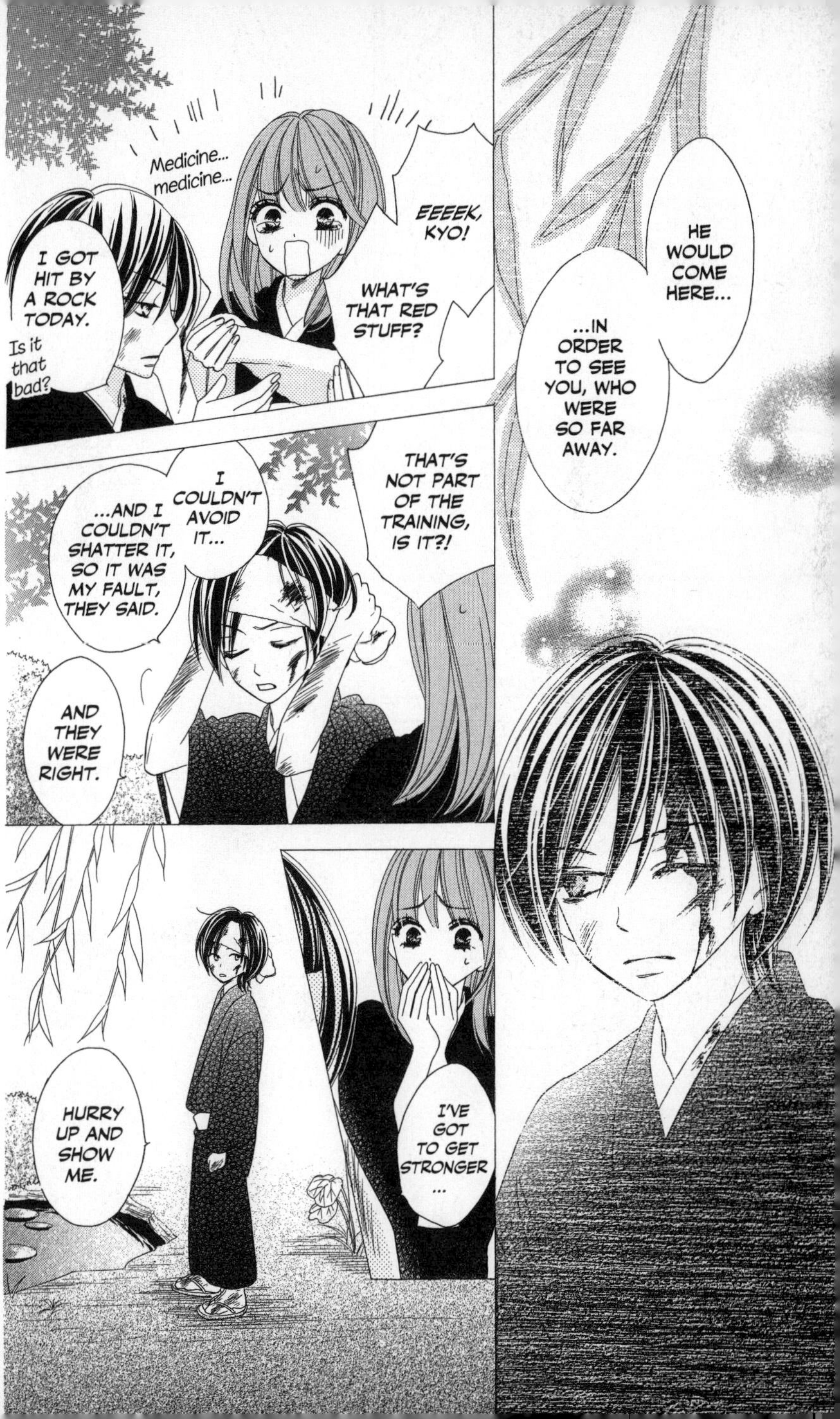
HE WOULD COME HERE...
...IN ORDER TO SEE YOU, WHO WERE SO FAR AWAY.
EEEEK, KYO!
WHAT'S THAT RED STUFF?
Medicine... medicine...
I GOT HIT BY A ROCK TODAY.
Is it that bad?
THAT'S NOT PART OF THE TRAINING, IS IT?!
I COULDN'T AVOID IT...
...AND I COULDN'T SHATTER IT, SO IT WAS MY FAULT, THEY SAID.
AND THEY WERE RIGHT.
I'VE GOT TO GET STRONGER...
HURRY UP AND SHOW ME.

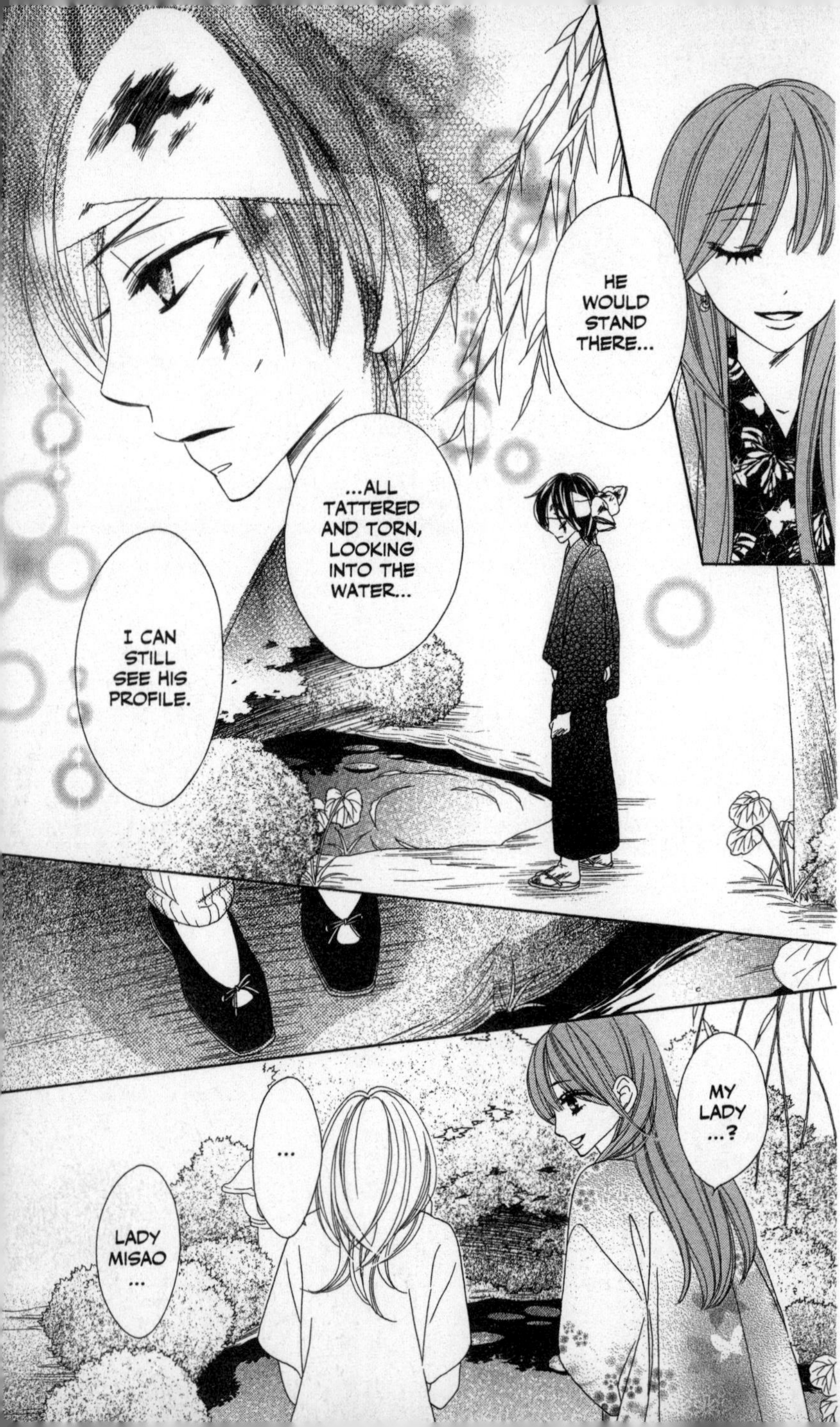
HE WOULD STAND THERE...
...ALL TATTERED AND TORN, LOOKING INTO THE WATER...
I CAN STILL SEE HIS PROFILE.
MY LADY ...?
...
LADY MISAO ...

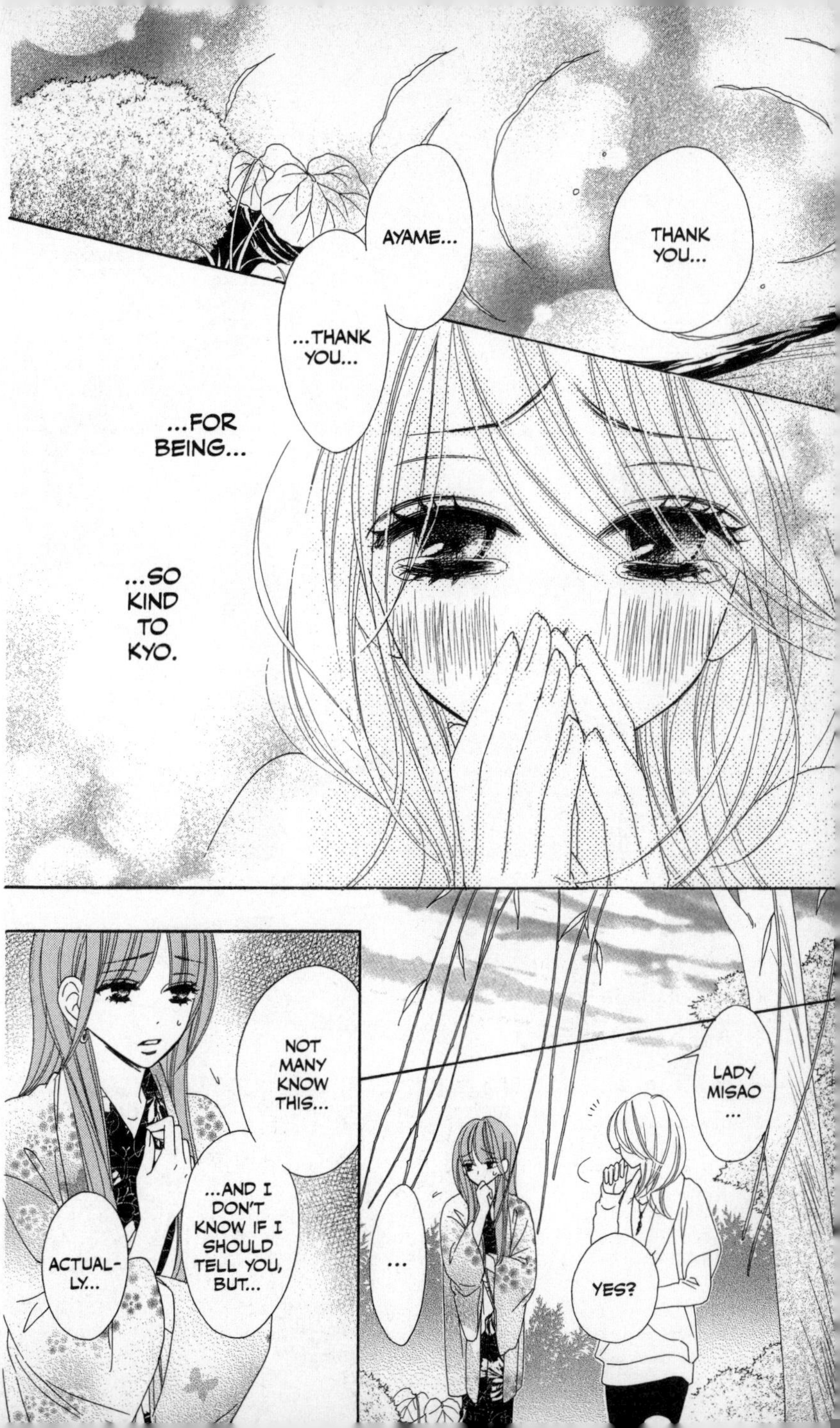
THANK YOU...
AYAME...
...THANK YOU...
...FOR BEING...
...SO KIND TO KYO.
LADY MISAO...
YES?
...
NOT MANY KNOW THIS...
...AND I DON'T KNOW IF I SHOULD TELL YOU, BUT...
ACTUAL-LY...

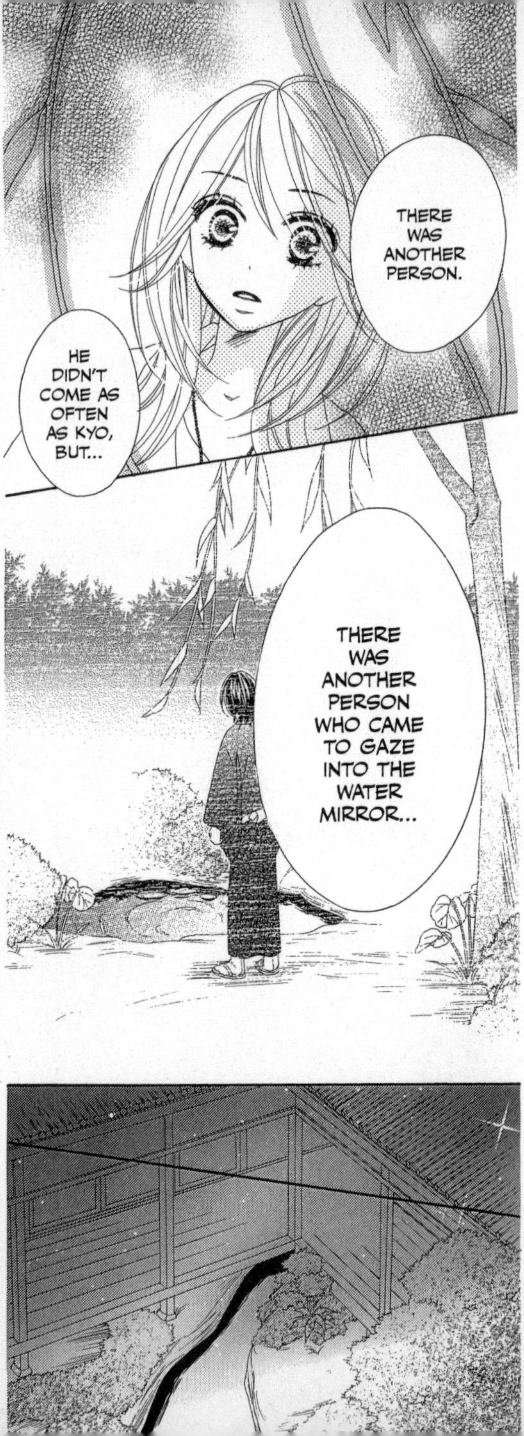
THERE WAS ANOTHER PERSON.
HE DIDN'T COME AS OFTEN AS KYO, BUT...
THERE WAS ANOTHER PERSON WHO CAME TO GAZE INTO THE WATER MIRROR...

Character Introduction

Ayame Usui
age: 23 height: 162 cm

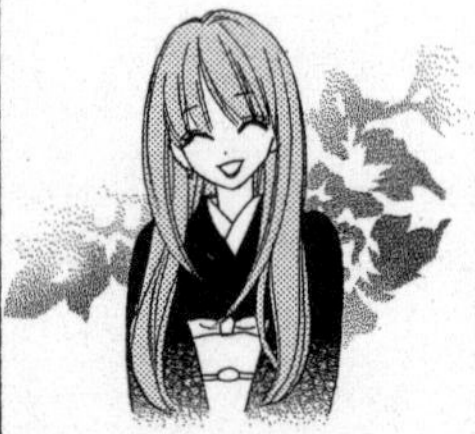

When I planned the characters, Sagami was supposed to be a married man. From time to time I made mention of someone back home being unwell and he was sent home periodically. Here, for the first time, I've been able to bring his wife into the story.

I enjoy drawing characters as honest as Ayame. Of course, there are those who said it was a surprise that she was Sagami's wife, but I love this sort of couple.

There were some who noticed that the two shared a pair of earrings. Thank you very much.

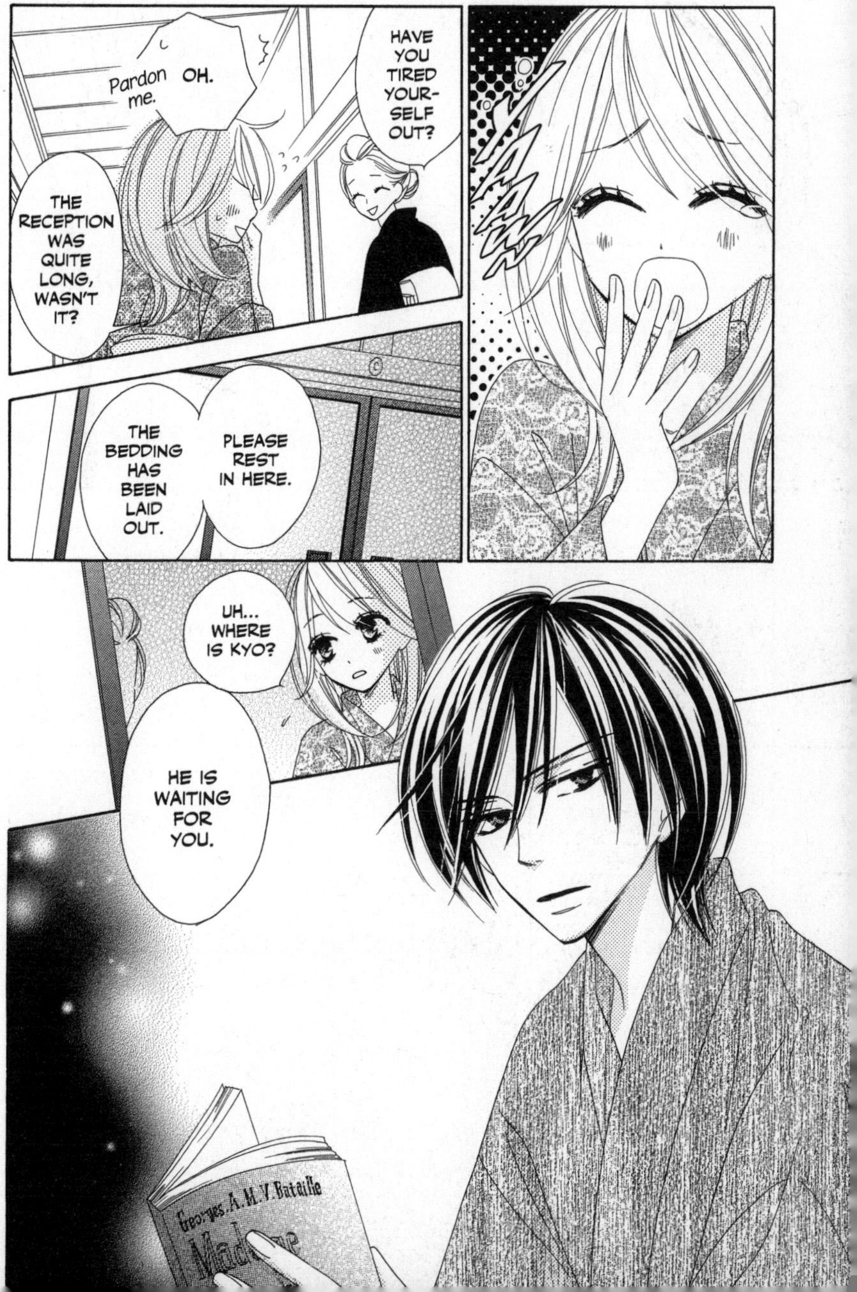
HAVE YOU TIRED YOURSELF OUT?
OH.
Pardon me.
THE RECEPTION WAS QUITE LONG, WASN'T IT?
PLEASE REST IN HERE.
THE BEDDING HAS BEEN LAID OUT.
UH... WHERE IS KYO?
HE IS WAITING FOR YOU.

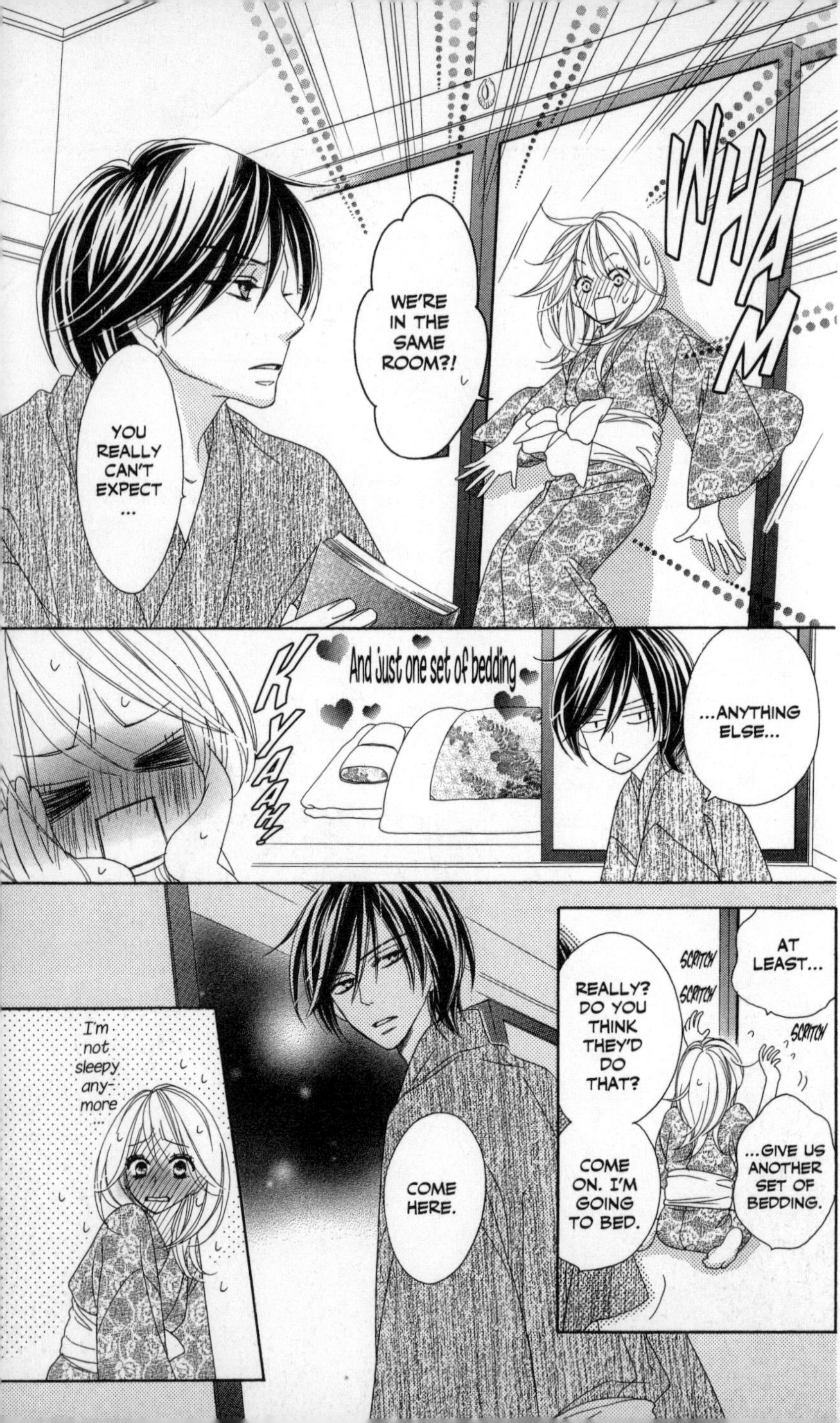
WHAM
WE'RE IN THE SAME ROOM?!
YOU REALLY CAN'T EXPECT ...
...ANYTHING ELSE...
And just one set of bedding
KYAAAH!
AT LEAST...
SCRITCH
SCRITCH
SCRITCH
...GIVE US ANOTHER SET OF BEDDING.
REALLY? DO YOU THINK THEY'D DO THAT?
COME ON. I'M GOING TO BED.
COME HERE.
I'm not sleepy any-more ...

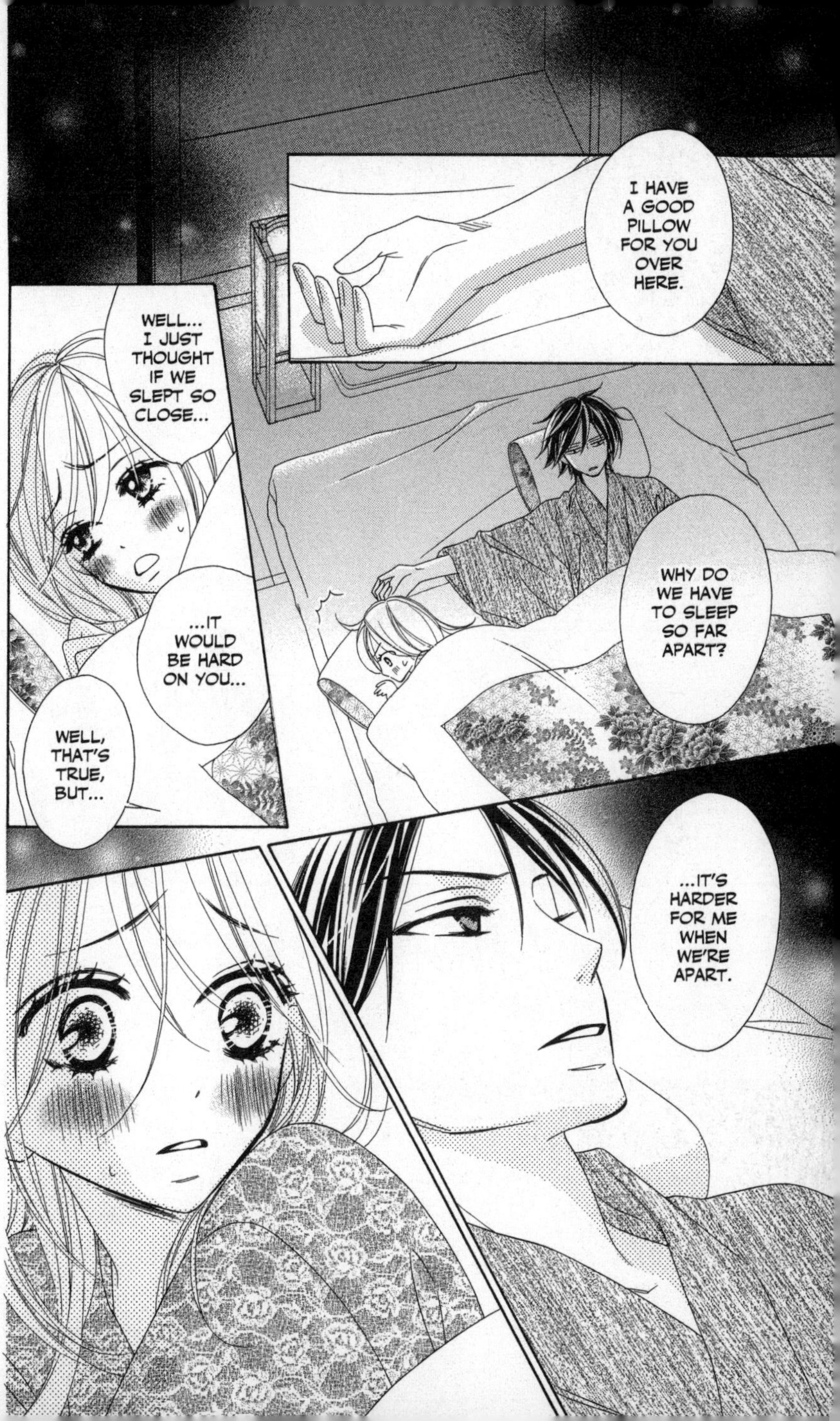
I HAVE A GOOD PILLOW FOR YOU OVER HERE.
WHY DO WE HAVE TO SLEEP SO FAR APART?
WELL... I JUST THOUGHT IF WE SLEPT SO CLOSE...
...IT WOULD BE HARD ON YOU...
WELL, THAT'S TRUE, BUT...
...IT'S HARDER FOR ME WHEN WE'RE APART.

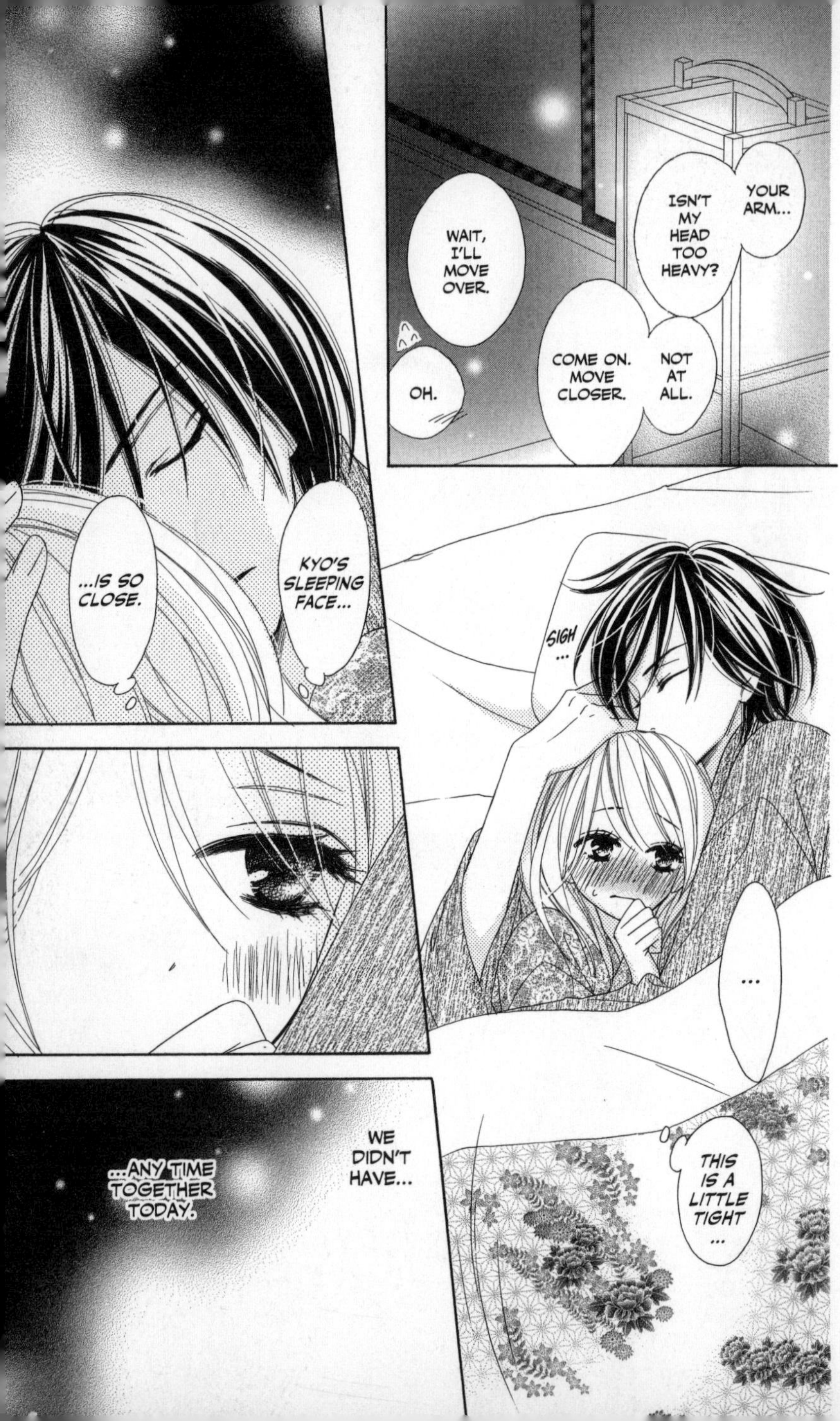
YOUR ARM...
ISN'T MY HEAD TOO HEAVY?
NOT AT ALL.
COME ON. MOVE CLOSER.
WAIT, I'LL MOVE OVER.
OH.
KYO'S SLEEPING FACE...
...IS SO CLOSE.
SIGH...
...
THIS IS A LITTLE TIGHT...
WE DIDN'T HAVE...
...ANY TIME TOGETHER TODAY.

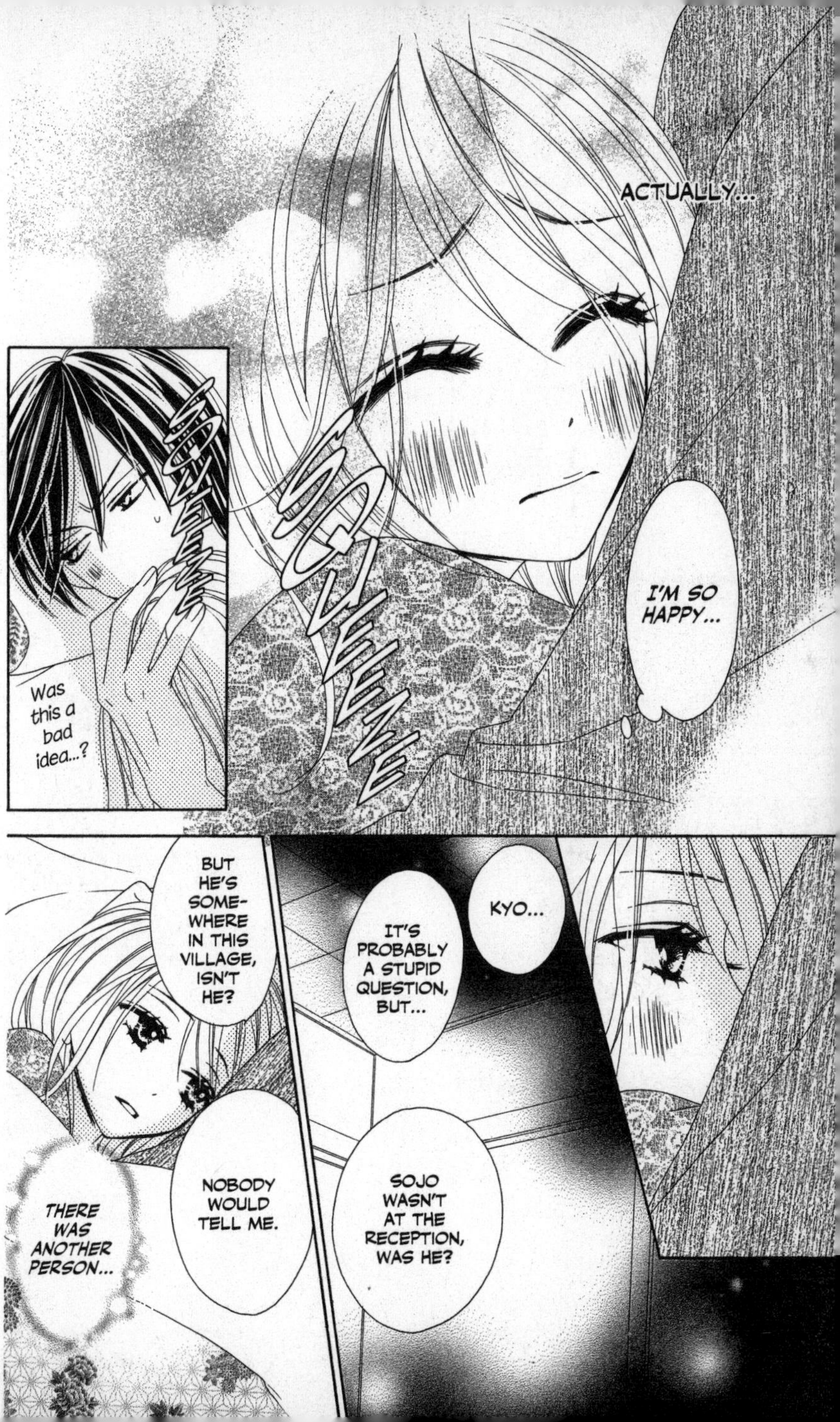
ACTUALLY...
I'M SO HAPPY...
Was this a bad idea...?
KYO...
IT'S PROBABLY A STUPID QUESTION, BUT...
SOJO WASN'T AT THE RECEPTION, WAS HE?
BUT HE'S SOME-WHERE IN THIS VILLAGE, ISN'T HE?
NOBODY WOULD TELL ME.
THERE WAS ANOTHER PERSON...

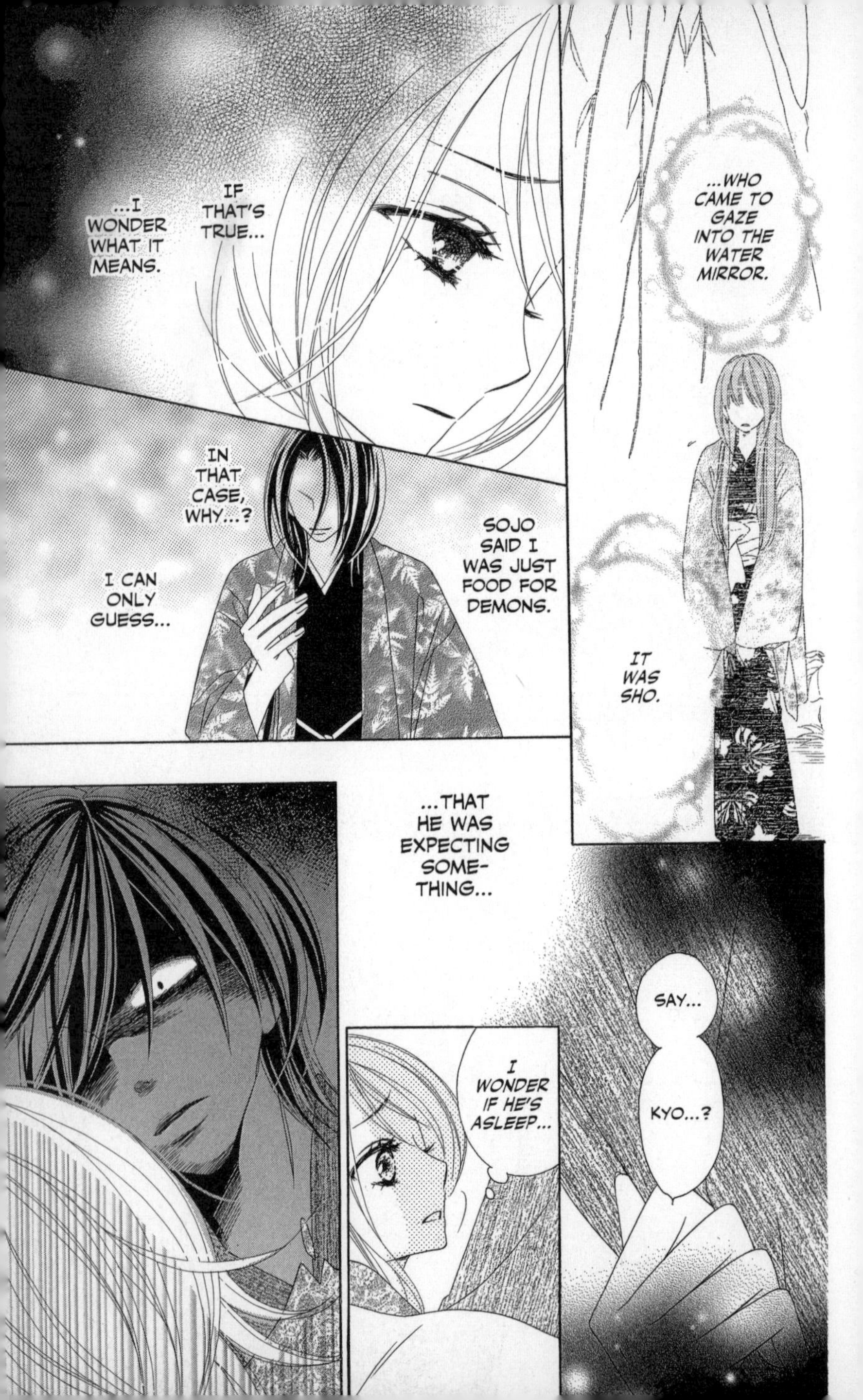
...WHO CAME TO GAZE INTO THE WATER MIRROR.
IT WAS SHO.
IF THAT'S TRUE...
...I WONDER WHAT IT MEANS.
SOJO SAID I WAS JUST FOOD FOR DEMONS.
IN THAT CASE, WHY...?
I CAN ONLY GUESS...
...THAT HE WAS EXPECTING SOME-THING...
SAY...
KYO...?
I WONDER IF HE'S ASLEEP...

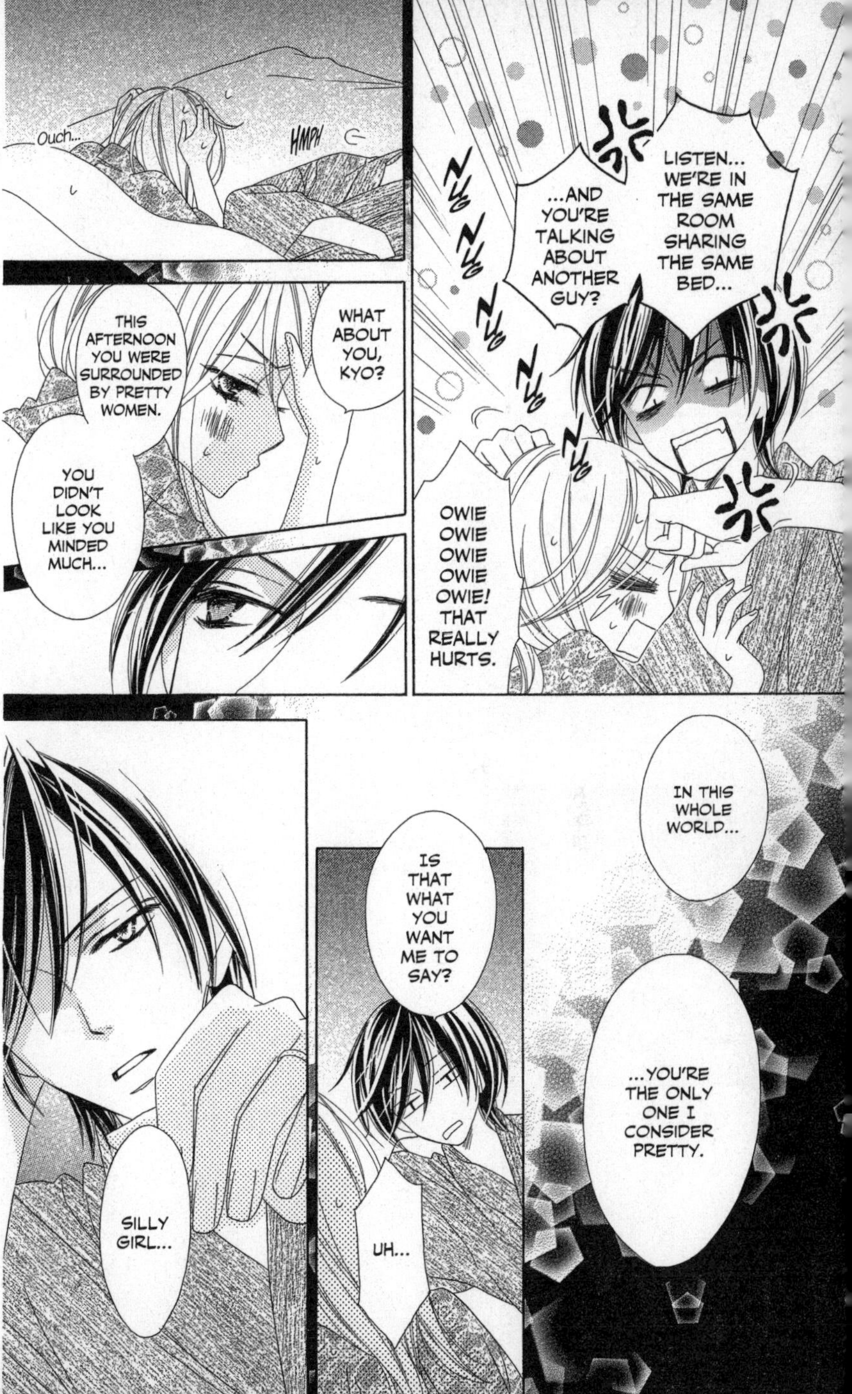
LISTEN... WE'RE IN THE SAME ROOM SHARING THE SAME BED...
...AND YOU'RE TALKING ABOUT ANOTHER GUY?
NUG NUG NUG NUG NUG NUG
OWIE OWIE OWIE OWIE OWIE! THAT REALLY HURTS.
Ouch...
HMPH
WHAT ABOUT YOU, KYO?
THIS AFTERNOON YOU WERE SURROUNDED BY PRETTY WOMEN.
YOU DIDN'T LOOK LIKE YOU MINDED MUCH...
IN THIS WHOLE WORLD...
...YOU'RE THE ONLY ONE I CONSIDER PRETTY.
IS THAT WHAT YOU WANT ME TO SAY?
UH...
SILLY GIRL...

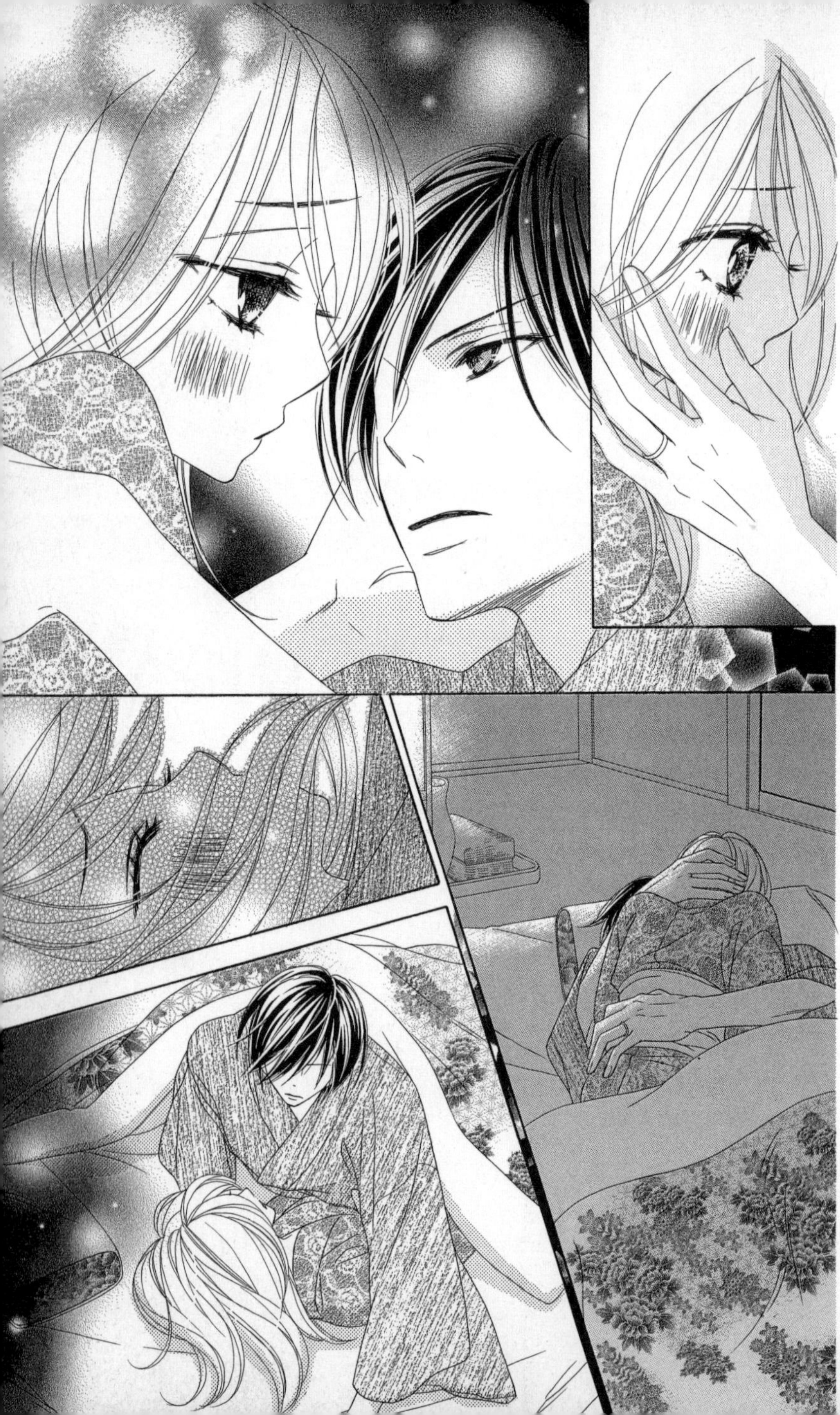

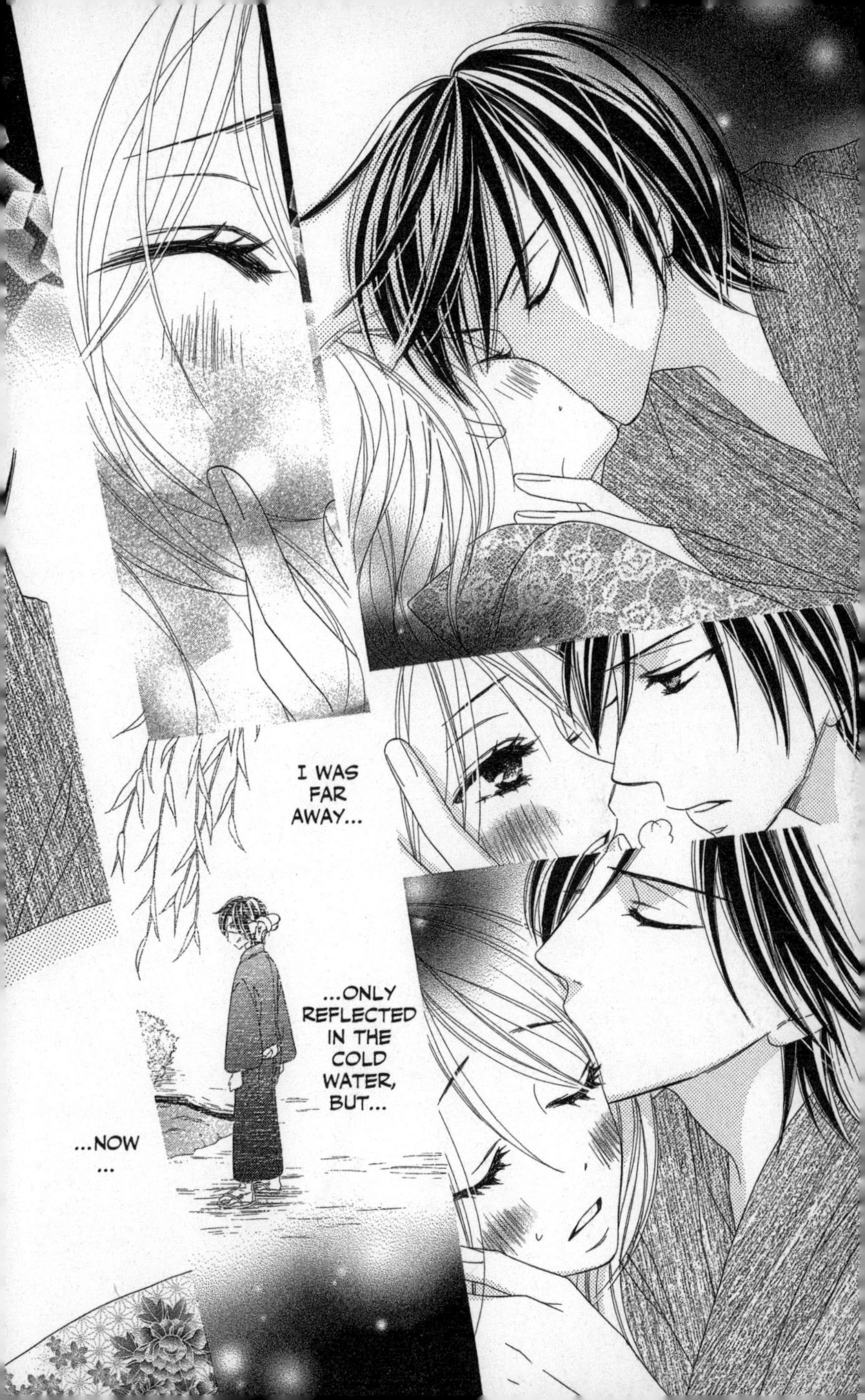
I WAS FAR AWAY...
...ONLY REFLECTED IN THE COLD WATER, BUT...
...NOW ...

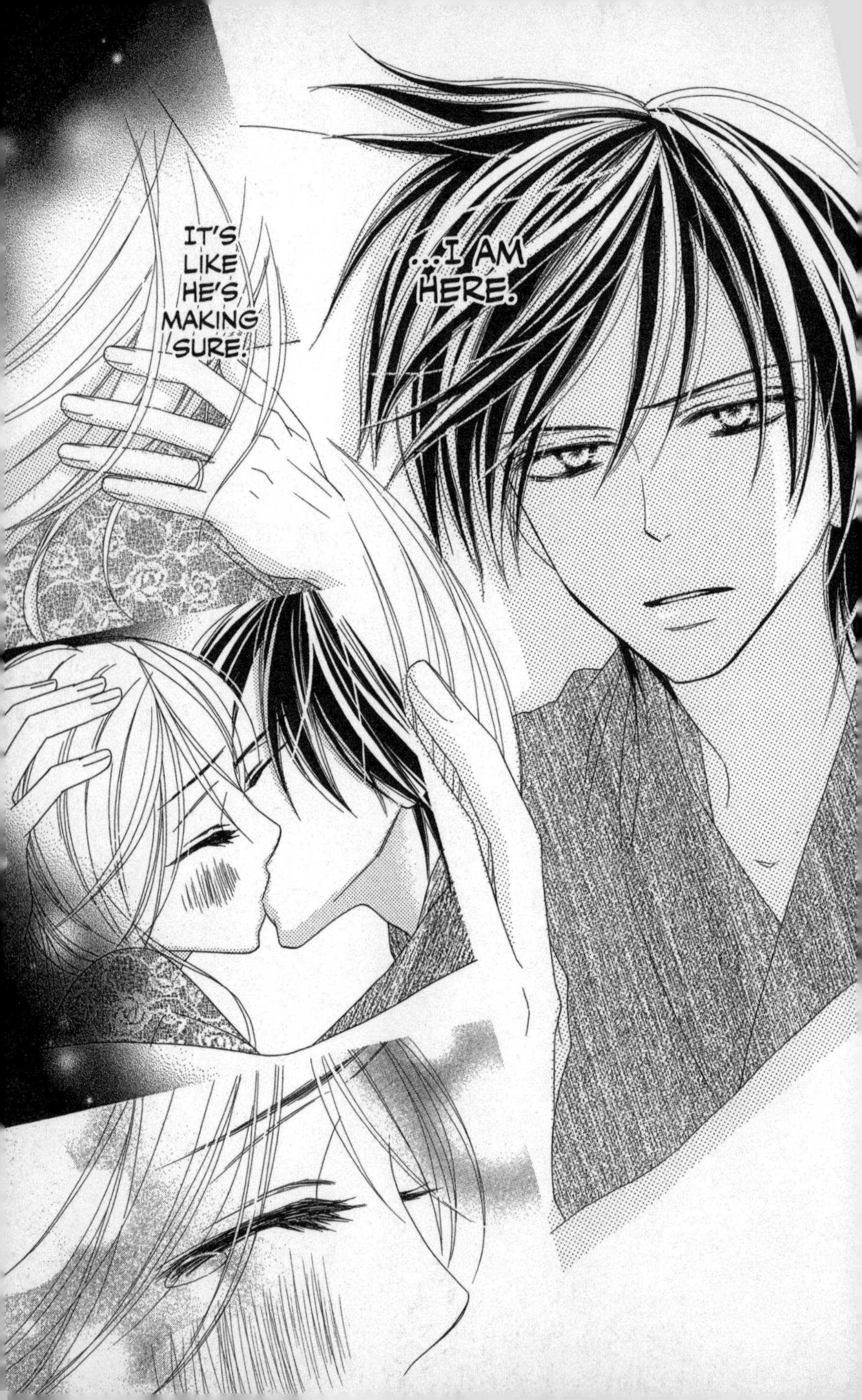
...I AM HERE.
IT'S LIKE HE'S MAKING SURE.

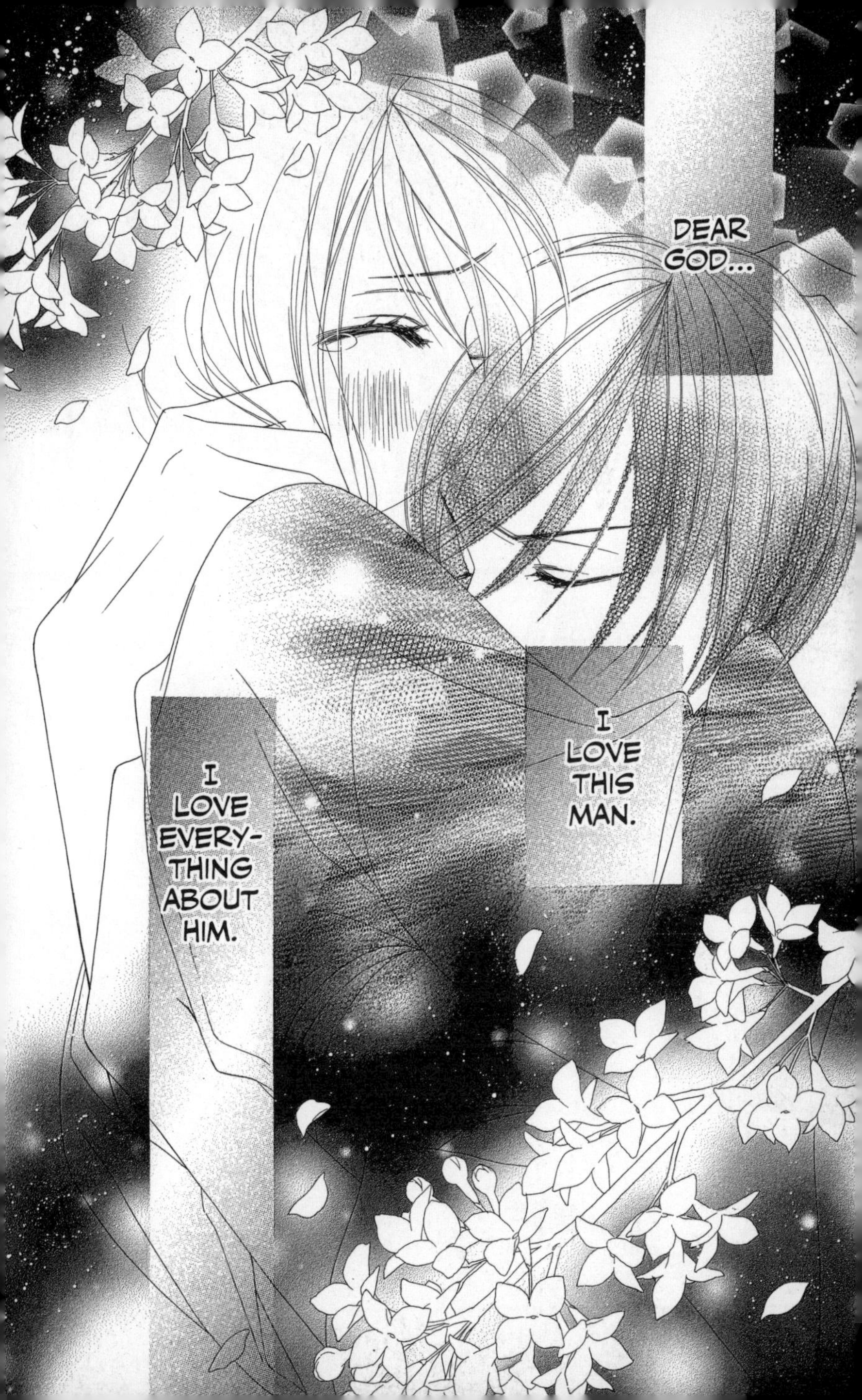
DEAR GOD...
I LOVE THIS MAN.
I LOVE EVERY-THING ABOUT HIM.

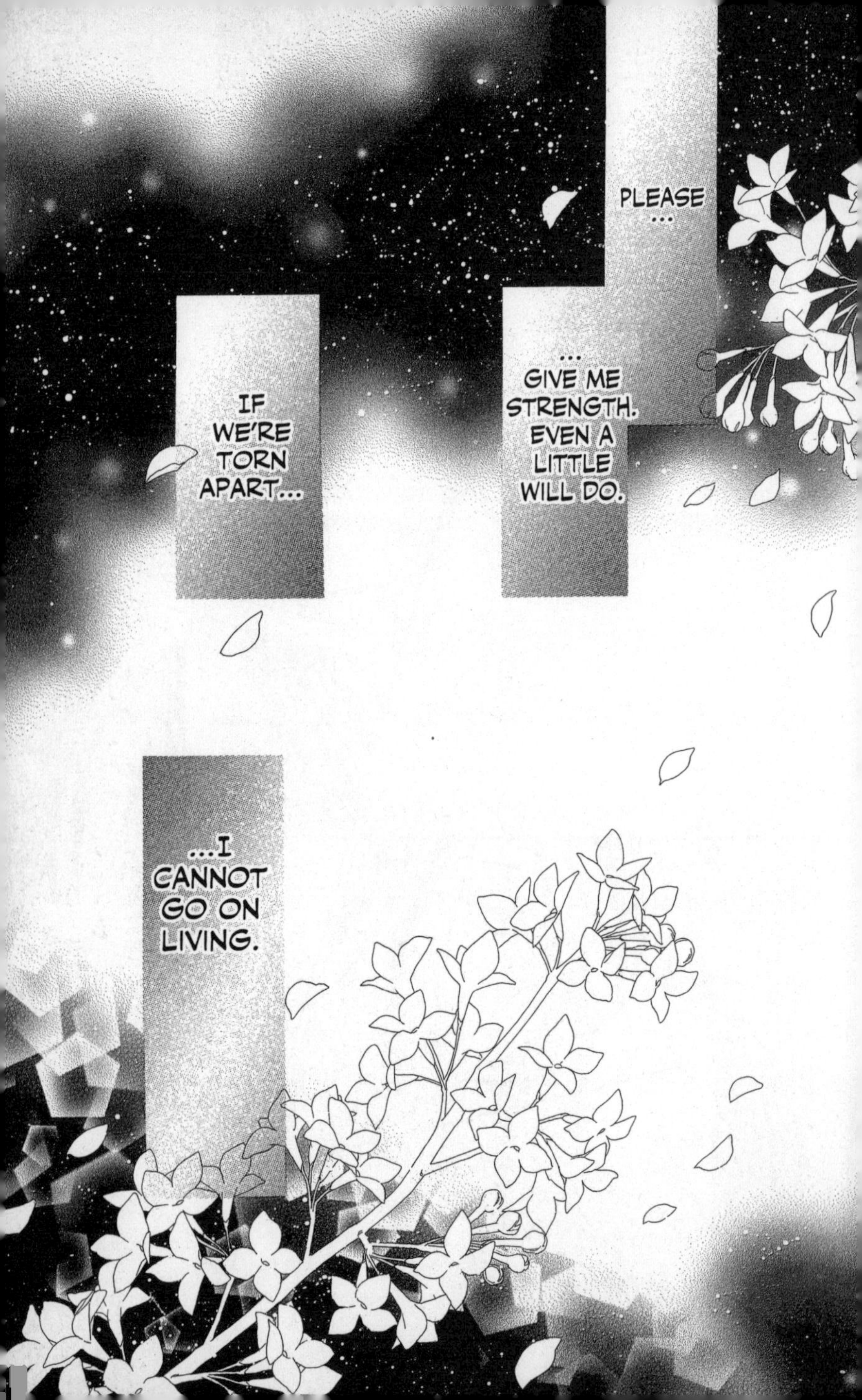
PLEASE ...
... GIVE ME STRENGTH. EVEN A LITTLE WILL DO.
IF WE'RE TORN APART...
...I CANNOT GO ON LIVING.

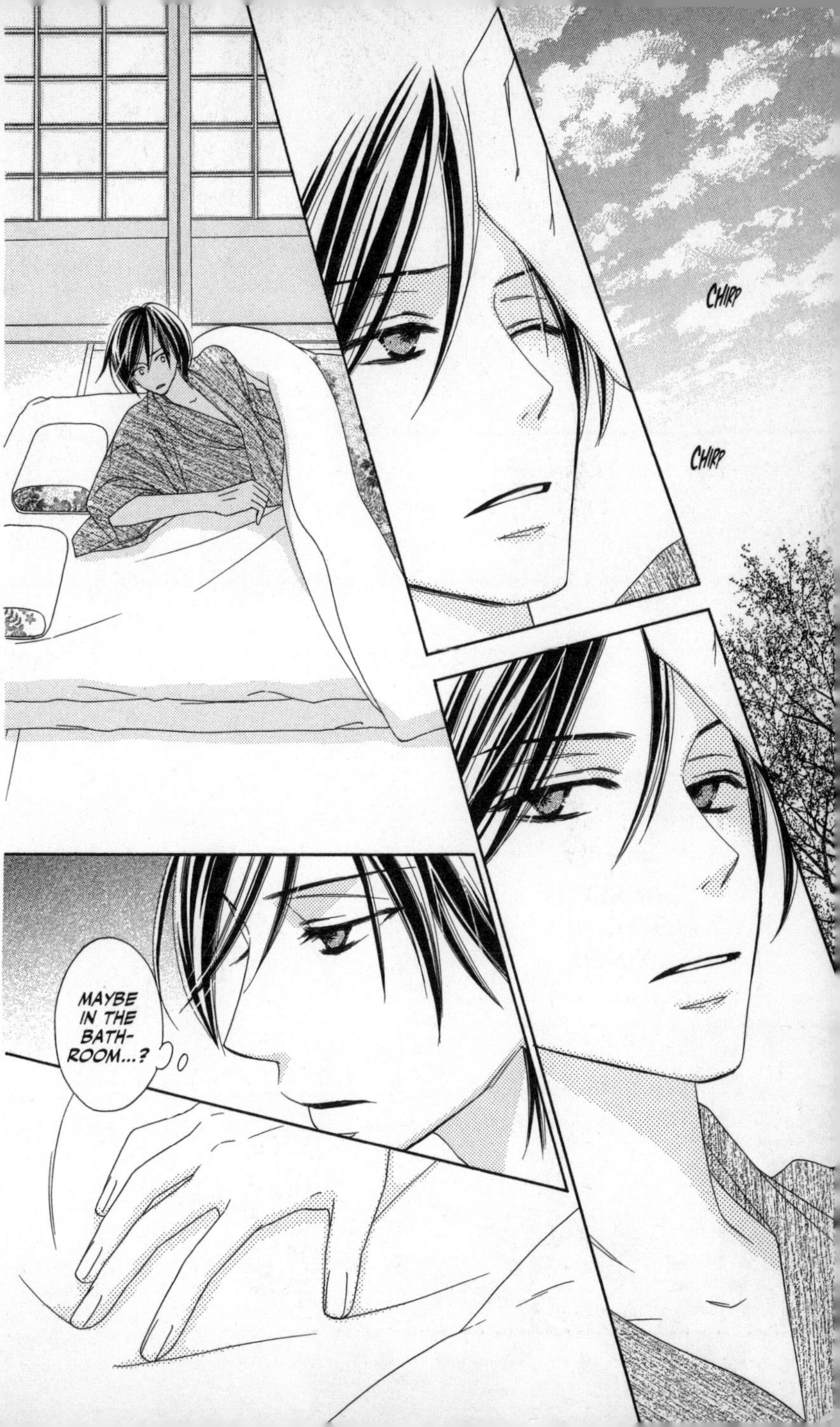
CHIRP
CHIRP
MAYBE IN THE BATH-ROOM...?

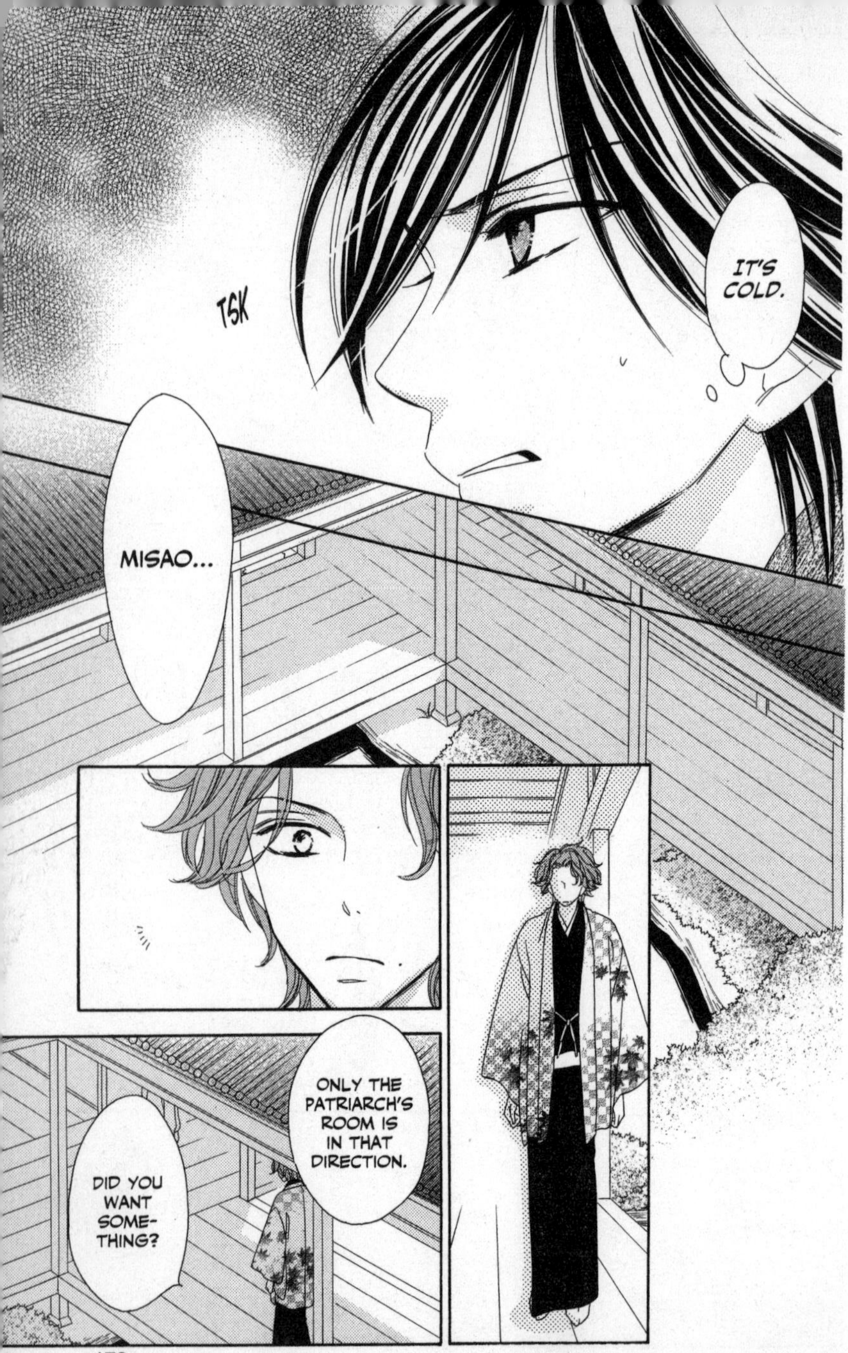
IT'S COLD.
TSK
MISAO...
ONLY THE PATRIARCH'S ROOM IS IN THAT DIRECTION.
DID YOU WANT SOME-THING?

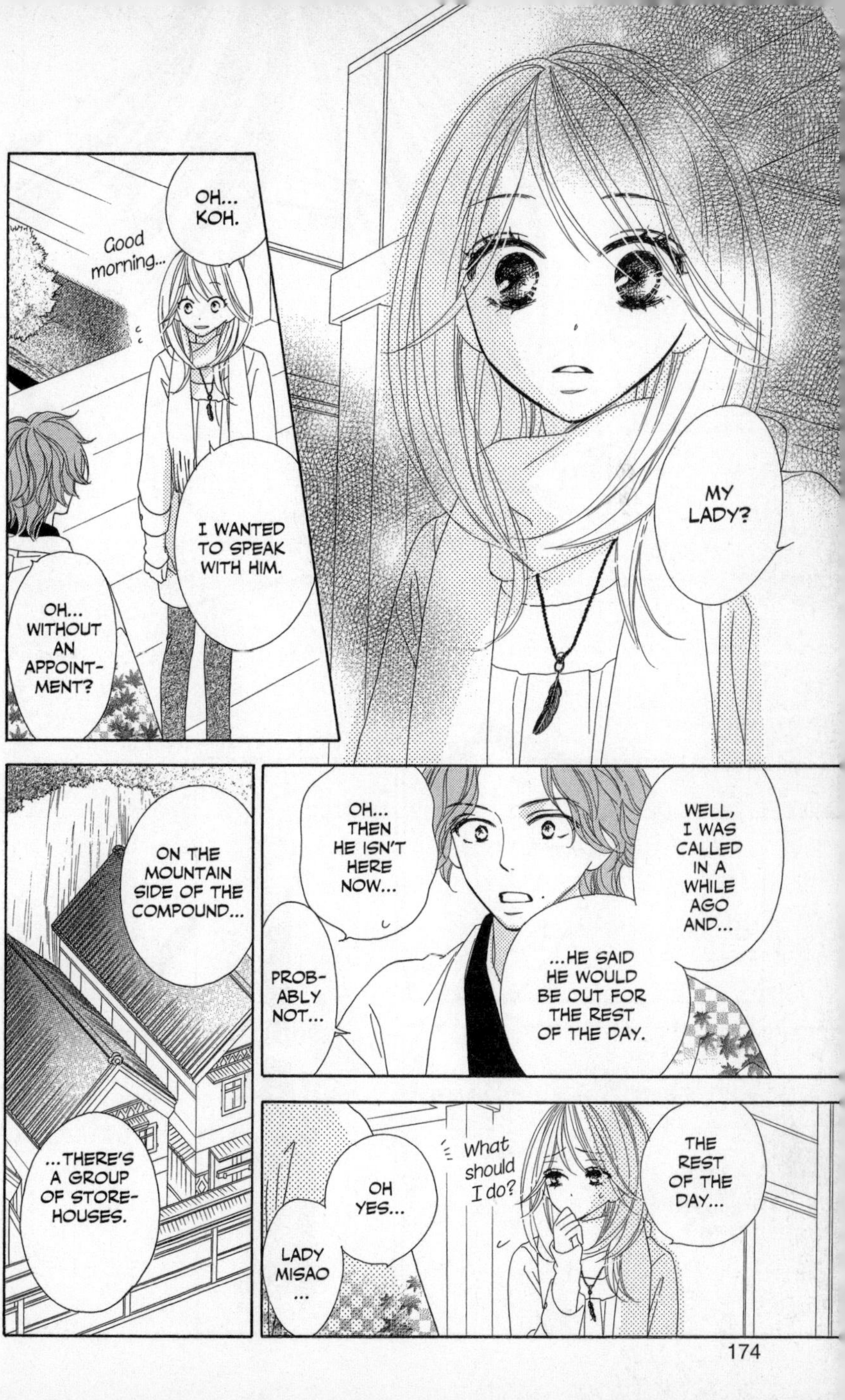
MY LADY?
OH... KOH.
Good morning...
I WANTED TO SPEAK WITH HIM.
OH... WITHOUT AN APPOINT-MENT?
WELL, I WAS CALLED IN A WHILE AGO AND...
...HE SAID HE WOULD BE OUT FOR THE REST OF THE DAY.
OH... THEN HE ISN'T HERE NOW...
PROB-ABLY NOT...
THE REST OF THE DAY...
What should I do?
OH YES...
LADY MISAO ...
ON THE MOUNTAIN SIDE OF THE COMPOUND...
...THERE'S A GROUP OF STORE-HOUSES.

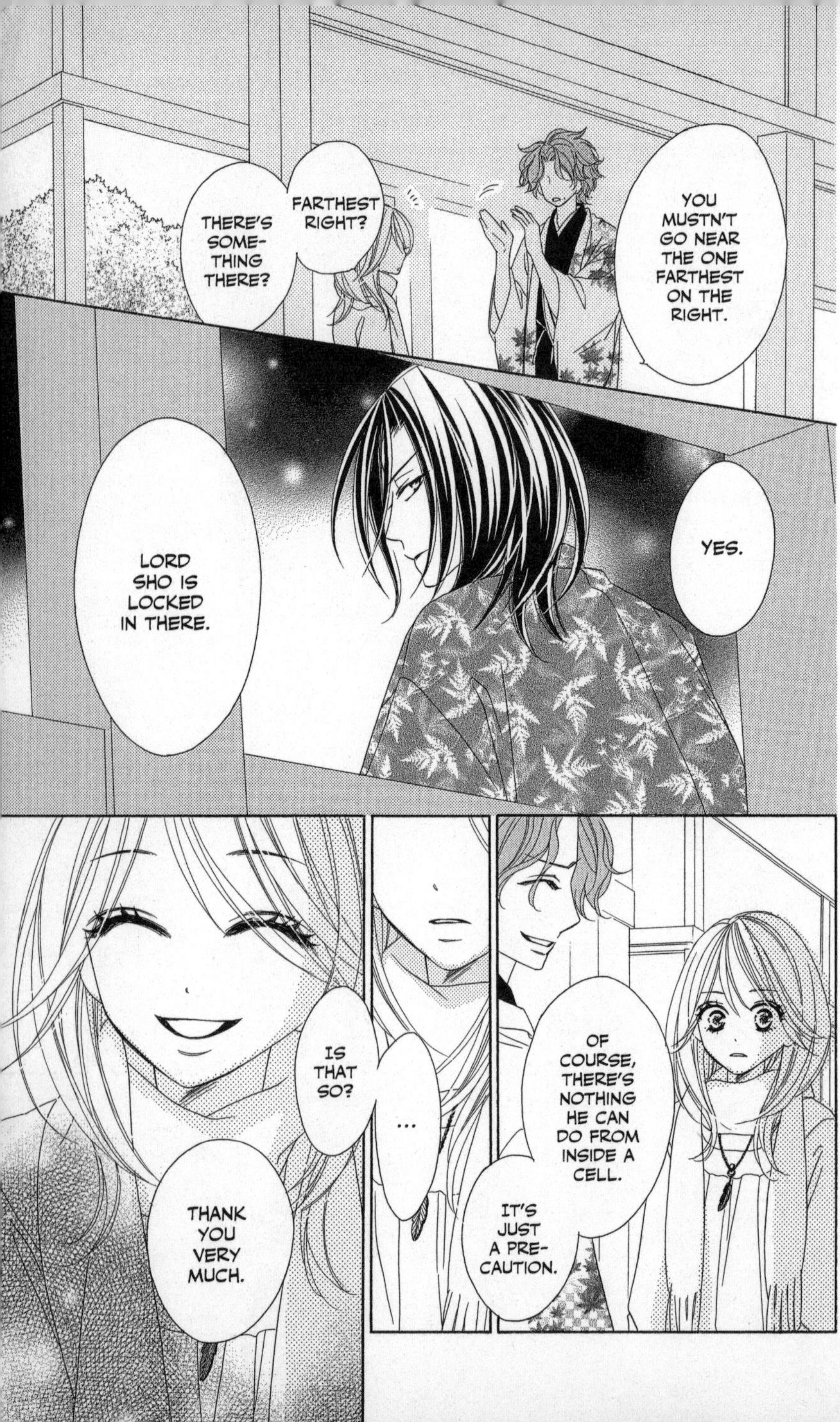
YOU MUSTN'T GO NEAR THE ONE FARTHEST ON THE RIGHT.
FARTHEST RIGHT?
THERE'S SOME-THING THERE?
YES.
LORD SHO IS LOCKED IN THERE.
OF COURSE, THERE'S NOTHING HE CAN DO FROM INSIDE A CELL.
IT'S JUST A PRE-CAUTION.
...
IS THAT SO?
THANK YOU VERY MUCH.

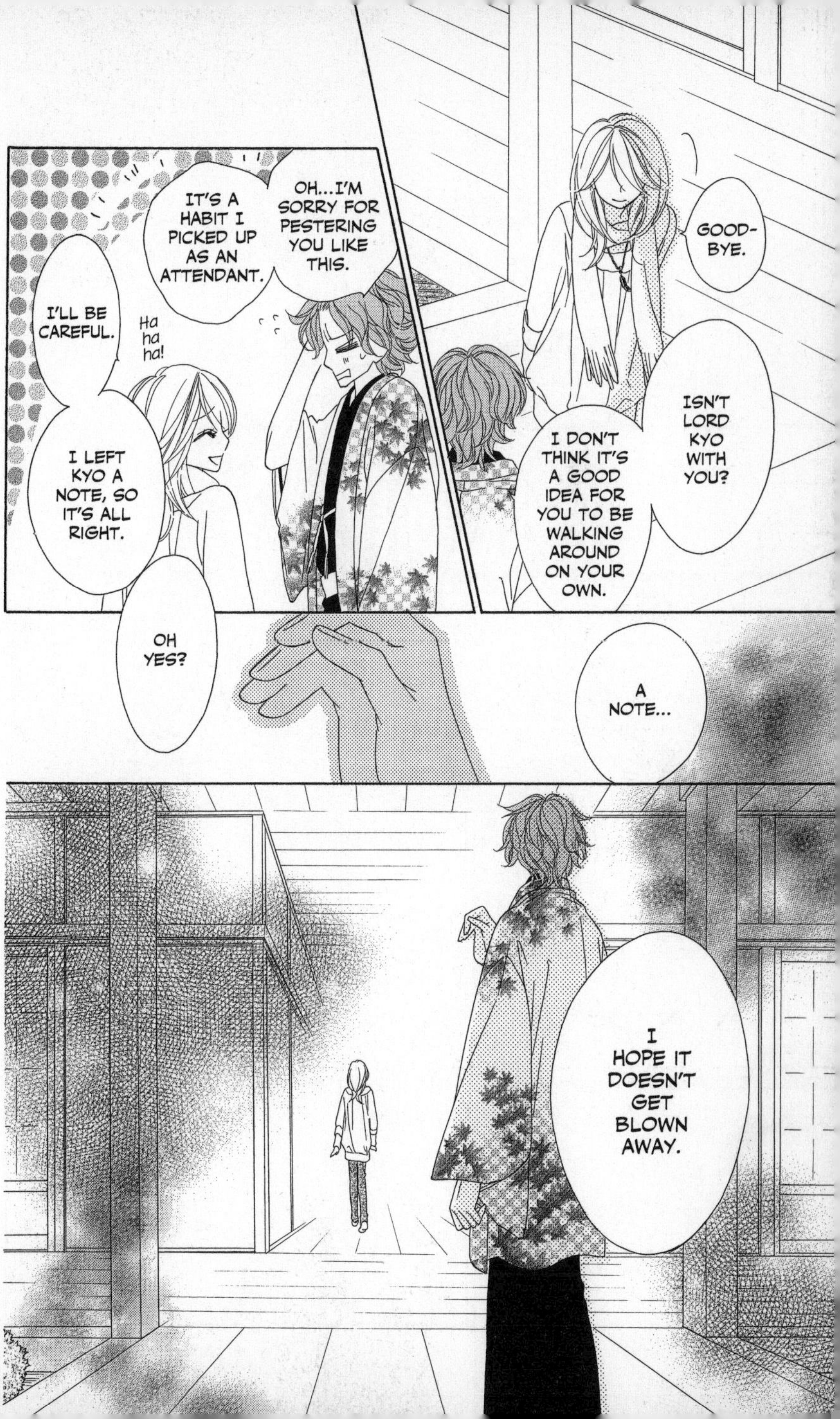
GOOD-BYE.
ISN'T LORD KYO WITH YOU?
I DON'T THINK IT'S A GOOD IDEA FOR YOU TO BE WALKING AROUND ON YOUR OWN.
OH...I'M SORRY FOR PESTERING YOU LIKE THIS.
IT'S A HABIT I PICKED UP AS AN ATTENDANT.
I'LL BE CAREFUL.
Ha ha ha!
I LEFT KYO A NOTE, SO IT'S ALL RIGHT.
OH YES?
A NOTE...
I HOPE IT DOESN'T GET BLOWN AWAY.

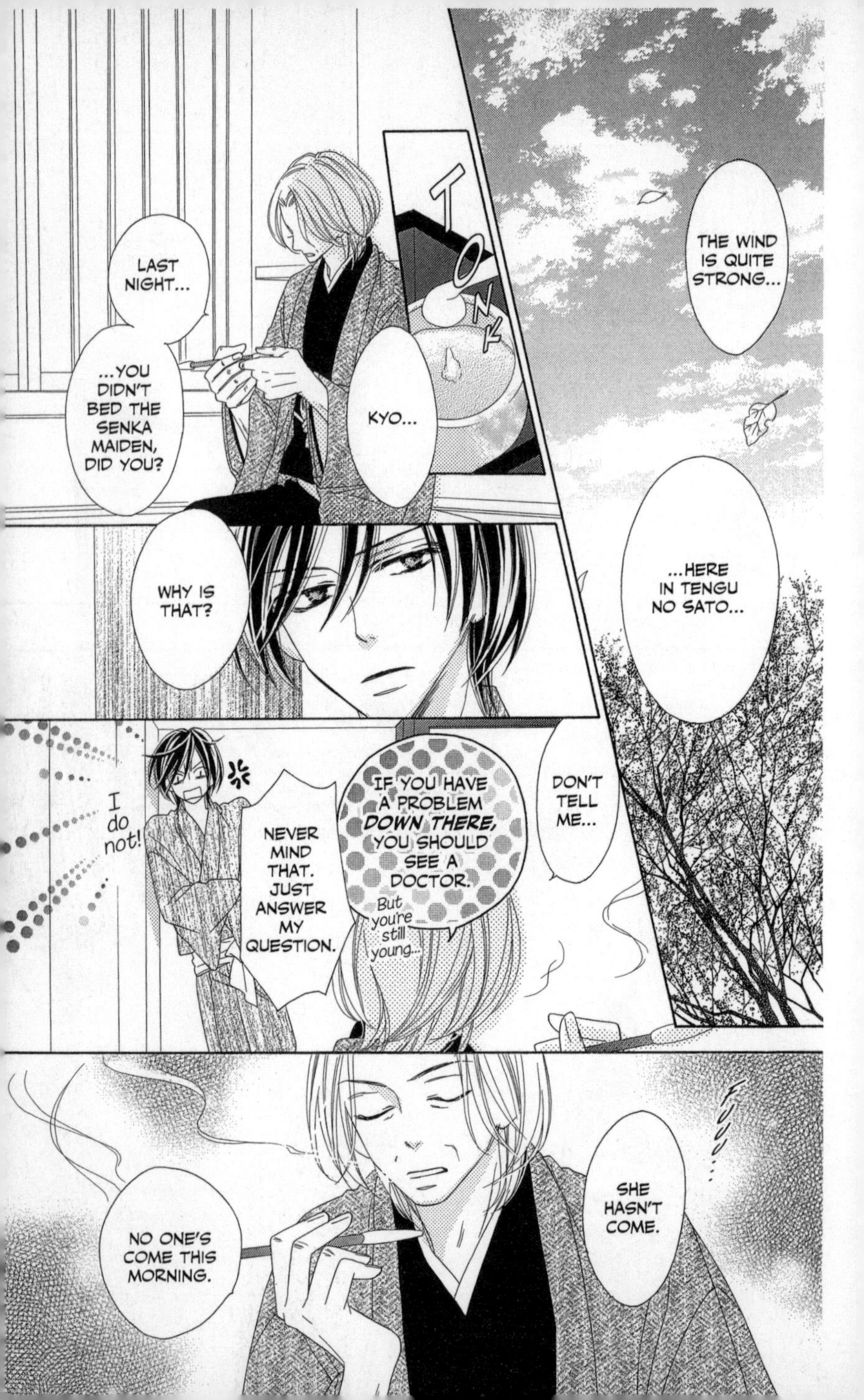
THE WIND IS QUITE STRONG...
...HERE IN TENGU NO SATO...
TONK
KYO...
LAST NIGHT...
...YOU DIDN'T BED THE SENKA MAIDEN, DID YOU?
WHY IS THAT?
DON'T TELL ME...
IF YOU HAVE A PROBLEM *DOWN THERE,* YOU SHOULD SEE A DOCTOR.
But you're still young...
NEVER MIND THAT. JUST ANSWER MY QUESTION.
I do not!
FUUU...
SHE HASN'T COME.
NO ONE'S COME THIS MORNING.

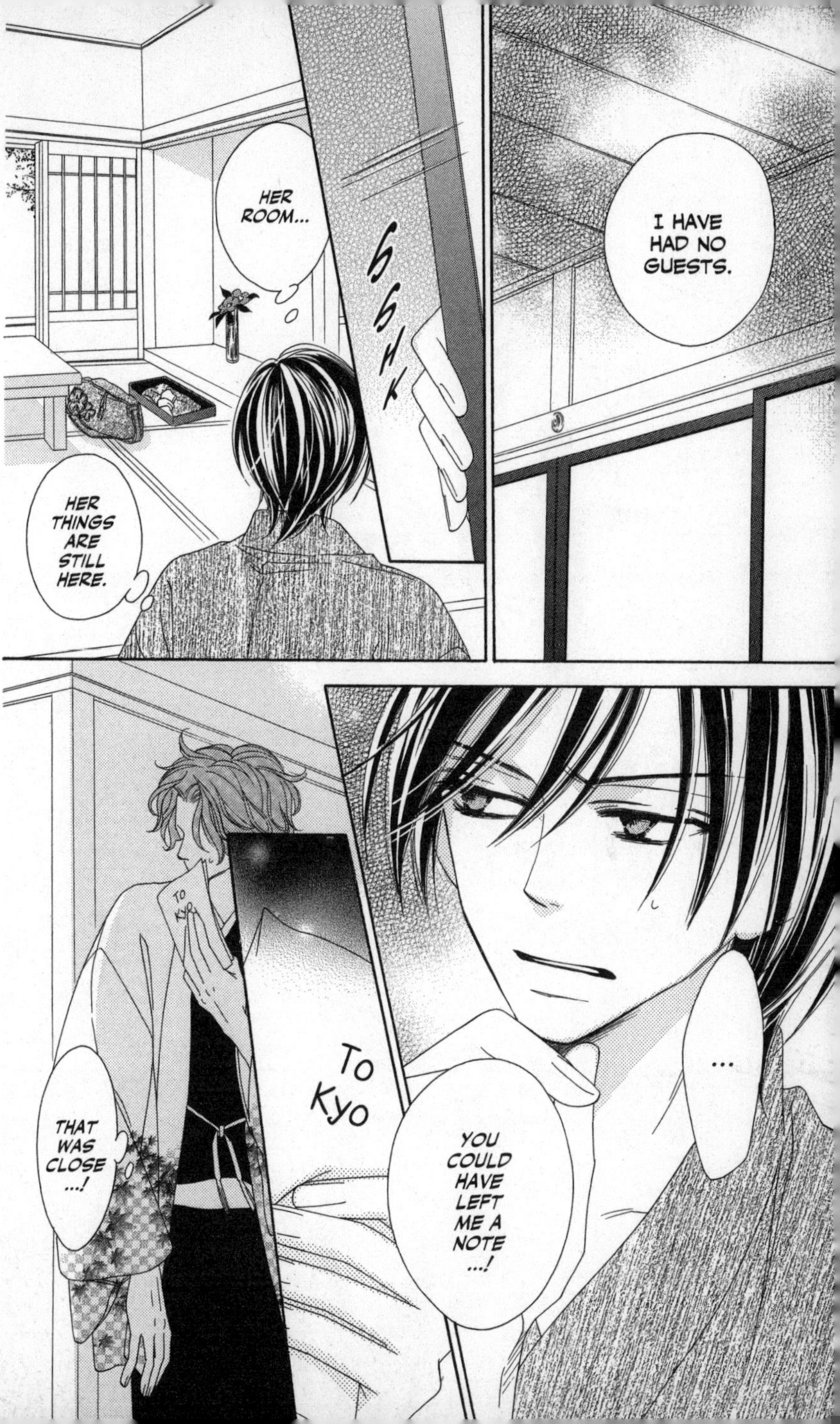
I HAVE HAD NO GUESTS.
SSHK
HER ROOM...
HER THINGS ARE STILL HERE.
...
To Kyo
YOU COULD HAVE LEFT ME A NOTE ...!
THAT WAS CLOSE ...!

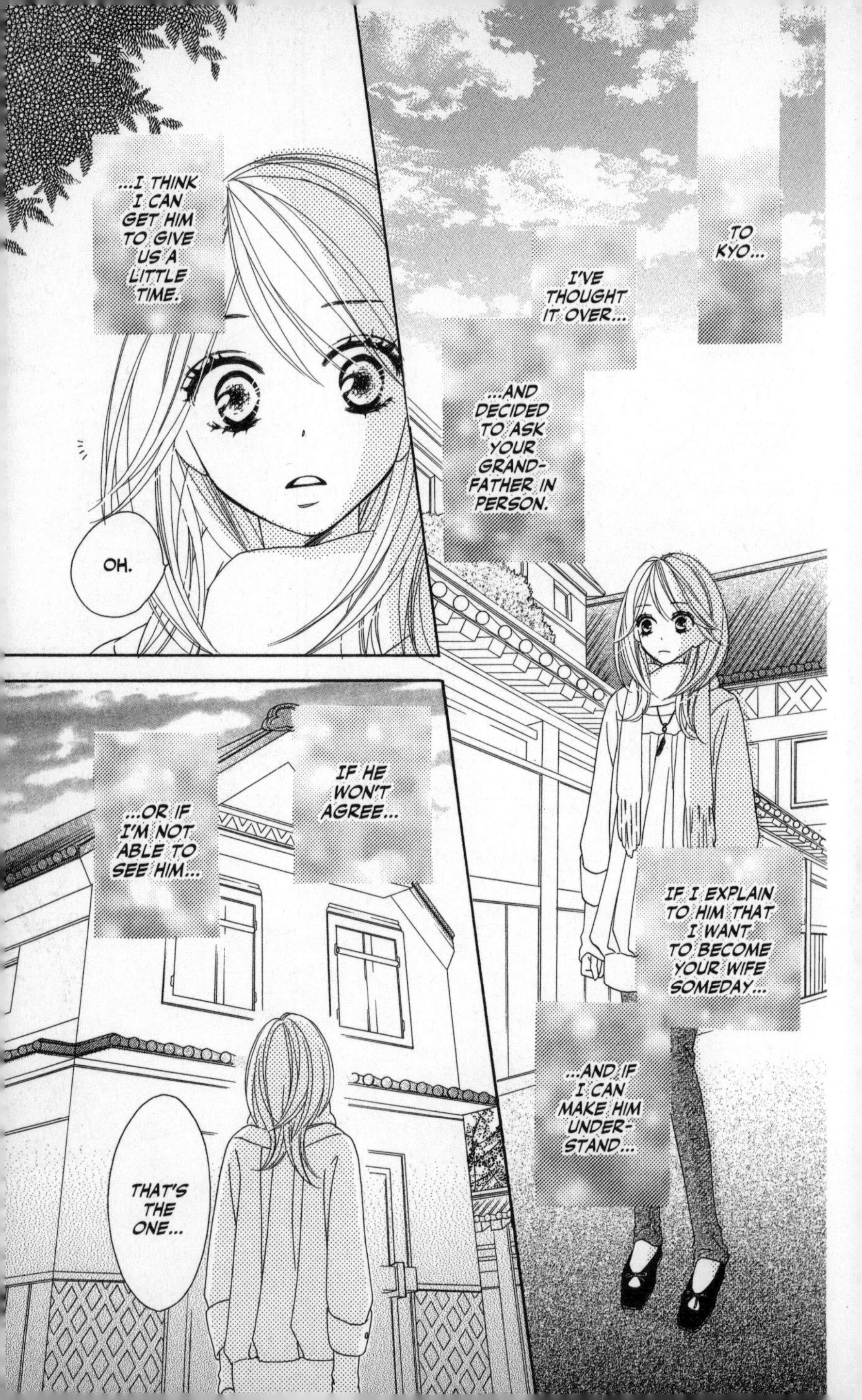
TO KYO...
I'VE THOUGHT IT OVER...
...AND DECIDED TO ASK YOUR GRANDFATHER IN PERSON.
IF I EXPLAIN TO HIM THAT I WANT TO BECOME YOUR WIFE SOMEDAY...
...AND IF I CAN MAKE HIM UNDER-STAND...
...I THINK I CAN GET HIM TO GIVE US A LITTLE TIME.
OH.
IF HE WON'T AGREE...
...OR IF I'M NOT ABLE TO SEE HIM...
THAT'S THE ONE...

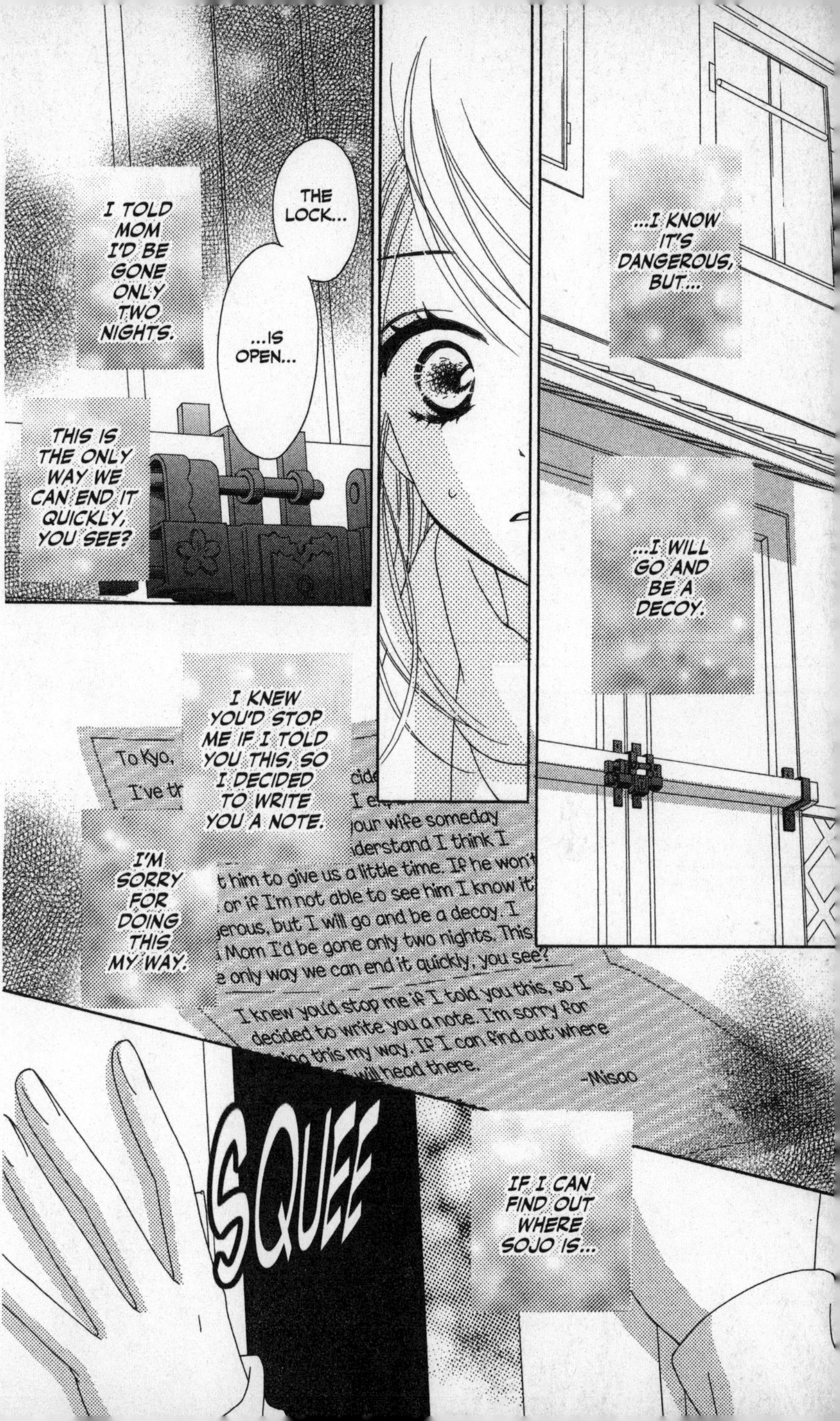
...I KNOW IT'S DANGEROUS, BUT...
...I WILL GO AND BE A DECOY.
THE LOCK...
...IS OPEN...
I TOLD MOM I'D BE GONE ONLY TWO NIGHTS.
THIS IS THE ONLY WAY WE CAN END IT QUICKLY, YOU SEE?
I KNEW YOU'D STOP ME IF I TOLD YOU THIS, SO I DECIDED TO WRITE YOU A NOTE.
I'M SORRY FOR DOING THIS MY WAY.
To Kyo,
I've tr
your wife someday
derstand I think I
t him to give us a little time. If he won't
or if I'm not able to see him I know it
gerous, but I will go and be a decoy. I
Mom I'd be gone only two nights. This
e only way we can end it quickly, you see?
I knew you'd stop me if I told you this, so I
decided to write you a note. I'm sorry for
this my way. If I can find out where
will head there.
-Misao
SQUEE
IF I CAN FIND OUT WHERE SOJO IS...

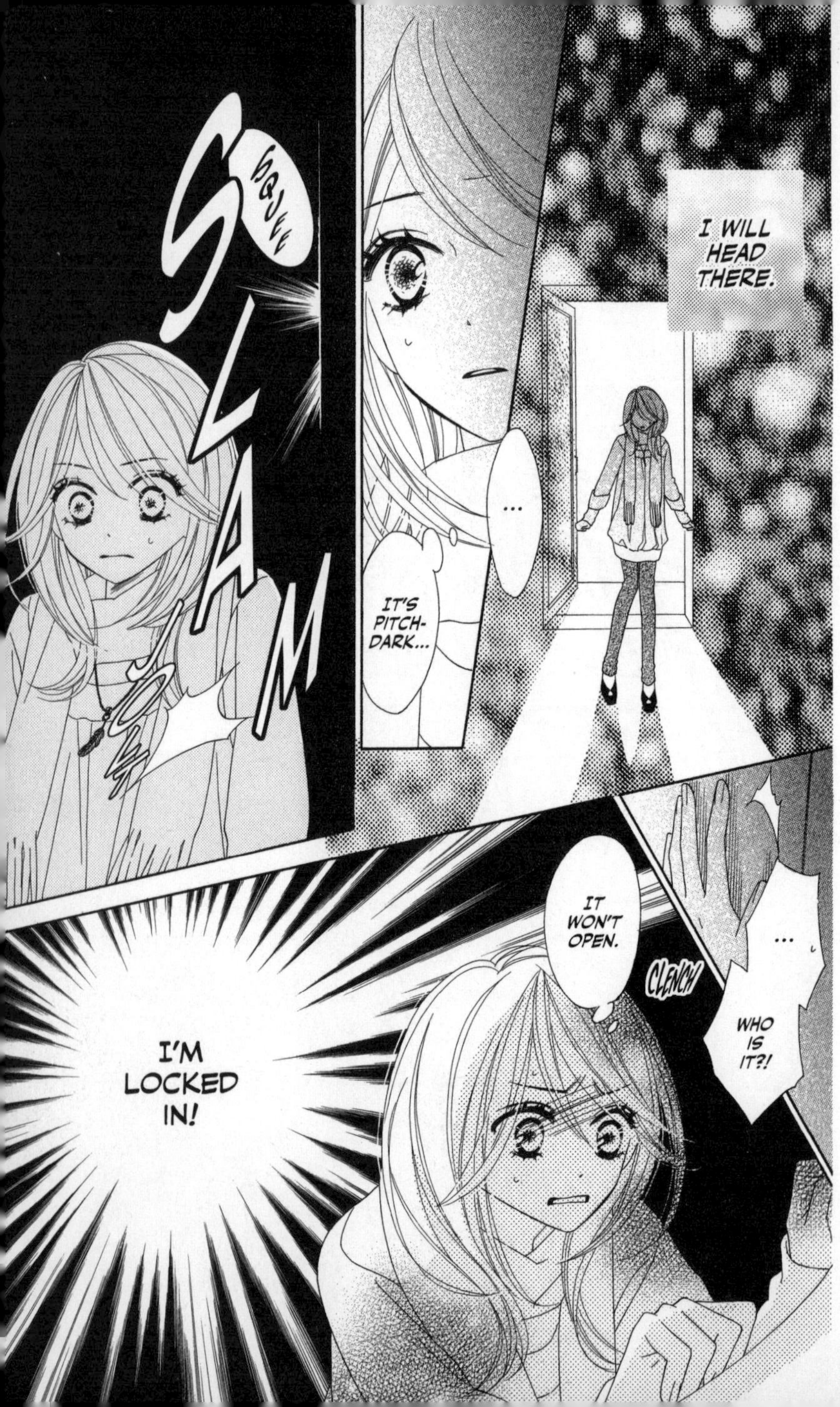
I WILL HEAD THERE.
...
IT'S PITCH-DARK...
SQUEE
SLAM
...
WHO IS IT?!
CLENCH
IT WON'T OPEN.
I'M LOCKED IN!

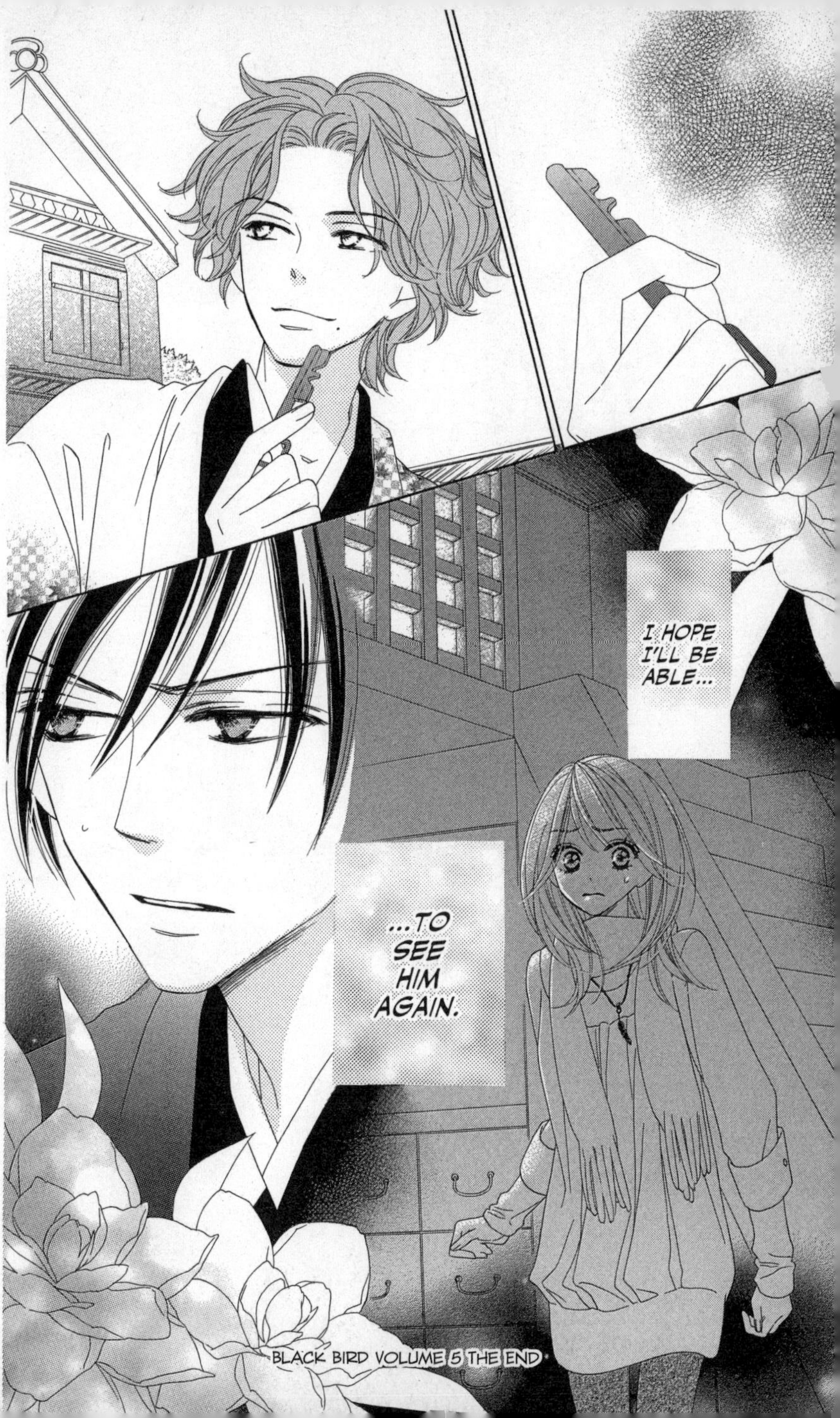
I HOPE I'LL BE ABLE...
...TO SEE HIM AGAIN.
BLACK BIRD VOLUME 5 THE END

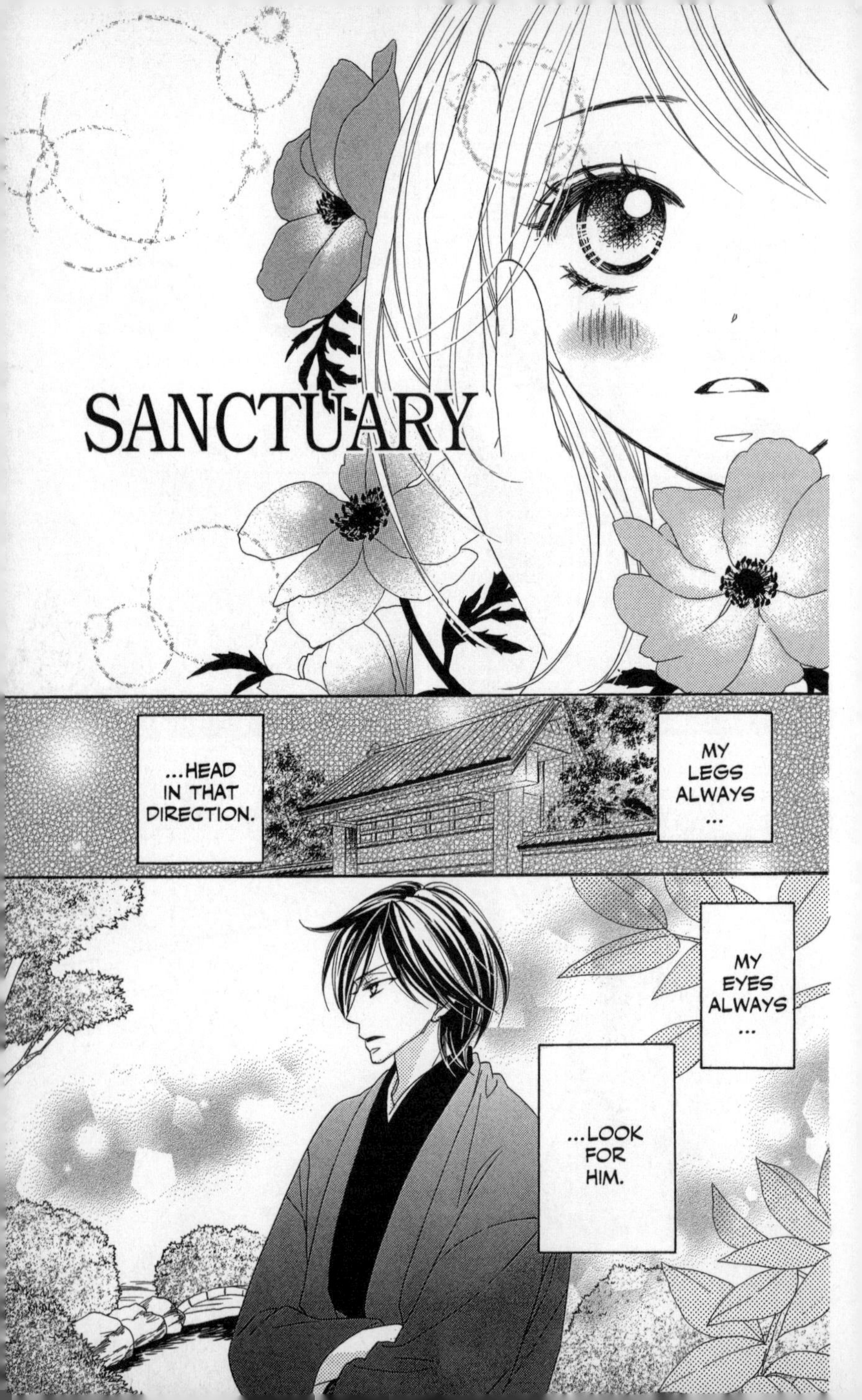
SANCTUARY
MY LEGS ALWAYS ...
...HEAD IN THAT DIRECTION.
MY EYES ALWAYS ...
...LOOK FOR HIM.

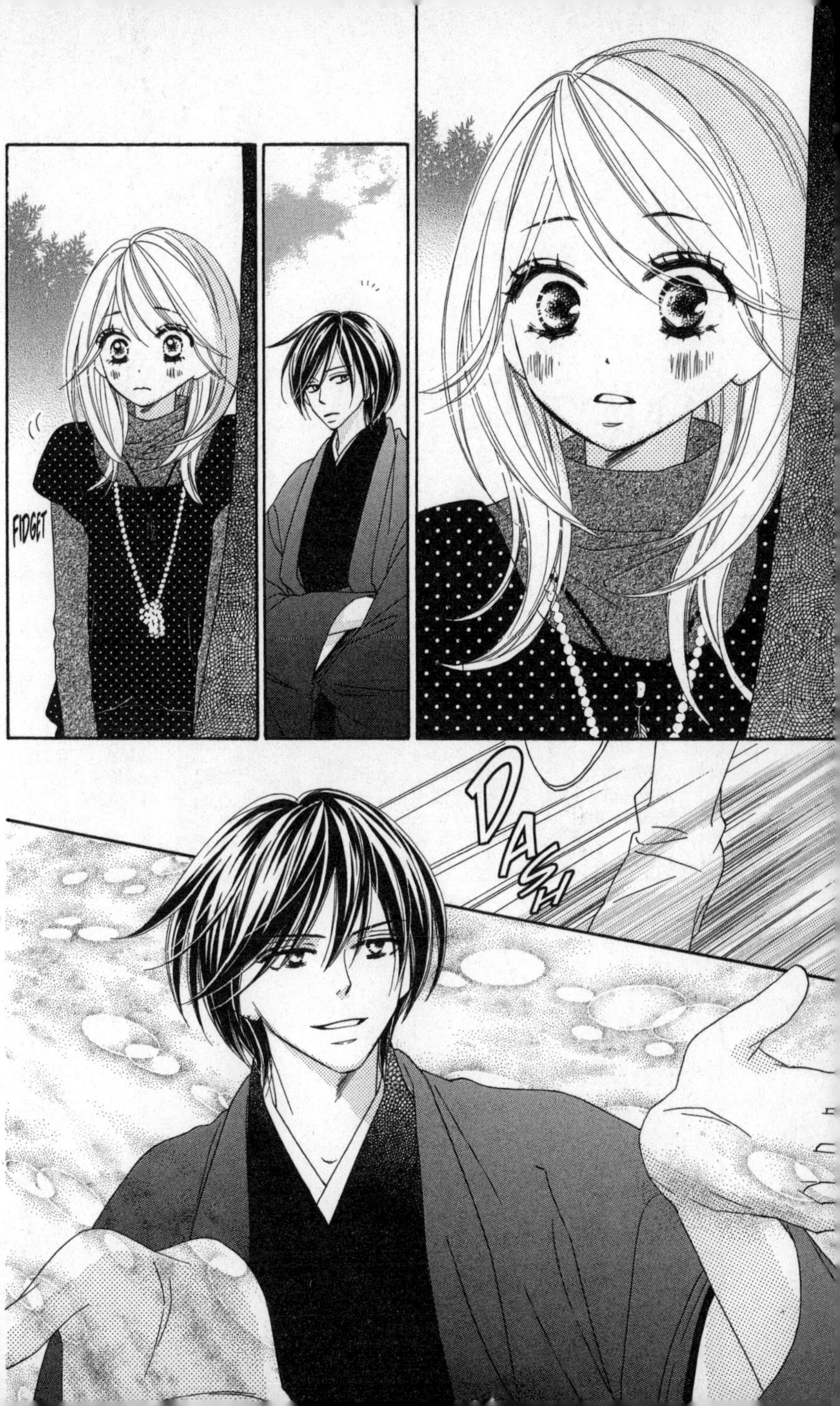
FIDGET
DASH

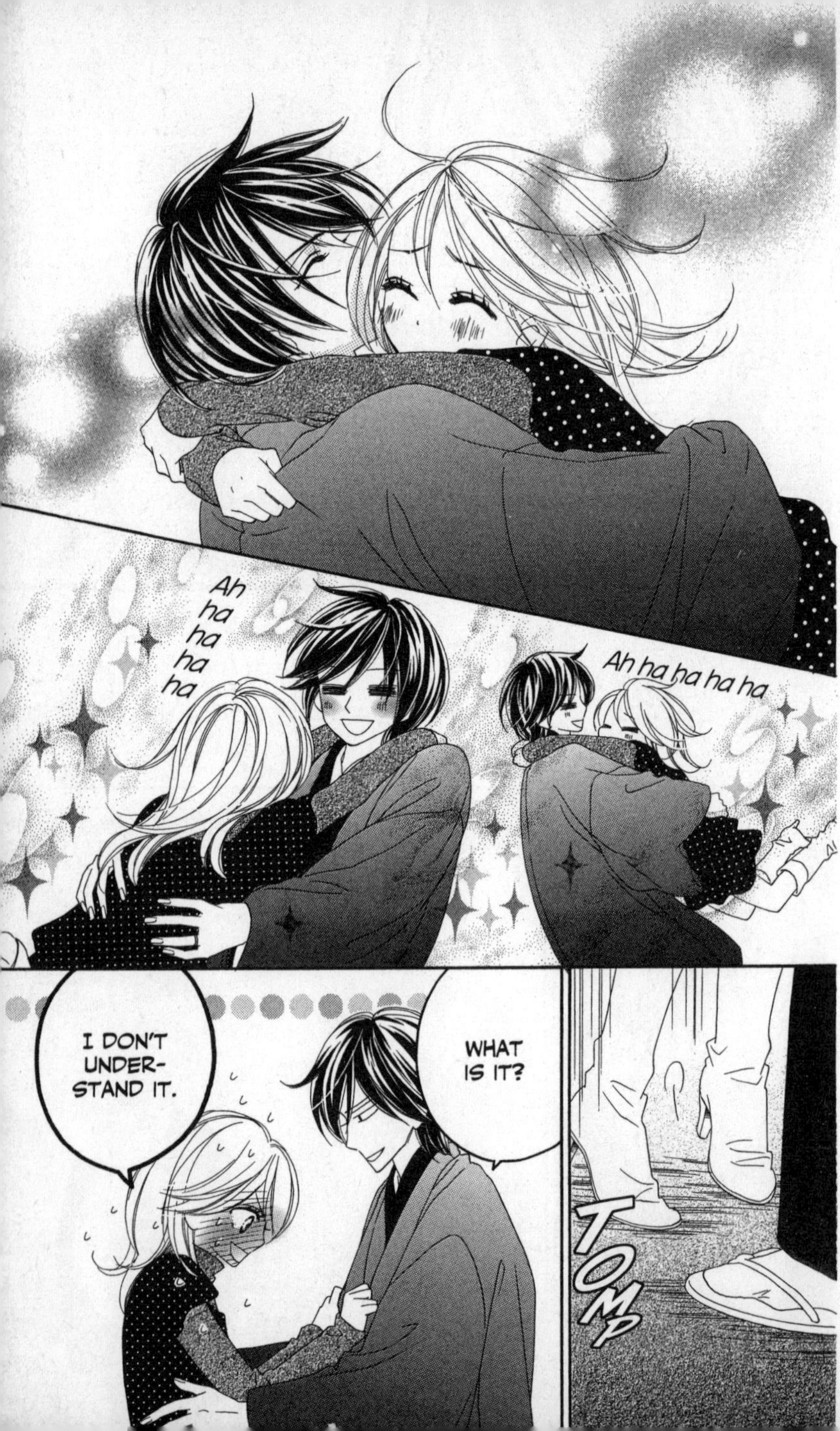
Ah ha ha ha ha
Ah ha ha ha ha
TOMP
WHAT IS IT?
I DON'T UNDER-STAND IT.

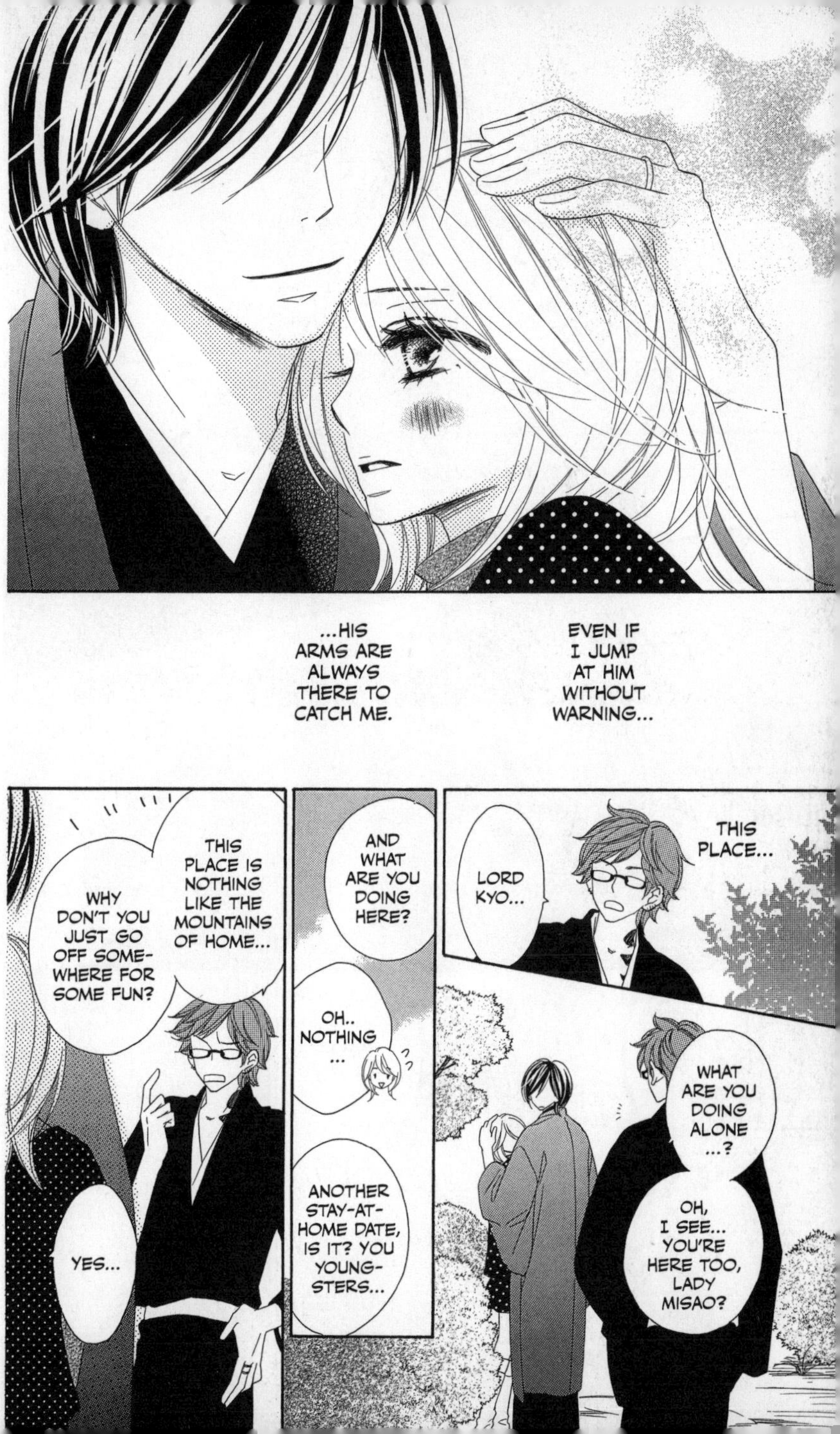

EVEN IF I JUMP AT HIM WITHOUT WARNING...
...HIS ARMS ARE ALWAYS THERE TO CATCH ME.
THIS PLACE...
LORD KYO...
WHAT ARE YOU DOING ALONE...?
OH, I SEE... YOU'RE HERE TOO, LADY MISAO?
AND WHAT ARE YOU DOING HERE?
OH.. NOTHING ...
ANOTHER STAY-AT-HOME DATE, IS IT? YOU YOUNGSTERS...
THIS PLACE IS NOTHING LIKE THE MOUNTAINS OF HOME...
WHY DON'T YOU JUST GO OFF SOMEWHERE FOR SOME FUN?
YES...

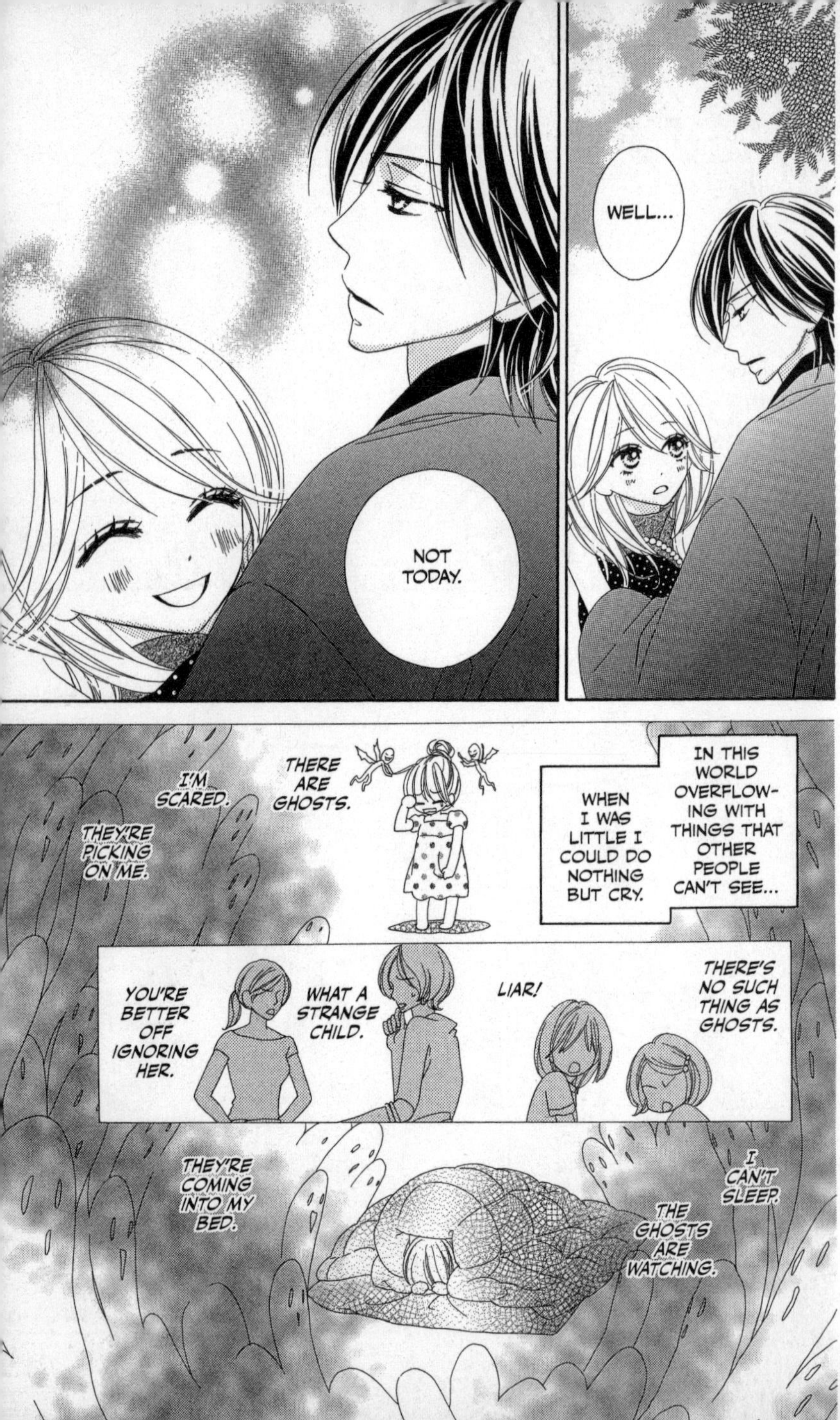

WELL...
NOT TODAY.
IN THIS WORLD OVERFLOWING WITH THINGS THAT OTHER PEOPLE CAN'T SEE...
WHEN I WAS LITTLE I COULD DO NOTHING BUT CRY.
THERE ARE GHOSTS.
I'M SCARED.
THEY'RE PICKING ON ME.
THERE'S NO SUCH THING AS GHOSTS.
LIAR!
WHAT A STRANGE CHILD.
YOU'RE BETTER OFF IGNORING HER.
I CAN'T SLEEP.
THE GHOSTS ARE WATCHING.
THEY'RE COMING INTO MY BED.

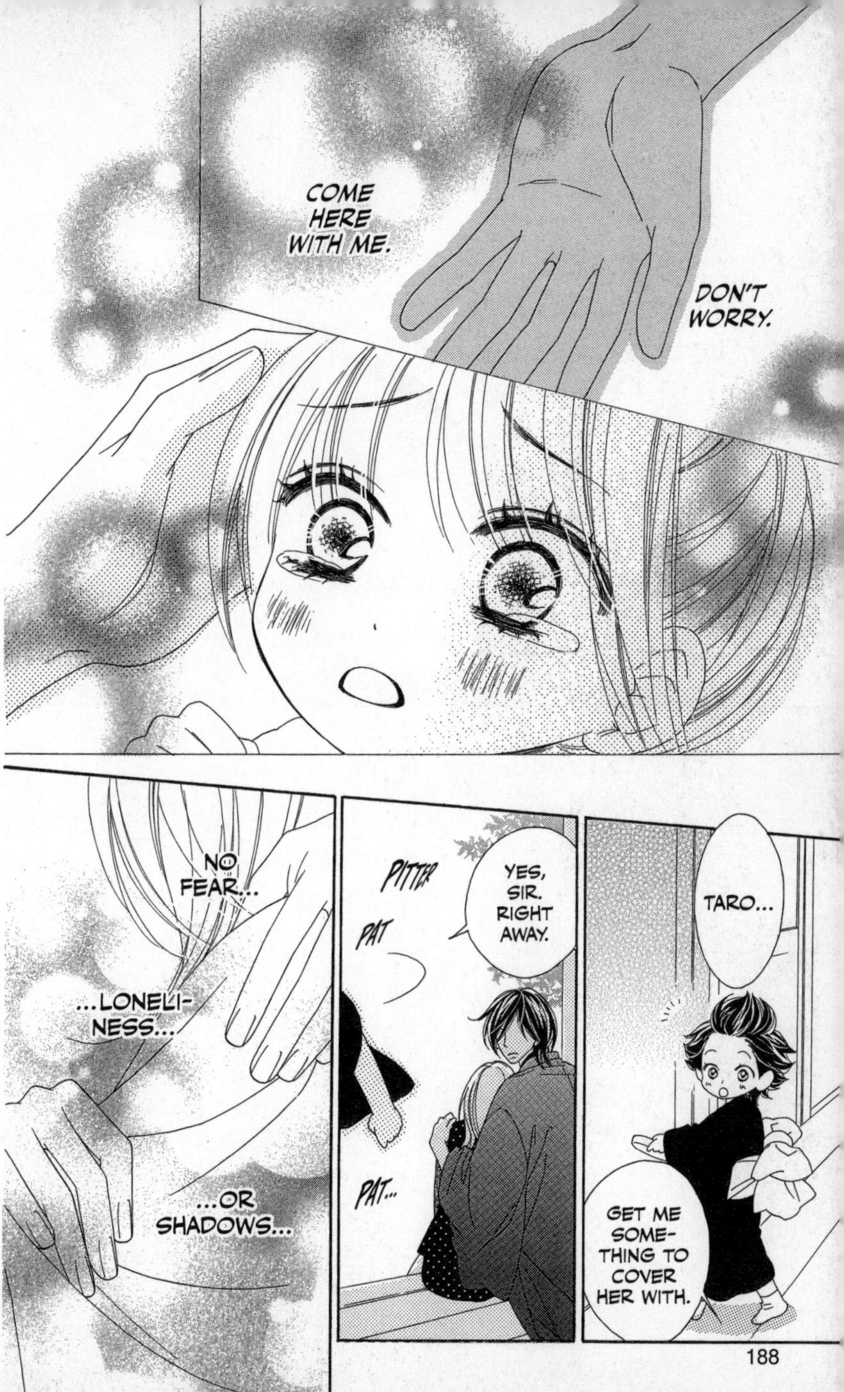
DON'T WORRY.
COME HERE WITH ME.
TARO...
GET ME SOME-THING TO COVER HER WITH.
YES, SIR. RIGHT AWAY.
PITTER
PAT
PAT...
NO FEAR...
...LONELI-NESS...
...OR SHADOWS...

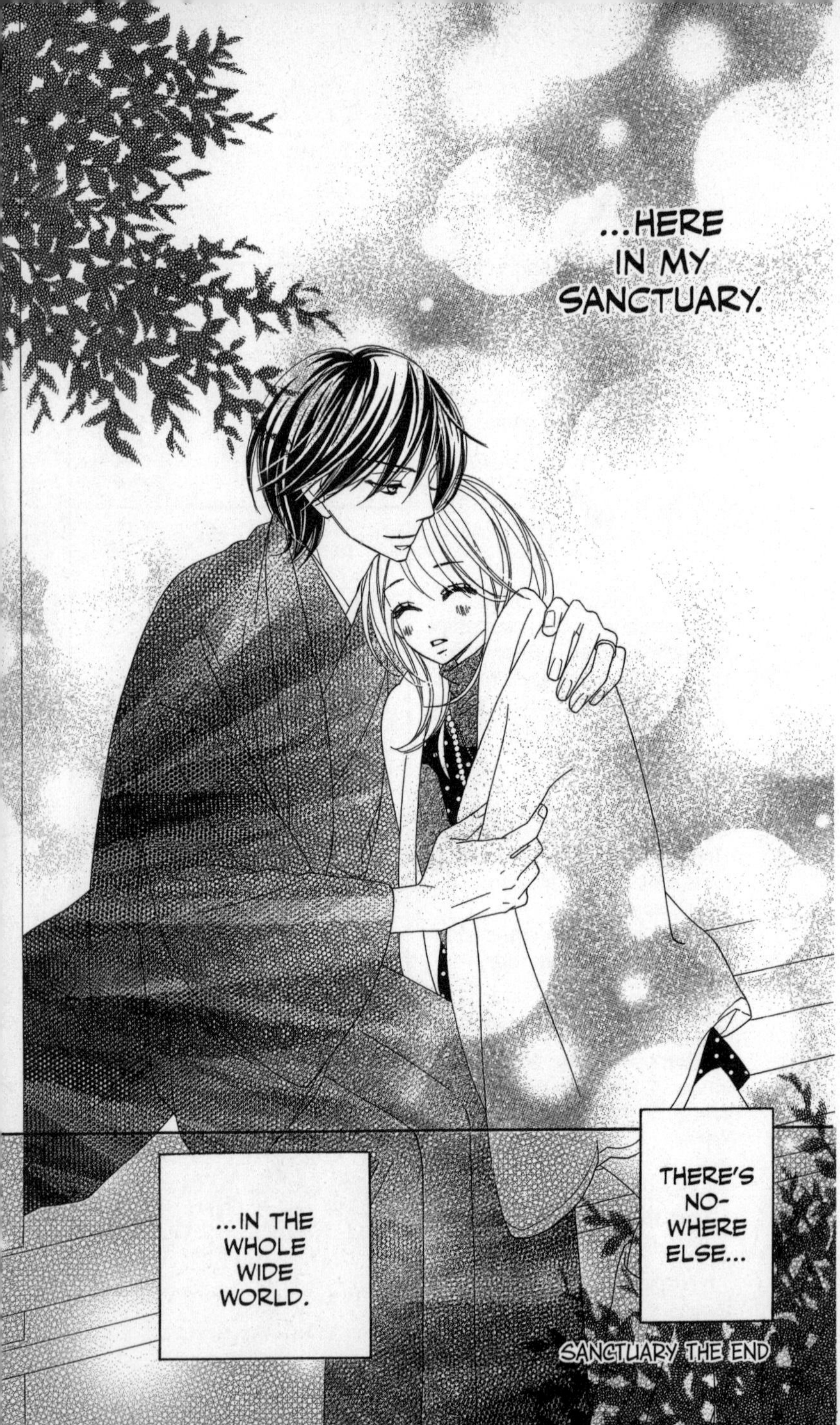
...HERE IN MY SANCTUARY.
THERE'S NO-WHERE ELSE...
...IN THE WHOLE WIDE WORLD.
SANCTUARY THE END

The title of the special feature, "Sanctuary", is *seiiki* in Japanese. The scenes were to be the same as the ones I used in the special feature I did in volume 4, but they weren't exactly the same. I'm sorry...

As the series continues to lengthen, characters that were not scheduled to appear and scenes that were never meant to be featured are making their appearance. I am very grateful for this.

Also, it seems this manga is being read by people of all ages. (The age range of people who have sent me letters and emails spans 40 years! ✧) This is completely unexpected, and I must say, I am very fortunate indeed.

The main story will continue in a more serious vein for a while longer. I hope you continue to follow the story. ♡
Please...!

I give my deepest thanks to all those who have had anything to do with me. ♡♡

An auspicious day, April 2008
Kanoko Sakurakouji
桜小路かのこ

You want to show us the dance you were supposed to do at our Christmas party?
Oh... Let's see it! Let's see it!
NOD
Thank you... ♡
At...
Ta...
ka...
sa...
go...
We hoist...
...the sail on this...
...small fishing craft...
...
"Takasago" is a Noh song. An auspicious song often sung at weddings.
Noh...?
He probably put a lot of thought into it...
Together with the moon...

Black Bird

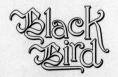

GLOSSARY

PAGE 15, PANEL 2: *Yasokyo*
An archaic term for "Christian." *Yaso* comes from the Japanese reading of the characters used to write "Jesus" in Chinese.

PAGE 15, PANEL 6: *Sexy night*
The Japanese for "holy night" is *seinaru yoru* (聖なる夜). Kyo thinks it is *seinaru yoru* (性なる夜), which means "sexy night."

PAGE 16, PANEL 1: *Hidden Christian*
Kakure kirishitan (隠れ切支丹), or "hidden Christians," refers to those who had to practice in secret when Christianity was banned from Japan in the 1600s.

PAGE 18, PANEL 3: *Spiral drawing*
The spiral figure on the right signifies "very good."

PAGE 21, PANEL 5: *Patriarch*
The Japanese is *sensen dai* (先々代) and means the leader of two generations ago. The current patriarch is Kyo's grandfather.

PAGE 94, PANEL 1: *Kyo-chan*
Chan is a type of honorific used to create diminutives. It is commonly used for and by young children and among friends. In this case, it can represent Misao's age and her close friendship with Kyo.

PAGE 125, PANEL 4: *Hiyoko*
There are well-known sweets of the same name in Japan. It is traditional in Japan to bring goodies such as these sweets when visiting someone's home.

Kanoko Sakurakouji was born in downtown Tokyo, and her hobbies include reading, watching plays, traveling and shopping. Her debut title, *Raibu ga Hanetara*, ran in *Bessatsu Shojo Comic* (currently called *Bestucomi*) in 2000, and her 2004 *Bestucomi* title *Backstage Prince* was serialized in VIZ Media's *Shojo Beat* magazine. She won the 54th Shogakukan Manga Award for *Black Bird*.

BLACK BIRD
VOL. 5
Shojo Beat Edition

Story and Art by KANOKO SAKURAKOUJI

© 2007 Kanoko SAKURAKOUJI/Shogakukan
All rights reserved.
Original Japanese edition "BLACK BIRD" published by SHOGAKUKAN Inc.

TRANSLATION JN Productions
TOUCH-UP ART & LETTERING Gia Cam Luc
DESIGN Courtney Utt
EDITOR Pancha Diaz

The stories, characters and incidents mentioned
in this publication are entirely fictional.

Printed in the U.S.A.

Published by VIZ Media, LLC
P.O. Box 77010
San Francisco, CA 94107

10 9 8 7 6 5 4
First printing, August 2010
Fourth printing, June 2013

www.shojobeat.com   www.viz.com

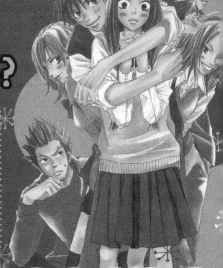
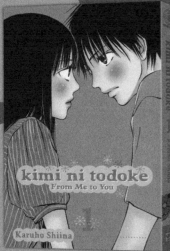
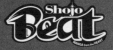

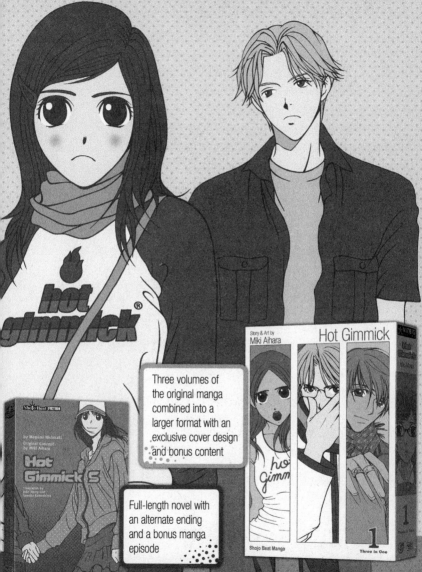
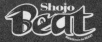

Hot Gimmick

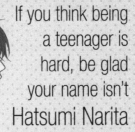

If you think being a teenager is hard, be glad your name isn't Hatsumi Narita

With scandals that would make any gossip girl blush and more triangles than you can throw a geometry book at, this girl may never figure out the game of love!

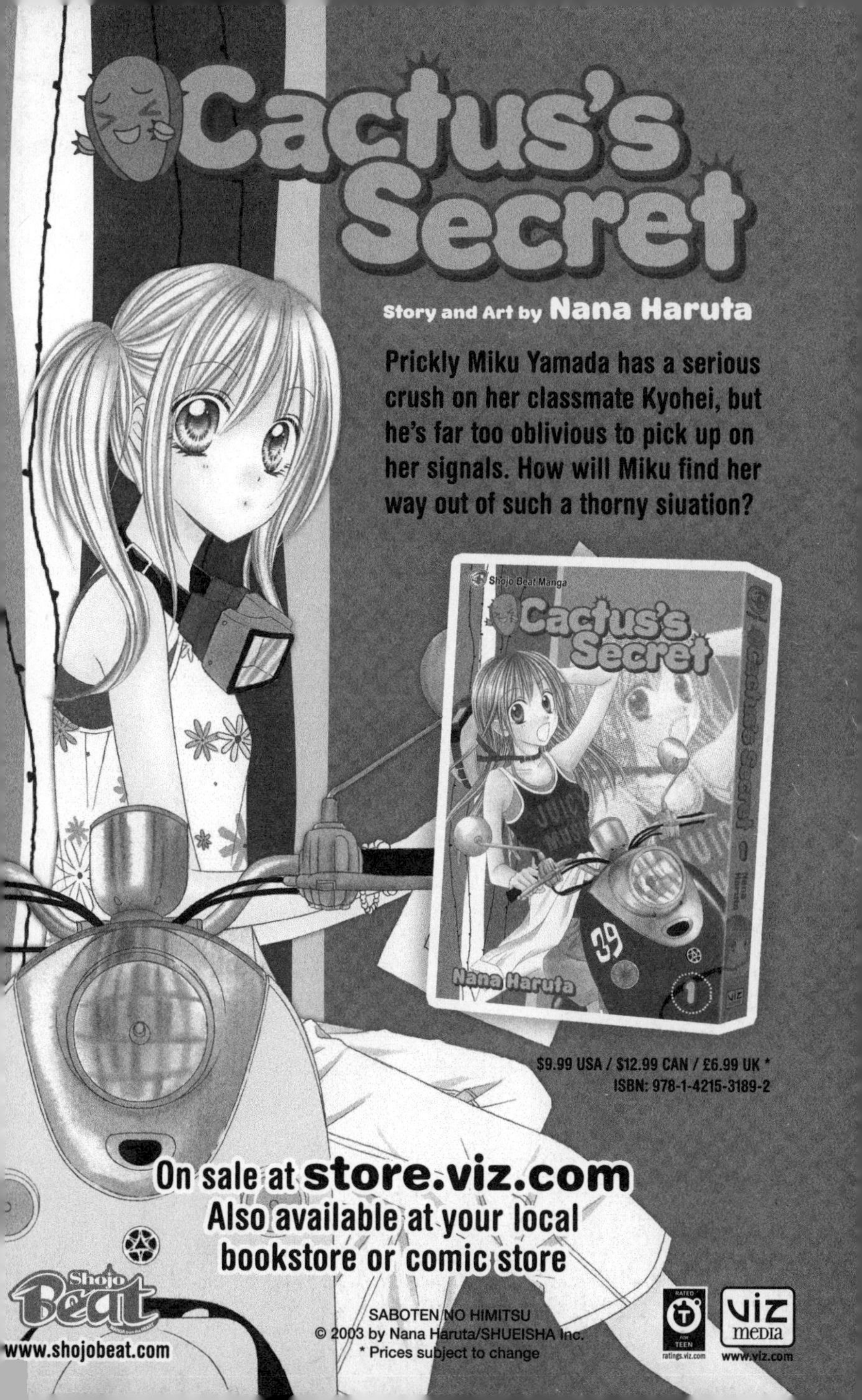
Cactus's Secret
Story and Art by Nana Haruta
Prickly Miku Yamada has a serious crush on her classmate Kyohei, but he's far too oblivious to pick up on her signals. How will Miku find her way out of such a thorny siuation?
Shojo Beat Manga
Cactus's Secret
Nana Haruta
1
$9.99 USA / $12.99 CAN / £6.99 UK *
ISBN: 978-1-4215-3189-2
On sale at store.viz.com
Also available at your local bookstore or comic store
Shojo Beat
www.shojobeat.com
SABOTEN NO HIMITSU
© 2003 by Nana Haruta/SHUEISHA Inc.
* Prices subject to change
RATED T FOR TEEN
ratings.viz.com
VIZ media
www.viz.com

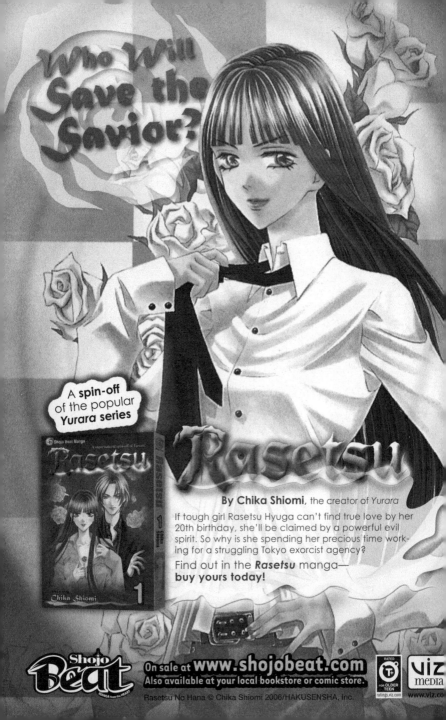

SURPRISE

You may be reading the wrong way!

It's true: In keeping with the original Japanese comic format, this book reads from right to left—so action, sound effects, and word balloons are completely reversed. This preserves the orientation of the original artwork—plus, it's fun! Check out the diagram shown here to get the hang of things, and then turn to the other side of the book to get started!

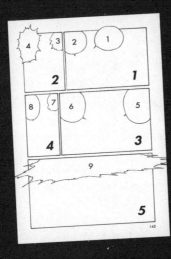